TRINIDAD HIGH SCHOOL
LIBRARY

22.00

Track and Field

D0731838

796.42
SCH 5t

Track
and Field

Edited by
Gerhardt Schmolinsky

TRINIDAD HIGH SCHOOL
LIBRARY

Sport Books Publisher 1993

27,676

Published under the auspices of the Department for Track and Field Events of the Leipzig College of Physical Culture (DHfK)

Contributors:

Dr. Dieter Deiss
Dr. Rolf Donath
Dr. Werner Fritsch
Klaus Gehrke
Heinz Hendel
Lothar Hinz
Gerhard Jeitner
Dr. Wolfgang Lohmann
Prof. Dr. Gert Marhold
Walter Meier

Dr. Dieter Nicklas
Dr. Hans-Günther Rabe
Dr. Manfred Reiss
Prof. Dr. Horst Röder
Gerhardt Schmolinsky
Dr. Manfred Scholich
Erhard Schumann
Alfred Sgonina
Max Weber

Canadian Cataloguing in Publication Data

Main entry under title:

Track and field: the East German textbook of
    athletics

1st Canadian ed.
Includes bibliographical references.
ISBN 0-920905-38-2

1. Track-athletics - Training. I. Schmolinsky,
Gerhardt.

GV1060.5.T73 1992   796.42   C92-095261-5

Copyright © 1992 by Sport Books Publisher
All rights reserved. Except for use in review,
no portion of this book may be reproduced in
any form or by any means without written
permission of the publisher.

Distribution worldwide by
Sport Books Publisher
278 Robert Street
Toronto, Ontario M5S 2K8
Canada

Printed in the United States

Contents

Foreword

"Track and Field" was compiled at the German College for Physical Culture (DHfK) in Leipzig in 1963 and appeared in 1980 in the 10th edition. For many years it has been one of the standard works of scientifically-based training and in many countries throughout the world it has become an indispensable aid in modern performance training. On account of the work's good international reputation it was adopted by the IAAF as official book for the training science of advanced trainers within the framework of the Technical Aid Programme.

The success of this book is linked with the high level of physical culture and particularly with the internationally-recognised standard of track and field in the GDR's Amateur Athletics Association (DVfL der DDR).

Prominent trainers and scientists have worked as coauthors, contributing their wealth of experience and scientific knowledge. This book can be recommended to all those who have enjoyment and interest in developing their sporting performance. It gives good broad insight into modern, scientifically-based training in track and field events. It imparts facts, relationships and laws of the theory and methodology of sports training so that everyone interested can avail themselves of broad practice-orientated material for their own work. In addition to general theoretical elements in which the principles of training and methods for developing sporting performance occupy a central position emphasis is placed on dealing with techniques and means of instruction in all track and field disciplines and on offering means and methods for developing general and specific sports performance.

All track and field disciplines have been dealt with in a uniform system which facilitates insight for the reader.

The 2nd edition of the English version corresponds to the 10th revised German edition. In my opinion it will find acclaim in track and field circles and will help trainers in the English-speaking world to further improve the level of training and sporting performance. It will also help to enhance the position of track and field in Olympic Games.

Prof. Dr. Georg Wieczisk
President of the GDR Amateur
Athletics Association (DVfL der DDR)

1. The Significance of Track and Field Events for Physical Culture

1.1. Track and Field Events as an Olympic Discipline

The first Olympic Games of modern times were held in Athens in 1896 on the decision of the first Olympic Congress which met in Paris in 1894 and followed the initiatives and aims of the Baron Pierre de Coubertin. The Olympic Games gave a new quality to international relations in sport for they were increasingly moulded by the humanist concern of the Olympic idea which corresponded with the longing of mankind for peace and understanding between the peoples. This idea was linked with the demand put upon all active athletes to maintain the ethical and moral values of sport through their own performance and behaviour.

Between 1896 and the present day the Olympic Games and the whole Olympic movement have developed enormously. This is evidenced by the increased number of events, disciplines, countries and athletes participating and by the growing demands on material and technical conditions. The swift and enormous improvement in athletes' performance and the international standing of the Games are also proof of this. These developments will continue as long as peace is maintained.

To mention but a few figures: in 1896 13 countries and 285 athletes competed in 10 disciplines in Athens for the first Olympic medals. Today some 8,000—9,000 athletes compete in 23 disciplines in the Olympic Games. The International Olympic Committee (IOC) has recognised over 145 National Olympic Committees (NOC) giving them the right to take part in the Olympic Games. This is indicative enough of the Olympic Games' prospects.

At this point mention should be made of two important facts which influenced the quality of the Olympic Games and which gave fresh impetus to the continued development of the Olympic movement. These were the inclusion of women's competitions in the Olympic programme—in 1928 in field and track events—and the participation of the socialist countries after the Second World War.

As early as in 1896 track and field events were predominant in the Olympic Games. A total of twelve various disciplines were included in the programme. Today there are some 24 disciplines for men and 14 for women. Competitions in track and field events are a highlight of the Olympic Games. Outstanding athletes from many countries have given the competitions the international standing they possess today. The spotlight has rested on many on account of their performances and personality and they have become examples to all those who are keen track and field athletes and who strive for good performances.

The constantly improving level of competition performance in all track

Major Games and Championships in Track and Field

Name of Fixture	Games Cycle (yearly)	1981	1982	1983	1984
African Champs	2	Lagos		Yamousakro	
African Games	4		Nairobi		
Asian Athletic Champs	2				
Asian Games	4		Delhi		
Balkan Athletic Games	ann.				
Central African Games		Tchad			
Central American Games	ann.				
Central American and Caribbean Games	4		Havanna		
Central American and Caribbean Champs	2	Santo Domingo		Havanna	
Commonwealth Games	4		Brisbane		
East and Central African Athletic Champs	ann.			Kampala	
European Champs	4		Athens		
European Cup Bruno Zauli	2	Zagreb		London	
European Cup—Combined Events	2	Birmingham		Sofia	
European Junior Champs	2	Utrecht		Vienna-Schwechat	
European Indoor Champs	ann.	Grenoble	Milan	Budapest	Göteborg
F.I.S.U. Universiade	2	Bucharest		Edmonton	
Lugano Trophy—Race Walking	2	Valencia		Bergen	
Mediterranean Games	4			Casablanca	
Olympic Games					Los Angeles
Pan American Games	4			Caracas	
Pan American Junior Champs	2		Caracas		
Pan Arab Games	4				
South American Champs	2	Lima		Panama City	
South American Junior Champs	2			Medellin	
IAAF World Championships	4			Helsinki	
IAAF World Cup	4	Rome			

and field disciplines is proof of the conscious endeavours being made in many countries. New standards have been set time and again—particularly at Olympic Games. From these comes the initiative to improve the training process through scientific knowledge so that the athletes' potential can be exploited more rationally and more effectively.

1.2.   Track and Field as All-Round Basic Physical Education

Athletic exercises and training have beneficial effects on the development of the human organism. During the educational process of physical training, properly selected events and their use in all age groups and in all fields of physical education guarantee the proper functioning and physical development of the human body. Walking, running, jumping and throwing help to develop and improve the cardio-vascular system and basic physical and technical qualities.

Learning motor activities in field and track sports helps to develop valuable new skills. They improve coordination and balance and help to perfect man's bodily abilities.

Track and field exercises and competitions also promote the individual's mental development. In training and competition knowledge of technique, tactics, hygiene, methodology and the role of sport in society is imparted to the athlete. Their application in training and competition further the knowledge and ability of the athlete and promotes their mental development.

Finally, practising track and field is, during training and competition, a means of strengthening will-power and character. The behaviour of athletes during training and competitions offers the sports teacher ample opportunity to help promote qualities such as will-power, perseverance, resoluteness, self-discipline, team spirit and readiness to perform. In the GDR's education system basic field and track activities (running, jumping, thrusting, throwing) are considered the best means of all-round physical education. They are a firm part of the curriculae for every age group in schools. Outside of school track and field training occupy a prominent position in children's and youth sport. The Spartakiad competitions, for example, are an important highlight.

2. Basic Elements of Track and Field Training

2.1. On the Unity of Instruction and Education in the Training Process

In the field of physical culture and sport training has the aim of developing all-round educated personalities, who are willing and capable of achieving high performances in sport. Promoting the personal qualities needed for this is determined to a large degree by the quality of instruction and education imparted by trainer, sports teacher and coach.

Training in sport is essentially an educational process. The athlete is instructed and educated by the trainer, the sports teacher and the coach. Here it is a matter of developing the pre-requisited essential for sport (personality, condition, coordination and tactical abilities, as well as coordinating and technical skills) in such a way that as a unity they guarantee optimal development in performance. This means that for example in reaching higher aims greater demands must be placed on the athlete, for example on his will-power and on his attitude to the higher demands of training and competition. The quality of his work must always be seen in conjunction with and in relationship to the level of his conviction, attitude, ideals and motives. Performance in sport reflects the state of development of physical and psychological pre-requisites for performance.

The structure of performance in sport:

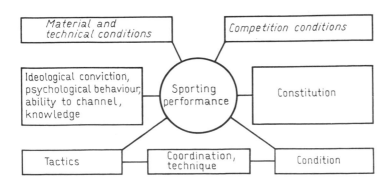

2.2.   Preconditions, Aims and Tasks in Instruction and Education

2.2.1.   On Characteristics of the Trainer's Personality

The trainer, sports teacher or coach guides the instructional and educational process of the athlete and exerts a considerable influence on his character and the personality as a whole. This places great demands on the trainer's quality of work. His authority, effectiveness and success depend to a great extent on the maturity of his personality, his educational abilities in coaching, psychological know-how, his knowledge, organisational abilities and allegiance to his responsible tasks.

2.2.1.1.   On the Trainer's Ideological Stance

Fundamentally the trainer's ideological stance must radiate all those qualities of personality which athletes regard as worthy of achieving. In sport these include clear and progressive convictions with regard to the social aims of sport and the tasks of national and international sport and identification with the humanist principles of the Olympic idea.

The ideological position exerts a strong influence on motivation, it promotes readiness to perform and determines behaviour and work as a whole.

In the ideological education of athletes the most important task is convincing them of the significance, goals and use of their training and in conjunction with this developing a positive and healthy attitude to the demands of training and competition and developing valuable ideals and personally and socially meaningful motivation.

2.2.1.2.   On the Educational Function of Guidance

In modern training thorough theoretical knowledge is essential for fulfilling the aims of training. Good educational guidance in the training process demands basic knowledge of a number of spheres. Here are a few examples of the many tasks and demands placed upon the educational work of the trainer:
— Imparting basic knowledge and creating valuable motivation.
— Improving performance effort in sport, in school and in career.
— Planning, managing and evaluating training and competition.
— Improving the athletes' condition, coordination, tactics and technical skills.
— Improving qualities of character and will-power, physical and psychological strain capacity.
— Improving readiness to perform, self-confidence and active cooperation in training and competition.
— Maintaining enjoyment of training and competition.

Fulfilling educational and instructional tasks means qualitatively developing character traits of the athlete. The trainer must form a clear picture of the athlete and deduce from this aims, tasks and methods of training. This requires sufficient knowledge of, for example, the state of the athletes' intellectual, political and physical development, knowledge of his or her interests, inclinations and motivations in sport, school and career and knowledge of behaviour and reactions in physically and psychologically strained situations in sport. A trusting relationship must exist between athlete and trainer based on the latter's knowledge and abilities, his comradeship, rationale and sense of justice.

For the trainer managing and organising training implies many organisational tasks. He must ensure that each training unit is carried out, he must channel the sporting activities of the group or individual athlete, select the correct forms of ordering and compiling, organise equipment and ensure their use and the safety of the athlete. The trainer requires experience in organising competition and knowledge and skills in refereeing. He also needs a certain organisational know-how and experience in organising trips to competitions and cultural events.

2.2.1.3. On the Trainer's Sports Knowledge and Skills

Every trainer, sports teacher and coach must be able to master his area of instruction both in theory and, if possible, also in practice—for purposes of demonstration. Specialised knowledge should focus on means and methods of developing the physical and psychological factors which determine performance, for example, condition and coordination, technical skills and tactical training, prophylactic and medical supervision as well as tasks linked to planning and management, organisation and evaluation of training and competition. This all requires a knowledge of educational science, psychology, physiology, biomechanics and motor activities.

The development of condition and coordination is one of the trainer's main fields of activity. This demands knowledge, experience and educational know-how in selecting and applying suitable means and methods of training. Only the correct build-up of sporting performance ability can lead to outstanding individual performance. For this reason the trainer must know and pay regard to the aims, contents and elements of training methods for each stage of development and breaking up training within the year (cf. 2.11. and 2.12).

Knowledge of physiology is of particular importance. With its aid one can estimate the effect of the means and methods of training used and one can reach an optimal strain load (cf. 2.4).

Technical instruction demands of the trainer that he knows modern techniques and that he is in a position to impart these to the athlete using suitable means and methods of training. In this a knowledge of biomechanics is valuable for it provides a rational basis for movement activities. Sports technique as the rational process for certain movements helps to make optimal use of condition and coordination (cf. 3., 4., 5. and 6.).

Particularly in competition tactical behaviour gains in influence on the application of performance potential. Every athlete must be made acquainted with competition regulations, basic tactical rules and behaviour in the relevant discipline and the trainer must tune the athlete tactically for competition (cf. 2.9.).

Medical and prophylactic supervision

helps to maintain the athlete's health and is the responsibility of the trainer in every stage of training. Regard to the didactic principles of training (cf. 2.3.) averts damage and muscular energy to a large extent. The trainer, however, must have a knowledge of prophylactic measures and their effects and must apply these in the correct manner, for example, alternating hot and cold showers, massage, sauna, solar radiation and pommades. Prophylactic measures and medical supervision as a whole increases with increasing load strains on the athlete.

The scientific planning and evaluation of training and competition occupy an important position particularly in competition sport. Proceeding from long-term planning of training aims, specific plans for specific segments of training weeks and years are deduced. Evaluation of training provides insight into ways of organising training more effectively (cf. 2.13.).

2.2.2. Selected Aspects of the Athlete's Personality Development

Sport promotes recreation, joie-de-vivre and performance and particularly in planned sports training helps to develop the personality.

2.2.2.1. Forming Convictions and Attitudes

Ideological education is inherent in sports training. It promotes development of the personality and is an important factor for creating clear convictions and attitudes to the aims and tasks in training and competition.

The aim of making the athlete think independently as an individual aware of his responsibility means, for example, in sport that they recognise the connection between sports and politics, that they grasp and advocate the progressive and humanist aims of the Olympic idea and that they respect athletes from other nations, show interest and consistency and training, improve their knowledge and skills and that in their behaviour they accord with the norms accepted for good amateur athletes. The trainer guides the process of sports instruction but with the athlete's increasing experience, knowledge independent and active personal commitment increases in significance and becomes a factor influencing performance. Educating oneself and the necessary self-control and self-evaluation presuppose firm ideological positions, sufficient knowledge and experience (cf. 2.3.4.).

2.2.2.2. On the Development of Character and Will

Preparing for and achieving high sporting performance places great demands on the character of the athlete.

According to RUBINSTEIN "the character is expressed in the basic positions of the person, in the fundamental active attitudes and tendencies which control and regulate the totality of the individual's expression. The character traits of the individual determine basic positions, mould his behaviour and express themselves in relations to other people, the world and oneself."

Sports training and competition in which maximum difficulties have to be overcome require and form many valuable qualities of character. The more consciously and consistently the trainer knows and makes use of the available opportunities the more successfully will he be able to influence those personality traits in athletes which determine performance. Qualities of character which are to be formed or improved can be divided up into three categories:

1. Qualities of character which express the athlete's relationship to training and competition (tenacity, industry, conscientiousness, will-power, readiness to perform).

2. Qualities of character which express the relationship to the collective, to other athletes and to oneself (fair sporting behaviour, modesty, optimism, honesty, politeness, readiness to help).

3. Qualities of character which reflect the athlete's relationship to his own country and to other countries and peoples (pride in sporting success and in representing one's country, recognition of athletes from other countries).

During sporting activities the athlete's qualities of character and will take on their own individual form. The trainer must carefully study the idiosyncrasies of the athlete and make use of these for instruction and education.

Will-power is at the heart of character. It is closely linked to other psychological phenomena (temperament, feelings, habits) and in particular to convictions, view of the world and morals. Feelings of responsibility vis-a-vis the state, the sports team, the trainers' collective and the individual trainer are forces which exert a strong influence on will-power. Tenacity and the ability to overcome difficulties are the hallmarks of will-power. Usually sporting activity is linked to overcoming difficulties. Particularly before and during competitions various and in part extreme physical and psychological difficulties and strains appear (excitement, inhibitions, fear, exhaustion, disappointment, opponent, unfavourable competition conditions) all of which the athlete must overcome to attain success. During training the athlete is often confronted with tasks which he can only fulfil by mobilising his full strength. This elucidates how important it is to promote will-power in order to attain high sporting performance.

Here in detail it is a matter of influencing the formation of motivation and the ability to make and implement decisions. It is also a matter of developing in the athlete a number of important qualities of will such as perseverance, activity, resoluteness, courage, the will to fight and win, and self-control. Here particular significance is to be attributed to the training process. The trainer must organise and manage this accordingly if he wants to school the will-power of the athlete to the highest degree. (For example, developing psycho-physical mobilisation capacity in runners in a state of advanced exhaustion.) The trainer and the athlete must know and make correct use of the physical and psychological effects of the means and methods of training used. In the training process overcoming high and very high general and specific training and competition strains promotes qualities of will-power, self-confidence and durability in training and competition all of which are typical of good athletes.

2.2.2.3. On Developing Conscious Creative Activity

Every trainer is interested in developing performance ability and in effective training. A precondition for this is the conscious and creative work of the athlete. It is certain that an athlete will only train responsibly and effectively when he understands and recognises his aims and tasks and the purpose of the training programme and when he is ready and willing to influence progressively training. To be able to do this theoretical knowledge is necessary as well as primarily practical experience in sport. They form the basis for insight, conviction and recognition and are essential for improving self-control and for the ability to evaluate and to correct oneself. This demands not only conscious but also creative work on the part of the athlete. This demands of every trainer that he provides his athletes with sufficient, useful theoretical knowledge and that he enables him to think and act independently in sport.

First and foremost theoretical instruction is concerned with social, technical and tactical aspects and with knowledge of methods and physiology in sport.

Training itself and planned group discussions best serve the theoretical instruction of the athlete.

In the training group discussions the necessary knowledge should be linked with current tasks and imparted with a conscious aim.

Here the knowledge and experience of the athletes must be taken into consideration. A useful basis for moulding the opinion of athletes are tables and evaluations of their training performance and competition results. Many various visual aids can provide support here.

An important part of theoretical instruction is training itself when the trainers bases his demands with hints and explanations when with thought out planning of training he supports the athletes' independence, mutual aid and support, when he makes effective use of coaching and checking and evaluates performance after training.

2.2.2.4. On Forming Psychological Load Strain

A precondition for sporting performance ability in competition is psychological load strain and competition stability. This is a complex quality which is determined by the state of training and development of character traits. The specific psychological load strain of athletes is developed by the demands of training and competition.

Each test situation in sport confronts the athlete with various external (competition atmosphere, conditions, opponents, spectators) and internal (nervous tension, excitement, joy, fear) influences. These release psychological reactions which either favour or impede performance. The state of the athlete prior to the start is an expression of psychological strain. Here it is clear how and athlete comes to terms with the various influences. The optimal state prior to the start is controlled excitement and tense expectation of the start. The athlete is favourably tuned to the competition in a way that promotes performance. Athletes who do not meet up to their performance expectations usually have not been able to come to terms with psychological strains prior to or during the competition and have failed on account of "nerves". This nervous failure, the inability to mobilise performance potential psycho-physically in competition, to release and exploit reserves can also be attributed to the fact that the psycho-physical demands of competition have not been trained to a sufficient extent in training.

Of interest for improving psychological strain load and stability are influences which mainly exert a positive influence on the psychological processing of strain and those which have a disturbing effect and impede performance. In the process of training athletes it is a matter of using the influences which favour performance (stimulus) and reducing and eliminating those which impede performance.

The influences which favour performance have been demonstrated frequently: they are, for example, high but realistic performance demands, good previous training and competition performance, success, spectators and trust in the trainer.

Those influencess which mainly impede performance are, for example, excess nervousness, fear, feelings of inferiority, so-called "fear opponents", frequent failure, poor previous training and competition performance, disagreement with the trainer.

Improving psychological strain load and stability comes about mainly in training and competition.

Specific demands on performance ability in training and competition and on the athlete's attitude and readiness to perform result in conjunction with relevant evaluations in opportunities for further improving psychological load strain potential.

Possibilities of improving psychological load strain and stability are first and foremost:

– Improving personality traits, in particular developing stable motivations and improving self-confidence and the ability to make self-evaluations. Creation of a good balance of success and failure performances.

– Structural aims of load strain training which accords with the expected psycho-physical demands of a specific competition.

Performance motivation influences the aims and content of an athlete's sporting activity and the intensity with which he uses his strength. It also has a substantial influence on will-power and performance behaviour. It is a precondition for success in sport. Knowledge and convictions of the usefulness of sporting activity are a point of departure for developing and improving performance motivation.

Success and failure can have positive or negative effects on the psychological constitution. Fundamentally success can be attributed to test situations which have been come to terms with in a positive manner. These have a positive effect. The contrary is the case when success leads to over-evaluation, feelings of superiority and bad training.

Failure has a mobilising effect when the athlete draws the correct consequences, when he feels motivated and eager to prove what he can achieve. Frequent failure depresses and inhibits the development of performance.

Praise, recognition and awards or criticism and punishment intensify success or failure.

Competition above all is the criterion for the attained state of psychological load strain and stability and is at the same time the best means of improving these. With high competition demands there arise test situations which can and should lead to high strains in the psychological sphere. Improving psychological performance potential presupposes "training" of these processes. On this account training using suitable means and methods should develop the specific psycho-physical qualities needed in competition to attain a certain performance. This is attained best of all by competition-orientated training.

2.2.3. Some Principles for Education in the Sports Training Process

1. Educational tasks can only be mastered successfully when they are planned and integrated in the training process. They must be laid down in unity with those of sports training in the training planning and implemented. Frequent analyses are essential.

2. Athletes are not simply the objects of education. They are consciously acting subjects. For the most part they have completed school and vocational training, have thorough knowledge and many varied inclinations and interests. This must be taken into account in educational work.

3. It is a matter of using the strength of the athlete's collective for educating the athletes. The collective offers the best pre-conditions for a high level of development of both personality and performance.

4. Educational work is only fully successful when all those who have a share in educating athletes proceed in unison.

2.3.   The Pedagogic Principles of Track and Field Training

The make-up of a training session is based on definite principles which should be seen as a logical unity, which ensures the unity of education and instruction in the class-room and in training. Such principles are the fundamental precepts of socialist physical education and didactic principles. During training these principles act much as they do in the teaching of general compulsory physical education, but assume particular forms. Mistakes in training schedules can only be avoided if all the principles involved are given due weight. General fundamental principles of training are:

The Principle of Versatility
The Principle of the Promotion of Health
The Principle of Utility
The Principle of Consciousness
The Principle of Repetition
The Principle of Systematization
The Principle of Durability
The Principle of Gradualness
The Principle of Age-Dependence
The order in which these principles have been enumerated is not related to their value. In the following explanations of these principles the close connection and interrelation between them are emphasized.

2.3.1. The Principle of Versatility

The socialist form of society sets high standards for the physical and mental development of the people. Therefore the principle of versatility receives great attention in the education and instruction of the socialist school system. The highly varied education and instruction is closely linked to the many-sided work of physical education and instruction. The great variety of instruction in polytechnics enables people to fulfil the increasing technological requirements of modern production. With general compulsory physical education in schools, various methods are applied which promote health, hardiness, fitness for work and national defence.

This is, however, only possible if people are involved in several kinds of sports (athletics, gymnastics, swimming, shooting, and others). Thus they can gain a variety of experience, acquire various physical aptitudes and improve their basic physical qualities. Versatility is therefore essential for a proper balance between mental and physical perfection. As a socialist process of education and instruction, training aims chiefly at the improvement of physical faculties; here the principle of versatility must be applied. In sports training, versatility can be:
1. Versatility in several sports
2. Versatility in one sport such as in track and field.

If a sportsman is good at several sports, one can speak about general versatility. Versatility in one sport, e.g. in track and field, may be designated as special versatility. Thus one avoids the confusion of ideas which often arises in the use of the terms versatility and specialization, or in the unclear definition of the word specialization, which can be:
1. Specialization in one sport or
2. Specialization in one event of the chosen sport.

OZOLIN [1] in speaking on specialization, says: "It is one-sided only in regard to its objective, while the way to it leads to a wide range of the most varied means and exercises." Specialization aims at achieving the highest performance in an adult on the basis of versatility. A wrong understanding of the term specialization can lead to a one-sided training of juniors in one particular event. Such youngsters are generally capable of achieving good results at a relatively early age, but often do not improve, as expected, their performances when they become adults.

Track and field athletes who have reached their best performances before the age of 18, have undergone the wrong training. In order to avoid this, the terms versatility and specialization should be well differentiated, clearly formulated, and properly applied during training. Therefore these two terms need to be further differentiated here.

If someone is trained to be generally versatile, we may speak of a general training versatility. If this general training versatility is also used for participation in competitions in several sports, we call the result general competition versatility. If one is trained to be versatile in one sport, the result is known as special training versatility. If several events of a chosen sport are tackled in competition, this we regard as special competition versatility.

1 N. Ozolin "Das Training des Leichtathleten", Sportverlag, Berlin 1952.

Specialization results then from general and special training and versatility in competition. Therefore specialization should be understood as training and competing in one selected event of the particular sport. Instruction in the compulsory physical education of our socialist school system is based on general versatility. The conditions for obtaining the official sports badge "Ready for work and the defence of our homeland" are devised on this basis. The principle of general versatility is specially applicable to the training of boys and girls. General versatility gives the background for a later specialization in one event. The broader the base is, the higher will be the standard in one special event.

The foundation training and build-up are recommended for the preparation of good athletic performance as shown in Table 1. There are obviously limits to the versatility requirement; it varies considerably in groundwork build-up and training for a good performance. We refer, on the one hand, to the general form of training and on the other to the selection of particular training means for the establishment of the training programme.

2.3.2. The Principle of Health Promotion

All young people fit for sport take part in general compulsory sports classes. Sports classes must, according to the principle of health promotion, be so organized that on the one hand a minimum intensity of activity produces in the body of the infant and adolescent the ability to adapt to different circumstances and, on the other hand, the avoidance of overwork by modifying the amount of exercise in particular cases as much as possible. The total load during the sports lessons must depend on sex and age and produce maximum possibilities of development. In the true spirit of physical culture, pupils are led to personal hygiene, toughening up etc. during the sports lessons and to training outside the lessons. Sports lessons are thus an important factor for improving public health. It can, however, be improved only if young people, thanks to interesting and good compulsory sports classes, can be persuaded to go in for sport during their leisure time at the various sports clubs. These sports clubs and training groups serve at the same time as the reservoir for top-class sport.

Training condition and health must be adequately improved and checked by a sports physician in close collaboration with the coach. The sports physician is required to inform the coach on the training and health of the athletes. The coach must give details to the sports physician of the training schedules and both together should plan the gradual and progressive training quota for the individual athlete or for a squad of athletes.

In the sports clubs a sports physician is at the disposal of the best athletes. In small sports communities a regular medical check-up is difficult, but the trainer or coach is nevertheless obliged to send the athletes at least twice a year for a medical check-up. The apparent well-being of the athlete does not always reflect a good physical condition. Ambitious young people especially do not always tell the truth about their health. The coach can and should therefore keep himself informed on the

Table 1 Training Structure According to the Principle of Manysidedness

Years of Age	Training in basic sports: Track and Field, Gymnastics with Apparatus, Swimming, Games in compulsory P. T. lessons	Extrascolar sport activities and Training
8–10	General manysidedness	General training and Competition manysidedness
10–12	General manysidedness 3 × 45 minutes weekly, sports badge, Olympic badge	General manysidedness; general or special competition manysidedness, 2–3 × 60 min. weekly, sports badge and Olympic badge for boys
13–14	General manysidedness 2 × 45 minutes weekly, sports badge, Olympic badge	General and special training manysidedness, 4–5 × 90 min. weekly, sports badge and Olympic badge for boys and classification standard
14–16	General manysidedness 2 × 45 minutes weekly, sports badge, Olympic badge	Special training manysidedness; special competition manysidedness, 4–6 × 90 min. weekly, sports badge and Olympic badge for Youths, classification standard
17	General manysidedness 2 × 45 minutes weekly, sports badge, Olympic badge	Special training manysidedness; special competition manysidedness, 5–6 × 120 min. weekly, special event, sports badge and Olympic badge for Youths, classification standard
18	General manysidedness 2 × 45 minutes weekly, sports badge, Olympic badge for men, for women	Special training manysidedness; special competition manysidedness, special event, 5–6 × 120 min. weekly, sports badge and Olympic badge for men, classification standard

health of his charges by measuring during training and immediately after a work-out the pulse-rate and recovery time.

Before a youngster or adult beginner starts training in any particular event, he should undergo a medical examination of his cardio-vascular system. The physician should measure his blood-pressure and the pulse-rate at rest, before and after physical effort and, if possible, determine his oxygen pulse. An ECG should be made and evaluated. The lungs should be screened or x-rayed. If no organic deficiency is detected, novices can start training without fear. Finally, it is necessary that the athlete studies himself during and after training. On the basis of the following intensity characteristics for judging the effects of daily training, or the intensity of the training schedules, every athlete can get a clear picture of the overall level of work in the training:

1st stage (active relaxation)
Relaxed, light-hearted exercises (as a matter of principle not in his special event), psycho-physical balance, relaxation (physical and mental recovery); appetite and sleep normal to very good.

2nd stage (slight increase in intensity)
Light training of a partly "playful" character, barely perceptible increase in intensity (with little demand placed

on the cardio-vascular system, neuro-muscular apparatus and concentration); after the training physical and mental well-being; appetite and sleep normal to good.

3rd stage (medium intensity)

Training with slightly noticeable increase in intensity (medium demands on the cardio-vascular system, neuro-muscular apparatus and concentration), giving the sensation of pleasant tiredness after training; appetite and sleep normal to very good.

4th stage (submaximum intensity)

Training giving the sensation of strong loading impulses (submaximum stress on the cardio-vascular system, neuro-muscular apparatus and concentration). Signs of fatigue during training, increased need of sleep and rest after training. Appetite and sleep normal to very good.

5th stage (maximum load—peak load)

Training giving the sensation of very high work-rate, very great stress on the cardio-vascular system, neuro-muscular apparatus and concentration and of signs of great fatigue accompanying effort, after which physical and mental freshness is re-established.

Neglecting rest periods and too frequent application of intensive work can lead to symptoms of overtraining.

We suggest the following rule: the lower the frequency of weekly training sessions, the higher the intensity of exercises should be. In the case of daily training, only two peaks of intensity (as described in stage 5) per week, at a maximum, should be reached. It must, however, be stressed that a training load which, from the feelings of the individual himself, could be characterized by stages 1 or 2, will, in the long run, not produce a training effect in the sense of a marked improvement in performance.

2.3.3. The Principle of Utility

Education and instruction in the general compulsory sports classes and during training must be pursued according to methods with a scientific foundation which ensure that the educational objectives of the classes or the training are attained. The utility principle means also, that sports lessons and training should be of benefit to a socialist society. This is, however, possible only, if theory and practice are at one.

The utility principle in sports classes and in training is fully effective only if, at the same time, the principles of versatility, consciousness, systemization and age-dependence are taken into consideration and complement each other.

The technical instruction must, for example, observe the utility principle in so far as the subject to be taught in a specific technical event consists of exercises which are indeed elements of the technique to be mastered and help to develop it systematically.

The ways and means to be applied during training for the development and improvement of condition and coordination must be chosen in the light of the utility principle and, with regard to age, training background, performance level and group of events, in such a way that a carry-on effect to the particular skills is guaranteed. This means that better competition results are obtained through a higher quality of condition and coordination and through the improvement of techniques. Sport classes and training must have as their objective the development of condition and coordination as well as of skills in an optimal relation to one another. This does not, however, prevent special emphasis being put on well-directed training for part of the time with the aim of developing condition or technique.

During build-up athletic fundamentals and training, for a specific event or events must form a unity. The training means must be chosen so that they promote development in the group of events concerned. For an intensive training in middle-distance races this means: no maximum strength training, but strength, endurance, and explosive force training in the athletic foundation. In hard training for the throwing events, no training involving a lot of continuous running should be taken on for the same reasons. The selection of so-called ancillary events should also conform to the utility principle.

The following ancillary events are recommended initially:

Sprinters:
Hurdles
Long jump
High jump
Javelin throw
Combined competitions

Middle distance runners:
Short-distance race up to 400 m
Hurdles
Long jump
Javelin

Jumpers:
Short-distance race up to 400 m
Hurdles
Javelin
Combined competitions

Throwers:
Short-distance race up to 200 m
Hurdles
Long jump
Triple jump
High jump
Combined competitions

● Test exercises

For testing physical condition the following exercises are recommended:

1. Maximum strength test
Press and clean the barbell; press in horizontal position on a bench; knee bends with barbell on the neck.
Not suitable for schools!

2. Explosive strength test
Press and clean and jerk the barbell. Knee bends with barbell (10 × for time); running jumps (10 to 20 × for distance); skip jumps (for height, not number); climbing and hanging on rope (for time); triple hop right/left; standing triple jump; long jump; high jump; standing shot put.

3. Speed test
30 m with flying start: 60 m from standing or crouch start; 30-m jumps on one leg (for time and numbers) or 10 jumps on one leg (measuring time and distance).

4. Strength-endurance test (suitable as maximum strength test in schools): climbing and hanging on rope (for time and numbers); front support (numbers); armpulls.

5. Speed-endurance test
100-m sprint from crouch start; 150-m, 300-m and 400-m run; two-minutes run (distance in metres); alternate hopping in front support and skip jump (for time and numbers).

The utility principle means furthermore that through training the readiness for work and defence, as well as for athletics, is constantly improved. The trainer should exert an educational influence to this effect on the athletes. In this his personal example is of the greatest value. In planning training the utility principle must also be taken into account. Training methods must help the athletes to achieve both short-term and long-term aims. Apart from planning the practical part of the training, this means planning the teaching of theory and tactics and the competition rules of the particular event.

2.3.4. The Principle of Consciousness

During sports classes and training the principle of consciousness plays a leading part in the education of athletes in the spirit of a conscious discipline, active collaboration, self-reliance and independent activity. The teacher or coach can only expect a conscious attitude and disciplined behaviour from his charges if he explains to them the social motivation of sports classes and training. The pupils and athletes must, by demands adapted to age and individuals, be induced to contribute actively to the success of classes or training. This can be done if pupils or athletes carry out the required repetitions of exercises by themselves in squads, if they observe and correct each other, if they in training complete the required training task by a proper understanding of the training demands. As long as the athletes are responding, they indicate that training is properly structured and planned. As soon as the normally keen athlete shows signs of reluctance or slackness,

it should be taken as a sign of incipient overtraining or an incorrect balance in the training schedules.

It must be made clear to the good athlete that he trains not only for his personal pleasure and perfection, but that outstanding athletic performances and correct conduct in competition, training and private life add to the prestige of his country.

Sports teachers as well as coaches must obey the principle of consciousness in their educational work, particularly by applying the educational methods of example and persuasion. Only then will a sports teacher be able to develop in his pupils the urge to take part regularly in sport or in training.

The principle of consciousness finally requires that the athlete balances his athletic interests with his professional, social and family life. One of the long-term aims must be not only to get to the top in sport but also to advance in his or her profession or trade. Thus the principle of consciousness in relation to the utility principle will lead the athlete to become not only a top performer but also a model worker or student.

2.3.5. The Principle of Repetition

The principle of repetition is particularly important for the development towards physical models. Through a gradually increasing number of repetitions, movements become automatic. At the same time strength, speed and endurance are improved through a fixed number of repetitions.

The number of repeats cannot be increased arbitrarily, since certain loads in a given period of time will bring about general fatigue and side-effects. How quickly symptoms of tiredness appear depends on the training level of the athlete and can be influenced by the alternation of effort and rest at adequate intervals.

Thus the principle of repetition governs the total load during a training session and the frequency of training sessions. For the correct planning of loads adapted to different age and training groups, the coach must know the degree of effort required for each type of training. This permits him to balance work and rest phases. The improvement of performance depends directly on interval work. After a certain amount of intensive training a performance plateau with respect to strength, speed, endurance and technique of various motion patterns is reached. The athlete cannot go beyond this performance plateau in spite of further intensive training. A further improvement in performance is only possible through more repetitions (volume stimulus), either in the form of more days of training per week or of more repetitions per day, or a greater intensity of training work (intensity stimulus) or by shorter breaks between repetitions (density stimulus). These changes in the loading factors lead to a progressive increase in the total work load and to an improvement in condition. The physical models are more quickly assimilated, not only by more repetitions, but also by better methods.

2.3.6.   The Principle of Systematization

In training this principle is applied to education, to the technical basis, and to improving condition and coordination: strength, speed, endurance, mobility, extensibility, and agility. The targets set for learning skills can only be reached by adhering to a system.

The quality of condition and coordination is improved by systematically raising the total load on the organism. This implies a well-planned development of physical abilities, building on experience gained in practice and according to laws substantiated by the research work of physiologists in the development of basic physical properties. Short-term and long-term goals must be considered in planning, and systematic means established for the maximum development of strength, speed, endurance, mobility and agility.

Practice shows that a cyclic arrangement of training demands gives the best results. A training cycle refers to the distribution of the total and peak loads over a week, month, training section, training phase or a whole training year.

The cyclic character of training implies that effort and recuperation or work and rest alternate at a given rhythm. As efforts must be gradually increased to a maximum in a given training cycle, this means that the total load will gradually lead to the peak load, after which the total work load must be reduced again to allow the body to recover.

The systematic increase of the amount of work during one training year or single important phase, as e.g. the preparation phase, must follow the principle of systemization and its two components—continuity and dynamics. Continuity in the increase in work means that work loads are consistently and gradually raised during a training phase. Dynamics in the build-up of work loads require that the planned

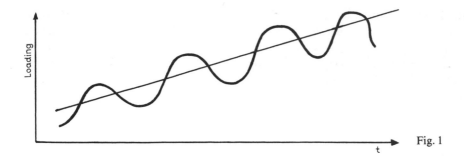

Fig. 1

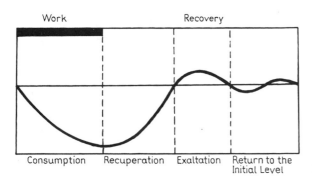

Fig. 2 Phases of alternating performance level during effort and rest

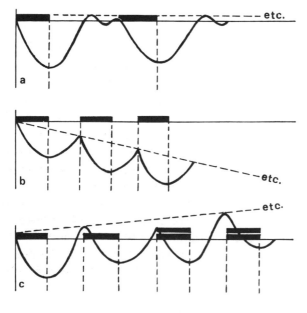

Fig. 2a Alternating functional potentialities in the execution of work during the phases of varying performance levels:

a) If repeats take place when the "remains" of the preceding effort have disappeared, there will be no change in the functional level;

b) If repeats take place before the organism has fully recovered, there will be a drop in the functional level;

c) If every consecutive effort takes place during the phase of "enhanced recovery" and with a gradually rising load level, the functional potentialities will increase accordingly.

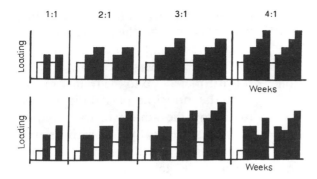

Fig. 3   Training cycles

consistent increase of loads in a training phase does not describe a straight line but rather an oscillating line (Fig. 1).

In a well-trained athlete the peak load acts in the same way as a strong single load, which first lowers the condition level, i.e. the normal performance capacity. The body then requires a longer rest period to return to its initial state by adaptive processes and to a longer recovery time in the so-called "over-compensation" phase. The relation between total work load and recovery is that the higher and stronger the intensity and volume of training, training cycle or training segment is, the longer the organism requires for recuperation and for further "over-compensation". This means that a new functional load must be applied only in the "over-compensation" phase, because a load stimulus, too soon renewed, may lead to deterioration or overloading (Figs. 2 and 2a).

Different commonly applied training cycles comply with the alternation of load and relative recovery. Such cycles are: 1 : 1, 2 : 1, 3 : 1, 4 : 1 (Fig. 3.).

Experience in training shows how the basic physical attributes can best be improved by the principle of systematization. Thus strength exercises without weights can be done daily, strength exercises with additional weight only every second or third day, strength exercises with barbell (near maximum) every second or third day. In training with high loads the main groups of muscles involved must be changed daily. According to the principle of systemization maximum speed development is permitted only on a rested nervous system. Speed exercises such as starts, accelerations, flying sprints and running with changes of speed should therefore be executed only after a good warmup at the beginning of the training session.

The systematic build-up of a continuous performance by running or strength exercises without additional load should follow a definite order: first method of continuous performance, then the method of extensive and intensive interval work. Thus the general or basic endurance and, building on it, the special endurance, is developed. If physical qualities are developed according to the principle of systemization and gradualness, the new qualities will be more lasting and the athlete's body will not be harmed. From this results a close relationship between the principle of systematization and those of improvement in health, gradualness, age dependence and durability.

2.3.7. The Principle of Durability

The principle of durability calls for a training structure which ensures the stability of acquired skills, condition and coordination over a long period of time, without changing their quality. The principle of durability is therefore closely linked with the principles of repetition and systematization. Only frequent repetition and systematic practice of a series of rhythmic movements will lead to stable physical performance. Rapidly acquired abilities are usually lost again after a short interruption in training. Skills become stable only if often repeated at short intervals. There are also skills that are so ingrained that they impede a further improvement in performance. This would be the case if a high jumper who did the western roll for years was to change over to the straddle technique. The old stereotype of the western roll will not only handicap the learning of the new jumping technique, but disturb the build-up of the new style in reaching a peak. In order to get rid of the old negative model the new technique must be frequently exercised when training, bringing work-load to its maximum. Only under these circumstances will it be possible to develop a new stable model. The durability of condition: strength, speed and endurance, at a high level, depends on the period of time over which the new level of this physical ability has been acquired. Experience shows that rapidly acquired strength, speed, endurance and physiological adaptive processes of the body are lost quicker than those acquired during a long, uninterrupted and constantly intensified training. Advanced athletes who interrupt their training deliberately or involuntarily for a long time can recover their previous good form quicker and improve it more rapidly than beginners.

It is ultimately up to the trainer to motivate the principle of stability, by encouraging the athlete to train consistently, systematically and with determination and to lead a real sportsman's life in order to bring his condition to that required by competition.

2.3.8. The Principle of Gradualness

In compliance with the principle of gradualness, the total load must be increased little by little in the training of each age-group, especially when training boys, girls and young people. This is the only way by which damage to the cardio-vascular system or to any other parts of the body can be avoided.

The principle of gradualness in the build-up of strength, speed and endurance is therefore closely linked to the principle of repetition.

In order to develop models according to the principle of gradualness, some general educational principles must be followed, viz. to proceed:

1. from simple to complicated forms,
2. from easy to difficult forms
3. from known to unknown forms.

To proceed from simple to complicated forms means that, e.g. the technique of a rhythmical movement is simplified for exercises. Hence a beginner will not be expected to master all the subtleties of an event after a short time. Each technique has its rough form. To "get it" will be the first training goal. Once it is roughly grasped, one may begin to smooth it out, i.e. to elaborate the more refined form until, finally, the basic technique takes on a personal note and the athlete's own style (linking the principle of systematization with the principle of gradualness).

To proceed from easy to difficult forms means, among other things, that easier conditions are created. A difficult rhythmical movement can be learnt quicker and better with a lighter implement (shell, discus, javelin, hammer) or with a lower apparatus (hurdle or crossbar). To proceed from easy to difficult forms sometimes requires the slower execution of a series of movements to be learnt, e.g. to do the five-stride-rhythm in javelin throwing first walking, then jogging and finally running.

To proceed from known to unknown forms means building on familiar movements or well-established skills before starting something new. Throwing a small ball or an Indian club, or the simple throwing of stones, can be good starting points for learning the correct technique of the javelin. The more difficult stage, the as yet unknown throwing of the javelin, is prepared by the similar technique of an already known movement of throwing. In the development of dynamic models the principles of gradualness and repetition also complement each other.

2.3.9. The Principle of Age-Dependence

The principle of age-dependence calls for different training methods for adults and juniors. The coach must take stock of anatomical and physiological variations and psychological differences at various stages of life, and organize the training accordingly.

The educational aims in all age-groups must be adapted to the physical and psychological level of development of the athlete. For meeting these requirements, different ways and means have to be applied. They must be adapted to the particular levels of groups or individuals. Thus the close connection between the principle of age-dependence and the principle of health promotion becomes evident. The coach and sports teacher must be aware that if boys, girls and young people react to proportionally similar work loads (per kg body weight) with a similar recovery and adaptation process as adults, the total of work load factors (intensity, volume, density and duration of stimuli) must for boys and girls be less than that of adults.

In establishing dynamic models in basic technical training the principle of age-dependence comes into play, as the sequence of movements has to be explained, bearing in mind the ability of the athletes to understand.

Age-dependence requires that the coach or sports teacher must demonstrate the movement with as little explanation as possible, while when giving instructions to adolescents and adults certain basic physical knowledge can be taken for granted.

Condition and coordination must also be developed according to age. This requires varied training and a gradual increase in the total volume of work.

Here it is clear that there is a close connection of the principle of age-dependence with those of improving health, versatility and gradualness.

2.3.10. Summary

The general training or basic principles apply not only to voluntary training of adults and adolescents in all branches of sport, but also to the training of basic sports in the compulsory sports classes of our educational system.

If these fundamental principles in the planning and structure of training are not correctly applied, or denied, mistakes in training may follow. These faults in training can lead to physical and psychological damage of athletes, especially the younger ones. Adherence to the fundamental principles must therefore be strongly emphasized by the trainer and sports master during sports lessons at school.

2.4. The Basic Physical Properties of Strength, Speed and Endurance and their Physiological Foundation

We introduce what we have to say on this subject by some explanation of the physiological functions which are of particular importance for the strength, speed and duration of muscular contractions. This can only be a very general survey; for more details we refer to the specialized literature [2].

2.4.1. Physiology of Blood Circulation

The muscles responsible for the support and mobility of the human body receive their impulses from the nervous system. The greater the number of impulses arriving at the muscle fibres in a given period of time, the faster and more strongly the muscle contracts. The impulses can originate from the pyramidal or extrapyramidal areas of the cerebral cortex. If they pass through the pyramidal tract, they trigger voluntary, conscious contractions; if they pass over the extrapyramidal tract, involuntary movements, as e.g. walking, are produced. When learning an exercise, one first performs separate movements consciously, i.e. the impulses pass along the pyramidal system. The stimulus for automated movements passes over the extrapyramidal system along certain grooved tracts.

Although the movements are performed involuntarily, they are controlled by the motor system that takes over immediately the conditions under which the movements occur normally change. The initial supply of energy for a muscle contraction originates from the breakdown of adenosine triphosphate (ATP). ATP-reserves in muscles are relatively small. Therefore ATP must be continuously resynthesized.

2 N. V. Zimkin "Physiologie des Sports" (Sports Physiology), Translation of a Manuscript, Instruction Material of the DHfK Leipzig, 1967. N. N. Iakovlev "Biochemie des Sports" (Biochemistry of Sports), Instruction material of the DHfK Leipzig, 1967. W. Rüdiger "Lehrbuch der Physiologie" (Text-Book on Physiology), Volk und Gesundheit, Berlin 1969. V. N. Satziorski "Die körperlichen Eigenschaften des Sportlers" (Physical Properties of the Athlete) in "Theorie und Praxis der Körperkultur", Annex 2, Sportverlag, Berlin 1971.

The energy required for this is obtained through the splitting of creatine phosphate and glycogen. Both substances are present in the muscle.

The breakdown of ATP and creatine phosphate is basically an anaerobic process and so is the breakdown of glycogen to pyruvic or lactic acid (glycolytic phosphorylation). Whether a further breakdown of lactic acid to the metabolic products CO_2 and H_2O will take place depends on the presence of oxygen, since this part of the muscular metabolism is exclusively aerobic (oxydative phosphorylation). The oxydative phosphorylation consumes much less energy than the glycolitic phosphorylation. Thus during the anaerobic breakdown of a glucose molecule to lactic acid 2 to 3 ATP-molecules, while during the further breakdown to CO_2 and H_2O between 30 and 38 molecules can be resynthesized.

Each endurance task of the muscle depends on the anaerobic metabolic process of the muscle and hence on the relevant supply of oxygen.

The glycogen reserve (stored carbohydrates) is about 200 gr in the untrained organism. It can be doubled by training. The muscular system and the liver share the storage of glycogen equally.

The nutrients required by muscles for their work are conveyed by the bloodstream. It acts as a medium between the environment and the cellular systems of the organism. The heart handles the blood flow as the motor of blood circulation. By rhythmical contractions of the heart blood is pumped into the large arteries, and flows, because of the fall in pressure it produces, through the smaller blood vessels (arteries, arterioles, capillaries, venoles)

and finally through the veins back to the heart. Blood drains all the organs of the body, enabling nutrients (e.g. glycogen), stored in the various organs, to be transported to other organs requiring them for work (e.g. muscles). Flowing through capillaries (fine and very porous tubes allowing water and nutrients to pass through their walls) blood supplies nutrients and oxygen to the adjacent cells. This gives rise to metabolic processes enabling these cells to work.

The activity of the cardio-vascular system is controlled by nerves which, according to need, increase the heart output (greater blood expulsion) and dilate the blood vessels. Responsibility for this control function rests with a pair of nerves of the sympathetic system, known as the sympathetic and the parasympathetic nerves. The sympathetic nerve is the so-called efficiency nerve and the parasympathetic nerve (or vagus) the recovery nerve.

Under the influence of the sympathetic nerve all organs of the human body are mobilized for successful physical activity. It raises the frequency of heart beats, strengthens contractions, increases the respiratory rate and volume. Acting on the stimulus-threshold of the motor end-organs at the muscle fibres, the sympathetic nerve enhances the reaction of muscles to stimuli. The cardio-vascular activity is furthermore increased by a hormone, produced from the adrenal medulla, called adrenalin.

Under the effect of the parasympathetic nerve the organism operates for the most part in overdrive.

2.4.2. Strength, Speed and Endurance

In what follows the condition factors (strength, speed and endurance) will, as is commonly done, be described separately, although in reality they are closely interrelated and interdependent. A sprinter must, for example, constantly strive to improve his speed. For this he does not only train his powers of endurance through repeated running, but also speed-endurance and strength, since the execution of each fast running stride requires a definite amount of strength. For top-class performances in a given event one or the other factor will have to be thoroughly trained, while others have to be neglected. The training capacity of the body, i.e. its ability to adapt to changing circumstances, enables it to improve particular factors depending on a given aim (to become a thrower, runner or jumper).

2.4.2.1. Strength

Strength can be defined as the capability of overcoming a certain resistance or of acting against it by muscular tension (the term capability is here used in the sense of functional potential). The manifestations of strength capacity are: maximum strength, explosive strength and strength endurance. Physically force is defined by the formula $F = m \cdot a$ (force equals mass multiplied by acceleration). From this formula it becomes evident that there are two possibilities of improving muscular strength:

1. By increasing the mass (m).
When the mass has reached a maximum, i.e. the highest value to be tack-led by an athlete with the maximum possible effort, one speaks of the maximum strength of the athlete. He thereby foregoes speed for heavy weights.

2. By an increase in acceleration (a).
The possibility of increasing acceleration plays a big part, particularly in the sprints, jumps and throws, since results in these events depend mainly on explosive force.

In answering the question which is often raised as to how much training is needed to reach maximum strength or explosive force performance, one must note that the difference in condition between athletes must be taken into account when determining training weights. In order to reach the maximum increase in strength only 78 percent of the muscular power which it is possible for an individual to achieve comes into play. The expenditure of muscular strength depends on some factors which can partly be influenced by training, namely:

1. On the type of muscle fibres and their percentage in muscles. It has been shown by research that the skeletal muscles are composed of two functionally different kinds of fibres, i.e. the phasic and the tonic muscle fibres. Both kinds of fibres are found side by side in almost all muscles. The phasic muscle fibres have a very short time of contraction but tire quickly. Therefore it is the muscle fibres which react in movements requiring speed or explosive force. The tonic fibres have a considerably longer time of contraction and tire much later than the phasic ones. The latter play a big part in endurance and strength-endurance work. Since phasic as well as tonic muscle fibres can be trained, it is advisable to rely on phasic qualities when explosive

strength is to be developed, meaning that the tonic muscle fibres must be adapted to the fast contractability of the phasic muscle fibres.

2. On the physiological cross-section of the muscle, i.e. on the number of muscle fibres of one particular muscle and their strength.

The number of muscle fibres is innate but their strength increases in the course of time. The increase in volume of the muscle fibres depends apparently on the amount of effort to which they have been subjected. It is a proven fact that muscular tension is the specific stimulus for growth in thickness and hence in the force increase of muscle fibres.

3. On the number of muscle fibres participating in the contraction.

Normally not all muscle fibres of one muscle participate in the contraction. They relieve each other in a combined action. The number of muscle fibres participating in the action can be influenced voluntarily and depends on the frequency of the impulse going from the central nervous system to the muscle.

4. On a good flow of blood in the muscle.

This applies particularly when contractions of long duration are executed with a high degree of tension. For a short time the muscle can work on energy reserves and without oxygen. Nutrients and oxygen must then be supplied by the blood stream and metabolic end-products eliminated. The energy reserves can be increased by training.

5. On the degree of muscular expansion.

Since muscles are elastic, the same principle applies as with rubber—the greater the stretching, the more strength is generated. This, of course, applies only within certain limits. Due to the function of expansion receptors (muscle and tendinous spindles) the muscle is protected against overstretching. In cases of intensive or sudden expansions the receptors bring about an immediate reflectory contraction of the muscle concerned (cf. knee-jerk). Pre-tension or preliminary swings are used in almost all physical exercises.

6. On the regulation of the muscle tone of sportsmen over the extrapyramidal motor system.

The lower the muscle tone of the sportsman, the easier and faster contraction can occur.

Finally some words on how strength is developed by static (supporting) and dynamic (motor) exertions. The cross-section of a muscle and consequently its maximum strength increase is much faster in static exertions, during which the greatest tension is produced. Owing to the continued contraction of the muscle the small blood vessels in the muscle are compressed, thus not allowing sufficient nutrients and oxygen to be conveyed by the blood. This hinders the elimination of metabolic residues with heat, so that fatigue sets in sooner. The uninterrupted flow of impulses sent out by the nervous system and conducted to the muscle, producing a constant contraction, leads naturally also to the exhaustion of the nervous system. Dynamic work, characterized by alternating contraction and relaxation, offers, on the other hand, great advantages. The muscle fibres which thicken during contraction compress the small blood vessels and press the blood into the veins; in the relaxation phase the pressure is relieved and blood flows again into the blood vessels. By this beneficial vascular massage the blood flow, and through it the supply of nutrients and oxygen to the muscular system, is improved. On the other hand the work of the nervous system is relieved, delaying the onset of fatigue.

2.4.2.2. Speed

Speed can be defined as the ability, on the basis of the mobility of the nervous system and the muscular apparatus, to perform movements at a certain velocity. Physically velocity is expressed by the formula:

$$V = \frac{\Delta D}{\Delta T} \quad \text{Velocity} = \frac{\text{change in distance}}{\text{change in time}}$$

A thorough analysis will show that results in most sports events are achieved by an acceleration of the body (or the body with an implement), which means that speed per unit of time is constantly increased. Acceleration is obtained by the coordinated strength and deployment of various groups of muscles, having imparted the highest possible speed to the body of the athlete or his implement in a given unit of time.

Speed comprises quick response, acceleration, maximum speed, and speed-endurance.

Since speed is generally considered as a collective term, it will not be further differentiated.

The speed of muscle contractions depends on the structure of muscle fibres and on the alternation of stimulus ("make way") and inhibition in the nervous system. The better the movements are coordinated, the faster excitations and inhibitions alternate in the nervous system, and the faster a movement can be performed.

When cyclical speed movements are performed (sprinting), the alternation of exertion and relaxation of muscles plays an important part in the duration of these movements. Only a muscle with a good adaptive capability can work at its maximum for a prolonged period of time since relaxation promotes the blood flow and thereby allows the muscle to recuperate. The suppleness depends on the type of nerve (ability to relax) and this can be trained to a certain extent.

The musculature adapts to speed training by increasing its glycogen and creatine phosphate contents. These substances are important factors for metabolic processes and enable the muscle to continue working without any further supply for a certain time, provided it has sufficient reserves. A further means of adaptation is the buffer property of the blood. Buffering is the ability to maintain the hydrogen ion concentration (pH-value) between 6.35 and 7.40 in the blood at a constant level. The high frequency of movements and the great effort applied in the execution of movements at the individually highest speed represents a very high physiological work rate per unit of time. The oxygen required for the transformation and supply of energy cannot be supplied in sufficient quantities. The muscle therefore works anaerobically, i.e. with only little or no oxygen. In the deployment of energy alkaline metabolic end and intermediate products are set free. They must be neutralized by buffering processes. In the 100 m sprint the organism requires, for example, about 8 to 10 l oxygen. Through respiration during running this oxygen requirement can be covered only to about 1 litre. The organism therefore works at an oxygen debt of about 90 % of the requirement. Metabolic processes in the muscles are to a great degree anaerobic. This hinders the work of the muscles and limits, amongst other things, the duration of the speed and explosive force performance. With great physical effort 90 percent of the whole metabolism take place in the musculature. The expenditure of energy for a 100 m sprint is e.g. appr. 210 kJ (50 cal.), i.e. a 200-fold increase compared to the B.M.R. (basal metabolic rate) of the value at rest. The longer the distances, the lower the expenditure of energy will be for each 100 m, because the running tempo also decreases. In the 400 m appr. 105 kJ (25 cal.) and in the 1,500 m appr. 46 kJ (11 cal.) are required per 100 m. The expenditure of energy for the total distance is, however, much higher

for 400 m appr. 410 kJ (100 cal.)
for 1,500 m appr. 700 kJ (170 cal.)
for 10,000 m appr. 2,950 kJ (700 cal.)

Warm-up before training or competitions contributes to improving the rate of muscular contractions. It furthers the blood flow, leads to the stimulus and activity of the nerve centres and nerve tracts involved and accelerates the metabolic processes.

This explains why far better results are obtained in the speed events in warm climates compared with colder ones.

In sustained speed exercises not only muscles and nerves, but also the vegetative systems, such as the cardio-vascular and respiratory systems play an important part, depending on intensity. In performing a-cyclic one-at-a-time speed exercises, much less strain than that required in cyclic speed exercises of longer duration is involved.

Quick response is particularly important for sprinters. It is the period of time from the perception of a stimulus to the time for the response and is composed of the transmission time from the sense organ to the nerve, the time needed to convey the excitation through the nervous system, the time required to switch over to the different nervous centres, and the time for the muscles to contract.

The time required for these switch-over processes depends largely on the type of nerve. The state of excitation of the nervous system is also important (different times of response in alert or sleepy states). Before the start, when the organism is working under the beneficial influence of the sympathetic nerve, the reaction time is shorter than under normal conditions.

2.4.2.3. Endurance

Endurance is the ability to carry out a given amount of work during a prolonged period of time without deterioration in the quality of such work. The build-up of endurance is always connected with the functioning of the entire organism which must work against the resulting fatigue. Although the effort per time unit is relatively low, in the long run the organism is subjected to a great work-load. The greater the endurance of an athlete is, the better he can resist fatigue.

For increasing endurance it is important to improve the functioning of the vegetative system, since the duration of the working ability of the muscular system depends largely on the supply of oxygen and nutrients as well as on the blood supply in general. Therefore the organism adapts itself to endurance training by increasing the number of capillaries in the muscle, thus improving the blood flow and the utilization of oxygen and nutrients.

The surplus quantity of blood needed in the active muscle is expelled by the heart. This places a larger load on the heart, which increases its size by enlarging the ventricles, and thickens the myocard (especially the muscles of the left ventricle). The increased blood volume of the heart enables it to expulse a bigger quantity of blood at each stroke, thus increasing blood supply to the circulatory system for its work. The greater quantity of blood supplied at every heart stroke during endurance training lowers the heart rate in a state of rest to 40 beats per minute. During rest the heart works with great economy by lowering its pulse rate and increasing the heart beat volume, thus obtaining greater reserves for work under stress. Under stress the pulse rate depends on the intensity of stress.

The above mentioned processes of adaptation by reduced vegetative function are enhanced by the release of heat during metabolic processes in the form of perspiration. The entire respiratory mechanism is also subject to the increased oxygen consumption. By endurance training the vital capacity is increased from the normal 3.5 to 4 litres up to 6 or 7 litres.

During long distance races an equilibrium of the metabolic processes in the muscular system is established. In physiology it is called "steady state". This equilibrium is expressed by the steadiness of the pulse rate, blood pressure and respiration. In this state the blood supply in the active muscle is ideal, sufficient nutrients and oxygen are supplied in response to needs and metabolic residues removed.

Thus the oxygen debt of a marathon runner is only about 4 to 6 % by comparison with the 90 to 95 % oxygen debt of a sprinter after 100 m. Endurance training involving long-distance races in the steady state leads to economy in the organic functions and metabolism. The nervous system can also economize its functions by endurance training. The coordination of movements between actions and reactions becomes harmonious. The impulses from the motor cells to the muscles operate with a regular rhythm and at a fairly low frequency. Furthermore, depending on the work load, nervous areas and muscle fibres alternate their activity (asynchronic activity), so that the exercise can be pursued for a long period of time. On this point ZIMKIN states: "The better the coordination of movements and the fewer muscles are involved in the performance of a given movement, the longer the work can be pursued". [3]

The links between endurance and the two other condition factors (strength and speed) are strength-endurance and speed-endurance. For both types of endurance the goal is to achieve a high performance during as long a period of time as possible. This can be realized by ensuring the participation of the circulatory system in the working process.

Having explained the effect of strength, speed and endurance training on the organism, we recommend that the coach is careful to train all these quali-

3   N. V. Zimkin "Physiologische Charakteristik von Kraft, Schnelligkeit und Ausdauer" (Physiological Characteristics of Strength, Speed and Endurance) in the Series "Sport im Sozialismus", Sportverlag, Berlin 1959.

ties, especially with athletes at the beginning of their careers, in order to influence the entire organism and not merely part to a greater and part to a lesser degree. Based on such a foundation a stable pattern of performance can be built up later on in a particular event, because, due to the allround training, the nervous processes function smoothly and the bodily functions adapt to the load. It is much easier for an athlete who has been given training which is flexible and manysided, than for an athlete with an intensely specialized preparation, to learn the technique of a particular event. For this reason the principle of versatility must be closely observed, especially when training boys, girls and young athletes.

2.4.3. Special Aspects in Training Women

Along with the constant improvement and the increasing concentration of world-class achievements, the strong development of women's sport is an outstanding feature of modern competition. This phenomenon becomes evident in track and field not only by the improvement of records in many events, but also by the considerable widening in the standard programme of the women's events. In recent years the Olympic programme has been expanded by the inclusion of the 400 m and the 1,500 m and the 4 × 400 relays and in the next European Championship the 3,000 m race will be added. During the last decade the press has informed us of the successful participation of women in long-distance races, up to the marathon, in which some women achieved better results than many of the men. These may be individual cases, but the development should by no means be regarded as fortuitous. It can be asserted that the conquest of endurance events by women, adopting a systematic approach to training for long distances, will develop naturally. We also consider it natural that this development— with the exception of some excellent performances of the top champions in the capitalist countries— is in general brought about by sportswomen from socialist countries. Like many other social processes this characterizes the potential for development in a socialist society. Thus sport for women can gain ground once it is freed from irrational biological and philosophical limitations and traditional prejudices.

The basis on which sport for women has developed has, without doubt, been considerably broadened in the GDR.

The work in large numbers of schools and in sports clubs has been brought about by the Spartakiad movement. Everywhere in factories, residential communities and social organizations women's sports groups have come into existence. The excellent performances of GDR sportswomen in top international competitions has set high standards for the physical efficiency of women.

The promotion of health for all citizens, a principle guaranteed by the constitution, requires great effort, particularly in the field of sport for women. It should not be overlooked that women have, apart from their jobs, many household duties. In spite of more household aids and service facilities, this puts an additional load on their shoulders; a purposeful and well-planned physical education becomes all the more important for women. Training should not only be regarded as a recreation activity, acting as a counter-weight to professional and household work, but as a well directed preparation, leading to mental and physical fitness. It is obvious that women age earlier and lose their proficiency if they neglect their bodies; this can be avoided by regular sports activities.

Track and field competition for women in our Republic has, for years, been famous throughout the world. The great importance of track and field as a basic sport lies in the manysidedness of its numerous events. With track and field exercises all the physical factors and coordination abilities, such as speed, strength, endurance, agility and mobility can be developed without special material expenditure, and the amount of work can be individually prescribed and controlled. The evidence of the results of training is easily established in track and field events. As forms of exercises and training means are very variable, they can be adapted to the requirements of women.

2.4.3.1. Morphological and Functional Differences Between Men and Women

Table 2 shows that in comparable track and field competitions women have results roughly 14 % lower than men. The reason for the lower general and physical efficiency of women is the morphological and functional differences between sexes. The most important ones will be outlined in what follows.

● Body Weight, Height and Physical Constitution

Table 2 Comparing Men's and Women's Performances (as of 1. 12. 1982)

Event	Men	Women	Per Cent
100 m	9.95	10.88	91.45
200 m	19.83	21.71	91.34
400 m	43.86	48.16	91.07
800 m	101.73	113.43	89.68
1,500 m	211.30	234.47	90.89
3,000 m	452.10	506.78	89.21
5,000 m	780.42	908.26	85.92
10,000 m	1,642.50	1,895.03	86.67
4 × 100 m	38.03	41.60	91.42
4 × 400 m	176.10	199.04	92.49
Weitsprung	8.90	7.20	80.90
Hochsprung	2.36	2.02	85.59
Average			88.88

Calculation of running results according to the formula:

$$\frac{100 \times \text{Men's Performances}}{\text{Women's Performances}}$$

The most vital differences between a man and a woman are to be found in body height (size, stature) and body weight. On the average women are 10 to 12 cm shorter and 10 to 15 kg lighter than men. These values apply to averages of the whole population and have been confirmed by a survey at the Olympic Games in Munich in 1972 (Table 3). Physical constitution is different in the two sexes (Table 4). The more abundant fatty (hypodermic) tissue in women gives them their typical outline. This fatty tissue is also differently distributed in women than in men. In men this is present mainly on the upper part of the body; women have it mostly on their thighs, hips and buttocks. This distribution of fat and their broader hips give women a stature that spreads downward.

Women have roughly 5 % less bone-

Table 3 Body Height and Weight of the Participants at the Olympic Games 1972 (according to H. Gundlach, Olympische Leichtathletik-Wettkämpfe 1972. DVfL der DDR 1973) (Olympic Track and Field Competitions 1972)

	Men	Women	Differences
Height (cm) of the 6 Best Performers (in brackets mean values of all participants)			
100 m	179 (175)	167 (164)	12
200 m	184 (177)	172 (166)	12
400 m	181 (178)	168 (168)	13
800 m	179 (177)	169 (168)	10
1,500 m	181 (178)	167 (166)	14
Long Jump	186 (182)	163 (170)	23
High Jump	190 (186)	179 (175)	11
Shot Put	192 (192)	177 (174)	15
Discus Throw	192 (190)	173 (174)	19
Javelin Throw	180 (181)	176 (173)	4
Combined Competition	184 (186)	176 (173)	8
Average	184 (182)	172 (170)	12.8
Weight (kg) of the 6 Best Performers (in brackets mean values of all participants)			
100 m	76.3 (69.8)	57.7 (55.7)	18.6
200 m	77.8 (71.2)	61.5 (55.4)	16.3
400 m	75.2 (70.9)	55.8 (56.0)	19.4
800 m	67.3 (65.8)	56.5 (55.8)	10.8
1,500 m	66.6 (65.0)	53.6 (52.6)	13.0
Long Jump	74.8 (74.1)	58.0 (59.7)	16.8
High Jump	80.1 (76.2)	66.6 (62.3)	14.1
Shot Put	120.2 (121.8)	86.8 (82.2)	33.4
Discus Throw	113.5 (108.8)	83.0 (80.2)	30.5
Javelin Throw	89.3 (87.7)	69.0 (68.9)	20.3
Combined Competition	82.3 (85.0)	67.5 (64.0)	14.8
Average	83.9 (81.5)	65.0 (63.0)	18.9

Table 4 Composition of the Human Body

	Man	Woman
Bones	20 %	15 %
Muscles	40 %	36 %
Fatty Tissue	20 %	30 %
Interior Organs	12 %	12 %
Blood	8 %	7 %

mass than men and the arrangement of the female skeleton renders it less suitable for physical exertions. The trunk is longer and the limbs are shorter. The female pelvis is broader, flatter and more protruding. Due to the arrangement of the pelvic bones the levering of the legs is less favourable, resulting in a less effective transmission of power, which becomes evident mainly in the sprints and jumps. Finally the legs have different bearing lines due to the sex-dependent position of the upper to the lower leg.

In the arms women have x-formed deviations from the straight line in the elbow joint, which are a handicap, mainly in throws (especially in the javelin).

The muscular mass in a woman is less than in man, only 36% of the total weight. This difference manifests itself in a smaller cross-section of muscles and in a reduced absolute output (effective work). In relation to body weight women achieve only 80 % of the performances of men.

In conclusion we may state that due to the shorter stature, lower body weight, a different material composition and the specific anatomical structure of the female body, women are inferior to men in physical proficiency.

● Details of the interior organs and functions

The interior organs are also different in the two sexes. The weight of a male lung is on the average 1.35 kg, that of a woman only 1.05 kg. The capacity of oxygen intake and elimination of carbon dioxide depends not only on the size of the pulmonary surface (in men approximately $90 m^2$ and in women $80 m^2$ or less), but also on the blood composition. The reduced respiratory volume can be demonstrated by measurements of the vital capacity. Women attain only 75 to 80 % of the vital capacity of men. This is due to the smaller thoracic circumference and also to the reduced respiratory width. In addition, the respiratory minute volume is about 25 % to that of men.

The male heart is more developed in all sections. In all age groups the weight of the male heart is higher than that of women. The average size of a male heart is of about $750 cm^2$ or $11.5 cm^2$ per body weight; while that of a woman is of only $550 cm^2$ or $9.5 cm^2$ per kg body weight. The smaller size and weight of the female heart results in a reduced force of contraction, reduced blood filling and hence in a lower output compared with that of a man. The capacity of oxygen-intake of the female lung is lower. In order to take up the same quantity of oxygen, the respiratory frequency of a woman must be higher than that of a man. This is physiologically unfavourable since the additional work of the respiratory musculature requires additional oxygen, because utilization of the inhaled air is poorer, since the increased respiratory frequency prevents a deeper inhalation and thus increases respiratory dead space (trachea, bronchi). A smaller heart also requires additional uneconomic work. The lower stroke volume also calls for a higher frequency. From these findings we conclude that the maximum oxygen intake of a woman is about 25 % lower than that of a man.

Blood, serving as a means of transport between the different organic systems, also plays an important role. The volume of blood in man is 70 to 80 ml/kg per body weight, in a woman 60 to 70 ml/kg. The composition of the blood is also different. In a man's blood there are about 5 million red cells per cm^3, in a woman's blood only 4.5 million. These red blood cells contain haemoglobin, a dye-stuff, the iron nucleus of which binds oxygen and conveys it through the body. The average haemoglobin content of a woman shows 13.7 g per 100 ml blood, and that of a man 15.8 g. The total quantity of haemoglobin in the female body is appr. 30 % lower than that in a man.

In summing up we can say that because of morphological and functional differences the physical efficiency of women must be considered as some 20 to 25 % lower than that of men. It is therefore a considerable merit of training if women athletes have been able to reduce this efficiency debt to 14 %. This result speaks for a good adaptability of the female organism to physical stress.

2.4.3.2. Sport and Menstruation

According to recent statistics menstruation (menarche) sets in usually at the age of 11½ years. In the first year menstrual bleeding is often irregular. This is purely physiological and is no reason for giving up sport, nor does sports training have to be put off if menstruation is delayed and sets in only at a later age.

Most women performers train—sometimes with a slightly reduced work load—also during menstruation. Many of them even take part in competition during this time, although evidently most of them are thereby handicapped.

The effects of the different phases of the menstrual cycle on the efficiency of the body have been the subject of many investigations. Dynamometric studies have revealed a drop in the muscular power prior to and after menstruation in about 50% of all women in sport. In some an increase of muscular strength was indicated during these periods.

EIDNER discovered that in 70% of the girl students tested during menstruation the explosive force, in 75% the throwing force and in 56% the strength of the hand grip was unaltered. On the whole one may say, however, that data on the timing of a proficiency optimum in the menstrual cycle varies considerably, partly due to differences in the conditions under which efficiency tests are carried out.

The results of these investigations also depend a great deal on those tested. Also relatively little attention has been given to the variations in time of the different phases of the menstrual cycle in relation to the duration of a complete cycle.

In general it is assumed today that one may count on a decrease before menstruation and a postmenstrual increase of performance ability.

According to latest findings (KISS) the character of menstruation undergoes a pathological change through competition only in 9% of women athletes; in another 6% the change is positive. KABISCH also emphasized the high adaptability of the menstrual cycle to high work loads.

Women athletes rarely have menstrual complaints, as compared to non-athletic women.

Negative changes are usually reflected in the development of ameno-, hypo- or oligomenorrhoeae and also in slight or delayed menstrual discharges. These are cases for the gynaecologist. Since this can be easily cured by proper treatment, it is rarely necessary to bar the women from participation in competitions and even less so in training.

2.4.3.3. Deferral of Menstruation

A postponement of menstruation is often desirable in view of the dates of major competitions, both because of reduced proficiency to be expected in some women athletes before or during menstruation and frequently for purely psychological reasons. There is no objection to this either from the gynaecologist or from the sports doctor. Since contraceptives are nowadays used all over the world, former ethical objections are certainly now not justified and the only problem the sport physician has to handle is whether the proficiency of the woman athlete will be influenced by administered drugs. Numerous experiments have shown that the hormone preparations used have no influence on the proficiency, neither in a positive nor in a negative sense. Therefore one cannot speak of doping, and contraception is certainly not injurious to the health of women athletes.

But one should keep in mind that the postponement of menstruation with reference to the fixture list should be prepared long beforehand.

2.4.3.4. Sport and Contraceptives

Many women athletes use hormonal contraceptives without harming their general condition or their special proficiency. On the contrary, oscillations in performance due to the cycle often become less frequent.

In some cases, however, (the percentage is not greater than in non-athletic women) slight menstrual disturbances (intermediate bleeding) and other signs of rejection have been observed. The reaction of a woman athlete to hormonal contraceptives in these cases must be given attention and a doctor consulted.

2.4.3.5. Sport and Pregnancy

Recent investigations (KISS, KOVACZ, ZAKHARIEVA) have, as against former assertions, proved that competitive sport does not influence the functioning of the inner sexual organs of women and their ability to conceive. Many women athletes have trained intensively for years before their first delivery, and then born their first child without any difficulty.

Furthermore, after the first delivery, the physical condition of a woman was better and more stable than before.

During the first three months of pregnancy more than half of pregnant women athletes experience no loss in athletics form. They should therefore be allowed to take part in training and in competitions during this time, but be kept under constant medical control. During this period exercises with vigorous pressing, forced strength workouts and jumps downward from appreciable heights should be avoided.

Women athletes who, in the first three months, complain of nausea, vomiting, hypertension, dizziness, headaches, loss of appetite, iron-deficiency or anaemia should be barred from training for competition. They should do exercises which are generally prescribed for the second period of 3 months.

These are easy movements without a combative character, such as gymnastics, swimming and water-games. During this time exercises requiring pressing, force and jumps or exercises with a sudden change of position should be dispensed with. At the same time one must bear in mind that a sudden inactivity may lead to functional disturbances in women athletes, called the "relief syndrome". Although naturally pregnancy means an increased physical load for women, this cannot take the place of that associated with sport. In order to prevent a considerable fall-off from the previously established development of the system, especially of the cardio-vascular system, and to satisfy the desire of a woman athlete to take exercise, she should be allowed to do light-hearted training during the second period of three months. It is of particular importance that she should remain in close contact with her club-mates, and the physical training instructor or coach must look after her health in view of her later reintegration into the competition squad.

The future mother will be considerably handicapped during the last three months. During this time the training programme should consist of gymnastics, swimming, deepbreathing exercises and extended walks.

In conclusion it may be said that competition and training during the first third of the pregnancy do not entail any more pregnancy complications than among non-athletic women.

2.4.3.6. Sport and Delivery

After thorough examinations the question as to how competitive sport during pregnancy affects the course of delivery, can also be conclusively answered.

It can be said generally that the duration of the delivery of active women athletes hardly differs from that of non-athletic women. While in highly trained women the first or "dilatation period" is generally prolonged, because of high muscle tone and reduced extensibility of the soft parts of the genital tract, the second or "expulsion period" is one and a half times shorter than that of non-athletic women.

Thanks to an improved preparation of women during pregnancy and good guidance during delivery, the delivery process is nowadays much shorter than it used to be. Serious complications due to sports activities have not been observed in athletes. One of the more frequent complications is the injury of the perineum of the pelvic floor muscles. On the other hand the striae gravidarum (cracks in the hypodermic fatty tissue on the abdomen and the thighs) are much less frequent than with non-athletes.

The children born by athletes do not differ from the children of non-athletes with regard to maturity, size and weight.

2.4.3.7. Sport, Childbed and Lactation

After a delivery without complications the athlete should immediately resume sports activities. She should, primarily, do exercises for strengthening the slackened abdominal and pelvic floor muscles, starting the first day after delivery, and gradually increasing the amount. After one month the athlete can start with strengthening exercises related to her special event and with technical training consisting of moderate endurance exercises.

Three months after delivery she can resume real exertion in her particular event; whether she will take part in competition will depend on the degree of efficiency she has been able to achieve. One may say that approximately six months after delivery her physical condition generally allows her to take part in competition.

Recent findings have proved that sports activities do not hinder a woman in nursing her child.

On the whole an athlete who expects and delivers a child cannot take part in competition for one year. Numerous athletic results of mothers prove that the general as well as the special proficiency of a woman is improved and more stabilized through pregnancy. Therefore proficiency in sports and motherhood do not exclude each other.

2.4.3.8. Sport and Abortion

In spite of all this a female athlete may, for several reasons, decide to have her pregnancy interrupted. Such an intervention calls for a special structure of the individual training programme.

If an athlete does not wish to continue her pregnancy she should continue her training until the day of the intervention. If no complications arise, a training break of two weeks is recommended. Athletes who compete should see the doctor for a follow-up examination, to make sure that the involution process of the uterus is concluded before resuming her training.

After abortion the training load should be increased by stages up to the level it was at before the break. Only when this is achieved should a woman athlete take part again in competition. Generally, if the intervention has taken a normal course, she should recover her full former efficiency after about six weeks.

2.4.3.9. Intersex Types and Sex Control

It is wrong to believe that the limit between the male and the female sex is completely plain and easy to determine.

There are, on the contrary, transitional forms which are recognized by a more or less marked difference of the sexual cells, the exterior and interior genitals and all exterior sex characteristics; these forms physiological science has attempted to classify. These intermediate sex types have become known in sport. They are physically superior to ordinary women and their participation in female competiton entails a real disadvantage for ordinary women. For this reason sex chromatine determination tests have been introduced which, beginning in Mexico-City, are compulsory for all women performers. A mucosal smear is taken from the mouth. One finds on the edge of mucosal cells a socalled "Barr-body" which is missing in all individuals with male chromosomes. This chromatine check has given good results, but there are also intermediate types which, according to the nucleus, are female or could be assigned to either sex. In such cases much more complicated examinations of the chromosome stock have to be carried out. Only thus can real disadvantages for other female athletes be avoided.

2.5.   Methods of Sports Training

An old Latin proverb says: "Many roads lead to Rome", meaning in other words, that many ways can lead to the same goal. Scientists, teachers or coaches use as roads different means for reaching a certain goal (i.e. the findings of research, educational aims etc.).

A scientist can use a variety of methods for examining an object. Due to the diversity of objects the methods of investigation vary considerably. But they have, nervertheless, a common methodological basis. [4]

4 Methodology is the teaching of the general laws of investigation of the objective world, the totality of methods and processes; it is based on dialectical materialism (see "Pädagogische Studientexte", Volk und Wissen, Berlin 1961).

796.42
SCH5t

Furthermore, the term "Method" refers to the presentation of the results of scientific investigations which, in teaching, assume the character of a branch of study. But a teacher or coach in his lessons or coaching sessions is concerned not only with the branch of study. He must, at first, sort the subject matter and then impart it to his pupils or athletes by appropriate methods. At the same time he must, during his teaching activity, ensure a unity of instruction and education in the lesson. Therefore fundamental differences between research work and teaching exist.

The method of presentation of science is called the "logico-systematical method" of presentation, the method of the classroom, the didactic method of presentation. The method of presentation of science will not be discussed further in this text-book.

What do we understand by the didactical method of presentation or the presentation method of teaching?

"By methods of teaching or instruction we designate the ways a teacher has to take, in order to direct the learning process of his pupils, i.e. the process of the absorption of knowledge, perception, convictions, abilities, skills and habits, and in order to lead them to optimal results". [5]

This definition of teaching methods applies also to the sports lesson and training. During the sports lesson and in training the pupils or athletes are taught many abilities and skills; they are also educated to become personalities in a socialist society. The unity of education and moulding of character in

5 "Pädagogische Studientexte" (Pedagogical Study Texts), Volk und Wissen, Berlin 1961.

the teaching lesson is thereby guaranteed. The general teaching methods for compulsory physical education also apply to training. But the methods of training are rightly considered to be a complex per se, since training as a specialized pedagogical process has a quality other than the pedagogical process of general compulsory physical education.

We therefore understand by training methods all those methods by which an athlete is educated to become a citizen in a socialist society and by which he is taught skills of movements and to develop and constantly improve his physical condition and coordination abilities such as strength, speed, endurance and their associated complex phenomena, as well as mobility, extensibility, suppleness, relaxation faculty etc. to a maximum, and to strengthen his qualities of will-power.

By the use of scientifically based methods of coaching an athlete is prepared physically and mentally to reach his personal best performance, to take part in competitions, and to safeguard the interests of a socialist society. Educational methods, methods for building up movement skills, as well as methods for further development and improvement of the factors affecting physical coordination and coordination abilities, form a dialectical unit during the process of training, i.e. the education, instruction and training methods are closely interrelated and interdependent.

The training methods combine two large bodies of methods:

1. Methods of political and character development
2. Methods of education

Trinidad High
School Library

27,676

a) Methods for building up movement skills

b) Methods for developing and improving condition factors and coordination abilities (strength, speed, endurance, mobility and agility)

c) Methods of training tactics and theory. The methods of the two bodies of methods complement each other not only in that only well developed condition factors and coordination abilities permit acquisition of the correct sequence of movements and development into proper skills, but also in that the methods of education are a great help in developing character, where certain methods of character formation are used in the training of technique or, for example, in strength training for moral education and development of will-power. Although the two complexes of methods form a unity in practice, they will be dealt with separately in what follows.

2.6.   Methods of Education

1. The method of instruction or persuasion

The method of instruction consists in giving guidance and enlightenment. It aims at the development of firm convictions. According to PETUKHOV the following educational means belong to the method of persuasion: Ethical and moral directions given by the teacher, explaining examples of proper conduct, summaries by the pupils of ethical problems, the dialogue on ethical problems and rules of conduct, the provision of extramural reading material, the influence of the media, i.e. of the theatre and cinema, and putting pupils into situations requiring conscious ethical behaviour. It is important to stress the emotional side of the personality.

2. Method of the living example

The method of the living example refers in the main to the example set by the teacher. It is only efficacious if the words of the teacher correspond to his own behaviour, and if he commands respect. The value of the living example for pupils depends on the trainer's or teacher's character. The example of the teacher should be strengthened by referring to personalities of great esteem and to their actions, so that they become familiar to the pupils.

3. Method of checking

Checking as a method of education in the form of control contributes essentially to the development of desirable habits such as careful, planned and responsible actions. The control must be consistent and continual and must become an integral part of the educational process and should unconditionally avoid being arbitrary.

4. Method of assistance

Assistance as a method of moral education is expressed by criticism and encouragement. This approach is more effective if backed by the whole squad. Encouragement becomes necessary when an adolescent or adult athlete lacks confidence and tends to give up easily.

5. Method of appraisal

Appraisal as a method of education is given in the way of praise or reprimand. There are many ways of doing this. Most important is that a proper amount be used, in that praise and re-proof never be given in the form of an absolute judgement and that adolescents or adult athletes be appraised uniformly by all persons participating in their education.

6. Method of demands

Setting targets is an essential method for the inculcation of moral qualities and rules of conduct. It applies at all ages and levels of attainment. When dealing with athletes who have been training for a long time or with adults, demands should be combined with persuasion. In the training process the method of setting targets should be made use of to carry through the planned volume of training.

The confrontation of an athlete with training and competition targets is an important educational means of developing his personality. This assumes, however, that the coach is well acquainted with the educational potential of the training means and methods and with specific schedules and that he applies them consciously during the educational process in training.

2.7. Methods of Instruction

During the process of instruction, in education, exercise is the main method [6]. Only by the repetition of a specific physical exercise, can athletic skills be trained, or factors affecting physical condition and coordination abilities be developed and improved. In special cases exercises with specific objectives will achieve simultaneously instruction and development of condition factors and coordination abilities and athletic skills. But usually, during sports classes and in training, exercises are set so that either the build-up of skills or the improvement of abilities are in the foreground.

When outlining the methods of education for sports lessons and training, both sides participating in the process, viz. teacher and pupil, or trainer and athlete, should be kept in mind. Therefore the methods of instruction in education are subdivided into several sections which complement each other. So, for instance, the methods of education or the build-up of skills are complemented by the methods of imparting and treating the subject matter.

2.7.1. Methods of Developing Motor Skills

2.7.1.1. Methods of Transmitting Knowledge

First there are a whole series of methods determining how the subject matter should be imparted. They concern the practical work of teaching and the relation between coach and athlete. Here we shall deal with the groups of methods regarding the approaches to be taken by the coach:

6 Cf. F. Trogsch "Die Hauptmethode ist das Üben" (The Chief Method is Practising) in "Körpererziehung", Nr. 12/1961.

1. Methods of presentation

Their task is to develop a good understanding of movement. It must be stressed that they should not only be applied at the beginning of the learning process. The main methods of presentation are the demonstration and the explanation. There are various ways of demonstrating:

– The *ideal demonstration* by the teacher gives to the pupil or athlete an allround impression of the exercise. In each case an explanation should follow. This method is not so efficacious when a movement is performed at great speed, for instance in the jumps.

– The *slow demonstration* of parts of movements completes the demonstration of the complete movement and underlines the main phases. This form of demonstration is chiefly used in the throwing events; for example the moment of release of the javelin can be demonstrated slowly while each single part of the movement is precisely explained.

– The *use of check marks* is eminently desirable in track and field events but unfortunately not yet widely practised. In almost all events check marks facilitate work. With the javelin a "trench" is used for learning the impulse stride. A radius drawn into the discus circle helps learning the turn on a straight line in the shot.

– With the help of *films and illustrations* the coach can explain an exercise more vividly. A film has great advantages over a single shot or series of pictures. The sequence of movements can be perceived in its entirety. Each group leader and coach in track and field should possess a good number of pictures and series of pictures of the most

important events and use them during training sessions.

– *Explaining* can be describing or analysing etc. The explanation should be short and concise, only emphasizing the main features. It must be logical and persuasive.

2. Methods of giving guidance

According to BURISCH [7] these methods comprise: setting the task (command, specification of the exercise, rules and aims of the exercise, homework), helping (by hints, encouragement, support), evaluation (appraisal, correction). They should be applied in accordance with the subject matter and according to the level of attainment of the athlete.

3. Methods of feat-finding

This is done by means of checking, examining and by awarding marks. Here competition plays a decisive role. The results of evaluation stimulate the athletes to further efforts and show the coach to what he should direct his attention.

2.7.1.2. Methods of Treating the Subject

The methods of treating a subject or of arranging it are, what the name implies. The structure of the exercise to be taught and its complexity decides how it should be approached. After reflection on this, the coach will decide on a series or sequence of exercises.

Such an approach is appropriate, because many track and field events are

7 Cf. I. Burisch "Zur Systematisierung der in der Körpererziehung (im Turnunterricht) vorwiegend verwendeten Methoden der Bildung" (On the Systematization of the chief Methods used in Physical Education during P. T. Lessons) in "Körpererziehung", Nr. 6/1961.

so difficult that they cannot be learnt in their entirety. The series of exercises may be shorter or longer. One should, however, strive to keep the number of exercises as few as possible. The individual exercises are elements of the total structure of the athletic skills to be absorbed. In the learning process the proper order in which single exercises are to be practised should be strictly adhered to. The degree of difficulty should increase from one exercise to the next. The series of exercises should be concluded with an exercise which is similar in form to the entire movement.

In practice there are several methods for arranging the subject matter.

In the *total learning method* the exercise is left as a whole. Its execution is simplified or made easier. Each exercise of a series corresponds in its basic structure to the whole movement to be learnt. This method has the advantage that from the beginning the "feel" for the proper rhythm and application of strength is produced. By means of this method usually only the rough form is developed. It is mainly applied in training boys and girls (example: hurdles).

In the *partial learning method* a new motion skill is acquired by several exercises corresponding to the various phases or parts of the total movement. Before moving on to the next exercise, the previous one must be mastered (compare with the basic exercises of the running jump).

The partial learning method is applied in very complicated movements (pole vault, discus throw) or in movements that can hardly or not at all be simplified (hitch-kick).

We must further look at the *analytico-synthetic method*. Here the teacher splits up the exercise into its elements, which must be specially practised. The athlete must thereby recognize the position of these elements in the total structure of the movement. The individual elements are then reunited as a whole. The shot put is, for instance, learnt by this method. First one practises the standing put, then the glide and finally the complete movement.

The methods mentioned so far are seldom applied in their pure form. It is relatively simple to assign the arrangement of the subject matter, up to learning the rough form, to *one* method.

If, however, we consider the whole

Table 5   *Spheres of Application of the different Methods of Treating the Subject Matter*

Application	Method	Procedure
Boys and Girls	Total learning method (preferable), partial learning method, analytico-synthetic method	deductive and inductive
Adults	Partial learning method, analytico-synthetic method	deductive and inductive
Learning the rough form	Total learning and partial learning methods, analytico-synthetic method	deductive and inductive
Learning the fine form	Combined methods	deductive and, in some cases, inductive

learning process right up to the assimilation of technique, we find that only *combined methods* are applied, viz. in learning hurdling, the complex learning method, the partial learning method and the complex learning method. At first the rough form is learnt in its totality. Then follow single movements which are trained specially (movement of the trailing leg in the hurdle stride) and finally the newly learnt elements are trained in the complete movement. This process can be repeated many times until the movement is fully stabilized. This is typical of training in track and field.

There is a further and second group of methods of treating the subject matter, to which belong the deductive and the inductive methods.

The *deductive method* means that the teacher, by setting an objective and demonstrating concisely, has the pupil carry out the prescribed movement immediately.

In the *inductive method,* on the other hand, the teacher sets the task for an exercise and gives an indication of the required movement, but allows the pupil to find out for himself the rhythm by trial and error. This would be the case in the javelin, where the athlete has to hit a target and is thus forced to throw the javelin over-head.

The *inductive method* is preferably used for boys and girls, the *deductive method* for adults, and for teaching the final form.

2.7.2. Methods of Developing Strength, Speed and Endurance

The second large complex of methods within the chief method of physical training are the methods for developing and improving condition and coordination abilities such as strength, speed, endurance, flexibility, extensibility, suppleness, agility etc. Through exercise, the level of the condition and coordination of an athlete are changed by his conscious movements. At the same time through the confrontation of the athlete with training schedules he develops not only functional skills but qualities of personality such as determination and will-power. Next to education and psychology, the most important sciences for the field of theory and methodology of sports training are physiology, neurophysiology, biochemistry and biomechanics. In the physiological bases of the methods for improving the quality of movement one starts with the fact that physical exercises as a means of training represent stimuli of development and load for all the organs of the body. The term load can therefore be differentiated according to its characteristics: intensity, density, volume and duration of a stimulus. At the same time the terms intensity (degree of load, maximum, submaximum, medium, moderate, tempo and density of the exercise) and volume (frequency of repetitions, training days, time, total of race kilometres, total of lifted weights) will be physiologically characterized more in detail.

The quality of a load on the body depends on the interrelation and balance of the load characteristics. These determine the physiological effects and bring about a specific training effect. There are also close interrelations between the different load characteristics. They represent a dialectical unity. This direct dependence of the load characteristics on one another is reflected in the basic methods.

The physiological work of the muscles is inseparably connected with the physical terms of work and proficiency. Therefore the concepts of work and proficiency are drawn into the designation of physiological characteristics and the basic methods for development and improvement of condition factors: strength, speed and endurance. These are the duration, interval and repetition methods. The essence of these basic methods within the scope of the chief method, which is exercise, are physiologically determined by the following load characteristics.

1. Stimulus intensity of the exercises

This is the intensity [8] with which the exercises (running, strength work with or without weights) are executed. The stimulus intensity is measured either in metre/seconds (m/s) during runs, in kilograms (kg) of a resistance (e.g. dumb-bell), in metre-kilograms (mkg) or in metre-kilograms per second (mkg/s), as well as by the number of repetitions per unit of time, that is, by frequency. The personal best performance of the athlete is converted into these units of measurement defined as 100 per cent. The stimulus intensity of a physical exercise, expressed in percentage, will always represent the necessary expenditure of effort in comparison with the expenditure of effort necessary for achieving a best personal performance.

2. Stimulus volume of the exercises

The stimulus volume results from the total repetitions of an exercise. In strength exercises without weights it consists of the number of repetitions

(e.g. 20 pull-ups, 30 push-ups). But the stimulus volume can also be measured in kilometres (total of race distance covered), or in kilograms (total of all lifts) in strength exercises with the dumb-bell.

3. Stimulus density of the exercises

By stimulus density of physical exercises we define the relation of the time sequence of movements to the rest interval. During exercises impulses are generated which cross the stimulus threshold once exerted continuously without a break but, another time, are broken by a short incomplete recovery, the so-called "worthwhile break" (REINDELL, KEUL, ROSKAMM, VOLKOV, CHRISTENSEN).

By "worthwhile break" physiologists regard about the first third of the time necessary for complete recovery. Under a medium or submaximum load the pulse rate is generally increased to about 180 beats per minute. Depending on the condition reached in training, after about 45 to 90 seconds, the pulse rate can drop to about 140 to 120 beats per minute. According to physiologists and training data, after a "worthwhile break" a new load phase can start (Fig. 4a).

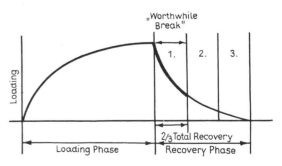

Fig. 4a "Worthwhile break"

8   Intensity = Strength, Force, Power

The "worthwhile break" must have an optimal length suited to the individual.

If, after a performance phase, the break is such that the pulse rate drops far below 100 beats per minute, the break is no longer incomplete, i.e. "worthwhile", but assumes the character of a real recovery break. Based on the different physiological effect, we distinguish the method of interval work and the method of repetition work.

4. Stimulus duration of the exercises

The stimulus duration is the time during which the physical exercise acts on the organism as a training stimulus. The weight stimulus can be very short but of great intensity and thus requires a longer pause and admits less repetitions. But it can also be very long and thus act as a sustained and uninterrupted stimulus, leading, at the end of training, to complete exhaustion. It can also be short with slight or medium stimulation intensity and thus admit a great number of repetitions with short "worthwhile breaks".

With the interval method, the duration of a training stimulus with an intensity between 50 to 70 per cent of the maximum performance capacity should not go much beyond 1 to 1½ minutes (REINDELL, ROSKAMM, KEUL, VOLKOV). In strength exercises the duration of stimulus is determined by the weight of the load. Heavy weights create a longer stimulus duration than lighter ones.

Among the different load factors there are close relationships. They will always act on the body as a self-contained unit. If a load factor is especially emphasized, other load factors must be prejudiced in its favour. Hence, for example, the stimulus intensity and stimulus volume affect each other so that in an exercise with maximum stimulus intensity, the stimulus volume cannot also be maximal simultaneously, and vice versa. At the same time, through the factors of stimulus intensity, density and duration the stimulus volume will always be limited. On the other hand, stimulus duration can influence all other load factors in volume, intensity and density. This method of continuous performance, the methods of extensive and intensive interval work and the method of repetition reflect the relationship of the load factors to each other. Each method can be used in its pure form or in a variant; the methods can also be combined. It is also possible to combine them with the methods of training with standard load, varying load, gradually increasing load and with the load of the combined change. [9] Finally, by assigning the basic methods to "circuit training", the respective variants result.

"Circuit training" and its variants are effective forms of practice for developing and perfecting the condition factors speed, strength and endurance and their complex forms, strength-endurance, speed-endurance and explosive strength. The practice is set up by coordination of a loading method with utilization of simpler and less complicated exercises; the exercises are put together as shown in Figure 4b into a schedule which can be carried out constantly for

9 For more details on this method see Novikov "Theory of Physical Education and of Training", Ch. VII, Moscow 1959, or Matveyev/Kolokolova "Allgemeine Grundlagen der Körpererziehung" (Fundamentals of Physical Education) in the Series "Sporterfahrungen des Auslands" (Sport Experiences in Other Countries), Sportverlag, Berlin, Nr. 6/1962

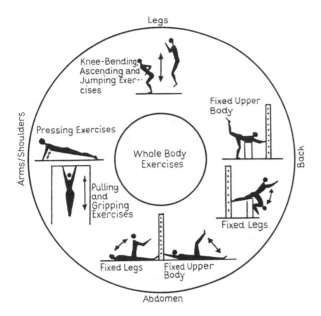

Fig. 4b

a longer time. In this the principle of progressive load is applied, so that the peak of the training load is set individually, taking into consideration physiological factors and starting from a so-called maximum test, thus avoiding overloading. Circuit training, either in a circuit or straight course, permits a large number of participants to carry out at the same time individual training, either in exact exercise periods with fixed pauses, or in progressively shorter total exercise periods, towards a so-called target time. Performance cards can be used to record the control of development on which the new training schedules are based. By practising circuit training regularly, it is possible to educate the athlete in honesty, independence, persistence, resolution and the development of his will-power [10].

These forms of schedules in no way

10   M. Scholich "Kreistraining" (Circuit Training), 2nd ed., Sportverlag, Berlin 1982.

change the essence of the basic methods with a physiological basis, because the load characteristics (stimulus intensity, volume, density and duration) produce the desired training effect. Between the different basic methods for developing and perfecting condition factors, there are transitional forms in the sequence:

1. Method of endurance work
2. Method of interval work
   a) Method of extensive interval work
   b) Method of intensive interval work
3. Method of repetitions.

The results of these methods are checked by the control method or competition method. By tests, test competitions or official competitions the training condition and the morale and will-power of an athlete are checked. Moreover the control of efficiency serves to adjust the load factors to the new and higher quality of the condition factors and to find out possible shortcomings or mistakes in the training schedules.

In the following chapter main features of the above basic methods are outlined, their physiological effects specified and concrete examples of their application given.

2.7.2.1.　The Method of Endurance Work

The method of endurance work is characterized by following features:

1. Stimulus intensity of exercises

The most characteristic form of activity exemplifying the method of continuous work are long-distance races. They are done at an intensity that corresponds to about 70 to 95 per cent of the maximum possible speed recorded in a competition or test race over a given distance (5, 10, 15, 20, 40 km).

In strength exercises with the barbell the intensity corresponds to about 25 to 50 per cent of the maximum barbell weight lifted.

Programmes composed of various different physical exercises (e.g. circuit training programme) are performed with about 25 to 75 per cent of the total repetition number recorded in the maximum test (MT).

2. Stimulus volume of exercises

The training volume measured in kms, mkgs, mkgs/s, kgs or tons is very high. Stimulus intensity and volume are contrasting quantities. One should therefore strive to build up the two load factors either consecutively or, if simultaneously, only with a gradual increase. The volume may also be recorded in minutes or hours as an overall time of the continuous work or as the total number of repetitions of a training schedule.

3. Stimulus intensity of exercises

The exercises are done without any interruption, neither by a rest interval nor by a "worthwhile break". Thus it is the same whether the training is characterized by an uninterrupted stimulus, as in a regular long-distance run, or by a uniform repetition of a specific physical exercise, up to the extreme potential, or by several different exercises, carried out consecutively without interruption.

4. Stimulus duration of exercises

The stimulus duration in training is very long. Depending on the age and physical condition of an athlete, the stimulus duration is, measured in time (15 minutes up to 5 hours) or in distance (between 3 and 50 km) during continuous runs.

In other conditioning routines the maximum repetition possible of uninterrupted exercise or the execution of a circuit training programme according to the method of continuous work are responsible for the long duration of the training stimulus. The main feature of exercise according to the method of continuous work is increasing fatigue, leading to a constantly increasing total load on the organism. Physical work will be stopped only when the state of almost complete exhaustion is reached (Fig. 5).

● Physiological foundation

The method of continuous work in training brings about physiological processes in the organism which improve the cardio-vascular regulation, capillarization, oxygen uptake of the blood, and muscular metabolism, adapting them to the continuous endurance work. The continuous struggle against the sustained stimulus during

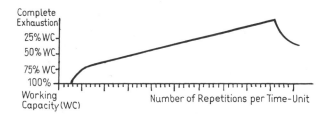

Fig. 5 Scheme of continuous work

training helps to strengthen psychological factors such as will-power, which often decides success, particularly in endurance events.

The method of continuous work is specially oriented towards an improved general endurance; at the same time it develops to a certain extent special endurance (local muscular endurance or endurance specific to a certain event) depending on the training condition of the athlete.

Continuous work must condition the organism to function uninterruptedly almost exclusively in a "steady state", i.e. at an equilibrium of oxygen, metabolism and functioning. This means that the body must be in a condition to cover its oxygen requirements for sustained muscular activity almost completely from its own reserves without foregoing a considerable oxygen debt. The circulation first reacts to the high oxygen expenditure by an increased pulse rate. Then the organism adapts to the permanent strain by an increased stroke volume and by dilatation of the heart with a reduced frequency. Sports doctors have established that the pulse rate drops by some 30 to 40 beats per minute, as soon as the adaptation processes are ended. A beginner should endeavour to keep his pulse rate at about 150 to 170 beats per minute during continuous work. This pulse rate is reached after a relatively "short" continuous performance. As adaptation to

continuous loads, work can be progressively extended and more strength applied without the pulse rate changing. A beginner who runs at a moderate tempo for 15 minutes may reach his efficiency limit after this time. Having trained 3 to 4 months (three times a week) with systematically increased loads, his condition will have improved to such an extent that he can either run 60 minutes uninterruptedly or cover a much longer distance in 15 minutes. Only after this part of preparatory training should the athlete, during continuous work, balance volume, intensity and density of the stimulus to each other so that his pulse rate increases to an average rate of about 180 beats per minute. The beginner must carefully watch his state of health, ensuring that the continuous work exerts an optimum stimulus on the body. The growing phenomena of fatigue are geared by the central nervous system and represent a protective reaction of the organism against overloading. This protective reaction must not be suppressed by the will during training. In measurements of performance (competitions, time trials), the runner must, through will-power, arrive at tiring himself to the extreme limit, so as to reach the state of critical stress.

If, after training, the athlete does not feel stiff, especially in the muscles involved in the continuous work, this is a sign of good local endurance, built up in these muscular groups through changes in the muscular mechanism. The structure is changed by the formation of new capillaries (fine tubes through which blood transports oxygen and nutrients to the muscle fibres). The total surface for gas exchange increases, thus ensuring a better oxygen supply to the muscles. By the improved capillary system in the groups of muscles, the metabolic residues produced in the muscles during endurance work can be better removed. They are partly expelled by the lungs and partly excreted by perspiration. Through continuous work, gradually increased from one phase of training to the next, the energy potential of the muscles improves, provided sufficient recovery time between training sessions is allowed for. Continuous work with high loads also develops the central nervous system. Central fatigue, as a sign of complete adaptation during the performance phase, sets in later, since after a certain period of training the central nervous system adapts itself to a frequently repeated continuous load. It is therefore important always to maintain the same total load during training programmes for a prolonged period of time. The organism learns to adapt itself to the standardized load via the vegetative nervous system and by connections via the central nervous system. It reaches a higher level of functioning that will reveal itself by better physical condition and by an improved cardio-vascular regulation, a higher heart-stroke volume and a better oxygen-uptake capacity of the blood, measured in tests of functions. In order to stimulate the body to a renewed qualitatively higher adaptation in the next phase of training, the total load, according to the method of continuous work, must place higher demands on the body since, by permanently even total loads, a so-called "exterior stereotype" of the organic functions is established (PAVLOV).

The method of continuous work requires that the total load be increased by gradually increasing the following load characteristics:

1. *Stimulus intensity*–same running distance but at higher speed.

2. *Stimulus volume*–same running speed, but increased running time or distance.

3. *Stimulus intensity* and *stimulus volume*–longer and longer distances must be covered in a shorter and shorter time.

If allround conditioning training means are applied (e.g. strength exercises without additional weights) in the place of runs, training must be built up so that the stimulus volume is increased through a growing number of physical exercises and through a growing number of repetitions. For improving general endurance by such all-round conditioning exercises, the means of circuit training, i.e. the principle of uninterrupted continuous exercise, involving successively different groups of muscles, can be applied effectively. This is also a good means for strengthening the cardio-vascular system and improving metabolism and oxygen-intake of the blood. Continuous physical work increases cardio-vascular endurance, as well as local endurance, mainly through the activity of constantly varying groups of muscles of the body.

Through allround conditioning exercise and training means according to the method of continuous work, the central and peripheral resistance against fatigue can be improved.

● Forms of exercise

Running (for beginners)

The basic principle in applying the method of continuous work with beginners consists in fixing the distance not in kilometres but in time. Start with about 5 minutes of uninterrupted continuous running at a medium pace and increase the demands gradually by stages (10, 15, 20, 25, 30, up to 40 minutes). Use a relatively even medium pace as a start. Greater changes in tempo should be avoided when starting. Continuous runs with changes in tempo may be applied only when training and performance levels of the athlete have been considerably raised, viz. not before 5 to 6 months of systematic endurance work.

For assessing the degree of effort required in continuous runs, beginners should try to do a certain distance out and back at the same speed. If the total time of such a continuous run is to be 20 minutes, 10 minutes should be used for running out and 10 minutes for running back. If the same time is recorded for both distances, the chosen tempo was right for the individual training and performance levels of the athlete. But if he can do the distance back faster, this means that he is generally capable of running faster or that the distance should be lengthened.

Only if, in spite of great efforts, the athlete cannot do the distance out and back in the same time, either the initial speed was too high or his actual performance level was not properly assessed.

Another means of judging the degree of load is to have the beginner measure his pulse rate after each run and the so-called respiratory pace rhythm during runs. Practical experience and medical research have substantiated that the demands in continuous runs may be designated as low, medium and/or high, when the pulse rate per minute and the respiratory pace rhythm are within a certain range (Table 6).

The respiratory pace rhythm describes the relation between the number of strides performed during breathing in and breathing out.

Beginners should carry out continuous runs so, that depending on their pulse rate and respiratory pace rhythm, the degree of load can be designated as medium. When the beginner is capable of doing about 30 minutes of uninterrupted running at a medium pace, he may, at the same time, check his performance and development by time-keeping.

Adequate distances are:

for boys and girls: up to about 8 km

for youths: 3 to 15 km

for adults: 3 to 25 km

Running (advanced athletes)

The main means of training uses the method of continuous work with runs through woods and parks, along streets with a flat or hilly course, at a relatively even or changing tempo. Depending on the targets set by training continuous runs should be undertaken

Table 6 *Pulse Rate and Respiratory Pace Rhythm*

Degree of Load	Pulse Rate/min.	Respiratory Pace Rhythm
Low	about 150 to 160	4 : 4
Medium	about 170 to 180	4 : 4/3 : 3
High	about 180 to 190	3 : 3/2 : 2

at 70 to 95 per cent of the maximum performance capacity, based on a comparable test course of 5, 10, 15, 20 or 40 km. The totality of continuous runs should, within the scope of a longer training period (e.g. the preparatory period) be in the region of about 80 to 90 per cent of the best performance. Also the distance should change from one training unit to the other. According to LYDIARD the dynamic structure of a training by continuous running is best achieved by changing the duration of runs from one session to the next.

In order to assess the running tempo, the following general rule applies: the longer the distance, the slower the average speed for the total distance must be and vice versa.

Advanced athletes should, in line with the criteria we have given for the dynamic structure of the training with continuous running and with the development of basic endurance in mind, use the following distances and running times, and gradually increase demands during the preparatory period (Table 7).

The application of strength exercises without additional weights (beginners and advanced)

General endurance can be improved by allround conditioning exercises, using the method of continuous work. Training programmes, composed of different allround conditioning exercises and executed according to the method of continuous work, ensure the complex development of condition factors and of general endurance at the same time as strength endurance.

In order to meet these targets strength exercises without additional weights are chiefly used with no breaks between exercises. This does not mean that the athlete should not relax and loosen his muscles before starting the next exercise. An uninterrupted continuous load on the cardio-vascular system and on other vegetative systems is thus ensured, so that these organic systems are submitted to a real continuous load. The different muscles and muscular groups are loaded alternately. The extent of loading of different muscle groups by exercise depends on the order of the exercises. It makes a difference whether each exercise has to be repeated with the highest possible number of repetitions or not. The systematic ordering of exercises must therefore correspond to the planned objectives. If the effect of training to be obtained

Table 7 Training with Continuous Running during the Preparatory Period

Event Group	Beginning of Preparatory Period		End of Preparatory Period	
	Distance (km)	Time (min.)	Distance (km)	Time (min.)
Short Distance	2–5	8–10/20–25	–	–
400-m Runners	2–8	8–10/32–36	up to 10	40–45
Middle Distance				
Women	5–15	17–20/55–65	10–18	35–40/70–85
Men	10–20	38–45/80–90	10–20	35–40/70–85
Long Distance	25–30	100–110/120–150	–	87–95/120–140

consists in developing endurance in a particular group of muscles (local muscular endurance), this exercise must indeed be repeated without a break to the limit. The aim of training in allround conditioning schedules consists mainly in getting a large number of groups of muscles to acquire power of endurance and to develop the condition factor of strength-endurance. The order of exercises should be such that different groups of muscles are loaded consecutively or alternately. The number of repetitions should only be sufficient to permit the execution of the whole training programme without rest intervals.

In practice the individual amount designated as $\frac{MR}{2}$ (half the maximum number of repetitions) has proved effective.

For developing condition according to this formula, the system is similar to that of "circuit" training. It is beneficial to the cardio-vascular regulation, muscular metabolism, general endurance and local muscular endurance. At the same time strength in its complex property of strength-endurance can be slightly improved. It is not the cross-section of the muscle that increases; rather in fact the muscle gets somewhat slimmer. The impression of increased strength results from the improved muscular mechanism, and from a better utilization of oxygen through the denser capillary network. Reflectory connections via the nervous system make the muscle more enduring and its work more effective.

Example of circuit training based on the method of continuous work

The sequence of movement can be so arranged that first the muscles of the shoulder girdle are activated and in the next exercises the main trunk muscles, the upper and then the lower extremities. One can also proceed the other way round—first load the lower and then the upper extremities. We give some examples illustrating the different possible variants in this group of exercises.

1st Example—Front support (upper extremities and shoulder girdle). Raising the trunk to an upright from a horizontal position—on wall bars, arms are held in front of the body or in the neck (abdominal muscles). Bending and erecting the trunk, in the sideways support on the bench (back muscles); Squat vaults (lower extremities).

2nd Example: Rope skipping from ankles with almost straight knees— Cossack's dance
Knee bending
Squat vaults (lower extremities)— Horizontal position—the hands grip the lowest bar of the wall bars—lifting and lowering legs.
Leg circling; leg circling describing eights (abdominal muscles)— Squat vault on wall bars
Lifting and lowering legs (back muscles)— Pull-ups— Hanging (shoulder girdle and upper extremities).

3rd Example: Front support— Squat vaults from squatting position, folding the legs to the chest— Front support— Squat vaults, folding bent legs to the chest etc.

2.7.2.2.   Methods of Interval Work

The condition factors: strength, speed and endurance can be developed by different methods. They are best improved by submitting the circulatory system, the nervous system and muscular metabolism not to one only stimulus during exercise, but to several stimuli. Training with intervals is the best form of practice for the complex build-up of strength, speed and endurance, as it ensures a regular alternation of effort and rest (Fig. 6).

The interval is a break between repetitions of exercises. Interval work in training has often been varied in the course of time. We shall here explain only the most up-to-date form of interval training and specify how it can be applied for beginners, youths and advanced athletes. According to physiologists (KEUL, REINDELL, ROSKAMM, MIES and others) it is not only characterized by the breaks between training loads but differentiated according to whether the break leads to a complete recovery or not. It has been established by medical research that the first third of the recovery break is particularly "worthwhile" (cf. 2.7.2., point 3). The method is also differentiated by emphasis, given in the application of loads. If, in interval work, the total load results from a great volume of work in time and space, we speak of extensive interval work; the intensive interval work is characterized by greater application of power and reduced volume in one unit of time. The distribution of loads in one training unit or the increase of loads in a phase of training should be as shown in Table 7 (p. 64).

Fig. 6   Scheme of the method of interval work

I. *Method of extensive interval work*
This method has the following load characteristics:
1. Stimulus intensity of exercise
Physical activity in the form of runs, strength exercises with and without weights, is performed with relatively low (medium) intensity, i.e. by runs with 60 to 80 per cent [11] and strength exercises with 50 to 60 per cent of the maximum performance capacity.
2. Stimulus volume of exercise
The low stimulus intensity allows for a greater volume. If physical work is done at medium intensity and with a "worthwhile" break, many repetitions are possible. This delays complete exhaustion. Symptoms of fatigue build-up gradually from one exercise to the other. DONATH [12] speaks of a "stored" fatigue (Fig. 7).
3. Stimulus density of exercise
Loading phases follow in close sequence. Breaks between repetitions are relatively short; they should be assessed for each individual separately and be of optimal length; the length of the "worthwhile" break is also an individual matter; it should not extend beyond the first third of the total recovery time. In advanced athletes it is usually between 45 to 90 seconds, in beginners between 60 and 120 seconds (or when the pulse has dropped to some 125 to 130 beats per minute in advanced and to about 110 to 120 beats per minute in beginners). The "worthwhile" break can be taken up with jogging, so that the training activity is not completely interrupted during this time.

11   Calculate by indirect rule of three.
12   R. Donath "Mittelstrecken- und Hindernislauf" (Middle Distances and Steeplechase), Sportverlag, Berlin 1960.

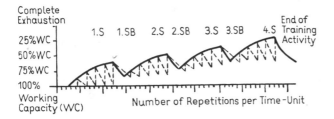

Fig. 7 Scheme of the method of extensive interval work (S — Series, SB — Serial break)

4. Stimulus duration of exercise

With running the stimulus duration is about 14 to 90 seconds over distances of 100 to 400 m. The total time of repetitions and jogging breaks leads to a long stimulus duration.

Stimuli produced by strength exercises are short. If exercise is done in a series with about 20 repetitions, the sum of individual stimuli will indicate the stimulus duration or the effective time of exercise.

● Physiological foundation

Programmes of tempo runs executed according to the method of extensive interval work develop, through their great stimulus volume, short intervals ("worthwhile" breaks) and the resulting long duration of the load, basic endurance. The effect produced on the body and the training effect of the programme depend essentially on the actual training level of the athlete, the distance length and planned speed of the tempo-run (e.g. the lower or upper limit of the intensity range of 60 to 80 per cent of the maximum performance capacity on the chosen distances). In relation with the above-mentioned factors the training effect may therefore consist, not only in the development of basic endurance, but also of special endurance (short duration, medium duration endurance). The level of every endurance phenomenon is influenced by the oxygen-intake capacity of the athlete. The demands placed on the cardio-vascular system by the great stimulus volume create an improved regulation of circulatory processes by gradual increasing the load doses. In beginners the higher oxygen demand required for great efforts is mainly satisfied by an increased heart-stroke frequency. After a long period of training the stroke frequency diminishes in favour of an increased stroke volume. This shows the adaptation capacity of the organism to loads. Contrary to earlier opinions, latest research on training children and adolescents shows that their organism has the same adaptation capacity. "Through training the heart of adolescents increases in size by a regulative dilatation, a greater stroke volume and greater capacity of the heart. This proves that the adolescent reacts to loads by the same adaptation phenomena as the adult."[13]

The complete exhaustion, which should occur only after many repetitions in the extensive interval work, depends on two factors:

a) central fatigue (nervous system)
b) local peripheral fatigue (muscles).

The central fatigue precedes the peripheral (local) fatigue. There are close

13 J. Nöcker "Grundriß der Biologie der Körperübungen" (Outline on Biology of Physical Exercises), 3rd ed., Sportverlag, Berlin 1959.

67

relationships between these two types of fatigue. Through acid metabolites produced during muscular activity, the stimulus conduction system and the nervous tracts are hindered in their work, because intermediate metabolic products are not sufficiently split or burnt, due to high oxygen demands which cannot be covered by sufficient supplies. The organism works at a so-called oxygen debt, which is relatively low in extensive interval work. The acid metabolic residues in the muscle increase from one performance phase to the next, since the oxygen debt is not completely covered during the "worthwhile break". These acid metabolites are conveyed to the nervous system with the blood. Through complicated biochemical processes the work of the nervous system is rendered difficult. It tires first. The impulses from the central nervous system (CNS) have difficulty in arriving at the motorial endplates in the muscle. This renders muscular activity uneconomic or impossible. Similar metabolic processes are probably taking place in the brain in the elaboration of excitations, so that this too can explain the central fatigue. Extensive interval work not only improves the cardio-vascular system by increasing the vital capacity of the heart volume, but also through long training the blood acquires the ability to bind more oxygen and to supply it to the muscles for the biochemical splitting of blood-sugar.

According to L. A. ORBELI, "the vegetative nerves have also the ability to exert adaptation-trophic influences on the muscle through metabolic processes, as they change not only the excitability of the muscles, but also their nutrition" [14].

Thus extensive interval work triggers adaptation processes and morphological changes in the muscle and in the whole body.

Muscles trained for general and special (local) endurance not only increase their cross-section, but increase the density of the capillary system. This improves the oxygen supply for metabolic processes in the muscle and postpones fatigue. In these adaptation processes various buffer substances, such as mineral salts and vitamins are of great importance. Through training, combined with a suitable diet, the ratio of these substances in the body, required for the buffering of acid waste metabolism, is improved. The entire body thus reacts to stress and tries to adapt itself to repeated efforts at regular intervals of time. The proof of this adaptation is that during training exhaustion sets in later and later, that the pulse rate after work drops quicker and sooner during the "worthwhile break" and that the pulse rate at rest becomes steadily lower.

The central fatigue may be regarded as a protective reaction of the body to overloading. It can be overcome by excessive will-power which may, however, lead to organic injury. Ignoring the protective reaction of the body through will-power will, invariably, end in collapse and, in rare cases, with the death of the athlete (e.g. the death of the first marathon runner Pheidippides).

● Forms of exercise

14 V. Zimkin "Physiologische Charakteristik von Kraft, Schnelligkeit und Ausdauer" (Physiology of Strength, Speed and Endurance) in the Series "Sport im Sozialismus", Sportverlag, Berlin 1959

The *running programme* may consist of running over distances between 100 m and 1,000 m. Typical of schedules in the past were frequent repetitions of runs over 200 m up to 400 m (e.g. 20 × 200 m or 10 to 20 × 400 m). They are usually executed in the form of interval endurance runs. Today world-class middle- and long-distance runners prefer to train using the method of extensive interval work, with a tend-ency to lengthen the distances of tempo runs, e.g. 10 to 20 × 600 m, 800 m or 1,000 m.

A series of short sprints over 30 to 50 m are partly done after each, or after several tempo runs, or the schedule is concluded with some sprints. Programmes of tempo runs usually postulate distances of varying length, as this makes the runs less monotonous. In its pure form extensive interval work im-

Table 8   Load Distribution (by association with Fred Wilt's "Run, run, run")

Training Means (Distance)	Stimulus Intensity Tempo (m/sec.)	Stimulus Volume Repetitions	Stimulus Duration Time scored (sec.)	Stimulus Density Duration of Breaks	Breaks to be taken up by:
1. Standard Distance	>	=	<	=	Walking
2. Standard Distance	=	>	= or >	=	Walking/Jogging
3. Standard Distance	=	=	=	<	Walking/Jogging
4. Running Programme with various running distances	> per Training unit of a training segment	to be fixed	variable	=	Walking/Jogging
5. Running Programme with various running distances	> within a training unit	will be fixed	variable	variable	Walking/Jogging
6. Running Programme with various running distances	> in the course of a training segment	<	<	variable	Walking/Jogging
7. The distances become shorter	>	> or <	<	= or >	Walking
8. The distances become longer	>	> or =	>	= or >	Walking/Jogging
9. The distances become longer	=	> or <	>	=	Walking/Jogging
10. Continuous run	=	>	>	to be omitted	to be omitted
11. Continuous run distance	>	=	<	to be omitted	to be omitted
12. Continuous run or Fartlek	variable	=	variable	to be omitted	to be omitted
13. Continuous run	>	>	>	to be omitted	to be omitted
14. Continuous run or Fartlek	>	<	< or =	to be omitted	to be omitted

Key to symbols used: = constant; > increased; < reduced

Table 9   Training for Beginners (Youths 14 to 18 years) and Advanced Athletes according to the Extensive Interval Work

Distance	Running Speed about	Break (Jogging) about	Repetitions about
Youths (14–16 years)			
100 m	20– 17 sec.	100– 60 sec.	10–12
200 m	42– 38 sec.	120– 90 sec.	8–10
300 m	60– 54 sec.	120– 90 sec.	6– 8
400 m	100– 80 sec.	150– 90 sec.	5– 7
Youths (17–18 years)			
100 m	16– 14 sec.	90– 60 sec.	12–15
200 m	36– 32 sec.	120– 60 sec.	10
300 m	56– 52 sec.	120– 90 sec.	8–10
400 m	90– 70 sec.	150–120 sec.	6–10
Advanced Athletes			
100 m	15– 14 sec.	60– 45 sec.	20–40
200 m	33– 29 sec.	90– 45 sec.	40–50
300 m	58– 48 sec.	90– 45 sec.	16–20
400 m	72– 60 sec.	120– 60 sec.	16–20
500 m	110– 80 sec.	120– 60 sec.	12–20
600 m	130–110 sec.	180– 90 sec.	10–20
800 m	160–140 sec.	180– 90 sec.	8–16
1000 m	205–180 sec.	300–120 sec.	8–12

plies only runs over one given distance in a fixed time, followed by a "worthwhile break" taken up with jogging. Workloads can be gradually increased by either reducing the "worthwhile break" stimulus density or by increasing the number of repetitions stimulus volume (see Tables 8 and 9).

Strength exercises with and without weights

With the method of extensive interval work a variety of strength exercises can be performed. This permits the development of general and special strength endurance. The higher level of strength endurance is caused not so much by an increased cross-section of the muscle (absolute strength), but by an improved metabolism in the working muscles and, through reflectory connections via the nervous system, by an improved relative strength [15]. At the same time the oxygen-intake capacity is improved. In developing condition through strength exercises emphasis should be focused on the greatest possible number of repetitions and on their constant increase. World-class athletes, advanced athletes and beginners (adults and adolescents) differ only in the number of repetitions. Thus an advanced athlete will, most probably, be able to do many more push-ups than an adolescent beginner. Using the principle of extensive

15   For more details on the absolute and relative strength see A. Tchudinov "Die Kraft ist die wichtigste Eigenschaft des Leichtathleten" (Strength is the most important quality of Track and Field Athletes) in "Theorie und Praxis der Körperkultur", Sportverlag, Berlin, Nr. 4/1960 und 5/1960.

interval work, strength exercises, in which the body weight must be overcome, should therefore be carried out up to complete or almost complete exhaustion. After a "worthwhile break" the same strength exercise is again performed up to complete or almost complete exhaustion; finally, after a renewed "worthwhile break" again as many repetitions as at all possible should be demanded of the body. Extensive interval work can be applied in strength exercises as in the following schedules.

1st Example: Push-up

1. Maximum number of repetitions possible = 30
2. Maximum number of repetitions possible = about another 15 to 20
3. Maximum number of repetitions possible = about another 7 to 10.

Breaks of about 60 to 90 seconds, devoted to loosening exercises, should be taken. Each exercise must be executed correctly and rapidly. In practice the number of repetitions possible will be divided into a series or done according to the system of circuit training.

Exercises in which the athlete's own weight must be overcome or exercises with additional weights can be performed in this way.

Exercises without apparatus:

Running up stairs
Hopping, bounding—
Hopping on one or both legs
Ankle-work
Knee-lifting runs
Exercises with medicine ball
Throwing and catching the ball with trunk-bending and stretching—
Throwing the ball sideways overhead from the left to the right hand—
Pushing the ball from right to left
Pushing the ball away from the chest (to a partner) with one or both hands, in an arched position—
Pass the ball to the partner over the head—
Throw the ball backwards through straddled legs
Push the ball upward with one and with both hands

Exercises with implements and on apparatus:

Pull-ups—
Uninterrupted upward circling on the horizontal bar from standing or hanging position—
Exercises for abdominal muscles on wall bars—
Exercises for abdominal muscles on bench in horizontal position—
Knee bending of one and both legs—
Climbing on rope or wall bars—
"Pumping" forward and backward on parallel bars—
Hopping and jumping exercises on track or over a bench—
Skipping from ankle-joints with almost straightened knees—
The same, but tucking the legs up to the chest—
Skipping in tucked position—
Cossack's dance—
From crouch to crouch—jump explosively from one leg and throw the other leg straight out.

2nd Example: Improving basic endurance and explosive strength.

For improving basic endurance and explosive strength, all the jumping exercises should be executed with many repetitions but only with medium effort. General and special endurance can be developed in various forms by practising in the gymnasium. Jumping exercises permit fairly precise loads for youths. Continuous jumps on to and off the box, followed by running, suits the outlook of the young. They are particularly enthusiastic about uninterrupted jumps combined with turns, catching the ball, somersaults and so on. These can be applied to athletes of various age-groups, only with the height of obstacles different (box, hurdles, etc.) and a changed duration of the uninterrupted jumps. The number of repetitions must of course be adapted to the particular age group. Such continuous runs can be arranged in the gymnasium in the form of a steeplechase. Forms of such steeplechases which are close to those of competition for the whole training group or for two partners are explained in detail in the section on intensive interval work (p. 73).

Examples:

Jumps on to and off the obstacles—
After landing return immediately to the start, run up again and jump on to the obstacle—
The same but in the form of jumping up steps—
Clearing the cross-bar—
Jumping on a track over parts of boxes or hurdles—
Jumping over medicine balls or long benches—
Different kinds of long jumps and triple jumps
Strength exercises with a barbell.
Extensive interval work in strength exercises with a barbell aims primarily at the development of strength endurance and, to a certain extent, general endurance.
The weights used in these exercises represent about one third of the body weight of the athlete.
Example: An athlete weighing 75 kg will practise with weights of about 20 to 30 kg. Each set of exercises must be repeated at least 20 to 30 times. The duration of the "worthwhile break" is of about 45 to 90 seconds.

Examples:

Jerking—
Snatching—jumping Jack—
Trunk bending and straightening with extended arms—
Trunk bending and straightening with weight on the neck—
Trunk circling with weight on the neck—
Lifting the heels with weight on the neck
In vertical or horizontal position (lying on a bench, box cover, inclined box or bench)—pushing barbell away from the chest.
Strength exercises with a barbell applied in training adolescent beginners.
Strength exercises with a barbell using extensive interval work are the main form of training adolescent beginners. The weights used (stimulus intensity) should not exceed one third of the athlete's weight. Horizontal bars can be used instead of barbells. Adolescent beginners can easily handle them. Do about 10 repetitions of a variety of exercises. In the beginning these implements are useful for learning the exercises. After some time higher loads can be used. Beginners must be able to stand 10 repetitions in three consecutive series, as otherwise training would not be that of extensive interval work. The duration of breaks between series should be for youths about 120 to

160 seconds and for juniors 60 to 90 seconds. They can be taken up with jogging and loosening exercises. Strength exercises with a barbell can be made attractive for youths by asking: "How often can each one of you do this exercise with a horizontal bar (beam, kettle bell, barbell)?" The method of extensive interval work requires the increase of loads by increasing the number of repetitions (stimulus volume) or by reducing the "worthwhile break" (stimulus density). If weights are increased (stimulus intensity), the exercise would come closer to intensive interval work.

II. Method of intensive interval work
This method can be described by the following load patterns:

1. Stimulus intensity of the exercises
Physical activities in the form of running, strength exercises with and without weights, are performed with a relatively high intensity. In runs about 80 to 90 per cent of the maximum performance is applied, in strength exercises about 75 per cent.

2. Stimulus volume of the exercises
The training volume depends directly on the stimulus intensity applied. Due to the high intensity with which the different performance phases are executed, the number of repetitions is much smaller than in extensive interval work. Complete exhaustion should be reached only gradually, as in extensive interval work. After the break there remains some fatigue. This residual fatigue is taken from one performance phase to the other and builds up. Fatigue (expressed in percentages in Figs. 7 and 8) is greater after the first performance phase than in extensive interval work (cf. Figs. 7 and 8). In intensive interval work the relatively long "worthwhile break" between repetitions leaves a greater residual fatigue after each performance phase (expressed in percentages in Fig. 8) and a reduced capacity for further work. This explains the smaller volume of training.

3. Stimulus density of the exercises
Due to the high intensity, the break between the different exercises is relatively long. But the principle of the "worthwhile break" is still adhered to. The duration of the "worthwhile break" is for advanced athletes about $1\frac{1}{2}$ to 3 minutes. The beginner requires about 2 to 4 minutes for an optimal "worthwhile break". It is taken up alternately with jogging and walking, so that the pulse rate does not drop below about 110 to 120 beats per minute.

4. Stimulus duration of the exercises
The duration of individual load stimuli is relatively short in runs of about 80 to 90 per cent of the maximum performance capacity. The stimulus duration should last only a little over one minute. In strength exercises which are executed at about 75 per cent of the

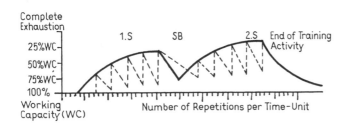

Fig. 8 Scheme of the method of intensive interval work (S – Series, SB – Serial break)

maximum performance capacity, the stimulus duration is increased through the greater load of weights.

● Physiological foundation

The method of intensive interval work aims at another training effect than that of extensive interval work. Intensive interval work mainly develops the various aspects of special endurance such as speed-endurance, short-duration and medium-duration endurance, strength endurance, speed and explosive force. During intensive interval work the body operates after each performance phase with a relatively high oxygen debt (about 10 to 12 litres, while the maximum oxygen deficiency is as high as 18 to 20 litres). The more intensive the muscular work is, the higher the oxygen debt will be. Thus the muscles are forced to work for the greater part anaerobically (with little oxygen). This places high demands on the blood for the neutralization of acid metabolic waste products and for buffering metabolic residues. During intensive interval work the oxygen debt can be made good in about 4 to 5 minutes. These findings of physiologists are important for determining the length of breaks after each performance phase and the exercises to be performed during the breaks.

The buffering capacity of the blood is important for the neutralization of the acid metabolic residues, just as it is responsible for the rapid elimination of carbon dioxide (CO_2). Apart from carbon dioxide, lactic acid and various other acids metabolic waste products are produced in the working muscle. Through strong load stimuli arising during intensive interval work, the body adapts itself to this situation by

increasing (via the vegetative nervous system) under the influence of the parasympathetic nerve, during recovery processes, the buffer capacity of blood and the supply of certain hormones for anticipated new load stimuli. During recovery, parts of the lactic acid are transformed into carbon dioxide and eliminated together with oxygen from the blood in the lungs to the respiratory air.

An athlete who trains regularly can feel the adaptation processes in his body by his ability to stand a higher training load. The adaptation-trophic influences, which the vegetative nervous system exerts on the muscles, are in intensive interval work similar to those experienced in extensive interval work.

High intensity of exercise (at least 75 per cent) in the performance phase not only changes the oxygen intake and buffer capacity, but also the muscular cross-section. The muscle, when subjected to tension, is probably induced to thicken.

Since in intensive interval work at least 75 per cent of the maximum performance capacity is applied in certain exercises with a given number of repetitions and suitable "worthwhile breaks", the expected training effect is not only improved speed, explosive force and endurance, but the complex development of condition factors in the form of speed- and strength-endurance. For the complex development of conditional abilities it is necessary that, despite the increased cross-section of the muscle, the surface of the vascular system in the muscle tissue retains its high oxygen-intake capacity. With training using intensive interval work, the number of repetitions must be sufficient to stimulate the formation of new capillaries and to make the capillary network denser. Each muscle fibre, in spite of an increased cross-section, must be surrounded by an increasingly dense capillary network. "This naturally leads to a greater cross-section of the muscle, resulting in a slower flow of the blood. The contact time between blood and tissue is prolonged, so that a greater amount of oxygen can be supplied. This must be regarded as one of the reasons for the increased arterio-venous difference of the oxygen content in the blood of trained athletes" [16]. If the vascular system is increased through training, it will react to renewed training loads or in general during muscular work, by a quicker vasodilatation, allowing more oxygen to pass. More mineral phosphates, potassium and ferments are supplied to the working muscle. This is also one of the reasons why, after a prolonged segment of training, the incidence of fatigue in the muscle becomes less and less. "Fatigue is therefore caused by (1) a more economical use, and a good adaptation of the muscles and (2) by an increased flow of blood, allowing more oxygen to the muscle and reducing metabolic waste products, such as lactic acid, which hinder the effective work of the muscle, to be produced. This postpones fatigue and accelerates recovery. The result of all these adaptation processes are an increased performance capacity, increased effectiveness and a reduced tendency to fatigue" [17].

Training using intensive interval work accelerates these processes of adaptation insofar as, after the optimal "worthwhile break", two thirds of the recovery processes are concluded, but a residue of fatigue is left in the muscles. The nervous system also does not recover completely during the "worthwhile break". In the new performance phase the body must therefore fight against a greater resistance. This forces the body to adapt itself. The sensomotor coordination (interplay between nerves and muscles) is trained by intensive interval work, thus improving speed.

● Forms of exercise

The duration of breaks will vary individually for beginners and adolescents between 14 and 16. Pulse rates should be taken

a) immediately after the run

b) after the planned break.

If after the supposedly optimal "worthwhile break" the pulse rate is still 130 beats per minute or more, the athlete must wait for the pulse rate to drop to about 110 to 120 before doing any more.

Running schedules may consist of runs from 100 m to 1,000 m. The "worthwhile break" can be taken up by jogging, slight ankle work, knee-lifting runs and particularly by easy bounding.

The intensity is increased by reducing the optimal "worthwhile break" during a training cycle. In the next training cycle the earlier length of breaks can be repeated and the running time shortened or 1 or 2 repetitions added. The amount of increased intensity depends on the training effect intended. If one merely keeps reducing the running time over identical training distances, the breaks must be at the same time steadily increased. This gradually changes

16   J. Nöcker, loc. cit.
17   J. Nöcker, loc. cit.

Table 10   *Method of Intensive Interval Work for Beginners and Advanced Athletes*

Distance	Running Speed about	Break (Jogging/ Walking) about	Repetitions about
Beginner and Youths (14–16 years)			
100 m	17–14 sec.	120– 90 sec.	6– 8
200 m	38–36 sec.	180–120 sec.	6– 8
300 m	54–52 sec.	180–120 sec.	4– 6
400 m	95–75 sec.	300–180 sec.	4– 5
Youths (17–18 years)			
100 m	14.5–13 sec.	120– 90 sec.	8–10
200 m	32–28 sec.	180–120 sec.	6– 8
300 m	52–45 sec.	240–150 sec.	6– 8
400 m	80–65 sec.	300–240 sec.	6– 8
Advanced Athletes			
100 m	13.5–12.5 sec.	180– 90 sec.	8–12
200 m	28– 26 sec.	200–150 sec.	8–10
300 m	48– 42 sec.	240–180 sec.	8–10
400 m	66– 58 sec.	300–180 sec.	8–10
500 m	90– 75 sec.	300–180 sec.	6– 8
600 m	120– 90 sec.	300–180 sec.	4– 6
800 m	140– 130 sec.	300–180 sec.	4– 8
1,000 m	180– 170 sec.	300–180 sec.	4– 8

the character of the intensive interval work to repetition work with real recovery breaks. Similarly the number of repetitions must then also be reduced.

The application of strength exercises with and without additional load to the athlete's own weight

If the method of intensive interval work is used for developing condition by strength exercises, the effort should correspond to about 75 per cent of the maximum performance capacity in the execution of this exercise, which should be done at high speed. Usually not more than 8 to 10 repetitions per series should be anticipated. The intensity can be increased by reducing the duration of breaks, or by a faster execution of the exercise within a given unit of time, or by using more difficult conditions (sandbag on the neck in jumps, weight vest in knee-lifting runs, snatching exercise and so on).

The intensity should, however, not be increased by more repetitions (stimulus volume), as this would go against the principle of intensive interval work. The strength exercises mentioned in the Section "Method of Extensive Interval Work" (p. 70) will serve as examples. They should only be executed more quickly, more powerfully or with a higher additional load to the body weight.

Exercises can be made more interesting and enjoyable for all age groups by competitions among the athletes of any training group. Running, jumping, hopping in all their various forms, wheelbarrow racing, exercises with a partner on apparatus, such as pull-ups, continuous upward hip circling, climbing on wall bars and ropes, hanging exercises on wall bars and so on can be carried out either in the form of relays or in a man-to-man contest. These can arouse great enthusiasm. Such relay games promote team spirit and plenty of action as well as developing conscious discipline by establishing the rule that at the end of a passage the winner is the team which stands in perfect order. Coaches or sports teachers must make sure that breaks are of the planned length. To increase the total stress on the body, the team may decide that the exercise is not concluded when each team member has performed once but to do two or several sequences one after the other.

Examples:

"Black-and-White": sprinting—hopping on one leg etc.

"Numbers": sprinting—hopping on both legs—hopping on one leg, walking on all fours—hopping in crouch position—bounding—two-step jumps (left-left right-right etc.), wheelbarrow races—pick-a-back etc.

"The wandering ball": in standing, sitting and in tucked position.

Jumping with additional load (sandbag or weight vest) over a track interspersed by parts of boxes or hurdles: two-leg jumps, snatching up knees—one-leg jumps—two-leg jumps sideways—bounding run-squat vaults from low crouch to low crouch.

Medicine ball relays: running game holding one or several balls in the hands—under the arms—rolling—pushing or driving the ball with foot—pushing with one arm—with two arms from the chest—overhead—same backwards—pushing and throwing the ball to the partner from arched position—with one arm overhead (javelin throw) and other games.

Steeplechase over various obstacles: long boxes (1.0 to 1.20 m high)—jump off on the right (left) side—land on the left (right) side of the box—continue running, landing on soft area (two mats) with somersault forward—running—different jumps (tuck, side-vault, straddle, straddle-jump exercise, hurdle stride) over the side horse with or without pummels—"pump" on parallel bars—upward circle on the horizontal bar or rings—run back to starting point.

Non-stop relays: in open-air or gymnasium. Experience with these forms of competition based on the principle of intensive interval work have shown that before starting a thorough warm-up is a must. Usually the same exercises are used for warming up. This reduces the training effect and increases the danger of injuries and of muscle soreness. The catch-as-catch-can with the medicine ball (2×5 min.) is ideal for warming up. Running for about 10 minutes, followed by some loosening exercises, is also well established as an effective warm-up practice.

If intensive interval work schedules are to be drawn up for each individual athlete separately, single exercises with a partner or in a group of not more than 4 persons (as an alternative) must be carried out according to the principle of intensive interval work. This is not as enjoyable and is unsuitable for youths. It should only be used for young athletes of 17 or more. The coach must try to make the exercise less monotonous by setting a variety of tasks and by encouraging the athlete verbally. The duration should not be more than 30 minutes.

Strength exercises with a barbell for beginners and advanced athletes

The method of intensive interval work is basically the same as when doing other strength exercises. If they are done with an additional load to the body weight (barbell) according to the method of intensive interval work, principally explosive force will be developed.

Depending on the weight used, the muscle working against great resistance will increase its cross-section. If done quickly and with a relatively great number of repetitions (8 to 10), this makes the capillary network denser in the muscular tissue. The method of intensive interval work, done by way of strength exercises with a barbell, permits the complex development of several facets of condition. The training effect depends on the weights used and on the type of exercise. These exercises help to build up

a) maximum strength

b) speed combined with strength = explosive force

c) explosive force combined with endurance = special endurance as strength endurance.

For a versatile foundation training in track and field for younger athletes strength exercises with a barbell based on intensive interval work are also of importance. They should be preceded by extensive interval work with weights. When the different exercises with a barbell of relatively light weight have been learnt and the muscles have become used to working against greater external resistance, one may pass from the extensive to the intensive form. For this the weights used invariably for a period of about 3 months in the exten-

sive form will be increased, the repetitions reduced and the duration of breaks lengthened. In the intensive interval work with the barbell with adolescents, series of about 8 to 10 repetitions at about 60 to 70 per cent of the maximum or up the half of the athlete's weight should be carried out. Barbell exercises using the method of intensive interval work should create the same development stimuli in all the muscle groups of 14 to 16 year olds. Only when training youths from 17 onwards the strength exercises with a barbell can be used for the development of certain of the main groups of muscles. These special strength exercises should not make up more than 50 per cent of the strength exercises with a barbell in a training cycle.

Examples of exercises for boys between 14 and 16 years and (with higher weights) for youths from 17 to 18 years

Scheme for track and field foundation—beginning November $(2 \times 1\frac{1}{2}$ hours per week):

The scheme should comprise for every training session half an hour of strength exercises with a barbell, half an hour gymnastics or track and field exercises and half an hour games. The plan for each session will be established according to the desired training effect.

Weight training in the extensive form for 3 months. The exercises selected must first be learnt. The weights are easily mastered. During the three months the total load of initially one series with about 10 repetitions is increased to three series with 10 repetitions each per exercise. The programme for about 30 minutes may, for example, consist of the following 10 exercises:

1. Clean and put down the weight
2. Jerk from chest upward in a stride position, alternately left and right
3. Knee-bending with weight on the neck
4. Snatching
5. Benchpress in horizontal position—pressing the weight from the chest
6. Jumping Jack
7. Trunk circling in sitting or standing position with weight on the neck
8. Squat vaults with weight on the neck from half knee-bend
9. Jerking the weight forward horizontally
10. Trunk bending (with weights on outstretched arms).

These 10 exercises will remain on the training programme for a long time. The increase in strength achieved through each exercise can thus be thoroughly checked. If after three months the 3 series with 10 repetitions each are properly mastered, weights can be gradually increased, repetitions reduced and longer breaks inserted between series. When increasing weights, one starts again with one series for each exercise and works up to three series in a further two months. The 3 series are then maintained, but weights increased by about 5 kilograms. The number of repetitions is at the same time reduced to about 6 to 8 in each series. Breaks between each series should be about 60 to 90 seconds. After 3 series of one exercise, a break of 3 to 5 minutes should be introduced, in order to prepare for the physiological effect of the intensive interval work and not to expose the young body suddenly to a relatively high resistance. Additionally it creates a feeling of success when the athlete finds out that the force he possessed at the beginning of the training has grown with the increased total load. This form of training with youths of between 14 and 16 has proved effective in our compulsory sports classes. We have built up a lot of beneficial experience with circuit training and with the body-building system. We distinguish these two systems by their different types of exercises.

1. The exercises chosen in circuit training are executed successively, i.e. first exercise 1, then 2, then 3 etc. in one to three passages. We call this form of exercise the circuit training system.
2. The exercises chosen in circuit training are executed in 3 series of about 10 repetitions each, side by side, i.e. after the first series of exercise 1 and a break follow the 2nd and 3rd series of exercise 1 and a break. Then the athletes change over to station 2 and there do exercise 2, etc. This way of organizing the training is that of the American body-building system. It mainly develops explosive strength. Here the training effect results from the relatively long breaks between series. The cardiovascular system is not strained so much as in the circuit training system. In the body-building system the total load is mainly increased by an increased intensity, in the circuit training more by an increased volume.

For advanced athletes the following principle applies: the weights must for sprinters and jumpers amount to about one half to two-thirds of the athlete's weight, in putters and throwers to about 75 to 80 per cent of the maximum performance.

Examples:

Sprinters (up to 400 m): For example 70 kg weight = 25 to 40 kg weight of barbell.

Approximately 10 repetitions (quick and neat execution of exercises); the duration of breaks after 10 repetitions is about 45 to 60 seconds, taken up with stretching and loosening exercises.

This develops explosive strength, special endurance as local speed-endurance (muscular metabolism, buffer capacity). Form of exercise: series
Exercises: jerking–snatching–jumping Jack–knee-bending; after extension the feet come off the ground–same, but as squat vaults–jumping into stride position (alternating legs)–raising heels with weights on the neck–standing on steps or edge of springboard–fast knee-lifting runs with weights on the neck.

Jumpers: e.g. weighing 70 kg = 30 to 60 kg weight of barbell.
Approximately 8 to 10 repetitions.
Duration of break after 8 to 10 repetitions: about 45 to 60 seconds, taken up with stretching and loosening exercises.
Development of jumping strength (spring) as local explosive force, special endurance as local strength-endurance.
Form of exercise: series
Exercises: Jerking in long-stride position, right-left, alternately–Snatching with knee-bending and straightening–Cleaning the barbell in front of the chest with deep knee-bending and straightening–Jumping Jack–Knee-bending–Squat jumps (on the spot, over obstacles)–Hopping–Bounding–Three-hops and five-hops.

Throwers: The weight of the barbell must be about 70 to 80 per cent of the maximum performance in the different lifting exercises, independent of the athlete's weight. About 8 to 10 repetitions (swift execution of exercises).

Development of maximum strength, explosive strength and strength endurance as local endurance for throwing events; increase of muscular cross-section and improvement of energy potential and of muscular metabolism
Form of exercise: series
Exercises:
Jumping–snatching–jumping Jack
Jerking several times from the chest upwards–
Pressing (swift execution)–
Knee-bending
Squat vaults–
Cleaning and putting down the weight

In all three event groups the total load can be increased by increasing the number of repetitions in a given unit of time.
Total loads can be increased either by more repetitions in a given unit of time or by heavier weights, without changing the number of repetitions or the time of the exercise. The desired training effect is to build up relative strength, (local) explosive force and (local) strength endurance. If weights are consistently increased, fewer repetitions and longer intervals between series are needed. This then comes close to the method of repetition work.
Summing up one may say that in training young beginners strength exercises with a barbell should begin with extensive interval work and lead up to intensive interval work. The systems to be applied are: for extensive interval work "circuit" training and for intensive interval work "body-building" training, bearing in mind that when taking up or resuming training, the body-building system should take on a more extended character.

2.7.2.3. The Method of Repetition Work

The method of repetitions is characterized by the following features:

1. Stimulus intensity of the exercises
Physical exercise in the form of running and of strength exercises with additional weights must be executed at high intensity. For each exercise at least 80 to 90 (occasionally 100) per cent of the maximum performance should be applied (running—90 to 100 per cent, strength exercises—80 to 90, occasionally 100 per cent).

2. Stimulus volume of the exercises
In view of the strong stimulus which each exercise exerts on the athlete's body, the number of repetitions should not be more than 3 to 6 for running and 20 to 30 lifts per training unit or 3 to 6 lifts per series for strength exercises with a barbell.

3. Stimulus density of the exercises
The very high intensity during this phase requires long rest intervals. The principle of "worthwhile breaks" is not applicable here. Depending on the amount of running, breaks after each performance phase should be between 3 to 45 minutes and in weight training with a barbell at least 2 to 3 minutes but not more than 5 minutes. Rest intervals can be taken up either by jogging and walking, or by walking alone. Breathing or easy loosening exercises can be done as alternatives.

4. Stimulus duration of the exercises
Each training stimulus varies in length. In running it may be only about 2 to 3 seconds, but can also be up to 6 or 9 minutes, while in strength exercises it should always be only a few second (Fig. 9).

● Physiological fundamentals

During training based on repetitions the athlete's body is submitted to very strong stimuli. They produce excitations in the cerebrum (central nervous system). If 100 per cent of the maximum performance is applied too frequently or if training is too often within the range of peak loads, excessively high stimulation producing maximum excitation in the nervous system can lead to inhibitions. In training using repetitions, the rule not to exceed 90 to 95 per cent of the maximum should be adhered to. High excitation resulting from strong load stimuli rapidly produces central fatigue, a process which is accelerated still further by other factors. Great efforts, near the maximum work rate or weight will soon develop a higher oxygen debt, forcing the muscles to work mainly anaerobically. Acid metabolic residues are thereby produced and increase central fatigue. The increased muscle metabolism requires more nutrients, buffer substances, mineral salts and vitamins, which must be available in sufficient quantities. In training the muscle metabolism, an ef-

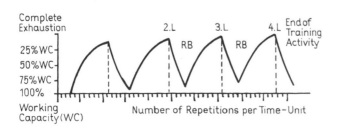

Fig. 9 Scheme of the method of repetition work (L – Loading, RB – Break)

fect is produced, which improves the local peripheral and central resistance to fatigue.

This results in a good interaction between the nerves and muscles (sensomotor coordination). If the repetition work is properly used, the quality of the following condition factors will be improved:

1. Speed
2. Maximum strength
3. Speed and strength combined = explosive force (special explosive force for single events).
4. Speed-endurance

● Forms of exercises

Running using repetitions in training young beginners and advanced athletes:

In training young athletes repetition work should be applied only under certain conditions. These are related to the particular requirements of the growing body. Under the effect of repeated efforts muscles work mainly anaerobically, so that the oxygen debt accumulated after each performance phase is very high. Although the bodies of adolescents have the ability to adjust to new conditions, it must be remembered that the vegetative nervous system of the young is still very unstable (NAGORNI, FILIN, MIES).

Research shows clearly that young athletes react better to medium load stimuli of short duration than to high stimuli of long duration.

In setting up training schedules of youths based on repetition work the following points should be noted:

Repeated runs in training boys between 14 and 16

Only the following distances should be included: 30 m, 50 m, 60 m, 75 m, 100 m, 125 m, 150 m. The longer the distances, the less repetitions should be planned. The following number of repetitions depending on distance lengths, are sensible and practical (R = Repetitions; RB = Recovery Break):

	30-m runs, R–8
RB	between runs–3–5 min.
	50-m runs, R–6
RB	between runs–5 min.
	60-m runs, R–5
RB	between runs–5–7 min.
	75-m runs, R–4
RB	between runs–7–10 min.
	100-m runs, R–3
RB	between runs–15–20 min.
	125-m runs, R–2
RB	between runs–15–20 min.
	150-m runs, R–2
RB	between runs–20–25 min.

Distances beyond 150 m should not be included in repetition schedules for 14 to 16 year olds.

As a means of training runs with changes of tempo can be applied in these schedules. Such runs should not exceed 75 to 150 m for 14 to 16 year olds. Not more than 2 to 4 repetitions should be planned for runs with changes of tempo. Suitable intervals between tempo-changing runs are 10 to 20 minutes. The length of intervals should be chosen according to the running pattern over a given distance. The distribution over a distance of 150 m should be:

50 m sprint–
50 m coasting–
50 m sprint
winding down
A very different pattern is:
30 m of brisk running–
30 m sprint
30 m coasting
30 m jogging

30 m sprint
winding down.

Only youths having undergone regular training over several months based on the duration method at relatively low intensity but with a lot of repetitions (extensive training) should be allowed to do repetition work. During this period the growing body has adjusted its oxygen-intake capacity to increased demands, so that repeated intensive muscular work under anerobic conditions involves less risk.

Youths, aged 17 or 18, who have trained systematically in the younger groups can do more repetitions. This will permit them to improve basic speed and special endurance in the spring and to conserve form in the main competition season. Repetition work should appear only once or twice on weekly training schedules with 6 training days. For 17 or 18 year olds repetition work should include 1,000-m runs in addition to the distances quoted for 14 to 16 year olds. These distances can be covered by fast runs, but also by runs with changes of tempo.

Examples: Repetitions for distances of 30 to 150 m
(examples for 14 to 16 year olds see 2.7.2.3.).
Tempo-runs
200-m runs, 2–3 sec. (sub-maximum)
Repetitions–2–3
Recovery breaks–30–45 min.
300-m runs, 3–4 sec. (sub-maximum) (to be determined by 100-m and 200-m best times or through test runs over 300 m).
Repetitions–2–3
Recovery breaks–30–45 min.
400-m runs–3–6 sec. (sub-maximum)
Repetitions–2–4
Recovery breaks–20–45 min.

Recovery breaks can be taken up alternately with jogging and walking and with easy loosening exercises. It is not advisable to remain completely passive during breaks, as the circulation must be prepared for the next performance phase.

If weather conditions permit, the athlete may also sit or lie down for a while. It is important, however, that he keeps warm for the next performance phase. This should be kept in mind when planning breaks. High load-exercises must be avoided during intervals.

Outline of *runs with changes of tempo* based on repetition work for 16 to 18 year olds:

200-m runs with changes of tempo
3–4 repetitions
10–25 minutes rest intervals
5 × 20 m sprints and 5 × 20 m coasting, alternately, or 50 m sprint–30 m coasting–20 m jogging–20 m brisk jogging
30 m sprint–50 m coasting
20 m sprint as finishing spurt–winding down
300 m tempo changing runs:
2–3 repetitions
20–30 min. interval
50 m accelerations up to sprint
50 m coasting
50 m acceleration up to sprint
50 m coasting
80 m acceleration
20 m finishing sprint
winding down
400 m tempo-changing runs:
2–3 repetitions
30 min. interval
100 m acceleration up to sprint
100 m coasting with deceleration and again acceleration, almost to sprinting speed, and so on.

The sprint after acceleration must be performed in an easy, relaxed style; after 10 to 20 m sprinting, coasting sets in immediately.

The application of tempo-changing runs in training youths and juniors requires a high sense of responsibility on the part of the coach and much understanding and discipline on the part of his charges. Only well prepared youngsters should be allowed to use this means of training and even then only with a few repetitions. One cannot caution strongly enough against the irresponsible application of such training means with a high stimulus volume which develop special endurance (speed-endurance). They should be included very sparingly in training schedules in the spring. Experience in the USSR has shown that the adolescent body is better able to resist loads over short training distances than sustained tempo runs and tempo-changing runs of very high intensity [18].

Hence, even in training well prepared 17 to 18 year olds using repetitions, it is advisable to use the above mentioned examples for 14 to 16 year olds. Speed over the 100-m distance (basic speed) and in all motor tasks should be developed at an early age. Specific endurance over distances from 800 m upwards should be trained for only after the 18th year. Once basic speed is well developed, special endurance as speed-endurance for middle- and long-distance running can build on it more easily. This naturally does not mean that one should avoid any repetition work over distances of 200 to 1,000 m as tempo- and tempo-changing runs with youths. The main thing is that these runs are used only occasionally with very few repetitions and long rest intervals (Table 11).

For the 3,000-m steeplechase the schedule for 1,500-m runners applies.

For 1,500-m and 10,000-m runners repetition work is applied only under certain conditions. For repetitions the programme of the 1,500-m runner may serve as a model, only with longer distances, easier running times and some additional repetitions. Up to 3,000 metres, 3 to 6 repetitions with longer rest intervals can be run.

Strength exercises with the barbell

When doing strength exercises with the barbell using repetitions, only 1 to 2 successive lifts or a series of 3 to 6 repetitions should be planned. The amount of weight lifted should be about 90 per cent (occasionally 100 per cent) of the personal best performance in the weight lifting event. This form of repetition work is also known as the weight-lifting method.

Rest intervals between lifts should last about 2 to 4 minutes. For physiological reasons these intervals should be taken up by stretching and loosening exercises. This is not yet widely recognized and one can often see athletes sitting around idly during intervals.

In track and field training schedules weight lifting is more and more used by jumpers, throwers and shot putters during conditioning training. The following world-class athletes have achieved excellent results in weight lift-

---

18 Cf. V. J. Ilyinitch "Verschiedene Varianten der Vorbereitung Jugendlicher in Sportarten, die hohe allgemeine und spezielle Ausdauer verlangen" (Different Ways of Preparing Youth for Events Requiring Great General and Special Endurance) from "Beiträge zu Trainingsfragen" in the Series "Sport im Sozialismus", Sportverlag, Berlin 1960.

Table 11 *Runs for Advanced Athletes according to the Repetition Method*

Distance	Running Speed about	Repetitions about	Recovery Break about
Sprinters up to 400 m			
30 m	maximum	6–8	3– 4 min.
50 m	maximum	5–6	3– 4 min.
60 m	maximum	4–6	4– 6 min.
80 m	maximum	3–4	5–10 min.
100 m	11.4–10.8 sec.	3–4	10–20 min.
150 m	19.0–17.0 sec.	3–4	10–20 min.
200 m	23.5–22.0 sec.	3–4	15–20 min.
300 m	40.0–36.0 sec.	3–4	15–20 min.
400 m	52.0–49.0 sec.	3–4	20–30 min.
500 m	75.0–65.0 sec.	2–3	20–30 min.
600 m	90.0–75.0 sec.	2–3	20–30 min.
800-m Runners			
100 m	12.2–11.5 sec.	4–6	10–15 min.
150 m	22.0–19.0 sec.	4–5	10–15 min.
200 m	25.0–23.5 sec.	4–5	15–25 min.
300 m	42.0–37.0 sec.	4–5	15–25 min.
400 m	58.0–53.0 sec.	4–5	15–25 min.
500 m	76.0–68.0 sec.	3–4	20–30 min.
600 m	110.0–80.0 sec.	3–4	20–30 min.
800 m	2:04.0–1:58.0 min.	2–3	45–60 min.
1,500-m Runners			
200 m	27.0–25.5 sec.	5–6	10–15 min.
400 m	60.0–54.0 sec.	4–5	10–15 min.
600 m	110.0–85.0 sec.	3–4	20–25 min.
800 m	2:08.0–2:00.0 min	3–4	20–25 min.
1,000 m	2:45.0–2:25.0 min.	2–3	25–35 min.
1,200 m	3:20.0–3:00.0 min.	2–3	25–45 min.
1,600 m	4:20.0–4:05.0 min.	2–3	20–45 min.
2,000 m	5:50.0–5:20.0 min.	2–3	20–45 min.
3,000 m	9:20.0–8:30.0 min.	2–3	20–45 min.

ing: Piatkowski, Oerter, O'Brien, Long, Gubner (throwers), Brumel, Kashkarov, Shcherbakov, Fyodoseyev (jumpers).

Some years ago the weight lifting method was also used by sprinters but has since been abandoned.

For middle- and long-distance runners the weight lifting method is out of the question, as it acts against the desired physiological qualities of these specialists.

Exercises based on the weight-lifting method

Apart from the Olympic exercises (two-arm jerking and snatching) various exercises for almost all the groups of muscles are generally used. Single exercises are almost identical to those described in the method of intensive interval work. The only difference is in the number of repetitions (stimulus volume) and in the weight of the barbells

85

(stimulus intensity). Exercises with the barbell are often combined with intensive interval and repetition work in conditioning schedules of athletes, starting with series based on intensive interval work.

Following some series with higher weights based on the method of repetitions, with only 1, 2, 3 or 4 lifts; then again 2 to 3 series of intensive interval work with about 8 to 10 lifts of some 70 to 80 per cent maximum.

The following training based on the "circuit" method has proved effective:

Snatching, bench pressing, jerking, deep knee-bending—executed successively in the order given. The barbell weight used will first only allow for 8 repetitions. When the weight is increased by 3.5 to 5 kg, only 6 repetitions are possible. By using higher and higher weights, fewer and fewer repetitions are possible (4,2,1,1, 1). When the maximum is attained, loads are again decreased by 2.5 to 5 kg. This permits, 2,4 up to 6 repetitions per series. The scheme 8−6−4−2−1−1−1−2−4−6 is thus obtained. Between series rest intervals of some $1\frac{1}{2}$ to 2 minutes are usual. It is advisable to record lifting times. After the maximum test new amounts are determined [19].

The application of repetitions in exercises with the barbell in training young beginners

The same pattern as for adults may be applied with just a few changes. Experience in the Soviet Union has shown that marked differences in the development of strength were found in young beginners after 3-months strength training (twice weekly), although one group (80 athletes) trained with medium loads and another group (60 athletes) with high loads.

The conclusion to be drawn from this is that in training young beginners use only medium (up to 60 per cent of the maximum lifting capacity) weights in the first training year. This appears sensible not only for health reasons, but also for the adequate development of strength. [20]

Investigations made in the USSR on young track and field athletes also confirmed that exercises with the barbell and with other weights should be performed from extensive via intensive interval work to repetitions. Repetition work should be included in weight training programmes for youths only occasionally, just to let them experience the gain in strength achieved through the barbell training. The increase in power is also reflected in the greater number of repetitions with the usual training weights or of faster lifts in a given unit of time. Young athletes naturally also wish to find out how much their maximum strength has improved by doing one or two lifts.

With 14 to 16 year old boys repetition work with weights will have more the character of test lifts. For youths from 17 years onwards repetition work with weights can, as for adults, be combined with series of extensive and intensive interval work, provided they have car-

---

19 For more details see M. Scholich "Kreistraining" (Circuit Training), 2nd ed., Sportverlag, Berlin 1982.

20 K.-H. Bauersfeld "Kraftentwicklung − eine wichtige Aufgabe der Leichtathleten" (Strength Development−an Important Task of Track and Field Athletes) in "Der Leichtathlet", Nr. 7/1961, Appendix "Der Leichtathletik-Trainer".

ried out the proper preparatory training as 14 to 16 year olds.

Repetition work with about 90 to 100 per cent of the maximum performance capacity involves essentially the following exercises with the barbell:

Two-arm jerking and snatching; one-arm jerking and snatching; knee-bends with weight on the neck; two-arm pressing from the horizontal position.

2.7.2.4. Organizational-Methodical Forms of Practising in Series

In modern training the methods of extensive and intensive interval work and of repetition work (except for running repetition) are usually undertaken in series. This improves the quality of training (per unit of time). It also permits to work both extensively and intensively on the same day and in one training session.

If the two methods of interval work are combined, the planning of quantity and intensity naturally becomes more difficult for the coach. He must be thoroughly familiar with both interval methods and with their physiological effects on the body, in order to devise series producing the desired training effect. Work in series makes the otherwise rather monotonous interval training more varied and interesting. We give some examples of extensive and intensive interval work and of the combination of these two methods. These examples are intended for adult athletes (about performance grade I).

● 1. The method of extensive interval work in series

Running: Overall objectives are 40 tempo runs (stimulus volume) over 200 m in about 32 to 36 seconds (stimulus intensity), followed by a "worthwhile break" of about 45 to 90 seconds (stimulus density). The runs can be split up into series, e.g. 4 series of 10 runs each.

Training examples: 30 minutes limbering up with gymnastics. 1st series:

10 × 200-m run in 36 seconds

"worthwhile break" 45 seconds, jogging

break 3 minutes, jogging.

2nd series:

10 × 200 m in 32 seconds

"worthwhile break" 50 seconds, jogging

break 3 minutes, jogging.

3rd series:

10 × 200 m in 34 sec.

"worthwhile break" 55 sec., jogging

break 3 minutes, jogging

15 minutes winding down.

Exercises with a barbell

(Exercising with a barbell weight of about one third of the body weight, i.e. athletes of 75 kg with 25-kg weights)

Optional exercises: jerking, snatching, jumping Jack, knee-bending

Training example:

30 minutes limbering up or game of basketball

1st series

10 × jerking

30 sec. break with stretching exercises

10 × snatching

30 sec. break with stretching exercises

10 × knee-bending

30 sec. break with stretching exercises

3–4 minutes break with light loosening exercises

2nd series

10 × knee-bending

30 sec. break with stretching exercises

10 × jumping Jack

30 sec. break with stretching exercises
10 × snatching
30 sec. break with stretching exercises
10 × jerking
30 sec. break with stretching exercises
3–5 min. break, jogging
3rd series
10 × jerking
30 sec. break, loosening and stretching exercises
10 × snatching
30 sec. break, loosening and stretching exercises
10 × knee-bending
30 sec. break, loosening and stretching exercises
10 min. loosening gymnastics
In all series the barbell weight should invariably be 25 kg, so that the total load in the three series quoted is 3,000 kg. Training effect: see extensive interval work (improved circulatory regulation, muscle metabolism and some gain in strength).

An increase of loads is obtained by fixing a definite time for the 10 repetitions, which is gradually shortened, or by doing more repetitions very quickly in the same time.

● 2. The method of intensive interval work in series

Running: Overall objectives are 10 runs: 5 runs over 100 m, 3 runs over 200 m and 2 runs over 400 m. The series can be arranged in various ways. One can start with 100-m runs, followed by 200-m runs and finally tackle the 400-m runs. This order can, however, also be reversed or one may start with two 100-m runs, then one 400-m run and finish with a 200-m run. This would then again be a 200-m run, a 400-m run and the last planned 200-m run. The training session would finish with 3 100-m runs. The variations do not influence the planned training effect.

Training examples (800-m runner)
Improving specific endurance at the end of the preparatory period:
30 minutes warming up
1st series
2 × 100-m run in 13.0 sec.
"worthwhile break" 90 sec., jogging
1 × 200-m run in 27.0 sec.,
"worthwhile break" 120 sec., jogging
1 × 400-m run in 63.0 sec.,
"worthwhile break" 120 sec., jogging
break 5 min., alternating walking and jogging.
2nd series
1 × 200-m run in 27.0 sec.,
"worthwhile break" 120 sec., jogging
1 × 400-m run in 60 sec.,
"worthwhile break" 120 sec., jogging
1 × 200-m run in 28.0 sec.,
"worthwhile break" 120 sec., jogging
break 5 min., walking and jogging alternately.
3rd series
3 × 100-m run in 13.5 sec.,
"worthwhile break" 120 sec., jogging
13.0 sec.,
"worthwhile break" 150 sec., jogging
12.8 sec.,
"worthwhile break" 180 sec., jogging
15 minutes, limbering down.

Exercises with the barbell

Examples for jumpers weighing 75 kg = barbell weight 30–40 kg.
The following exercises are employed:
jerking–snatching–jumping Jack–knee-bending–
squat vault.
Arrangement of series for developing explosive power.
Training example: 30 minutes warm-up, e.g. by games (basketball)

1st series
10 × 30 kg jerking
45 sec. break, loosening exercises
10 × 30 kg jumping Jack
45 sec. break, loosening exercises
10 × 30 kg jumping Jack
45 sec. break, loosening exercises
10 × 30 kg jerking
45 sec. break, loosening exercises
5 min. break, walking and jogging,
loosening and stretching exercises.
2nd series
8 × 40 kg snatching
60 sec. break, loosening exercises
8 × 40 kg knee-bending
60 sec. break, loosening exercises
4 × 40 kg squat vaults
60 sec. break, loosening exercises
4 × 40 kg squat vaults
60 sec. break, loosening exercises
5–10 min. break, jogging and walking,
loosening and stretching exercises.
3rd series
6 × 50 kg snatching
45 sec. break, loosening exercises
10 × 30 kg jumping Jack
45 sec. brcak, loosening exercises
10 × 30 kg jumping Jack
45 sec. break, loosening exercises
6 × 50 kg snatching
45 sec. break, loosening exercises
10 × 30 kg jumping Jack
45 sec. break, loosening exercises
loosening exercises–stretching exercises–walking–jogging.

*Combination of extensive and intensive
interval work in the arrangement of
series*

Running: Training example for improving basic endurance (for high performance athletes of grade 1)
30 minutes limbering up
1st series
8 × 200-m run in 34 sec.,

"worthwhile break" between each run
90.0 sec.
5 min. break, alternating walking and
jogging.
In the "worthwhile break" after
45.0 sec. jogging, after every second
200-m run from jogging a flying sprint
over 30 m.
10 min. break, alternating walking and
jogging.
2nd series
1 × 100-m run in 13.5 sec.,
"worthwhile break" 90 sec., jogging
1 × 200-m run in 36.0 sec.,
"worthwhile break" 90 sec., jogging
2 × 100-m run in 15.0 sec.,
"worthwhile break" 90 sec., jogging
1 × 200-m run in 30.0 sec.,
"worthwhile break" 90 sec., jogging
1 × 100-m run in 15.0 sec.,
"worthwhile break" 90 sec., jogging
Serial breaks 10 min. walking and jogging, alternately
3rd series
1 × 300-m run in 55.0 sec.,
"worthwhile break" 120 sec., jogging
2 × 200-m run in 30.0 sec.,
"worthwhile break" 120 sec., jogging
1 × 100-m run in 13.5 sec.,
"worthwhile break" 120 sec., jogging
3 × 50-m run all out,
"worthwhile break" 90 sec., jogging
10 minutes limbering down.

Exercises with the barbell

Training example for a sprinter
(Athlete weighing 75 kg–12 st.)
Training effect:
1. Speed by improved sensomotor coordination
2. Special endurance as strength-endurance
3. Explosive strength
30 minutes warm-up (basketball)
1st series

10 × 25 kg jerking
execution at max. speed,
45 sec. break
20 × 25 kg snatching
execution at max. speed,
45 sec. break
10 × 25 kg knee-bending
execution at max. speed,
45 sec. break
Serial break 10 minutes, loosening and some stretching exercises.
2nd series
10 × 25 kg squat vaults
execution at max. speed,
60 sec. break
5 × 50 kg snatching
execution at max. speed,
60 sec. break
5 × 50 kg knee-bending
execution at max. speed,
60 sec. break
5 × 50 kg snatching
execution at max. speed,
60 sec. break
10 × 25 kg jumping Jack
execution at max. speed,
60 sec. break.
Serial break 10 minutes taken up by walking, jogging and quick response exercises (2 to 3 sprint starts from easy hopping diagonally across the gymnasium).
3rd series
3 × 10 snatching exercises (left, right, left),
then 90 sec. break
10 × 30 kg jumping Jack
60 sec. break
3 × 10 snatching exercises (right, left, right),
then 90 sec. break
10 × without additional load on the long/triple jump run-up (6 parts of boxes or 6 hurdles)—walk back. Shake out legs! Long/triple jump run-up:

clear first with both legs in tucked position, then from crouch to crouch–squat vaults (next sequences alternating 1 and 2). Loosening gymnastics, short sprint starts, a few stretching exercises.

● 3. Applying different forms of interval work in series in training with youths

As a matter of principle the various forms of interval work in series can be used with youths between 14 and 18 during training. This makes training more varied and interesting. The different forms of interval work in series can also be combined, as shown in the examples for advanced adult athletes (about grade I level). Consideration of the following points is imperative when training youths.

1. The combination of the extensive and intensive interval work in training runs in series leads to a high load, so that

a) the number of repetitions for both interval forms must be reduced,

b) the serial breaks must be lengthened,

c) breaks between series must be lengthened.

2. The coach or team leader must measure the pulse rate of athletes after each series and determine their capacity to recover and their degree of fatigue.

3. For strength exercises the variants of "circuit" training should be used. This permits young athletes not only to practise at individually fixed intensities, but also to check their improving performance by the use of the control cards.

4. In planning training schedules and quantity and intensity of work all the fundamental principles of training must be taken into consideration.

2.7.3. Importance and Development of Mobility

Flexibility is defined as the ability to fully utilize the range of movement around the joints. Other synonyms such as suppleness are sometimes used.

Not everyone is endowed with the same degree of flexibility; it depends on the physical characteristics of the individual. There are great differences in the form of bone structures and in the length and extensibility of muscles and tendons. The greatest differences are chiefly found in muscles and tendons. Those with bulky short muscles are prone to a certain lack of mobility, which can only be overcome by great effort. Other persons are quite flexible without doing much exercise.

Good *allround flexibility* is achieved when movements about all the joints are flexible. Technical skills of some athletics events require a special and exceptional flexibility in single, usually limited parts of the body. This is the *special flexibility* found in hurdlers and high jumpers.

Special flexibility can only be developed to perfection on the foundation of a good general flexibility.

2.7.3.1. The Importance of Mobility

Good flexibility facilitates the achievement of a maximum range of swing in all swinging movements and the movement of different parts of the body (especially arms and legs) economically in performing skills.

Because of the reduced resistance of antagonists (provided the technique is properly mastered), a higher velocity of the movements is achieved.

The role of special flexibility in the economic performance of skills is obvious in some events. It would thus be impossible to perform a good hurdle stride or the extended swinging leg action in the straddle jump, or the pull of the arm in a straight line in the javelin without excellent flexibility at the hip joint.

In all other technical events the influence of flexibility, although not so clearly visible, has a bearing nevertheless on the quality of techniques. An economic landing in the long and triple jump is only possible if trunk and legs are jack-knived as far forward as possible.

In running events flexibility contributes to the looseness, velocity and length of strides. The frequently expressed opinion that a high intensity of flexibility exercises adversely influences strength has not been confirmed by TOPULIAN's studies [21] and is probably based on a certain amount of neglect and lack of recognition of the importance of flexibility.

2.7.3.2. Methods of the Developing of Mobility

Flexibility can only be improved if the required exercises are performed persistently with great intensity and endurance. If gymnastics are interrupted for an appreciable period of time, flexibility will soon return to the initial natural values. Improvement is slow at first. Stretching produces disagreeable

21 Topulian "Methoden zur Entwicklung der Beweglichkeit beim Hürdenläufer" (Methods for the Development of Mobility in Hurdlers), Thesis delivered by the Author for his Degree (Translation, Library of the DHfK, Leipzig).

sensations in the muscles, leading to soreness or even pain. Will-power is important for improving flexibility. Exercises for flexibility have much in common with gymnastics and may be divided into two groups:

1. Passive stretching exercises
   (kneading exercises)

In these exercises motion and extension are not produced by the muscles themselves, but by outside forces:

a) constrained position (e.g. hurdle seat)

b) partners

c) pulling or pressing the arms (e.g. trunk bending forward by grasping the ankles with both hands and pulling the trunk forward until the head touches the knees).

These exercises should be executed slowly and carefully in the early stages so as to avoid injuries.

2. Active stretching exercises

In this group of exercises movements are produced by the muscles. They must be executed quickly and energetically so as to approach the limits of flexibility. By these drills the antagonists and their tendons are stretched and lengthened. At the same time the muscles producing these movements become stronger and faster.

Straight, circling and rotating swinging movements also belong to this group.

The tempo of these exercises gradually increases with growing flexibility.

When doing flexibility exercises in training, the following principles should be adhered to:

1. Every training session should be introduced by a certain number of flexibility exercises. In daily training sessions the exercises should be frequently changed. This creates favourable conditions for developing skills and for reducing the risk of injuries. For improving flexibility it is, however, not sufficient to do gymnastic exercises before training sessions.

2. Daily morning and evening gymnastic exercises are a good way of developing flexibility.

3. Before beginning special exercises, the athlete must warm up until he is perspiring slightly. Warming-up must be more intensive in the morning than in the evening, because muscles are less extensible in the morning.

4. Each exercise can be performed in series of 10 to 20 repetitions.

5. Loosening and relaxation exercises after each series help to overcome soreness in the muscles quickly. Then the next series follows.

6. Depending on the athlete's special event and individual characteristics each part of the gymnastics may involve some 150 to 300 repetitions (10 to 15 exercises with 15 to 20 repetitions each).

7. When taking up training, passive stretching exercises are the most important. With growing athletic perfection and specialization, active stretching exercises come more to the foreground; they should be considered as the principal form of flexibility exercises of track and field athletes.

8. Special flexibility exercises for one specific event should be very similar to the technical structure or parts of it.

2.7.4.   Importance and
          Development of Agility

Agility is a necessary prerequisite for all physical exercises requiring the participation of the whole body and the interplay of all the groups of muscles.

MEINEL defines agility as follows: "Agility must be understood as a good coordination of the kinesthesis of the whole body." [22] It therefore plays an important role. Good general agility in an athlete is his ability to grasp the technique of a new sequence of movement in its rough form very quickly and often at the first attempt. Special agility builds on the foundation of such general agility. It is known in track and field as "jumping agility" or "hurdling agility".

Characteristics of special agility are:

1. Outstanding coordination ability in one training complex (running, jumping or throwing).

2. Excellent orientating in all phases of a movement of the special event (high jump, hurdles etc.).

3. The capacity to adapt successfully to various conditions (situations, layouts, implements etc.).

4. Superior composure in the face of unexpected incidents in the execution of movements of the special event (wind, being impeded by other participants, unevenness of the track etc.).

Summarizing one may say that an athlete with good special agility can execute new parts of movements or variants in his special event without appreciable loss of performance. He is able to immediately adapt to unforeseen changes of conditions by slightly varying his usual movements.

2.7.4.1. The Importance of Agility

Agility plays a significant role in the training of technique and in competi-

tion. The aim in training skills is to bring the athlete closer and closer to the ideal form of the sequence of movement. An athlete can only make the required corrections successfully if he possesses excellent agility. One may say *that without further systematic development of special agility, which can be improved only on the basis of a good coordination, progress in the special technical training of the top-class athlete can hardly be expected.*

During competition situations may arise which force the athlete to change well-established series of movements. The different texture of tracks in jumping and running and different layouts in the throws, tactics of opponents in middle- and long-distance races all require, for example, good adaptability. All these qualities are mainly found in athletes who possess a high degree of special agility. The development of agility must therefore not be left to chance but promoted systematically through suitable exercises.

2.7.4.2. Methods of Developing Agility

General agility is developed during childhood or adolescence. In this period of life the young should be taught a wide variety of movements. This is one of the reasons why so much emphasis is laid on the training of versatility in boys, girls and youngsters. Adult athletes who are lacking general agility can hardly develop it to a marked degree later in life. Improvement of general agility and development of special agility are ensured during foundation training in a special event. This influence diminishes, because the athlete gets used to frequently repeated exer-

22 Team of Authors (Chief Editors: K. Meinel/ G. Schnabel) "Bewegungslehre" (Kinesology), 2nd ed., Volk und Wissen, Berlin 1977

cises. Special exercises for developing agility must then be included in the training programme.

Since agility rapidly reduces with growing fatigue, it is advisable to do the special agility exercises at the beginning of a training session. They should be chosen according to the following precepts:

1. The athlete should acquire a rich and versatile repertoire of movements.

2. These exercises should enable him to react quickly and correctly in unforeseen situations.

3. Exercises setting several tasks within a complex of movements should be chosen with the purpose of developing quick coordination.

For the development of *general agility* we recommend:

Sports games requiring a quick response, principally basketball, handball and football on a small pitch, volleyball, football-tennis, punch-ball etc.

Apparatus work permitting different combinations of movements for improving coordination. The varying structure of movements of gymnastic elements has a particularly beneficial effect on the development of agility.

Skiing with its great variety of possible movements and varying conditions (snow and terrain) is an ideal and enjoyable agility exercise.

The training of versatility in athletics every athlete should tackle. Particularly suitable events for developing agility are: hammer throwing, pole vault and hurdles.

Special agility is acquired in training by learning and practising many different sorts of movement, which have a similar structure (e.g. jumps in a variety of forms). This gives an indication of the means at one's disposal.

Carefully chosen variations of the technique, its components and the practising of the technique of similar events assist in the development of special agility. We mention here only the main possibilities (further examples can be found in the sections on physical conditions and training means in the different events):

Open-field exercises, e.g. jumps over pits and bushes, throwing stones.

Practising the special event under unusual conditions, e.g. sprints and starts on sandy ground, long jumps on grass and so on.

Practising the special event under constantly changing conditions, runs with and against the wind, with different kinds of shoes, throws with different or heavy implements, jumps with changing run-ups etc.

Mirror exercises. These are the reversed execution of movements. Competitions should be organized during training in which the results of throws of the right and the left hand are added.

Practising novel movements, e.g. running sideways or backwards. Exercising antiquated high-jump techniques, complicated jumps over apparatus, backward and overhead throws etc.

With growing specialization such exercises often help to vary the technical training.

2.8.   Technical Training

To teach technique, one must know the sequence of movements and the laws governing it. Track and field experts have come more and more to the opinion that every beginner should learn the must up-to-date technique. Numerous tests on boys and girls have proved this to be possible. Every coach and sports teacher should therefore be thoroughly conversant with the features of modern technique and with the laws on which the learning of new movements is based. These are primarily neurophysiological processes, researched and enunciated by PAVLOV and his school.

PAVLOV's theory is based on the concept of reflexes. According to his theory each movement is, from a neurophysiological point of view, a chain of successive reflexes, of which the conditioned reflexes are of main interest. They are the response of the organism to external and internal stimuli. Reflexes are acquired, subject to changes and limited in time.

Each stimulus produces an excitation in certain areas of the cerebral cortex (central organ of nervous activity). If the excitation is new to the body, which is the case in the learning of each new movement, irradiation of the excitation to adjacent areas of the cortex will occur. The exterior signs of this process are uneconomic movements accompanying first trials of a new movement. The course of practice limits the excitation centres in the cerebral cortex; inhibition processes develop, which cause the extraneous movements to disappear. These excitation and inhibition processes become differentiated but not yet clearly distinct from one another.

This state is defined as the differentiation of excitation and inhibition processes.

Through further exercising, single excitation and inhibition processes, relatively independent of each other, come into play. This state is called the concentration of excitation and inhibition in definite centres in the cerebral cortex. It results in the activity of certain muscles to the exclusion of all others.

By repeated practice the system of excitation and inhibition becomes stabilized. It fixes the proper sequence of movements and the coordinated work of all the muscles involved in the movement; in other words, it leads to the mastery of patterns of movement. This system is also known as the dynamic stereotype.

The Learning Process

In this process an athlete acquires mechanical skills and learns to master the technique of an athletic event. This may on occasions take some time; at other times it can be quite quick. It is influenced by different factors, the complexity of the sequence of movements to be learnt, the learning capacity of the athlete, and the effectiveness of the teacher.

Here the level of physical ability is of great importance, but is only one factor. Not every agile and strong athlete learns a new movement in a short time; we know that versatile athletes acquire new skills more quickly, due to a special faculty of the cerebral cortex, known as plasticity. Plasticity is the ability to create new complexes of conditioned reflexes and to modify existing ones. The more complexes there are, the greater is the plasticity.

A guiding principle can be deduced from this for the training of technique: the more varied and numerous the dynamic stereotypes which an athlete has acquired through his manysided athletic training, the greater is the capacity to learn new movements and to modify known patterns. The appropriation of new mechanical skills takes place in three phases, which are not always clearly distinct, merge into one another and are of varying duration.

These phases are [23]:

1. Rough coordination of the movements
(absorption of the basic elements of a movement in their rough form)

2. Smooth coordination of the movements (correction, smoothing out, differentiation)

3. Stabilization of the movement
(driving home and adapting to changing conditions).

1st Phase—rough coordination of the movement

The first phase corresponds to the irradiation. Prior to learning a new movement it is usually demonstrated in its separate parts. The athlete follows attentively every phase of the movement to get a clear understanding of it. At first he only sees what is done but does not yet know how to do it.

To get a clear understanding of the movement, the athlete must attempt it himself. The perceptions of the eyes and ears must be coordinated with those of the muscles; only in this way can a movement be properly grasped. This relationship is often disregarded

23   According to "Bewegungslehre", loc. cit.

in practice in two ways:

1. Some coaches like to explain an exercise in great detail and to demonstrate it many times before allowing the athlete to have a go at it.

2. Others have the athlete practice it along with them. They explain and demonstrate the exercise only initially, assuming thereafter that the athlete has a good model of the movement in his head.

This is a big mistake. The more experience an athlete has, the more important will explanations and demonstrations of a new movement be for him. The right grasp of the movement is acquired only in the course of exercise and training. This fact is important to know and crucial for successful learning.

The rough coordination of the movement is, according to MEINEL, characterized by much effort and little quality, as well as by uneven performance (some trials are successful, others fail). In developing the rough form, emphasis must be concentrated on the main phases of the movement. Such phases are e.g. the push-off with the rear foot in running, the take-off in the jumps and the release in the throws.

2nd Phase—smooth coordination of the movements

The second phase corresponds to the differentiated excitation and inhibition processes. Through many repetitions the rough form is developed into the refined form. The refined form is the efficient movement. It is economic, energy-saving, and becomes easy for the performer. The development of the refined form is a consciously geared process and takes a long time. There are many ways and means of getting there.

The second phase is marked by conscious practising. The teacher draws the attention of the athlete to individual parts of the whole movement. His chief aim is to detect wrong movements and to correct them.

The correction of wrong movements should not be unsystematic. First serious mistakes are corrected. Such mistakes are easily detected by the application of the following criteria:

1. Are the movements of the main phase correct?
2. Is the direction of the movements right?
3. Is the rhythm of the application of power correct?

Reasons for mistakes can be:

1. Incorrect understanding of a movement
2. Low level of basic physical qualities
3. Poor coordination of the movements
4. Wrong application of power
5. Lack of concentration
6. Outside factors (layout, implements).

By correcting a mistake it is sometimes possible to set right other movements. But this may also have an adverse effect. In drawing attention to particular phases, other phases, which were previously right, suddenly deteriorate or even the complete movement goes wrong. This is a natural occurrence. One thing the coach should never do is draw attention to several mistakes simultaneously.

In the second phase of the learning process the athlete should gain a right understanding of the movement. With the help of a good grasp of the mechanics—helped by hints from the coach—the athlete learns to distinguish between right and wrong movements; he should now be able partly to check his movements himself.

3rd Phase—stabilization of the movement

This phase corresponds to the concentration of excitations and inhibitions to certain areas of the cerebral cortex. In this phase the movements reach a high degree of accomplishment. They are stabilized and consolidated.

According to MEINEL this means:

1. they have greater homogeneity in space, time and dynamics,
2. they are better protected against external and internal disturbances, including disturbances by mental processes.

Consolidation is the result of automation.

Automatic movements are fast, confident and economic. To the onlooker they appear effortless. Typical of automatic movement is also the consistent and rhythmical application of power; there is a change in rhythm, since the main movement is executed in a shorter time.

The consolidated and stabilized movement is furthermore protected against all external influences. Every single movement must be "competition-proof". The nearer an athlete gets to this state, the better his chance of attaining his best performance in competition.

A fully automatic movement is performed without conscious thinking. This allows the athlete to concentrate on certain crucial points of the movement (MEINEL), as, for instance, the take-off in jumps.

In perfecting the technique of an event, the whole structure of movement changes when *one* factor is improved or enhanced. One can therefore never really say that an athlete masters a skill to perfection. When a pole vaulter with a consolidated technique considerably improves the planting action and the take-off, the structure of all other movements is altered. When a hurdler does a faster hurdle stride, the whole hurdles race will achieve a new quality. Every coach should be aware of this, because it may happen that an athlete becomes faster and stronger and yet does not improve his performance. He must start afresh, which is more difficult than learning from scratch.

2.9. Training Tactics

Tactics in track and field try to create an approach to competition which will achieve good results against opponents—tactics involve the sensible application of the athlete's own strength which will ensure the best possible success of the individual.

2.9.1. General Hints

When drawing up tactical plans for competition the following factors should be taken into consideration:

1. The current physical and mental condition of the athlete (how can one attain the best performance or ensue success?).
2. The level of accomplishment of his technique (slackening of performance with growing fatigue or at high speed must be considered).
3. The athlete's competitive experience.
4. The potential of the opponent (analysis of previous starts, studies on the adversary's morale, e.g. his susceptibility to feints, "stability" of his tactical approach and technical skills under pressure).
5. The nature of the competition (championship, international competition, eliminating contests, European championships, Olympic Games, qualifying contests, heats, finals).
6. The condition of the competition layout, wind conditions and other climatic influences.

The tactical preparation of the athlete in a broad sense takes place throughout training, but particularly in its quantity and intensity. Apart from improving the athlete's skill and abilities, his readiness to perform should be constantly stimulated (strengthening self-confidence, trust in his coach and in the plan of campaign). The "impetus training" as a means for attaining superior results at a given date is clearly a tactical question.

Qualification contests in the early morning of competition days are a good example. Detailed competition timetables are known well in advance. The athlete should adapt his training to the particular time of the day and prove repeatedly at a given hour that he is fit to achieve the required minimum performance in this event almost in his sleep (sprints, long and triple jump, shot put, javelin, discus and hammer throw).

An athlete should also know exactly how much time he needs for his warm-up in the morning and in the afternoon and after how many trials in jumps and throws at different hours of the day he anticipates his results.

During heats and finals of long- and triple jumps, shot put and throwing events, it is good tactics to "shock" the opponents at the first trial by an outstanding performance. On the other hand the athlete should not allow his opponent's results to depress him but must try to improve his performance from trial to trail. By a careful analysis of competitions the coach and his charges recognize the significance of tactical moves and of their consequences. This prevents athletes from becoming victims of their own tactics (e.g. intermediate spurts in middle- and long-distance runs).

2.9.1.1. Racing Tactics

The tactical approach in races may be divided into result tactics and winning tactics. Result tactics have as their purpose not only victory but also the achievement of good performances. A given distance must be covered in the shortest time possible and with predetermined intermediate times.

Winning tactics are intended to help the runner to victory and take into account the opponents' potentials. The athlete can, as an example, within the scope of competition rules, try to prevent his opponents from fully exploiting their strong points. Here the competitive experience of an athlete plays a paramount role.

Short-distance races

It is clear that tactics are less important in sprints than in middle- and long-distance races. In 100-m heats and semi-finals the sprinter must mainly run for a placing, not so much for "time".

In the 200-m race about 80 to 120 m are covered at maximum speed. If a runner is clearly superior to his opponents at that point, enough time is left for energy conservation over the remaining distance.

In the 400 m the right distribution of energy is of vital importance. Good results depend on the adherence to an optimal conservation time (intermediate time minus best time). In the 400 m the conservation time is about 0.5 sec., i.e. the first 200 m are run 0.5 seconds slower than the best 200-m time.

Middle- and long-distances races

The first half in 800-m and 1,500-m races is usually faster than the second. Experienced runners regularly attain better results if they are too fast over the first half than if they are too slow.

With winning tactics a "tempo" runner will wear the rival "fast finishers" down by speed right from the start. The "fast finisher" by contrast, strives to make full use of his strong finishing qualities at the finish. Only in a very fast race will he take the lead in order to slow the pace down (e.g. MATU-SCHEWSKI).

Performers and coaches have established a great number of "Golden Rules" for tactics over the years. We mention some below:

1. Run in the inside lane so as to prevent the opponent from passing on the inside and so as to avoid being boxed in.

2. Keep close to the leading runner and do not look back.

3. Do not lead against a head wind and avoid passing on the bend.
4. Concentrate fully on the race and do not allow anything to divert you.
5. Start the finish with a burst and take advantage of your rival's unguarded moment; never give up in this most important phase of the race.

2.9.1.2. Tactics in some Jumping Events

In the high jump and pole vault international rules have a greater influence than in all other events on the tactical considerations of coaches and athletes. So a competitor may "commence jumping at any height and then clear every further height as he chooses. After three consecutive failures, irrespective at which height, the competitor is eliminated for all further jumps". The effect of this rule is that an athlete can, after the first failure, omit the second and third trials at a given height and compete at later heights.

When several competitors clear the same height, placings are decided as follows [24]:

a) The competitor with the lowest number of failures at the height last cleared is awarded the highest placing.

b) If, however, there is still a tie, the competitor with the lowest total of failures, including the height last cleared, is awarded the highest placing.

c) If the winner has still not been found, a tie-breaking competition must

be carried out, but only to ascertain an outright winner. [24]

Tactical considerations are also of the greatest importance in competitions where participation in heats or finals depends on the qualifying standard. If the qualifying standard is achieved by less than 12 athletes, the best of those not reaching the standard will be nominated for the final. If several competitors have equal results, they all take part in the final, so that then more than 12 athletes may participate in it.

Therefore high jumpers and pole vaulters should not omit the last height before the qualifying standard.

The following examples of the high jump and pole vault clearly show the significance of tactical considerations.

Pole vault examples

In Stockholm, 1958, Landström (Finland) began the final at only 4.20 m. With 4.50 m, he became European Champion in front of Preussger (GDR), who vaulted the same height. Up to the height of 4.50 m, Landström only needed a total of 7 vaults, whereas Preussger needed 11.

Suutinen (Finland) was obviously too self-confident. He jumped 4.0 m in his first trial, missing out at 4.10 and 4.20 m. At 4.30 m he had three failures and had finally to be content with the 19th place! In Rome (1960) Preussger and Laufer, having cleared 4.20 m passed, in the qualifying round, 4.30 m and then failed at 4.40 m!

The qualifying standard of 4.40 metres was reached by ten competitors. Subsequently four vaulters were admitted to the final who had jumped 4.30 m at the first attempt. Among them was the later silver medal winner Morris (USA).

24 Cf. "Wettkampfbestimmungen des Deutschen Verbandes für Leichtathletik der DDR", published in 1977, and Amendments according to "Athletic Rules for Men's and Women's International Competitions", London 1982.

Preussger and Laufer overestimated their strength and neglected the time factor. Between the 4.20-m jumps and those of 4.40 m 3½ hours had elapsed!

2.9.2.   Tactics

Obviously the most astute tactical insights cannot lead to success if the basic physical qualities are insufficiently developed.

But one should not, on the other hand, underestimate tactical training. The absorption of "tactical thinking" and application of corresponding decisions must be part and parcel of the training process. Frequency and volume of exercise must be adapted to the level of fitness and competitive experience of the athlete as well as to the forthcoming competitions.

Firstly physical shortcomings must receive attention. This requires an exact assessment of one's own capacity. A runner will, for instance, focus his attention on the development of special endurance etc. The jumper will work on the improvement of his jumping power and agility, the throwers and putters will try to improve their throwing or putting power. All athletes should train frequently under near competition conditions.

Exercise pattern for runners

Handicaps with fixed tasks, e.g. to pull up and overtake the partner–races with constantly changing leads–test races of 300, 500, 600, 1,200 m for middle- and long-distance runners, keeping strict intermediate times for the development of pace-judgement; in group training: fast races with sudden intermediate spurts–

fast first stride from standing start (start in groups)–"trying to get clear" (a runner is boxed in on the inner lane)–competitive races over 200 to 400 m without lanes–training competitions with heats and finals (with time intervals of 40 minutes to 6 hours, depending on the distance).

Exercise pattern for jumpers

Run-ups and take-offs from a take-off board at maximum speed against the wind and with following wind in long and triple jumps–hitting the take-off board exactly in training competitions at the first trial and achieving a specified distance–training competitions of long duration (1 to 3 hours) at all hours of the day in high jump and pole vault–clear several times heights corresponding to best performance or just below it–in high-jump training competitions: begin only at a height which is some 20 centimetres below the best performance (pole vault: 40 to 50 cm below best performance)–training competitions at all hours of the day and with very long interruptions between trials (4 to 6 hours) and breaks between the various jumps (1 to 3 hours). Insert longer breaks when jumping lower heights.

Exercise pattern for throwers and putters

Throwing and putting from throwing circles with different surfaces–reach certain qualifying standards in training competitions–longer breaks between the different trials–use different exercises for "keeping warm" between the trials in training competitions (jogging, easy acceleration runs, exercises with weights, throws with the competitive implement, etc.)–maximum concentration during each trial in spite of many diversions (e.g. noises, spectators)— warm-up of varying duration and intensity—measurement of the throwing and putting readiness (after how many trials were the best results achieved?).

2.10.   System of Exercises in Training Track and Field Athletes

In track and field, as in all other sports events, the coach has a great number of exercises at his disposal. He can therefore vary his programme and make training interesting.

Yet it is not always easy to choose, out of the multitude of exercises, those corresponding best to given training standards and aims which promise the best results.

Organizing the exercises into suitable groups gives a better overall view and facilitates convenient selection (compare the statements made on technical training in track and field events).

Each group of exercises will be used for tackling specific objectives in the general and special training of an athlete, without restricting their effect to this alone. The above sequence is followed as a general guide, but in the long process of training the exercises often run parallel to and complement each other. This is particularly true of the special training. Individually these groups have the following characteristics:

General Preparatory Exercises are the simplest physical exercises, hardly requiring any marked coordination (used chiefly in circuit training as an auxiliary task and in stationary training). They help to build up motor qualities and are musts for whole groups of events (throwing, jumping etc.).

Special Preparatory Exercises are also simple physical exercises, but the similarity with different phases of the technique to be learnt is evident. They are essentially simple basic forms of the main phase of the sequence of movements and are demanding with regard to their technical aspects when directed towards a special event (high jump, shot put etc.). They are meant to develop certain types of movements as well as basic athletic ability.

Basic Exercises form a logical set of ex-

Basic Training Exercises	*Development of*
1. General preparatory exercises	Qualities
2. Special preparatory exercises	Qualities and skills
3. Basic and auxiliary exercises	Skills
Special Training Exercises	
4. Complementary exercises	Skills
5. General conditioning	Qualities
6. Special conditioning or special exercises	Qualities and skills

ercises, selected and put into a proper sequence. They are arranged according to the principle: "from easy to difficult forms". These are either simplified forms or correspond to certain elements of the sequence of movement to be learnt.

The sequence of exercises is designed to teach the rough form. It should be kept short, but the degree of difficulty increasing from exercise to exercise should not get beyond the intellectual grasp of the learner.

Auxiliary Exercises are in principle very simplified variations of the basic exercises (assistance by partners, slow execution of movements, etc.). They are related to particular basic exercises and applied only when some learners cannot master the new challenge.

Complementary Exercises are generally the difficult core of a series of movements. By introducing obstacles, changing the normal routine conditions, or by exercising some phases in sets, particular elements of the technique are made especially difficult and exercised with special emphasis.

General Conditioning Exercises are practiced under higher loads (great number of repetitions or additional weight etc.). They help to build up motor qualities, mainly strength and endurance, and are intended to round up the varied training of the athlete and bring it to a higher level. They include general force and endurance exercises, etc.

Special Conditioning Exercises or Special Exercises are usually complicated exercises which correspond, or are very similar, to various important phases of the complete movement of certain events. They are always worked at with high loads, sometimes with weights (sandbag, heavy implements, etc.), as a rule in groups and based on the interval method. They serve primarily for the development of special qualities but are, owing to their pattern, conducive to the improvement of motor skills. These are special strength exercises, special endurance exercises and so on.

The last two groups of exercises appear in the chapter on training of track and field events under the heading: "Means of Developing Physical Properties."

2.11.   Systematization of the Training Process

Great proficiency in any track and field event requires training over many years. The athletic age of top performers is therefore relatively high. In the track and field competitions of the 1972 Olympics, the average age of the six best men was between 23 (200 m) and 33 (20-km walk), that of women between 21 (100 m) and 28 (discus).

Today training extending over 6 to 10 years is required to reach the top in sport. The training must therefore be planned for a long period of time, and broken up into different segments. In track and field a subdivision into *foundation, build-up,* and *top performance training* has been shown to be effective.

2.11.1. Foundation Training

Foundation training covers the initial training process in track and field.

It can take the form of:

1. goal-directed and event-oriented training in centres where young talent is prepared for quality performance;
2. track and field training for children and youth groups of sports communities of the GDR Gymnastics and Sports Federation (DTSB); or
3. an organized track and field training outside educational institutions.

The foundation training of young talents is mostly completed during childhood. But athletes who first turn to track and field during adolescence must begin with foundation training. Consequently athletes who have completed foundation training range from children between 9 and 10 to youngsters between 15 and 16 years. Individual training programmes must be established which are determined by the age and training level of the particular athlete.

The length of the foundation training depends on the age of the athlete, his general training background, and on the volume and intensity of workouts. It usually lasts 3 to 4 years.

The structure and specificity, that is, the quantity of work and the ways and means applied in the different age groups, also depend on the age and training level of the athletes.

All foundation exercises have obvious common features, as follows:

– Top athletic performances are not the only purpose of track and field activities; others are the build-up of a broad base of general physical fitness and sporting achievements, the promotion and maintenance of health and pleasure from life, and the awakening of a lasting interest in sport.

– To reach this goal a great number of the most varied exercises and specific methods of track and field practice are applied.

– The level of success achieved is measured mainly by results in competition.

– Another criterion of proficiency is achieving the conditions for the GDR Sports Badge.

– The level and structure of training are built on the curriculum of the compulsory sports lessons of the ten year general polytechnical schools (6 to 16 years old), twelve-year extended college preparatory schools and vocational institutions (6 to 18 years old).

– Training is basically organized on the same principles; it has, for example, a group character and is based on voluntary participation, independent of the standards. These common features mainly determine the principles used in setting goals for the foundation training in the various age groups.

2.11.1.1. The Aim

Athletics activities for children follow the objectives set by society for the education and instruction of the young generation. Next to their main task—developing children and youngsters into athletes—they have the task of moulding the general personality in a socialist society.

Training is therefore a comprehensive teaching process, which must be systematically planned and directed within the framework of education and instruction. From this process grow demands for raising the quality of exercises, training and competition.

Foundation training must give the young athletes a solid foundation over a wide spectrum of physical, mechanical, psychological and moral factors, i.e. prepare them for the achievement of good results in athletics through the development of ability, skill and character.

2.11.1.2. Tasks

Given these objectives foundation training must fulfil the following tasks:
- develop condition and good coordination;
- impart to the athlete skills in the main track and field events, sufficient to ensure successful participation in competition;
- impart movement patterns of athletics' training exercises and basic skills of other types of sport;
- develop a general capacity for hard work and the adaptability of the body through properly directed exercise contributing to good health;
- form important personal qualities such as readiness to work for peace and friendship among peoples, team spirit, discipline, honesty, solidarity, courage, determination and willingness to withstand the rigours of athletics training;
- foster the desire to go in for sport regularly through enjoyable exercise and training and through highlights in training and competition which make it a pleasant pastime and awaken interest in the particular event;
- gain experience in competition and the right attitude towards competing (friendship first, competition second);
- teach the fundamentals of exercises and procedures in such a way that the athlete can practise alone;
- find talented children and youngsters for future performance training.

The aims and tasks require that some aspects of the foundation training be emphasized.

Special attention must be given to versatility in training; this requires that the budding athlete possesses a variety of athletic abilities and skills and that the sports leader employs a great number of ways and means. Through greatly varied training in athletics the physical abilities (strength, speed, endurance and mobility) must be developed to high levels. The means are all-round training, including exercises of other types of sport, but chiefly using the routines and rhythmical movements of athletics which correspond to the age and standard of the athlete concerned. It is of particular importance to utilize fully the plentiful store of track and field exercises from all events.

In the build-up of physical qualities speed stands out, as it has been proved, that it can best be developed during childhood and adolescence. The improvement of agility and of coordination in general must also receive special attention.

The best way of achieving this can be found in training skills. Children and youths should learn the rhythmical movements of all track and field events during the age when this is easiest. They can thus gain the right sort of experience and improve their coordination. The series of movements can be learnt in simplified forms or in parts of movements and developed to a degree which permits youngs athletes to participate successfully in competition.

The principle of versatility applies to

the whole of track and field for children and young people. As they get older and their experience of training grows, the wide spectrum of routines should be gradually reduced. The training becomes more and more directed towards particular objectives but the principle of versatility should never be fully abandoned in training children and young people.

Eventually practising other sports loses its importance for track and field training, mainly when the child passes to adolescence. This is the time when emphasis should be switched more and more to track and field events and training be extended to all of them.

Apart from this determining principle of versatility the content of the foundation training, particularly in the transition phase to the build-up training, must have the following features:

– work should acquire more specific traits of athletic training (e.g. systematic planning, continuous and cyclic increase in intensity);

– training should be more directed towards top-class performance in track and field events;

– the volume of training should be considerably increased (from once a week to three or four times a week) and the training intensity as well;

– methods should gradually become more specific;

– the initial concentration on developing skill should be widened by gradually including exercises for training condition;

– the participation in competition should measurably increase and gradually be limited to a small number of events (one-event group).

2.11.2. The Build-Up Training

The build-up training is the second phase of the overall training process.

2.11.2.1. The Aim

The aim of build-up training is to perfect the acquired qualities, abilities and skills and to prepare the athletes for superior performances in top level training, building on the foundation training.

At this point the young athlete will specialize (running, jumping, throwing); the single event to which he will finally turn is fixed later.

During this time the athlete must try to get good results, corresponding approximately to those of performance grade I. It is essential that he reaches such high performances through advanced training and not by specialized training. An athlete who wants to achieve good results in the shot put should not only be able to put the shot 15 metres at the end of this phase, but must also attain the following performances:

100 m	12.0 sec.
long jump	6.00 m
high jump	1.65 m
110-m hurdles	16.5 sec.
400 m	56.0 sec.

Build-up training starts generally at the age of 13 or 14 and takes about 4 to 6 years. It can be regarded as concluded when the athlete is physically and mentally fit for top level training, when he is able to attain the performances asked of him and when he can prove he has reached a sufficient level of allround track and field training.

An athlete should not complete advanced training before he has reached the age of 17, nor later than at the age of 22. There is little point in beginning too late, since it has been amply demonstrated that the best results in any event can be reached only up to a certain age. The age alone should, however, never be the only consideration for changing from advanced to top level training.

An adolescent who takes up track and field training late must complete the advanced training first, as he would, otherwise, build his training on shaky foundations.

2.11.2.2. Tasks

For the sake of clarity we shall deal with the different tasks separately. In practice they form a unit, but depending on the athlete's standard or the periodization, one or the other task may be temporarily emphasized.

– Socialist education

The political and moral education of athletes to become personalities in a socialist society is continued. [25]

At this stage we are dealing with adolescents who are already better acquainted with social relationships.

There are two outstanding points to inculcate: a good spirit in training and strong will-power. A good spirit in training implies regular attendance at all training sessions and active cooperation during them. This will ensure good preparation for competition and adaptation of the whole personality to the requirements of superior performance. In one word training must become a real need and difficulties

25 Cf. "Über Aufgaben, Inhalt und Methoden der sozialistischen Erziehung im Jugendtraining" (On Tasks, Content and Methods of Socialist Education in Training Youths) in "Theorie und Praxis der Körperkultur", Nr. 9/1961.

should provide no reason to give up. It is precisely during the advanced training that the adolescent is faced with numerous difficulties. When the young athlete takes up an apprenticeship or has to go for military service, he will have to change his residence and his coach and may face further problems.

Closely connected with the first task is the task of strengthening the athlete's will-power, to inculcate in him the unbending will to overcome any difficulty in training, to fight to the last against opponents, and to give up a good many creature comforts. Lost ground in the education of will-power during this time can hardly be made good.

It has been explained under what conditions an athlete can start with the top level training (see section 2.11.2.1.). To this we should add that an athlete who does not possess enough will-power at the end of the advanced training, and who does not have a conscientious attitude towards training and is not ready to fulfil still higher training demands should not start top-level training. His time and the time of his coach will be wasted and can be used in better ways. The education for independent action should also be stressed. Young people should not merely be regarded as an object of education, but as thinking and acting people.

The methods of education applied in advanced training are very much at variance with those used in the basic training. In the latter adaptation and demands were in the foreground, and now persuasion takes their place.

Excursions, attendance at important competitions, training camps etc. should also be used for educational purposes.

– Versatile athletic training.

The task of manysided athletic training in advanced training is to develop harmoniously condition and coordination, i.e. strength, speed, endurance, agility and mobility and to differentiate and specialize them for the specific branch of the sport, in order to build up the physical fundamentals for good results and the requirements for top level performances (THIESS).

It is advisable to divide the advanced training into two phases. In the first phase—covering about two years—general and varied athletic instruction stands in the foreground. The achievement of physical fitness and readiness of the body to undertake intensive work is the task here. Allround developing exercises take a major place (work with apparatus including barbell, gymnastics and games).

In the second phase, means for the specific athletic training become more important; these are mainly exercises developing the groups of muscles and organs submitted to special stress in a particular event. These special exercises (which will be described under the various events) facilitate the execution of the movements of an event with accuracy, maximum force, and great speed. The share of special exercises is gradually increased.

Since performances in track and field are determined first by the level in highly varied athletic training, its share in advanced training is fairly high. Initially 30 to 50 % of the total available time should be used for exercises in other branches of sport. This share will be reduced to 20 to 30 % over the course of years. The remaining time is used for track and field exercises. This training has mainly a multi-disciplinary charac-ter, where the time is evenly distributed between racing, jumping and throwing.

But in the second half of advanced training, work in the other athletic events must gradually adopt a more specialized character, i.e. elements from other events which create the requirements for the special event are given preference.

A balanced development of all the physical qualities does not mean that they are all developed to the maximum. Depending on the special event, the age, the individual standards and the period of the training year, this quality or that is stressed more. The build-up of explosive power takes first place. The emphasis now is shifted to exercises with the barbell (especially for future throwers and allrounders, but also for jumpers).

It is quite difficult for the coach always to know which means to apply for the general and highly varied basic training. He has to keep rethinking it and checking his work.

The same means can serve different tasks. Here the method applied is highly important. For example it is possible to use 200-m runs for developing general endurance (method of extensive interval work) and for the development of special endurance (repetition work). [26]

– The technical training

Through technical training the movements must be so accurate that the young athlete is able to attain a standard of final advanced training, on the basis of good versatile athletic standards. In special events the form which will be reliable in competition must be attained.

26 Cf. Chapter 2.7.2.

The athlete now undergoes the third stage of the learning process. In events where top level performance is at a relatively low age, the dynamic stereotype should be striven for (see 2.8.1.). For this purpose the most up-to-date technique is taught in each case. At this age the ability to learn new movements is still good. Therefore necessary changes in the technique should be carried out in advanced training, because even if we assume that modern technique was taught in the basic training, new findings in biomechanics (O'Brien-technique) or new implements (fibre-glass poles), occasionally require a complete modification. The chief method of training technique in advanced training is the use of the exercises. In doing this the coach should keep the following in mind:

To learn and improve movements successfully, conscious learning is indispensable.

The principle of versatility requires learning many movements. Numerous experiences enable the athlete to learn new movements quicker and to correct his faults more easily.

The principle of durability requires that a stereotype is consolidated by repeated practice. Practising under changing conditions is of great importance.

– Tactical training

The tactical preparation in advanced training involves more than just preparing future middle- and long-distance runners for victory in a race. The foundations are laid which enable the athlete to become a strong competitor. In middle- and long-distance races the training is directed toward defeating the opponent by sustaining a fast pace (tempo).

In field events (jumps, throws) the target must be to win in crucial competitions under great stress, under different environmental conditions and with top performances. Necessities are a versatile athletic training level, mastery of the technique, strong will-power, independence, creative activity, and socialist awareness.

It is important that an athlete is faced with many different competitive situations and stands up to the test. Therefore competitions and a thorough subsequent analysis are the most important means of tactical preparation. Important are also training under near competition conditions or a training competition under the most varied—including infavourable—conditions.

2.11.3. High-Performance Training

The high-performance training is the last phase of the whole training process, to which those athletes turn who have successfully coped with advanced training. The others need not give up the training; they can take part in less exacting competition and prepare themselves accordingly.

The aim of this training is to enable the athlete to take part in national and international competitions and to enable him to set records and best performances.

The athlete should be educated to become someone who is loyal to our workers' and farmers' state, lives according to the laws of socialist morals, has strong will-power, and is successful in both sport and work.

The manysided athletic training and technical training develop qualities which are favourable for the highest specialized perfection. The means for special and versatile training play a major role in this. The nature of the top-level training varies greatly between the various events. This is why we shall deal with it more in detail in later chapters.

2.12.　Periodization of Training

A training plan for a year is divided into periods. The various periods serve to prepare and build up systematically the athletic condition and skill as well as attitudes towards competition.

This periodization of the training year is adapted to the most important competitions. These are for the majority of athletes district and county championships; for the leading athletes national championships or international competition. Periodization helps to plan and solve consistently different training tasks, training means and methods in such a way that the athlete is ready and able to produce personal best performances at a date fixed in advance. There are three major periods in a year:

The preparatory period,

the competitive period,

the transition period.

On principle the annual plan of training and competition can be divided as follows:

1. Preparatory period (November to April)

1st phase (November and December)

2nd phase (January and February)

3rd phase (March and April)

2. Competitive period (May to September)

1st phase (Pre-season–May)

2nd phase (Main season–June, July, August)

3rd phase (Late season–September, possibly October)

3. Transition period (October)

In the various periods the training and competition demands increase from year to year, thus tending to improve best performances.

2.12.1.　The Preparatory Period

In the preparatory period the foundation is laid on which performances can be built up. The preparatory period cannot be ignored. Athletes who, because of illness or injuries, are forced to interrupt their training must catch up and should start with competitive activities only later, if they wish to be successful in their athletics careers.

The preparatory period is absolutely necessary for arriving at a new stage of development. It is used for perfecting physical abilities by systematic development of technique. It creates the necessary condition for success in the coming season.

During the training phase general and specific training means dominate. Emphasis is given to the perfection of strength, endurance, speed, mobility and agility through various track and field exercises, conducted in the gymnasium, on the sports ground, through woods and in the countryside. Exercises of other sports events, such as gymnastics, acrobatics, weight lifting, apparatus work, games, skiing, etc. should be integrated into the programme, to make training more varied and interesting. During the preparatory period the athlete is not confined to the gymnasium, but should be allowed to exercise as much as possible outdoors, even when the weather is bad.

During this period organize control competitions and separate fitness tests to discover any weaknesses and to assess the progress made in training.

The preparatory period is usually divided into three or four segments of equal duration.

1st segment

In this phase training should be varied and carefree. General training to improve good allround fitness predominates.

2nd segment

In this segment the training means become more specifically directed; emphasis shifts to the development of special fitness. The total training load starts to increase by increasing the volume and intensity of training. The great physical stress involved in this training calls for special attention to health and rules of conduct.

3rd segment

This is the segment in which the athlete is prepared for competition by a near-to-competition training. His body must be conditioned for maximum stress in the special event. Form is checked and perfected by some conditioning competitions. These competitions are not a goal in themselves but a means of training. The special fitness level should not be allowed to drop too much during the preparation period but be continuously raised. The athlete must make it a point to improve his standard from segment to segment right from the beginning of training.

The best results of the preceding year should already be achieved during indoor competition. This applies above all to athletes who are engaged in build-up training.

2.12.2.   The Competition Period

Consistent form with top results in particular high-level competitions should be achieved during the competition period. This period can also be divided into segments: short early season, main season (covering three months) and late season.

Competitions during the short early season are not specially prepared for; they represent limbering up for subsequent major competition. Training will not be interrupted or reduced prior to these competitions.

Top-level competitions during the main season are specially prepared for. The preparation time is between two to four weeks. During the three weeks' preparation the amounts of work should be gradually increased in the first, become very high in the second and drop off in the third week. Prior to competition there is usually a period of active rest of two to three days. General and versatile training predominate during the first part, special exercises during the second part. Recovery intervals will always be longer during the competitive period and hence the volume of training reduced by comparison with the preparatory period.

2.12.3. The Transition Period

This is a short period (of about 2 to 4 weeks) of active rest after intensive training and competitions. Many athletes require such a phase of recovery and relaxation to recuperate. This is the time when they are being prepared and tuned up for new training and competition tasks. The standard achieved, especially that of physical fitness, should not be allowed to drop drastically during this period. Some regular relaxed exercise should therefore be maintained. More attention can be given to personal wishes in the training arrangements during this time, provided they do not conflict with training objectives.

2.12.4. Special Features of Periodization

Periodization, particularly during the main season, must take into account the highlights of the fixture list. From this result some differences between top-performance and build-up training.

2.12.4.1. Special Features of High-Performance Training

The periods already given are often slightly modified during high-performance training and adjusted for the training of athletes who are getting ready for several major competitions in the course of a year. Although the division into three main periods is basically maintained, the special preparation of major competitions requires in many cases a special approach. Thus training principles of the preparation and the transition phase (active rest) can be applied for a relatively short time during the competition period. This procedure ensures the maintenance and build-up of essential physical abilities during the season as well, while stress and (active) recovery are kept in their proper proportions.

2.12.4.2. Special Features in the Build-Up Training

In the periodization of the build-up training some special features deriving from training goals and from the fact that the yearly training schedules of adolescents (this being the age at which build-up training usually takes place) must be adapted to school curricula. What consequences result from this?

1. The demands placed on the periodization of top-performance training, which are adapted to certain definite dates (championships, Olympic Games) at which superior results must be achieved, do not apply here. The differences between periods in regard to intensity of training, choice of means, tasks etc. are therefore not so marked.

2. To realize the aims of the build-up training, a sufficiently long preparatory period must be allowed for. This guarantees a good allround conditioning. Competitions during the preparation period are themselves a means of training.

3. In order to maintain the athlete's interest in training, he should be allowed to take part in a great number of competitions, not only during the competitive period, but also during the preparatory period (indoor competitions, cross-country races or combined competitions) to check on his allround

standards; these competitions are not specially prepared for.

4. Training throughout the year is indispensable for good results. This must be specially emphasized, because some youngsters interrupt training during school holidays and are sometimes even encouraged by coaches and other officials to do so.

The following periodization of the build-up training, which has, of late, been widely adapted to top-performance training, can be recommended:

1. Preparatory period—end of October to January
1. Transition period—December (two weeks)
1. Competitive period—February
2. Preparatory period—March to April
2. Competitive period—May to beginning of August
2. Transition period—August
3. Preparatory period—August to Sept.
3. Competitive period—September to beginning of October
3. Transition period—October (2 weeks)

2.13. Planning and Evaluation of Training

Planning is the crucial means of balancing and directing all aspects of sports practice, theory and science towards a definite goal in performance training. It serves as a basis for checking proper progress and for analysing possible causes of mistakes. Planning sets the aims which determine the whole range of the athlete's personal, sporting and professional development. A system of planning and evaluation is applied for several years, based on the best current knowledge and scientific methods. What follows is an outline of an up-to-date system of planning and evaluation of training.

2.13.1. Programmes for Several Years

The direction of training and development of athletes over several years towards a particular goal requires plans extending from foundation, through build-up to high-performance training.

In this planning system the structure for building up to a high standard is determined.

Developing the athlete for top performances requires, in general, a period of 6 to 8 years. The structure of a plan for several years must, in the first place, satisfy the demands of the foundation and build-up training. Plans can be established for a group of several athletes (running, jumping, throwing).

In order to achieve top-class results individual training plans must be established, extending usually over 4 years (between two Olympics) and taking due account of the experiences of the best coaches and experts. These plans over several years serve as a basis for future work and every coach is expected to train his charges in such a manner that they attain their best results at their best athletic age, i.e. in top-level competition (European Championships, Olympic Games).

The principal item of the plan for several years is the annual plan. From it is obtained the overall concept for the build-up for top-class performances. The plan is based on the rough periodization of the training and competition year. It contains main indicators for physical conditioning and training intensity during the preparatory and competitive periods; these are mainly indicators of the frequency, volume and ratio of speed-training, of general and special endurance training and of general and special strength training and of the technical and more versatile athletic training. Training loads are listed in a synoptical table. Training emphasis may change from one year to another, but a systematic gradual increase in intensity is a general requirement.

2.13.2. The Individual Year's Plan

The individual outline plan covers the ensuing training and competition year in which the tasks contained in the several years plan are made definite. It takes into account the personal characteristics and standards of each athlete (physical fitness and efficiency level, capacity for hard work, personality traits, will-power, competitive spirit etc.). The following points should be considered in the formulation of the individual plan:

1. Evaluation of the preceding training and competition year.
1.1. Appraisal of determination and personality traits.
1.2. Appreciation of physical fitness and technical accomplishment in the light of results and through appraisal of the intensity of training.
1.3. Assessing the development of the athlete's personality, using as a criterion his progress at work, team spirit, behaviour in public, political and moral attitudes.
1.4. Evaluation of the allround development within the framework of the longer term plan.
2. Planning the main tasks for the coming training and competition year.
2.1. Fixing the main tasks and methods to be given special attention in educational, professional and class-room work.
2.2. Periodization of training following consideration of courses and highlights of the fixture lists.
2.3. Establishment of an individual plan based on the longer term plan and on data of the preceding year's plan.
2.4. Information provided by the sports doctor, data on injuries, planned experiments, research, etc.

Yearly plans

The individual plan is based on the periodization of the training and competition year and split up into several cycles (of about 6 weeks each) in the preparatory and competitive periods, giving due consideration to the most important competitions. Indicators for the different cycles—first for the preparatory then for the competitive period—should be planned and main tasks for the physical and technical training fixed in advance. A more detailed weekly schedule for the ensuing training cycle, fixing average intensity and quantity for each week, depending on the actual training condition and standard reached by the athlete, should then be established. This permits the amount of training to be planned in recurring cycles (cf. section 2.2.6.), i.e. to plan high, medium or average loads for the different weeks (see section 2.2.2.). In the cyclic planning of training due consideration must be given to the capacity of each athlete. This should, by no means, become cut and dried.

The preparation for a major competition often takes between two to four weeks and should be organized carefully for a proper distribution of effort.

2.13.3. The Weekly Schedule

Based on the values of the yearly outline plan, a specific weekly allocation of time can be made. The weekly schedule must be flexible, giving the coach the opportunity to increase or reduce the amount of training according to condition requirements, without losing sight of the basic concept. The cyclic character of training should be kept up also in the weekly training programme, provided training takes place daily or almost every day of the week (see "Load Stages" in section, 2.2.2.).

2.13.4. Evaluation of the Training

Without a thorough recording and evaluation of the training session, modern training directed towards a goal is inconceivable. This evaluation is the source from which the coach draws conclusions about the efficiency of his work in the light of competitions and trials (cf. 2.2.3.); it allows him to plan the right quantity of training and systematically build-up training schedules. Training results should be evaluated by a chart in which the most important training results can be recorded and evaluated. For a systematic workout the average load of training per week should be recorded also when training in groups.

The weekly evaluation of the records of training sessions permits the coach to find out whether the projected values of the outline plan have been adhered to.

2.14.   Content and Structure of the Training Session

The training session is not only the primary form of organization in the process of education and instruction during foundation and build-up training, but also during top-performance training. It may be regarded as the smallest unit in the organization of the training process. All targets set by the training programme are implemented during training sessions.

2.14.1. Principles for Preparing a Training Session

In the preparation of training sessions, as in the planning of all the training, the coach must be guided by the main training principles (cf. chapter 2.3.). If one of these principles is disregarded, the preparation of the training session is incomplete and mistakes may creep in.

Without dwelling on the different

principles, we only wish to emphasize some particular features deriving from these principles for the preparation of the training session. In preparing training sessions for boys, girls and youngsters the coach or group leader should give due consideration to the principle of age dependence. All other training principles are subservient to it. Special attention must be given to the interests of boys, girls and youths and to their development, in order to arouse a lasting interest in regular sports activities and to win acceptance for personal sacrifices to this end. The process of growth, affected by a variety of external and internal factors, must also not be neglected. Special tasks results from this for the structure of the training session for boys, girls and young people; all known educational methods, as well as training methods must be specially adapted to this particular age group.

Manysided and interesting sport activities, satisfying the requirements of general versatile training (cf. 2.3.1.) should be given preference. One particular aspect in the preparation of the training session arises from the principle of the education of athletes for a socialist society. The best methods of education are those in which the personal interests of the young coincide with the general tasks and goals of training. This aspect of a uniform process of education and instruction is often neglected in practice. The coach can obtain precious information for his educational work from a careful analysis of every training session. Various tasks reflected in the preparation of training sessions result from the cycle of periodization (see chapters 2.14.2. and 2.12.). Besides age, physical fitness and technical accomplishment levels, it is periodization

that determines the application of one or the other type of training session. One of these factors in training is the right alternation between tension and relaxation. This factor is often neglected in the preparation of training sessions. Breaks must be planned for the training session like any other component. It goes without saying that the coach must pay heed to the degree of exhaustion of his athletes. If these factors are considered in setting up training schedules, work will be successful and injuries or damage to health largely avoided.

During different periods of the year other training tasks have to be fulfilled. This applies chiefly to the competitive period. Prior to competition the arrangement of training sessions differs from that after competition.

Also of importance for the content and structure of the training session is the training frequency. If training is for four or six days a week, a better differentiation of training tasks is possible than when training is say only twice a week.

Other matters which should not be neglected are the distance of the training site from the place where training material is prepared and distributed. It is of educational value if the athletes take full charge of this task under the proper guidance of the coach.

Summarizing one may say that successful training is only possible if all the factors influencing training are prepared and executed on the basis of the track and field training principles.

2.14.2. The Main Types of Training Sessions

In order to achieve good or outstanding results, excellent condition and coordination must be acquired in a special event.

These two factors are developed and constantly improved during training, being the two facets of a uniform educational process. They are closely correlated and interdependent. One of the two factors may naturally, at times, receive priority during training. But there is no training in which only motor faculties (skills) are trained, just as there can be no training exclusively for developing physical qualities.

Since physical qualities are the basis for the acquisition of technique, greater attention must be given to their development. This is particularly important when training children or adolescents, but also in training adult beginners. It is also important, although on a higher level, for advanced athletes who have reached a level of mechanical skill corresponding to their basic physical abilities. Training technique on a higher level presupposes a higher quality of physical abilities.

The development of mechanical ability must receive greater attention when it no longer corresponds to the development of physical abilities or when the latter are not optimally applicable. A long jumper, for example, who possesses explosive force and great speed, but does not have the necessary ability to combine explosive strength and great speed with a technically correct take-off, must practise this element until he masters it completely.

During foundation and build-up training the acquisition of technique is very tricky. On the one hand the proper age for absorbing new skills should be fully utilized, while on the other technique can be built only on well developed physical abilities. During this stage the training session should be so arranged, that besides the intensive development of basic physical qualities mechanical skills are absorbed, leading youngsters very quickly to the mastery of the rough form of various events. With growing specialization, more emphasis is given to the training of technique. The training of skills, alongside the development of physical abilities, creates the basis for a continuous improvement of performance.

Basically three types of training sessions may be distinguished:

1. The training session in which special attention is given to physical qualities;
2. The training session stressing chiefly mechanical skills (technique);
3. The combined training session.

All three types of training sessions are applied during foundation and build-up training, as well as during top-performance training with adult athletes. The combined training session completes the training of athletes, whereas the first type of training session is the most important in the training of boys, girls, young people and adult beginners.

The training session in which chiefly mechanical skills are developed, is becoming increasingly important in the training of advanced athletes.

The application of one or the other main type of training session therefore depends above all on the standard of the athletes. But independently of this, differences in training sessions may occur during the year, resulting from the main tasks of the various training periods.

Accordingly during the first months of preparation the training session stressing mainly mechanical skills (technique) prevails, while during the last months prior to competitions a considerably greater amount of training is devoted to technical training. The application of one or the other main type of training session therefore depends also on the main tasks of training during the yearly cycle.

2.14.3.   Structure of the Training Session and Contents of its Parts

As a rule the training session is divided into three parts:
1. Preparatory part
2. Main part
3. Concluding part.

The main part may, in regard to its principal content, consist of two parts with special tasks, e.g. in a combined training session.

It is therefore necessary to divide the preparatory part into a general and a special preparatory part.

– The preparatory part of the training session

In practice, but also in theoretical publications, the terms warm-up and limbering up are often used as synonyms for the preparatory part of the training session. These terms do not, or only incompletely, define the essence of the training instructions. Warming up is certainly a necessary part of the introduction and is, in some training sessions, a sufficient preparation; in most training sessions it is, however, only one part of the first section of the training hour. The words "introductory part of the session" define exactly the character of the introduction. It comprises the general preparation of the athlete (warm-up in the form of walking, jogging and other running exercises or of general gymnastic exercises), as well as its special preparation which is leading up directly to the main training section, overlapping with its content and often containing special training elements (e.g. splits of the hurdler).

The special task of the introduction is therefore the preparation of the athlete for the principal tasks to be tackled in the main part. The athlete's body must be prepared systematically for undergoing stress. The preparation is therefore an important part of the training session and should definitely not be omitted. If the athlete is submitted to great stress without due preparation, injuries may easily result.

The preparation must not be left to chance, but submitted to the same principles as the main part and should always be seen in relation to the main objective. If intensive work is planned for the main part of the session, the preparation must be carried out with the same intensity. This is the case when using repetition work. In this case the amount of training must also be systematically increased in the preparation, which often merges into the main part. A fast game (basketball is very popular) can naturally also be used for warming up at the beginning of the training session. The main thing is that the body and especially the muscles involved in the main part are properly exercised. On the other hand it goes by no means against training principles if, before a main section, with a relatively low total amount of work, preliminaries requiring great physical effort are undertaken.

Possibilities for a general preparation are provided by runs of all types. They serve at the same time as special preparation for short-, middle- and long-distance runs, steeplechasing and hurdling.

The coach must bear in mind that the introduction requires about one fourth or one fifth of the training time. All this leads to a considerable amount of time throughout the year. It depends on the coach whether this time is used effectively, say for the improvement of definite qualities (e.g. in the form of a permanent schedule for improving mobility in javelin throwers lacking suppleness in the hip- and shoulder-joints), or whether he allows this section to be filled less formally, by letting the athletes do what they like.

– The main part

During the main part of the training session the chief tasks fixed in the training plan must be fulfilled. Its content is therefore a section of the cyclical plan. The most important training methods are applied in the main part of the training session; this determines its role in the training of physical abilities, technique and tactics. The choice of training means depends on the event, the main tasks of the respective training cycles on the age and standard of the athletes. The more advanced an athlete is, the more specialized will be the tasks of the main section.

Independently of the training frequency and content of training sessions, the principle applies that exercises and parts of exercises requiring the greatest effort and concentration should be carried out at the beginning of the main section. This is the time when the reactions, coordination and concentration of the athlete are greatest, provided he has received adequate preparation during the first part of the session. The duration of the main part varies in the normal training session (some $1\frac{1}{2}$ to 2 hours) between two-thirds and three quarters of the total work. If the training tasks demand high (approaching the maximum) stress on the body, the main section is, as a rule, shorter than when the stress is less intense, since a longer time of preparation and return to the normal functioning of the body in the subsequent part of the session are required. Apart from this, other factors are vital for the duration of the main section, e.g. the capacity of the athlete, his physical and psychological condition, his age etc.

– The concluding part of the training session

Basically the concluding part of the training session has the task of bringing the body back to its normal state after intensive work. This must be provided by an arrangement of this part of the session, which itself results from the character of the main part. This does not mean that fast games should not be played at the end of the training session. If games are chosen, they should represent a different type of work, be enjoyable and permit athletes to relax after considerable stress.

The content of the concluding part therefore varies. Loosening exercises (e.g. after intensive work) easy warming down (e.g. after running at great speed and for a long time) or games are often used.

In the execution of the concluding part, the principles of track and field training apply, as for all other parts of the training session.

3. Walking and Running

3.1. Fundamental Mechanics of Walking and Running

Walking and running are cyclic movements in which two consecutive strides or one double stride make up a complete cycle of movement. In a double stride all the separate phases of the running movement are performed; the new cycle follows without a break. In this cycle both legs have alternately supporting and driving functions.

The main difference between walking and running is that in walking one foot always touches the ground; in running this ground contact is temporarily broken (non-supporting phase). The basically similar patterns of movement permit us to confine ourselves in what follows to running.

3.1.1. The Most Important Phases in a Cycle of Movement

The cyclic running movement has two main phases: the supporting and the non-supporting phase. The vertical moment, i.e. the vertical projection of the point of support in relation to the body's centre of gravity (CG) is regarded here as the demarcation between the phases. This is the instant when the free driving leg passes the foot bearing the weight of the body.

In the running movement the function of one leg is always in marked contrast with the function of the other. Thus during the closing support phase of the front foot the rear swinging phase is being concluded simultaneously. The rear swinging phase is again linked to the forward support phase. During the last part of the rear support phase, the knee reaches its highest point in the anterior swinging phase. Immediately after the push-off this leg begins its rear swinging phase. At this moment the front leg has not yet touched the ground but still continues its forward swing. The runner has no contact with the ground and is now in the non-supporting phase, i.e. in the second main phase of the running motion.

3.1.2. Importance of the Push-Off Force

Forward movement is mainly achieved by the alternating push-off action in the rear support phase. By stretching the push-off leg at the hip-, knee- and ankle joints, a force, greater than that of the body weight, which is directed back- and downward, is exerted against the ground. Due to the resist-

120

ance of the track or ground this force, resulting from the exertion of the muscles, produces an effect in the opposite direction, which we call the supporting reaction. This generates the push-off force, viz. kinetic energy, which acts on the body's centre of gravity. The speed at which the moving leg bends and stretches at the joints is a function of the magnitude of this force.

The quicker the push-off action is performed in combination with the forward swing of the moving leg, the greater will be the push-off force. The gluteal muscles, the triceps of the leading leg, the muscles at the back of the ankle joint and the tendons of the longer toes are mainly involved in this action. The push-off angle (angle between push-off leg and track surface) is around 50 to 55 degrees.

Several factors determine the effect of the push-off on the running speed, one of which is the condition of the track. On a firm, elastic track the effect will be greater than on soft ground. By wearing spikes, the athlete has a stronger hold on the ground in the supporting phase and this enhances the effect of the push-off action. However the action of the driving leg has also a considerable influence on the push-off force. The forward swing must be rapid and powerful, so as to produce a momentum capable of assisting the push-off force. The speed of a sprinter in this swinging phase (approx. 20 m/sec.) is well in excess of the average racing speed. Great assistance to the push-off force can be provided by the arm movement. During the forward swing the arms must be moving in the running direction and not towards the centre of the body. Finally the proper carriage of the upper body must allow an optimum transmission of the push-off force on to the runner's centre of gravity. In track events this is achieved by an almost erect position of the upper body. A marked forward lean would create a better basis for the push-off action, but hinder a fast and efficient movement of the swinging leg.

3.1.3. Economy of Movement in Running

A running action is considered to be economic when the runner's energy is expended solely on overcoming the forces of resistance he encounters.

The greatest expenditure of energy takes place during the push-off phase. Further components of the running movement which require the expenditure of energy are the anterior swinging phase (knee-lift phase) and the anterior support phase. Energy is further required for overcoming the air resistance, which increases with the running speed, and for coordinating the various parts of the body.

Fluctuations of the body's centre of gravity adversely affect the straightness of the run. During the extension of the push-off leg the runner's CG at first moves more forward and upward. Through the effect of gravity the direction of movement will change during the non-supporting phase into a more forward and downward direction. In the anterior support phase the movement is again horizontal.

Running should involve a rapid change of muscular contraction and relaxation. A fit and technically competent runner avoids unnecessary muscular tension and applies his energy more effectively.

Table 12   Scheme of Phase Structure of a Double Stride

Phase	Beginning	End	Function	Points to note
Leading foot support phase	Landing of foot	Vertical moment = mid-support `	Supporting function, absorbing impact of body weight on landing	Active, striking, "pawing-like" elastic contact on the outer edge of the ball of the foot, body weight is elastically absorbed at the knee- and ankle-joints; no contact of the heel with the ground
Rear foot support phase	Vertical moment	Toes coming off support area	Supporting function; development of optimal push-off force	Optimal extension at ankle-knee- and hip-joints (50–55°); upper body almost erect (85–80°)
Rear Swinging phase	Toes coming off support area	Vertical moment; thigh of strongly bent leg points vertically downwards; it is level with the thigh of the supporting leg	Swinging function, relaxation	1. Easy but fast back- and upward swinging of leading leg to buttocks 2. Beginning of loose but active forward swing of thigh, when leading leg is just about parallel to the ground
Forward swinging phase	Vertical moment	Landing of foot on forward support area	Swinging function: 1. forward swing for knee-lift 2. Lowering of thigh and bringing leading leg down and backward in preparation for landing	1. The strongly flexed leg drives forward and upward near to the horizontal 2. Forward swing of leading leg, beginning to lower the thigh 1. Cocked foot at the end of forward swing of leading leg 2. Backward swing of leading leg, active, "pawing-like" landing of foot on vertical projection of line between knee- and ankle-joint

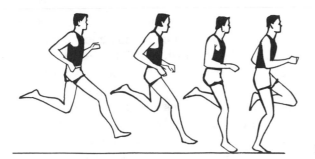

Fig. 10

The ability to relax is therefore of vital importance in an economic running movement.

3.1.4. Relationships between Speed and Stride Pattern in the 100 m

Speed is a function of stride length and stride frequency (number of strides in a given unit of time). The athlete who wishes to gain speed will either take longer strides, increase the frequency of his strides or use a combination of the two. This, of course, is of much greater importance for sprinters than for middle- and long-distance runners.

Investigations have substantiated differences in the stride pattern (the length and frequency of strides in relation to the running speed) of 100-m runners of varying performance levels (grade I and II). [27]

27 H. Gundlach "Untersuchungen über den Zusammenhang zwischen Schrittgestaltung und Laufgeschwindigkeit bei 100-m-Läufern und Läuferinnen unterschiedlicher Qualifikation" (Investigations on the Relation between the Stride Pattern and Running Speed in 100-m Sprinters of varying Qualifications), in "Theorie und Praxis der Körperkultur", Nr. 3/1963 and 4/1963.

Depending on their performance, the runners were classified into six groups (see also Figs. 11, 12 and 13):
Group A—the fastest men
Group B—all the men
Group C—the slowest men
Group D—the fastest women
Group E—all the women
Group F—the slowest women

The curve of stride length in this study illustrates three definite phase: a phase of high acceleration, a relatively constant phase and a phase of renewed acceleration. The duration of the first phase (starting section) is clearly dependent on the runner's standard. Top sprinters can increase their stride length up to the 45-m mark, whereas untrained or poorly trained athletes will come to the constant phase—phase of almost even stride length—as early as 25 m. In all sprinters this phase ends after 92 or 93 m. The greater stride length during the third stage (the last 3 or 4 strides) is dependent on the stride frequency and reflects the runner's endeavour to counteract the loss of speed (Fig. 11).

The curve representing the stride frequency also shows three typical phases: the phase of maximum acceleration, the phase of gradual deceleration and the phase of increasing loss of speed

(Fig. 12). The graph shows that in comparison with the stride length, a much slighter increase (only about 6 to 10 per cent from the 2.5-m mark up to the maximum) is achieved. The widely prevailing idea that in the 100 m the sprinter reaches the highest stride frequency during the first strides is definitely wrong. One should bear in mind that there is also a difference between beginners and top performers in so far as beginners attain maximum speed after as little as 10 to 15 m, whereas top performers reach it only after some 25. During the second stage the curve for all runners is similar and in some cases even parallel. The reduction in frequency with respect to the maximum lies between 4 and 10 per cent. In this respect top performers showed the least decrease in frequency. The greater decrease in frequency during the third

stage invariably appears between 90 and 95 m. This phenomenon is related to the lengthening of strides over the final stretch, to which we have already referred (see also Fig. 11).

The variations in speed in the 100-m race can also be subdivided into three stages: the first acceleration, the second maximum speed and the third reduction in speed. In 100-m sprints speed is actually increased to the maximum, followed by a slight slow-down. This drop in speed is particularly slight in experienced sprinters who achieve almost top speed long before the actual maximum is reached. It would therefore appear sensible to define speed on a section yet to be determined as the phase of maximum speed. The most striking difference between speed curves of experienced and less experienced runners is that acceleration in the starting section

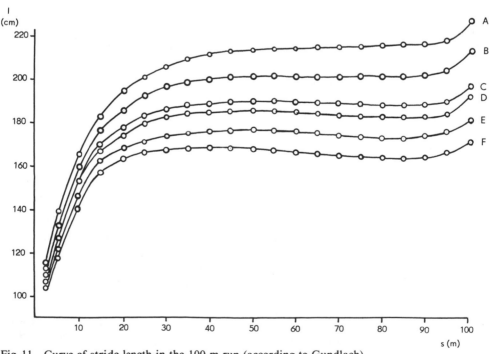

Fig. 11   Curve of stride length in the 100-m run (according to Gundlach)

is much more marked in top performers. Furthermore they are in a position to continue to accelerate when beginners have already reached the phase of their maximum possible speed. The switch to this stage will, depending on the ability of the individual, be somewhere between 22 and 35 m. The distance to the stage of maximum speed also varies greatly. While this amounts to only some 20 m for beginners, top 100-m sprinters reach it at 45 m and more. We also find a similar graduation with regard to the maximum speed. Beginners reach this peak already after 30 m, whereas the best male sprinters reach it somewhere around 55 m. This is in agreement with the widely expressed opinion that the speed of a top sprinter is achieved only up to about 70 m and that then—over the last 30 metres—speed endurance be-

comes decisive for the overall performance. Therefore the length of the phase of deceleration depends on the experience and ability of the sprinter. The speed decrease is of the order of 3.5 to 9.5 per cent. This means that in the final phase the speed decrease in top sprinters amounts to only 0.1 sec. and in beginners to 0.5 sec. (Fig. 13).

If we then look at the relationships between stride length, stride frequency and running speed, we will find that experienced runners achieve a higher speed by the increase of both length and frequency of strides. There are only gradual differences from one runner to another with regard to qualitative changes in the length and frequency of strides. Too much emphasis on the increase of stride length and frequency in training would be a mistake. Emphasis should be more on the devel-

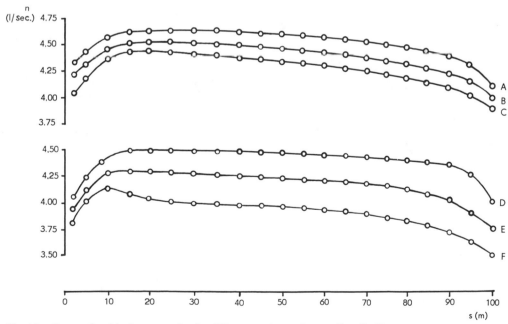

Fig. 12   Curve of stride frequency in the 100-m run (according to Gundlach)

opment of explosive strength of the muscles allowing the athlete to take longer strides in a shorter time.

The slow-down in the second half of the distance may be considered as an upset balance in the stride rhythm (length and frequency of strides), the reason for which is clearly a decrease in stride frequency. It may surprise the reader that the decrease in stride frequency is nearly independent of the standard of the runner. Experienced runners are better equipped to level out this factor which tends to lower performance by picking up somewhat on the stride length during the second half to the stretch. The question arises as to whether a decrease in the stride frequency in top performers must be regarded as unavoidable or whether there are training means by which a consistent stride rate right through to the finishing line can be achieved.

As previously mentioned the question of the relationship between stride pattern and running speed is less important in middle-and long-distance races. Over these distances the stride length and rate should be balanced with the running speed. This implies that the strides become shorter and their rate lower the longer the distance to be covered and the slower the speed chosen. With regard to stride length we may therefore find that differences up to 0.60 m e.g. from 2.30 m to 1.70 m have been found between short-and long-distance runners.

3.1.5. Classification of Running Distances

Running events laid down in rules of competition are mainly differentiated by the length of the racing distances.

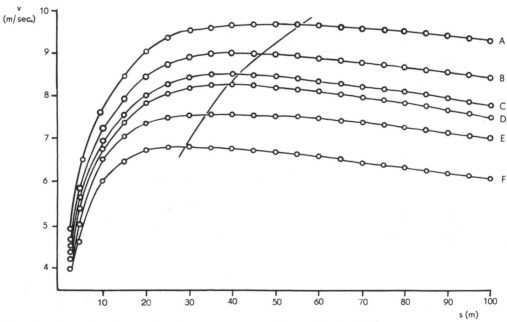

Fig. 13 Curve of stride speed in the 100-m run (according to Gundlach)

126

Running competitions for men and women are held over distances from 100 m to 42,195 m (Marathon).

We know by experience that the various distances cannot be covered at any speed. In order to achieve a good competition result, viz. to cover the distance in the shortest possible time, the middle- and long-distance runner should strive to maintain the initially adopted speed (optimum speed) up to the finishing line. In 100-m and 200-m sprints the maximum possible speed should be reached rapidly and held throughout. In competition the running speed depends on the duration of physical effort. The intensity of effort therefore varies over the different distances, so that running events are classified as follows:

Short-distance races
100 m, 200 m, 400 m 110-m hurdles (men), 400-m hurdles, and 100-m hurdles (women)

Middle-distance races
800 m, 1,500 m

Long-distance races (men)
3,000 m, 3,000-m steeplechase, 5,000 m, 10,000 m, Marathon, walking (all distances).

The results in all running events are mainly influenced by the level of development of the runner's qualities of speed and endurance.

Running velocity is the highest possible speed a runner can attain; endurance is his power to resist fatigue. Maximum speed can, experience shows, be maintained only over short distances—some 40—50 metres beyond the distance required for acceleration. So even in a 100-m race the result will depend on the runner's power of endurance. The less a sprinter's maximum speed is reduced over the distance, the better his endurance. The endurance in a short-distance race we will call speed endurance and is particularly important in 200-m races. A sprinter who takes say 5.0 sec. over a distance of 50 m with a flying start could cover 100 m in about 10.8 sec. (5.0 sec. + 5.0 sec. = 10 sec. + 0.8 sec. time lag at the start = 10.8 sec.!) The time lag at the start is the difference in time between a run with a flying start and one with a crouch start. Theoretically a time of 20.8 sec. (4×5.0 sec. + [0,8 to 1.0 sec]) should be possible. In practice double the time taken in the 100-m race (21.6 sec.) can be considered as a good 200-m performance. From this it may be concluded that the optimum competitive speed in middle- and long-distance races cannot be identical with the runner's maximum possible speed. If, for example, an 800-m man started his race at the highest possible speed, an inevitable and crucial slow-down would already set in after some 200 m. The result would either be a poor performance or the athlete would prematurely exhaust his strength and have to give up before reaching the tape. It is therefore of great importance that middle- and long-distance runners manage the race distance at an optimum speed, i.e. realize their full potential in both speed and endurance for a successful performance.

The longer the race distances, the more endurance assumes priority over speed. Even for a 1500-m specialist not the sprinter's speed but the specific endurance he has acquired by training is of paramount importance. His speed must only be developed to the extent needed to achieve good results over the next shortest distances, i.e. 400 or 800 m in relation to his capacity over his particular distance. This counts inasmuch as high quality performance over the next shorter distances will also effect the results in his special event.

3.2. Walking

Rules have been laid down for differentiating walking from running, which must be adhered to by walkers. Walking is defined like this in competition regulations: Strides must be taken in such a way that one foot is in contact with the ground all the time. The foot must meet the ground with the heel first. The supporting leg must be straightened at some time during the stride.

It is the task of walking judges to check the proper sequence of movements and to issue warnings or disqualify a race walker who breaks the rules.

A technically accomplished walker need not pay attention to these rules but can and must fully concentrate on performance.

Race Distances

Walking distances in the Olympic Games and in European Championships are over 20 and 50 km, but for the Montreal games; in 1976 the 50-km distance was eliminated from the Olympic programme.

Championships in walking

Age group (years)	Distance
11, 12, 13	3,000 m
14, 15	3,000 m, 5,000 m
16, 17	10 km, 20 km
Men	20 km, 50 km

3.2.1. Technique

The technique of walking must be perfectly mastered if good results are to be achieved. Importance must therefore be attached to the training of technical skills, as shortcomings in this respect can impair further improvement at a later stage in an otherwise fit walker.

If pace work is started too soon, mis-

takes will creep in, which are difficult to discard and may even become irreparable.

3.2.1.1. Leg Movements

A long and economic stride is achieved by an accentuated pushing off with the trailing leg. Attention must be paid to the correct push-off right from the beginning. The forward thrust necessary for a long stride is achieved by a complete ball-to-toe roll of the foot. Just before the foot is lifted off the ground the front leg should touch the ground with the heel. The so-called double-support phase is an outstanding feature of correct walking.

The foot plant must be soft and should occur before the leg is completely stretched. A braking effect which would hamper the forward thrust can thus be avoided.

After the landing of the front foot, the rear leg is swiftly and slackly brought forward without describing an arc by outward turning of the foot or the knee joint. In order to obtain a "flat" low stride, an exaggerated lifting of the thigh must be avoided. Also an excessively high or wide forward swing of the foot can induce "jumping". On the whole the measured, flat leg action is characteristic of a good walker.

The following principle should be observed: Increase the stride length in line with the increase of the pace and not vice versa!

3.2.1.2. Trunk Carriage

The upper body is erect or has a slight forward lean. Too much body lean leads to running.

A backward lean of the trunk is wrong and indicates poorly developed abdominal and dorsal muscles. There is the danger of breaking the necessary contact with the ground.

3.2.1.3. Arm Action

By their rhythmical movements the arms assist the stride rhythm. The faster the pace, the more the arms are bent. This of course varies from individual to individual. The arm movements should aid the body thrust forward which is introduced by the push-off from the ground. This must involve the shoulders which have to counteract the movement of the pelvis and have thereby a beneficial effect on the stride length (Fig. 14).

A natural swinging of the arms almost to the mid-line of the body is the best

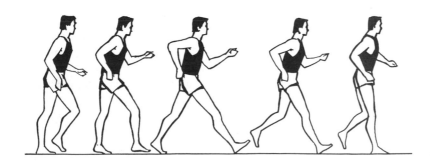

Fig. 14

129

form. A hunching of the shoulders must be avoided, since this leads to an unfavourable shift of the body's CG and tends to pull the walker off the ground.

A beginner with a short, unsteady stride who tends to "jump" should be advised to keep his arms lower and less bent, since he can thus counteract the technical errors we have just mentioned.

3.2.1.4. Hip Action

Good flexibility in the hip joints is decisive for a smooth and steady pace. A walker should attempt to put one foot before the other in an almost straight line. To accomplish this the athlete must learn to walk with a rotary movement of the hip joints. At every stride, when the rear leg swings forward, the hip must make a dodging movement to the other side. Apart from the body twist occurring in running, there is a horizontal shift in the hip an shoulder axes in walking (Fig. 15). This combined movement is a characteristic of

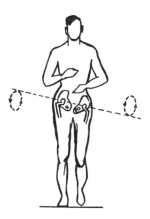

Fig. 15

the style of a race walker. It is a purely economic movement and does not appear unnatural or tense in a good walker. An exaggerated lateral shift of the pelvis must be avoided. It is not only unaesthetic, but hinders the forward movement.

3.2.2. Technical Training

Although race walking differs greatly from walking in everyday life, both have the same basic characteristics. The special technique in race walking is the result of an increased pace rate and has been fixed later by competition rules.

Most of the characteristics of walking, such as arm and hip actions, are caused by the fast speed. It is by no means the case that the "walking rules" were there first and merely had to be observed. They developed from kinetic and style considerations. Beginners should keep this in mind! When beginning to learn the technique, they should not try to simply reproduce the movements they have observed, but should just attempt to walk quickly. This inevitably leads to a sequence of movements which is close to the walking technique. Experience shows that it helps if a coach or another good walker walks alongside. A beginner can be more easily monitored and corrected while in motion than during training breaks. It is advisable to start learning race walking in early years. Children and adolescents learn it much easier and more quickly than sportsmen in a later age.

From the beginning emphasis should be on a slack swift movement and according to the principle: technique before speed!

3.2.2.1. Special Preparatory Exercises

These comprise all those exercises strengthening the back-, leg- and abdominal muscles. Exercises lumbering up the hip and shoulder muscles and strengthening the ankle joints should also be included in work-outs. Walking itself is, of course, the best and most specific means of preparation. A race walker can also derive benefit from running, but he should thereby follow certain principles. This applies mainly to beginners.

If a former runner wishes to take up walking, he should avoid running during his training until he has a good command of the newly acquired walking movements and performs them automatically.

In all preparatory exercises and in walking emphasis should be on exercises which not only strengthen the limbs but also improve slackness and extensibility of the leg muscles.

We now give a selection of exercises:

1. Walking at increased pace.

2. Walking on a straight line painted on the track surface in order to learn how to keep the feet straight and parallel.

3. Easy shift of body weight in normal position from one foot to the other on the spot getting the feeling for leg extension and hip gyration.

4. Same exercise but with powerful strides and corresponding arm movements.

5. All kinds of games for improving suppleness and slackness, gymnastic exercises for increasing the extensibility of leg muscles.

3.2.2.2. Basic Exercises of Technical Training

The following set of exercise is recommended for developing walking technique:

— Exercise 1: Marching
Aim: Learn the fundamental elements of walking.
Points to note: Easy pacing with erect upper body.

— Exercise 2: Marching at gradually increasing pace.
Aim: Higher speed requires a more vigorous arm action and a corresponding push-off with the trailing foot.
Points to note: The arms should be flexed 90 degress at the elbows; longer strides; more accentuated roll of foot.

— Exercise 3: Walking at medium and fast rate.
Aim: All characteristics of walking should be applied and smoothly coordinated.
Points to note: Unbroken contact with the ground and economic sequence of movements.

— Exercise 4: Walking with change of pace.
Aim: Consolidation and perfection of technical skills.
Points to note: Keep unbroken contact with the ground; when speeding up avoid shortening of strides. Slack walking.

Faults or shortcomings in the sequence of movements or in posture may be due to physical factors or the training mistakes. If the walker makes mistakes which break the rules or hinder an economical sequence of movement, they must be eradicated. If points of style of a walker are involved, they deserve little attention, as much time may well be required to overcome them and, in any case, success may be doubtful.

3.2.2.3. Fault—Reason—Correction

— Fault: Breaking contact with the ground.
Reason: The chosen pace is not consistent with the athlete's skills. He does not yet master the correct sequence of movements.
Correction: Reduce pace rate and improve style.
— Fault: Too much backward lean (hollow back).
Reason: Fatigue, underdeveloped dorsal and abdominal muscles.
Correction: Devise special exercises for strengthening the groups of muscles involved.
— Fault: Body lift. The runner's body describes a wavy line: the result is a tendency to jump.
Reason: Stretching of rear leg before the heel-ball-toe roll of the foot is completed. Thus thrust is directed upward rather than forward.
Correction: Pay attention to a proper heelball-toe rolling. Keep leg in the rear position as long as possible, carry arms lower. Strengthen ankle joints by special gymnastic exercises.
— Fault: Legs too wide or walking with feet turned outwards.
Reason: Natural tendency of individual or wrong arm movements.
Correction: Walk on a straight line and watch parallel arm action.
— Fault: Persistent knee bend of supporting leg.
Reason: The chosen pace is beyond the walker's abilities, poorly developed leg muscles—hence fatigue.
Correction: Pay attention to a fully stretched leg at the knee joint, if necessary reduce pace; general strengthening of leg muscles.
— Fault: Hard landing of leading leg, leading to heel trouble.
Reason: Incorrect hell-ball-toe action of rear foot. The front leg is stretched too soon before touching the ground. As a consequence the walker jogs into the stride instead of gliding into it.
Correction: Pay attention to "soft" walking. Land high on the outer edge of the foot, keep leg in the rear position as long as possible and complete foot roll.
— Fault: Very short strides.
Reason: Lack of special strength. Wrong arm action; fatigue.
Correction: Gradually lengthen strides, try to make wide strides and, if necessary, improve arm action.

3.2.3. Physical Requirements and Training Methods for Improving Performance

3.2.3.1. The Importance of Physical Condition in Walking

For successful performance in walking, tall athletes have an advantage over shorter men because of their longer stride. The typical efficient walker is generally a tall, lean, wiry athlete with endurance.

● Endurance

The chief attribute of a successful walker is endurance. It can only be acquired through an extensive training programme in which efficiency is strongly emphasized and influenced by the mental qualities and will-power of the athlete. The latter attributes are, alas, much more difficult to acquire and are often the limiting factor in the athlete's response to training and expectations of his performance.

- Strength

In walking the role of strength consists mainly in increasing endurance potential. This means that training should not be designed primarily to stimulate the building of muscular bulk but to improve the economy of muscular work, permitting the muscles to perform during a long period of time with the smallest possible effort. Nevertheless a walker should have well developed dorsal, abdominal and leg muscles for covering distances (up to 50 km) according to the rules and at a relatively quick pace, or else it might happen that with growing distance he slackens off more and more, so that he can hardly keep his arms up and fails to achieve the necessary forward thrust.

- Speed

The term speed is a relative one and should, particularly over such long distances, be considered with some caution. One may say that, strictly speaking, every walker is fast enough and that it is merely a question of endurance and fitness how long he can keep up his pace.

Special speed training is today used less and less. Athletes, especially beginners who particularly like to practice it, should be restrained.

Naturally a walker will not be able to cover the 20 km distance in less than 1 : 34 unless he is capable of walking the 5000-m distance in some 23 minutes. This is, however, a question of fitness and not the result of speed training.

3.2.3.2. Means for Developing Physical Properties

- Endurance

This can only be achieved by a lot of training in a programme which is properly adjusted to the athlete's age and training background. Although special (competition directed) endurance, basic endurance and general endurance are closely related to each other, we shall, especially for the benefit of beginners, first indicate the means of developing basic and general endurance:

1. Long marches at a good pace (youths up to 20 km, raised to 35 km for 20-km walkers and up to 60 km for 50-km walkers).
2. Walking over the same distances. The beginner should not be overconcerned with achieving a fast pace, but with acquiring correct technical posture and a smooth walking style (vary the walking distances).
3. Walking and marching alternately, depending on the terrain and on the runner's condition.
4. Running on paths through forests over some 15 to 20 km (especially in springtime).
5. Skiing.
6. Participating in cross-country competitions.
7. Continuous swimming.
8. Circuit training, using the duration method.

All the training methods should be applied at low or medium intensity. The main aim is to obtain proper circulation and metabolic rate, to increase the oxygen intake capacity, to build up the proper mental attitude towards walking long distances over a long period of time.

Basic endurance should be trained for

throughout the year; during the competition season its part in the total volume of training is reduced to switch to competition directed endurance training.

Special endurance can be developed by training schedules in which the pace corresponds to that of competition or is slightly faster. The distances in training are usually shorter than in competitions. The interval or repetition methods, as well as the duration method including fartlek, are utilized. As a rule training on these lines is started in March or April.

– Examples of interval training:

1. Frequent walks over stretches at racing pace (or slightly above it) in quantity with short recovery intervals, e.g. 20×1000 m with 60 to 90 sec. recovery.

2. Walks of 4×5000 m or $2 \times 10,000$ m with longer recovery intervals.

The above examples are for adults; reduce the volume for adolescents de-

pending on their race distance and fitness.

– Examples of the duration method:

1. Walks over $^1/_2$ to $^3/_4$ of the race distance at near competition pace.

2. Walks of a fartlek pattern with pace accelerations close to competition speed.

Distance for adolescents about 10 to 15 km, for adults 15 to 30 km.

3. Competitions over shorter distances.

● Speed

Special speed training is rarely used today. Distances to be covered at a considerably higher pace are included in the training for competition-directed endurance (e.g. 10 to 15×400 m).

● Strength

A sportsman with a good athletic background is at an advantage also in race walking. Junior walkers should particularly bear this in mind when plan-

Table 13   Weekly Schedule of Training during the Preparatory Period (about February) (Build-up Training)

Day	Training Objectives	Training	Total km
Monday	Basic endurance	20-km walk	20 km
Tuesday	Supplementary training	Game 10-km walk	10 km
Wednesday	Basic endurance	30-km walk possibly with accelerations	30 km
Thursday	General and specific strength	30–50 min. exercises with medicine ball, ankle workout, 10-km run	10 km
Friday	Supplementary training	Game	
Saturday	Basic endurance	35-km walk	35 km
Sunday	Supplementary training	Game, gymnastics, possibly easy walking	10 km
			115 km

ning their training build-up. We distinguish between general and special strength exercises, the former being of greater importance, especially for beginners.

General strength exercises

These are exercises which are particularly suitable for every young sportsman. Important examples have been stressed in the section 3.2.2.1. It should be noted that workouts with excessively heavy weights should not be the main concern; preference should be given to exercises which do not only strengthen the muscles but also increase their extensibility and flexibility at the joints.

An implement that can be used in many ways and satisfies almost all demands is the medicine ball.

Exercises

1. With barbell on the neck (low weight, large number of repetitions). Trunk bending forward—trunk turning left and right sideways.

2. Exercises with medicine ball: e.g. throwing with both arms forward and backward; holding the ball between the feet in a sitting position; leg circling.
Game: Throwing the medicine ball over a string. The ball must not be dropped.

3. Following other track and field exercises.

Special strength exercises

Exercises which are directly related to the walking movements or serve to strengthen specific groups of muscles.
The best strengthening exercise is, of course, walking itself. Great benefit can be drawn from walking in hilly country against a strong headwind or on slightly upward sloping streets. Particularly the latter requires a strong push-off with the rear foot, which again contributes to the strengthening of the ankle joints. Wearing heavy clothes in winter time will serve the same purpose.
There are also specific jumping exer-

Table 14   *Weekly Schedule of Training during the Competition Period (Build-up Training)*

Day	Training Objectives	Training	km
Monday	Basic endurance	20-km walking	20 km
Tuesday	Special endurance	15-km walking fartlek or pace walking	15 km
Wednesday	Basic endurance	20-km walking	20 km
Thursday	Basic endurance	15-km walking	15 km
Friday	Special endurance	Interval training 10 × 1,000 m 5 × 2,000 m	20 km
Saturday	Basic endurance	25-km walk	25 km
Sunday	Supplementary training	possibly 10-km run	10 km
			125 km

cises which may be recommended for strengthening the ankle joints.

When setting up a weekly training programme the level of development of the athlete (beginner or advanced) as well as the training, depending on the periods of the year with their corresponding tasks, must be taken into consideration.

The following examples of a training week are intended for an athlete in the build-up period of training (see Tables 13 and 14). Special distance: 20 km, best time recorded approximately 1 : 34 : 00.

Coordination capabilities

The development of coordination capabilities both general and specific occurs in conjunction with the development of condition, i.e. on the one hand through varied training and on the other through taking into account the specific demands of the event.

The following are suited to developing specific coordination abilities:
—walking on various surfaces (ash, tarmac, paths, streets)
—walking up and downhill at different speeds
—walking alone and in the group (adaptability).

3.3. Short-, Middle- and Long-Distance Running

3.3.1. Sprinting Technique

Sprinting technique comprises starting, running and baton-exchange. As in all other track and field events, a high level of technical training is one of the decisive factors in producing proficiency.

A sprinter's performance is mainly determined by the force and rapidity with which muscles can contract and relax and, as a consequence of the cyclic motion, the correct timing of the change from tension to relaxation. The outward sign of good sprinting is the seemingly effortless and economic movement. Optimal tension at maximum effort is an important principle in training sprints and a major criterion marking off top sprinters from beginners.

3.3.1.1. Technique of the Sprint Stride at Maximum Speed

The most important phase in the sprint stride is the rear foot support phase (push-off phase) (Fig. 16, Pos. 2 and 3). The velocity of propulsion depends mainly on the intensity and direction of the push-off force. The rear foot support phase is technically correct when the ankle-, hip- and knee-joints are extended to the utmost. A line drawn between the ankle joint and the hip point to the supporting area (track surface) should, in this phase, make an angle of about 50 to 55 degrees. The upper body is generally almost erect with only a slight forward lean at an angie of some 85 to 90 degrees. When the tip of the take-off foot has left the ground, the rear support phase is followed by the non-supporting "floating" phase. In this phase the shank of the push-off leg folds tightly toward the hips, coming close to the buttocks. During this movement, which may be described as "heeling", the muscles of the rear leg should be completely relaxed. After the push-off and before beginning the forward swing the thigh of the rear leg at first moves slightly backwards and upwards. Only when the leading leg is swinging almost up to the horizontal as a result of the push-off force, the thigh begins to move forward. The leading leg continues to fold up toward the buttocks. The nearest approach between the lower leg and the thigh must take place at the moment when the thigh points vertically to the ground (Fig. 16, Pos. 8 and 9). This phase should be regarded as a decisive technical element. The strongly flexed leg now forms a kind of short pendulum with its point of suspension in the hip. It can therefore be thrust forward and upward at maximum speed. In good sprinters the velocity of the forward swing is up to 20 m/sec. This quick forward drive of the strongly flexed leg, which reaches almost twice the average sprinting speed, is of great assistance to the power of the push-off leg. During the forward drive the thigh and the lower leg should remain relatively long. When the thigh has reached the maximum possible for the individual in the knee-lift phase, the lower leg swings forward in a relaxed movement, during which the thigh begins to move down. The cocked foot at the end of the forward drive of the leading leg is typical of good sprinters.

After this the thigh and the lower leg with the slightly upturned cocked foot are swept backwards and downwards

Fig. 16

in an active pawing-like action. The foot meets the ground lightly. Now that the leading support phase begins, contact with the foot is made on the outer instep of the ball of the foot. Then, under the impact of the body weight, the pressure area moves towards the inside of the foot and the whole of the ball of the foot makes contact with the ground. The length of the leading supporting phase depends on a further balancing of the body weight, which is a special mark of a good running technique. International class sprinters, by virtue of their well developed calf muscles, balance, in this phase, their body weight in such a manner that only the ball of the foot touches the ground in the mid-support phase (vertical moment) (Fig. 16, Pos. 10). The distance between the ground and the heel varies in individuals from a few millimetres to about 3 or 4 cm. After rigorous contact with the ground the pressure remains on the ball of the foot. As a result the landing movement can be continued by a kind of traction movement. The point of the runner's hip tends to drop less, his centre of gravity moves faster in the mid-support phase and the rear support phase can be started relatively early. The total time of the support phase is thus reduced and the energy impulses of the push-off phase, which are necessary and decisive for the running speed, can be triggered in quicker succession.

Arm action. The powerful, speedy drive of the legs should be ideally matched by an equally powerful and speedy action of the arms. The arms should be bent and kept close to the body and move forwards and backwards in a straight line; the shoulders should be kept as steady as possible. The angle between the upper and the forearm does not remain constant in the forward and backward movement. At the limit of the forward swing it is between 80 to 85 degrees. During the backward drive, when passing the point of the hip, the arms tend to open out a little. By the time the arms reach the limit of their backward swing, they should regain 95° angle at the elbow. The rule may be applied that the closer the angle remains, the quicker the arms can be moved forward and backward. This is an important factor since there is a direct relation between the speed of the arm and the leg movements. The arm muscles must not be tense. The hands are therefore either loosely cupped or the thumb rests lightly on the bent index finger and the other fingers are very lightly bent underneath. A relaxed carriage of the head in natural alignment with trunk and shoulders prevents tightening of the facial and neck muscles. The lower jaw is allowed to sag by opening the mouth.

3.3.1.2. The Start and the Acceleration Section

This section comprises the movements beginning after the starting pistol is fired and ending after the runner has achieved the major part of his acceleration. Good sprinters reach this point at approximately 30 to 40 m. The strides have now reached optimal length and the runner's upper body is almost erect.

After this point a further acceleration is still possible and should be attempted by those striving for top class performances. However the maximum rate of acceleration is clearly achieved over this first section of the distance at about 30 metres from the start; this is considered to be the limit of the acceleration section (compare Figs. 11 and 13).

● The crouch start

The crouch start is used in all running events up to the 400 m. It allows the runner, through proper positioning of his centre of gravity in the "set" position, to respond most quickly to the gun and start the race. A fast start and a superior capacity for acceleration often decide the final result of a short-distance race. The starting velocity depends partly on a good technique, but mainly on the level of development of strength, capacity for concentration and reaction as well as on the enthusiasm of the runner for his event.

Two kinds of starting positions are used in modern starting technique: the "bunch" and the "medium" starting position. They differ in the spacing between the starting blocks and the distance from the blocks to the starting line. The "elongated" start, although still known, is hardly used nowadays. The medium start has largely taken the place of the bunch start. When training beginners it is recommended that both be practised. The figures in Table 15 give only approximate values. The angle of inclination of the blocks must

Table 15   The Position of the Starting Blocks

Starting Position	Starting Blocks	Distance from the Starting Line (feet)
Bunch	Front Block	2
	Rear Block	2.5–2.75
Medium	Front Block	1.75–2
	Rear Block	3–3.5

guarantee a good push-off, i.e. they must permit full pressure of the ball of each foot against the surface of each block. Front block angles of 45 to 50°, which are still in use, do not always guarantee this. If necessary, the angle of the front start block can be altered by placing a pad under its rear part.

The medium starting position. Research shows that the medium starting position produces a somewhat higher initial speed than the bunch start. This is due to a better distribution of the body weight over the limbs in the "set" position, the more favourable angle of the legs and a more effective straightening action of the leg.

Upon the command "on your marks", the runner assumes the initial position for the crouch start. He takes a position directly in front of the starting blocks and places his hands on the ground much as in a press-up. Then the foot—usually the foot of his stronger leg—is placed on the front block and the foot of the other leg on the rear block. Care should be taken that only the tip of the foot touches the ground and that the foot is pressed firmly against the block. The knee of the rear leg is now placed on the ground. Both knees should point in the running direction. Both hands (shoulder width apart) contact the ground with the thumbs and the index fingers just behind the starting line. The thumb and the index finger are spread so that they form a high bridge. The arms are extended and the knee of the front leg is close to the arms. Head carriage is relaxed and the eyes are focused on a point on the ground. The initial position has no particular bearing on the start. It only allows the runner to assume a favourable "set" position. At "set" the runner raises his hips by lifting the knee of the rear leg off the ground. The body weight is distributed almost evenly over the four supporting areas. The head remains in a natural relaxed position. The "set" position conveys to the runner's body the preliminary tension necessary for a powerful start from the blocks. The runner's attention is fully concentrated on the start. In order to achieve a high initial speed, the angles of both legs are of particular importance. An angle of about 90° at the front knee and of about 110 to 130° at the rear knee will be appropriate (Fig. 17, Pos. 2).

At "go" the sprinter starts without unnecessary delay. A quick response to the gun is of major importance for a fast start. In good sprinters the reaction time is about 0.12—0.18 sec.

The power exerted on the blocks when starting will transmit to the runner's body the highest possible initial velocity. This is brought about by an explosive pushing of both legs against the blocks. When measuring the push-off force exerted by each of the two legs, higher absolute values are often obtained for the rear leg than for the front leg, although the front leg is exerting force on the blocks longer and has therefore a greater influence on the initial velocity.

The main technical skills in the leg action are as follows: after coming off the rear starting block, the push-off leg starts to drive forward, i.e. the thigh is rapidly drawn forward and upward. At first the leading leg remains in an approximately horizontal position. Only when the foot passes the stretching leg (Fig. 17, Pos. 4), that is, when the visible lifting of the thigh begins, will the leading leg begin to come forward somewhat. The front leg completes its extension as the rear leg completes its swinging action. In this stretching phase, which typifies the crouch start, the thigh of the swinging leg forms in most sprinters almost a right angle between the thigh and the trunk and between the thigh and the lower leg (Fig. 17, Pos. 5). The power produced by the extension of the front leg must act optimally on the runner's centre of gravity. This implies that the extended leg and the trunk must form a nearly straight line. The "starting angle" of a good sprinter is about 42 to 45° in relation to the track surface.

Proper arm action: The arms have an important function in helping to produce the starting acceleration. Special attention must therefore be paid to the correct action of the arms. The movement of the swinging leg requires that the respective arm swings forward and upward. The arm tends to bend increasingly at the elbow until it reaches an angle of about 90° in the final phase of the movement. In this process the fist swings towards the forehead. The el-

Fig. 17

bow has a slight outward spread. The opposite arm performs a corresponding counter-movement backwards.

● *Running in the acceleration section*

We describe the stride pattern after the crouch start. There is an optimal ratio between stride length and stride rate for every sprinter, which is extremely important for the acceleration of the body. Many sprinters find out for themselves the ratio that is best for them by plenty of training. Certain requirements and rules of thumb, should, however, be stressed. In the first stride the foot meets the ground from the vertical projection of the runner's centre of gravity at a point which is generally at about 1.5 to 2 feet behind the starting line. In the second stride the foot is brought down below the runner's centre of gravity (in some cases somewhat ahead or behind). In all further strides the foot meets the ground in front of the vertical projection of the runner's CG. Generally during the first few strides each successive stride is longer by half a foot.

At the beginning of the acceleration phase the runner has a marked forward body lean. With an increasing rate and length of stride this angle of inclination gradually decreases, so that after 20 m the runner reaches his normal sprinting position. The forward body lean should be at its maximum when the front foot

comes off the starting block and during the initial strides. A good body lean is a function of the power exerted by the push-off force during the first few strides. The greater this force, the smaller will be the angle between the runner's body and the ground. Runners with a poor push-off force will come to an upright position sooner. If they persist in keeping a marked forward lean, they tend to stumble or fail to make full use of their sprinting capacity. In some cases runners with a good push-off force prematurely assume an upright position, because they raise their heads immediately after the start in order to look up to the finish. The head must always be kept in a relaxed position. During the first strides the runner focuses his eyes on a spot somewhere down on the track.

3.3.1.3. Special Features in Middle- and Long-Distance Running Technique

● *Standing start and running in the acceleration section*

The start in middle- and long-distance races is invariably from a standing position. The technique of the standing start is less complicated than that of the crouch start, since the runner may remain in his standing position.

Upon the command "on your marks" the runner steps up to the starting line and adopts a relaxed striding position. This often corresponds to the medium start position in the crouch start. The body weight is either distributed over both legs or is already over the front leg.

Upon the command "set" the flexion of the front knee is in most cases increased and in all runners the body weight is now over the front leg. The upper body is bent forward. If the time lag between the commands "set" and "go" is long, the danger of a false start due to a further forward shift of the body's centre of gravity will result.

After the pistol shot the athlete's body should adopt a body lean in order to assist the stretching movement of the legs and, in particular, the forward swing of the leg. Body lean is a function of acceleration. The more importance the acceleration phase has for an event, the greater will be the athlete's body lean. However, in general, the acceleration phase loses its importance as the race distance increases.

● *Special facets in running technique*

In middle- and long-distance running economy of energy is the most important consideration. All wasteful, hindering movements must be excluded by the use of a rational technique. The way the foot lands on the ground varies according to the rate and length of strides. Middle- and long-distance runners make contact with the ground with the foot close to the vertical projection of the body's centre of gravity. The longer the distance, the flatter the foot will be on impact. Middle-distance runners will first make contact with the ground high up on the metatarsus. Shortly after the first contact, the body weight presses the whole of the foot for a short moment down to the ground. The slight flexion in the knee-joint during the leading support phase is neutralized by the extension of the leg in the rear foot support phase.

During the run the upper body has only a slight or no forward lean (85 to 95°). The arms assist the running movement rhythmically by an efficient angle at the elbow. It does not matter whether the arms move parallel to the body or slightly inwards in front of the body. Nor is it wrong if a runner makes some use of the shoulder girdle in the movement.

3.3.2. Technical Training in Running

Man learns to run as a child. Therefore, in contrast to all other events, pupils of the first form already have vast practical experience in this particular event. Because of this emphasis in running exercises should, from the start, be focused on the maintenance and further build-up of existing ability guided by technical knowledge.

3.3.2.1. Special Preparatory Exercises

We are primarily concerned here with the wide range of games involving running [28] which aim at the development of the basic physical skills (above all strength, speed and agility). At this stage less attention is paid to technically correct running.

The following wide variety of exercises can be increased further by changing the initial position, e.g. by lying horizontally, squat and knee stand, straddle- and stretched leg position.

In the following exercises certain facets of running technique are stressed [29].

28 See S. Rauchmaul "100 kleine Spiele", 13th ed., Sportverlag, Berlin 1971.

29 Cf. M. Scholich "Richtig sprinten", in "Körpererziehung", Volk und Wissen, Berlin, Nr. 8/9 1969.

1. Walking
—with sprint-like arm action and marked heel and toe roll of the foot;
—with arms behind the neck and accentuated stretching of hips;
—on tip-toe, with arms lifting high and accentuated stretching of hips;
—on the lateral aspect of the foot.

2. Jogging
Bouncing walk on the ball of the foot, taking short steps, slow progression, sprint-like arm action.

3. Ankle-joint action
Running on the ball of the foot with springy push-off from the ankle joint with moderate arm and leg movements. Set feet on the ground accurately in running direction. Stretching hips and knee-joints of the standing leg.

4. Running with knee-lift
—moderately high knee lift at medium cadence of legs and arms. Short steps. Sharply angled landing of foot, then brief descent on the whole sole of the foot.

5. One-leg hopping and jumping
—Hopping on the ball of the foot in slow progression;
—Hopping by lifting the take-off leg to the chest;
—Competitive hopping and jumping.

3.3.2.2. Basic Exercises of Technical Training

With the following exercises the most important elements of the running stride can be trained.
—Exercise 1: Jogging
Aim: Getting acquainted with the complete movement in a relaxed manner.
Points to note: Start on the ball of the foot with the body completely upright. Chin and shoulders are relaxed. The properly bent arms are close to the body; the feet are kept straight. Run on the ball of the foot and cushion body weight elastically; the heels have no contact with the ground, the shoulders are in a fixed position.
Hints: Begin slowly, then continue at a moderate pace.
—Exercise 2: "Heeling"
Aim: Train the rear swinging phase. Raise leading leg high at the back with heel close to the buttocks.
Points to note: Consciously rapid but loose kicking upwards of lower leg with heel touching buttocks; the thigh is pointing vertically downward. Balance between leg and arm action. After "heeling" the lower leg drops down loosely; landing on the toes with heel off the ground. Variants of "Heeling":
a) Heeling left (right) without strides in between
b) Heeling left-right continuously, without knee-lift.
—Exercise 3: Acceleration run after backward kick with accentuated transition to the knee-lift phase (up to medium speed).
Aim: Learn the driving run; forward swing of the strongly flexed leg, gradually increasing speed and knee-lift. Build-up of the forward swing of the leading leg in the last section of the acceleration; striking, "pawing-like" movement of the foot.
Points to note: The acceleration is started with a heel-to-buttocks-kicking; with gradual increase of speed corresponding knee lift. Note relaxed performance of the forward swing of the leading leg.
—Exercise 4: Racing at medium speed, starting with backward kick-up.
Aim: Development of technique in doing the whole movement at an even moderate pace.

Points to note: Pay attention to the proper position of head, chin, trunk and shoulders and arm work-out. High "heeling" behind after fast forward drive of a strongly flexed leg; high knee lift, loose swinging of front leg, upturned foot and active "pawing-like" action of foot; the heel is off the ground.

Hints: After about 3 to 5 m jogging with "heeling" the rhythm is gradually increased to medium speed.

–Exercise 5: Acceleration run up to maximum speed

Aim: Develop running technique at higher speed. Develop feeling for rhythm.

Points to note: Train to relax also in all-out efforts. Demonstration of all technical elements mentioned above.

Hints: Increase rhythm gradually but steadily to maximum speed. Maintain speed over 20 to 30 m coasting without putting in effort. Slow down if movements become tense or technically wrong.

–Exercise 6: Race at under maximum and at maximum speed

Aim: Build up running technique at a high constant speed and develop "feel" for running.

Points to note: See above. Optimal ratio between stride length and stride frequency.

3.3.2.3. Ancillary Exercises

These are intended to help learn the running technique from the acquisition of the rudiments to the finishing touches and to perfect that technique at high speed and under a variety of conditions.

1. Acceleration run with final section at maximum speed (20 to 30 m), followed by a running out over 20 m.

2. Acceleration run with medium section (20 to 30 m) at maximum speed, followed by coasting over 30 m.

3. Runs at speed over distances between 50 and 150 m at something under maximum speed from standing start or after some preliminary strides.

4. Runs with changes in tempo over 100 or 200 m distance.

Examples: 150-m run: 80 m below top speed–30 m coasting–40 m maximum; over 100 m: 40 m maximum–20 m coasting–40 m max., or similar combinations.

5. Wind-sprints or sprints with a flying-start over distances between 20 and 50 m after an acceleration run (acceleration section) of some 20 to 50 m.

6. Runs at speed under various conditions.

Example: running in the curve, on grass, cinder and Tartan tracks, against headwind and with a following wind, solo and in a group.

3.3.2.4. Fault–Reason–Correction

–Fault: Insufficient leg extension at the push-off, the runner "sits".

Reason: Inadequate power transmission: the push-off is not powerful enough and too hasty.

Correction: ankle-joint work in forward movement; running and hopping, running and jumping, bouncing, special strengthening exercises.

–Fault: Feet turned outwards excessively

Reason: Faulty running form

Correction: Running in lanes. Walking, jogging and slow running with toes turned slightly inwards

–Fault: "Bouncing" walk with marked vertical swaying

Reason: The push-off force is directed too much upward.

Correction: Longer push-off, hitting chalk marks at regular intervals, starting exercises, increase stride frequency.

—Fault: Too wide forward swinging of leading leg and flat foot plant.

Reason: Forward thrust of the leading leg.

Correction: Running with impact on the ball of the foot.

— Fault: Backward lean of the trunk

Reason: Poorly developed trunk and thigh muscles, build-up of fatigue.

Correction: Snatching of thigh in diagonal support with and without additional load; high knee lift under difficult conditions, e.g. in deep snow, sand, uphill, with heavy boots, with weights on the thigh and lower legs, strengthening exercises for the trunk muscles.

— Fault: Ineffective arm movements (transverse arm movements, excessive backward swing of arms, hunched shoulders).

Reason: Too much shoulder movement; insufficient flexibility in the shoulder joints.

Correction: Practice proper arm movement with easy strides or side-straddle position and in jogging.

— Fault: Head thrown back or chin on the chest.

Reason: Stress due to fatigue; wrong understanding of movement.

Correction: Normal and erect head carriage, eyes focused ahead.

3.3.3. Training of Crouch Start

Beginners have usually much more experience in the running movement than in the crouch start. The rudiments of these starting movements must therefore be systematically developed.

3.3.3.1. Special Preparatory Exercises

All the examples in this part of the book are designed to improve reactions and coordination and to help develop acceleration from a position of rest. Fast movement with attention to style is a prerequisite for the effectiveness of these exercises.

Examples:

1. Standing start and start from various positions on the ground e. g.
2. Start from run-up quarter-, half- and full turn.
3. Start with tipping the man ahead.
4. "Chain reaction" (the athletes are lined up; the man on the extreme right or left starts and the start of his neighbour takes place in reaction to this first movement).
5. "Group start" (execution much as in "chain reaction"). The athlete in the middle starts and his right and left neighbours start as soon as they become aware of the slightest movement by him.
6. The last athlete dashes forward upon a signal (whistle or similar). The sportsmen run in file.
7. Falling start (can also be executed as a "chain reaction" or as a "group start" (see exercise 4 and 5). In the initial position the feet are parallel; pressure is on the ball of the foot. Almost straight forward dip of the body, explosive starting stride when the body has reached the correct angle (no sagging at the hips!).
8. Standing start (individually or in groups, with and without starting or-

ders). Train fast starts in middle- and long-distance races and in relays. Medium stride position; the body weight is over the front (the stronger) leg. Upon the command "set" the front leg assumes the position with pressure on the ball of the foot. The trunk is bent well forward, both arms are hanging down loosely to the sides or the opposite arm to the front leg is brought forward ahead of the body. After the gun goes the leg extends forward and upward in order to obtain an effective body lean; powerful push-off with the rear leg and powerful swing of the front leg, counterbalanced by the arm movements.

3.3.3.2. Basic Exercises of Technical Training

The following series of exercises is recommended:

– Exercise 1: Starts without starting blocks from the "set" position (starts in groups as in a competition).
Aim: To get a proper understanding of the complete movement.
Points to note: The feet and hands are set on lines drawn on the ground (about medium starting position). The arms are stretched, the rear knee is on the ground. For the "set" position the hips are gradually lifted, the body weight is evenly distributed over the arms and legs.
– Exercise 2: Assume the initial position after the command: "on your marks".
Aim: To become familiar with the starting blocks, with the spacing between the blocks and from the blocks to the starting line; to assess the best spacing between starting blocks for the individ-

ual; to find out the proper initial position.
Points to note: See also description of initial position for crouch start (3.3.1.2.).
– Exercise 3: Adopt the "set" position. Start from this position without command. Cover 10 to 20 m by sprinting at a little less than maximum effort.
Aim: Practice so as to find the best starting position for the individual.
Points to note: The angles at the knee joints of both legs (front leg 90°, rear leg 110 to 130°) may serve as criteria for a correct posture in the starting position. Deviations from these angles must be corrected by changing the height of the pelvis, the distance of the blocks from the starting line or the spacing between the blocks.
– Exercise 4: Practise the complete sequence of movements in the crouch start without command (run over 15 to 20 m).
Aim: Train a fast start from the "set" position with optimal body lean.
Points to note: Explosive push-off from starting blocks with both legs: full stretching of the front starting leg, active forward swing of the rear starting leg, good forward lean; fast first stride of optimal length.
– Exercise 5: Crouch start with command and burst over 30 m.
Aim: Quick response to the gun.
Points to note: Abide by competition rules (e.g. avoid false starts by proper posture in the "set" position); explosive response to the pistol shot, marked forward lean up to about the 10th stride, powerful strides, touchdown on the ball of the foot.
– Exercise 6: Crouch start in competition conditions (starting in groups with point scoring, clocked runs).

Aim: Improve the starting procedure and the acceleration phase at near competition conditions.

Points to note: Apply all the skills acquired in exercises 1 to 5 for optimal acceleration.

3.3.3.3. Ancillary Exercises

The complementary exercises for the crouch start serve mainly to improve speed of reaction, the start from the "set" position and the first strides after the start.

Improvement of reaction:
1. Starts upon acoustic signals of varying intensity (whistles, clapped hands, pistol shot, starting device).
2. Starts with various intervals between the commands "on your marks" and "set".

Improving the starting speed by concentrating on certain parts of the whole movement, as follows:
1. Rapid forward and backward swing of the appropriate arm.
2. Fast forward swing and touchdown of the rear leg.
3. Extension and forward swing of front leg as fast as possible.

Improving the push-off force:
1. Starts on a slightly rising track
2. Starts wearing a weight vest
3. Starts with impeding harness
4. Starts on sand.

Perfecting stride frequency:
1. Starts on a slightly inclined track
2. Starts with traction or following wind.

Improving Stride Length:
1. Hit check markings during the first strides
2. Starting exercises with powerful strides and a good forward lean of the trunk.

Improving the forward lean of the body:
1. Optimal balance of the thigh and the trunk in body lean.
2. Complete stretching of the front starting leg in the ankle-, knee- and hip-joints (attempting to see the tip of the front foot).

3.3.3.4. Fault—Reason—Correction

— Fault: The hands are too wide apart in the initial position.
Reason: Incorrect understanding of movement
Correction: Set well extended arms shoulder width apart just behind the starting line.
— Fault: The effective angle of 90 degrees at the knee-joint of the front leg is not achieved in the "set" position.
Reason: The pelvis is too high or too low
Correction: Change height of hips
— Fault: Arms support extremely heavy weight in the "set" position.
Reason: Too much weight transferred forward.
Correction: Bring hips more upward than forward. Straighten arms and distribute body weight evenly over arms and legs.
— Fault: Unnecessary tension in dorsal muscles by backward lean of head.
Reason: Imperfect understanding of movement.
Correction: Keep head normally aligned; focus eyes on the track.
— Fault: "Jumped" first stride.
Reason: Too high push-off angle. Upward thrust too steep.
Correction: Increase forward lean. Watch position of head and line of vision. Accelerate movement of rear leg.

– Fault: Coming to the upright position too soon.

Reason: Inadequate push-off force, wrong carriage of head.

Correction: Improve push-off force; consistently maintain forward lean of trunk; eyes focused on the ground, no lifting of head.

3.3.4. Physical Requirements and Training Methods for Improving Performance in Sprinting

3.3.4.1. The Importance of Physical Condition

Analyses of training of the world best sprinters have demonstrated that top performances in short-distance races are, as a rule, not the result of spontaneous or incidental physical development. Success was not achieved by one or two years of training only. An intensive training with specific objectives over many years were the main reasons for getting to the top.

Certain anatomical and physiological factors are necessary and important attributes for top performances. Yet innate physical qualities (structure of muscles, quick response to stimuli and the capacity to perform fast movements) would be of no avail if not developed by efficient, directed practice, by educational processes into skills which permit the athlete to achieve top-class results in competition through conscious will-power. The development of individual aptitudes into athletic skills is achieved by the process of properly planned training which covers all sides of the athlete's personality (physical, mental and moral) and leads him to top performances by systematic instruction and education.

Through well-planned and directed training it is possible to improve the racing speed of all athletes over short distances. The predominant physical attributes of sprinters are speed and speed endurance; their level of development is mainly a function of the quality of muscular power and of the smooth and elastic functioning of the corresponding processes of the nervous system.

● Strength

Muscular strength is an important factor for rapid movements. For its systematic build-up weight training must be included in workouts. By improving his strength qualities, the sprinter can achieve better results in sprints. Good training methods are general and special strength developing exercises, executed with quick, explosive movements. The athlete should do strength exercises with and without additional load to his body weight (e.g. sandbags, weight vests, barbells etc.). The amount of additional load should be adapted to the physical training level of the sportsman. Inadequately developed muscles can be strengthened by using high additional loads (approximately 75 per cent of the maximum load). In modern training strength exercises could not be missed; they should, however, not become an end in themselves, but must have as a specific objective the improvement of sprinting.

This kind of training must by no means lead to a onesided emphasis on strength, since power is only one of the determinants of speed. Under certain circumstances an exaggerated or me-

148

thodically poorly structured training for strength may lead to a deterioration in performance (see sections 2.7.2.2. and 2.7.2.3.).

● Speed

Fast movements require an excellent motor coordination, the outward sign of which is fluent relaxed movement. A fast and purposeful interplay of the muscles involved in a movement is often the result of much training; it is based on the accurate timing of tension and relaxation, of excitation and inhibition, respectively, of the working nerves and muscles. Running speed only becomes fully effective when the athlete masters an economic running technique. Speed determines almost exclusively the performance in sprints. Sprinting velocity is characterized by the reactivity, acceleration capacity and maximum speed of a sprinter (ef. 3.1.4.).

● Endurance

Basic endurance is not a distinct and crucial factor in sprinting, but together with all the other aspects of training it forms an important basis of training for sprinting. This is the basis which largely determines the ultimate capacity and hence the potential of an athlete. The general endurance training has to fulfill two main tasks within the framework of sprinting schedules. On the one hand it serves to improve the functioning of the cardio-vascular system, and on the other hand to offset the effects of intensive training and competition by improving looseness in the joints and motor-coordination.

Speed endurance contributes to the outcome of a sprinting race. The reason is that after some 60 or 70 m covered at maximum speed even good sprinters experience a gradual decline in speed, due to the build-up of oxygen deficiency which reduces the rapidity of processes in the nervous system. This has a more harmful effect on beginners than on experienced athletes. With suitable training the resistance to fatigue can gradually be improved through processes of the adaptation in body. This becomes of increasing importance, especially in longer sprinting distances. (Ratio of the 100-m to the 200-m performance. Rule: double the 100-m time ± 0.2 sec = 200-m time.)

● Extensibility

An optimal muscular contraction must be matched by an equally good extensibility of the muscles. At every movement certain muscle groups come into play. When one muscle contracts, the other will extend and vice versa. If an antagonistic muscle is not relaxed, it will impede the contraction of the respective synergist.

OZOLIN [30] writes: "The better the antagonistic muscles expand and the less resistance they offer to an energetic movement, the faster this movement can be performed." Extending muscles improves the flexibility at the joints. Muscles that have to continue doing rapid work should not, however, be stretched beyond a certain extent. Gymnastic exercises with and without additional loads are recommended for improving the extensibility of muscles. The importance of gymnastic exercises for improving mobility, extensibility and looseness has sometimes been un-

30 N. Ozolin "Das Training des Leichtathleten" (The Training of the Track and Field Athlete), in "Der Leichtathlet", Nr. 11/1959, Annex "Der Leichtathletik-Trainer".

derestimated in sprint training, although it is a known fact that they reduce the liability to muscle injuries and can improve the length of stride.

● Age, Height and Weight

The majority of sprinters who have been trained as juniors will reach their top form between 18 and 25. Best performances over the 100-m distance are usually achieved sooner than over the 200-m distance, because the development of speed endurance has to build on speed. Height and weight vary greatly from one athlete to the other, so that the values given below should not be regarded as rigid standards.

The chart on this page gives a general idea of the age, height and weight of sprinters at the 1972 Olympic Games in Munich.

3.3.4.2. Methods of Improving Performance over Short Distances

● Strength

The methods used in strength workouts are chiefly determined by the demands placed on the athletes over a particular race distance. The typical and essential attribute of a sprinter is explosive power. This quality must be developed according to the athlete's age and training level with regard to general and special strength.

In setting up strength training programmes for different age groups, the following pattern may serve as a guide: For 15 and 16 year-olds (including beginners): develop in the first place strength endurance by the extended interval method and build up a good general basis of strength.

For 17 and 18 year-olds (including advanced trainers): here the intensive interval method with occasional use of repetition running is paramount.

The chief objective of strength training consists therefore in developing explosive power and maximum strength.

There are correlations between the attributes of strength, endurance, explosive power and maximum strength. Thus strength endurance has also a certain bearing on explosive power and vice versa. Correlations exist similarly between explosive power and maximum strength while strength endurance and maximum strength are in a sense in opposition to one another (see 2.7.2.).

Knowledge of these general correlations is important for the coach if he is to determine the most rational training method best suited for a particular level.

Training for the 400 m requires special consideration, because in this event the

Table 16 *Mean Values of Age, Height and Weight of the 6 Best Performers at the Olympic Games 1972*

	Men					Women			
	100 m	200 m	400 m	110 m H.	400 m H.	100 m	200 m	400 m	100 m H.
Age (years)	24.5	23.2	25.0	24.2	24.7	21.0	22.0	21.8	29.2
Height (cm)	179	184	181	186	186	167	172	168	167
Weight (kg)	76.3	77.8	75.2	87.0	75.0	57.7	61.5	55.8	58.3

performance is influenced both by explosive strength and by strength endurance. Both these qualities must therefore be constantly improved even for superior performers.

General strength exercises

1. From the horizontal position (floor, bench, box) raising the trunk to a vertical position with and without additional load (medicine ball, kettle bell and sandbag).
2. Raise and lower (tuck and stretch, circle) the legs with and without additional weights (medicine ball, weights on wrists, exercise rope, sandbag and partner) – from the horizontal position on the floor (box, bench) – from stretched hang backward and wall bars.
3. With legs apart bending of trunk sideways with barbells, kettle bell, sandbag or medicine ball (on the neck or with arms up).
4. Overhead throwing backwards of medicine ball (also kettle bell)
– from legs apart with impetus
– from horizontal position on box (medicine ball).
5. Throwing medicine ball up with legs apart.
6. Lifting barbell by bringing trunk into vertical position (arms and legs remain stretched).
Exercises for developing shoulder muscles:
1. Double-arm snatching of barbells
2. Pressing barbell (in standing, sitting, lying positions)
3. Lifting barbell (kettle bell or sandbag) with outstretched arms
– standing
– from horizontal position on the box
4. Lifting two weights sideways with outstretched arms

– from standing position
– from horizontal position on box.
5. Hammer swinging with both arms (kettle bell, sandbag, hammer).
6. Arm-bends in push-up position on finger-tips.
7. Double-arm and barbell pushing upward forward
8. Pull-ups with ordinary grasp and undergrasp.
9. Snatching barbell to the chest (without clearing) from straddle-stand.
10. Arm stretching and bending with kettle bell

Special strength exercises

Exercises promoting sprinting posture and running rhythm:
1. Running with impeding harness over approximately 30 to 100 m. The athlete's movement is braced by a skipping rope or a tire pulled by a partner.
In order to avoid cramp and to acquire a proper feel of movement, running with more or less vigorous bracing effects of this kind should be included in every workout.
2. Running and jumping up and down stairs
– running on stairs with accentuated knee-lift (3 or 4 steps in one stride) at reduced and at full effort
Distance involving some 8 to 10 double strides
– One-leg jumps (two steps at a time), approximately 10 to 15 repetitions for each leg
3. Bouncing on straightaways (soft ground) Emphasize knee-lift, the active "pawing- like" foot plant and the rapid push-off and pull-through forward. Distance length: 30 to 100 m or 10 to 20 repetitions for performance.
4. Jumping on one leg

– Continuous jumps on one leg 20 to 50 m or 10 to 20 repetitions (performance test in metres).
– Jumps on one leg alternating (i. e. left-left, right-right) covering about 30 to 60 m.
5. Running uphill or in sand (not too steeply, otherwise good running form will be sacrificed).
Distance length: 20 to 30 m, for improving acceleration;
– Distance length 80 to 150 m, for improving special endurance.

Fig. 18–20

All these runs should be performed flat out and be timed by someone.
6. Knee-lift runs
– taking short strides, in slow progression with emphasis on lifting the thigh roughly to the horizontal and with a fast sequence of strides.
– taking long strides, medium to top speed; accentuated knee-lift with normal stride length. Distances: approx. 50–100 m.
7. Coasting. Ordinary hang-up, if possible free hanging on horizontal bar. Running with accentuated knee-lift. Strength exercises for sprinting based on corresponding running movement. Exercises for developing stretching force:
1. Squat vaults from medium knee-bend forward or upward (with and without additional load)
2. Squat vaults over obstacles (box, bench, hurdles)
3. Tiered jumps
4. Knee-bend with barbell
5. Ankle-stretching exercises with additional load (barbell) (Fig. 18)
6. One-leg knee-bends (loading by partner or barbell) (Fig. 19)
7. "Stair-stepping" with and without additional load (barbell, partner) (Fig. 20)

8. Horizontal position on box, one leg hanging down sideways, burdened with loads of 10 to 20 kg (sandbag). Repeated backward and upward swinging of leg (Fig. 21). Exercises for developing lifting strength:
1. Quick forward and upward snatching of thigh, almost to the horizontal from wide oblique forward support on wall bars. Repeat this exercise very quickly and frequently without load. Additional load provided by sandbag or bicycle inner tube placed across the thigh and fixed at the other end (Fig. 22).
2. Jerking of thigh to the horizontal from standing position on a bench. On the lifting leg should be hung a kettle bell of 10 to 15 kg weight or a sandbag (Fig. 23).
3. In horizontal position on box; one leg, loaded with sandbag, hangs down sideways. Repeated forward and upward swinging of leg with weight (Fig. 24).
4. Sitting position. Support from hands in rear position or hands gripping a bar. From this initial position both legs are slightly lifted, drawn to the body, then stretched again; or only stretched and moved up-and downwards (Fig. 25).

5. Back hang on wall bars, lifting legs beyond the horizontal (either stretched or bent at the knee). Additional load of medicine ball or sandbag (Fig. 26).

6. In horizontal position on a mat. Hands grip bars. Tuck the thigh up to the horizontal against resistance by partner (partner holding on the athlete's foot).

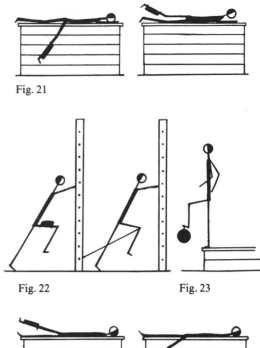

Fig. 21

Fig. 22   Fig. 23

● Speed

Based on the speed pattern of 100-m sprints two forms of running must be practised in sprint workouts:

Running to improve acceleration
— Crouch or high start with bursts over 20 to 40 m
— Games requiring strong acceleration over 20 to 40 m
— Bursts over 20 to 40 m, from walking or jogging
— Long-jump run-ups
— Relay starts over 30 to 40 m

Running schedules for improving (maximum) speed
— Runs at speed from crouch start over 50 to 80 m
— Flying sprints over 20 to 40 m
— The approach run up to maximum speed is of about 40 to 50 m length
— Run-ups with baton in relay training over 50 to 70 m
— Maximum acceleration over 30 to 50 m, followed by coasting.
Coasting must be performed in an easy, relaxed way, without visible slow-down.
— Acceleration runs over 100 m with a maximum or less than maximum section of some 30 to 40 m.
— Acceleration runs over 100 to 150 m at maximum or submaximum speed with a medium section of 20 to 30 m, followed by 30 m coasting.

Fig. 24

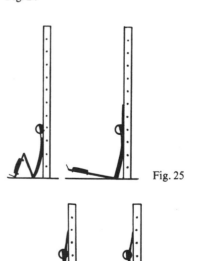

Fig. 25

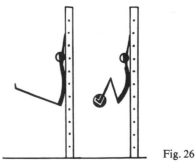

Fig. 26

Table 17 Weekly Schedule of Training for Sprinters during the Preparatory Period (Build-up Training)

Day	Duration (min.)	Training Task A = Preparation B = Main Part C = Finishing Phase	Training Details
Monday	15	A Warm-up	Game (Basketball, Rugby, Football)
	15	B Agility exercises	Floor exercises, gymnastics
	45	Strength build-up	Obstacle runs
	10	C Relaxation	General, very varied strength training, gymnastics, jogging
Tuesday	15	A Warm-up	Jogging, ankle-strengthening work, jumps, acceleration working, gymnastics
		B Endurance build-up	Runs at low speed (300–500 m), mainly cross-country
	10	C Running-out	Jogging
Wednesday	15	A Warm-up	Jogging, knee-lift run, acceleration work, gymnastics
	60	B Speed development and technical training	Starts up to 50 m, wind-sprints up to 50 m (crouch start, relays and hurdle technique)
	10	C Running-out	Jogging
Thursday	15	A Warm-up	Games
	15	B Agility exercises, Strength development	Floor exercises, obstacle runs, general and special strength exercises
		C Relaxation	Gymnastics
Friday	15	A Warm-up	Jogging, acceleration work, gymnastics
	30	B Speed development and technical training	(same as Wednesday)
	30	Endurance	High-speed runs at medium or low speed (100–400 m)
	10	C Running-out	Jogging
Saturday	60	Supplementary training	Track and field athletics, jumping and throwing events, games etc.
Sunday		Rest	

● Endurance

Running forms for developing special endurance:
They follow the pattern of the intensive interval method or the repetition method (see 2.7.2.2. and 2.7.2.3.).
– Speed runs at high or medium speed: for 100/200-m runners distances between 100 and 300 metres; for 400-m men mainly between 200 and 600 metres.
– Changes in tempo runs at high or medium speed: for 100/200-m runners preferably between 100 and 250 m.
For 400-m runners mainly between 200 and 450 m (Example of such runs over 150 m: 50 m maximum, 50 m coasting,

Table 18 Weekly Schedule of Training for Sprinters during the Competition Period (Build-up Training)

Day	Duration (min.)	Training Tasks A = Preparation B = Main Part C Finishing Phase		Training Details
Monday	20	A	Warm-up and gymnastics	Games, gymnastic exercises
	10	B	Strength	General and special strength and agility exercises
		C	Running-out	A few runs at low speed up to 200 m
Tuesday	20	A	Warm-up	Continuous run (CR), 10–15 min.
	40	B	Endurance	High speed runs at low speed (200/300 m)
	10	C	Limbering down	Easy continuous running
Wednesday	25	A	Warm-up and gymnastics	Jogging, ankle-joint work, knee-lift run, bouncing run
	40	B	Speed build-up and technical training	Acceleration runs, crouch starts, baton-changing and hurdles
	20		Endurance build-up	High-speed runs at high or medium intensity (150/400 m)
	5	C	Limbering down	Jogging or easy continuous run
Thursday	15	A	Warm-up	Game or run-in work
	40	B	Explosive power build-up	Various jumps
	30		Supplementary training	Putting and throwing events, swimming, gymnastics etc.
	10	C	Limbering down	Gymnastics, loosening exercises
Friday	15	A	Warm-up	Same as Tuesday
	30	B	Speed build-up and technical training	Acceleration runs, crouch starts, baton exchange, hurdles
	30		Endurance	Paces at high or medium intensity (80/150 m)
		C	Limbering down	Jogging
Sunday			Competition	100/200/400-m hurdle races, relays

50 m maximum; and over 400 m: 150 m high speed, 150 m medium speed and 100 m high speed).
– Acceleration runs over 150 to 200 m
– last 60–80 m full-out.
– High speed runs with special objectives. Example: a 200-m distance must be covered at a predetermined time of say 23 sec., of which the first section of 100 metres is at moderate speed (e.g. in 12.5 sec.) and the remainder really fast (10.5 sec.).

Running forms developing basic endurance

The best forms of training the human body for basic endurance are through continuous running and extensive interval work. They improve the capacity of enduring a sustained effort under aerobic stress. For both methods the required intensity demands must be satisfied. Pulse rate control serves as a criterion. After stress loads pulse rates should in all these runs be not more than 160 to 180 per minute (See also sections 2.7.2.1., 2.7.2.2. and 3.3.5.2.).

– Continuous runs (CR) are runs without a rest, carried out mainly through woods and parks. They are designed to develop the sprinter's capacity for running uninterruptedly for a period of some 30 minutes; this will mainly be achieved by increasing the volume stimulus (running time or running distance) and not the stimulus intensity (running intensity). A beginner who runs say 1 km in 10 minutes will, after a fair amount of training, run some 2 km in 10 minutes. When he manages a continuous run for 30 minutes, his endurance capacity can be further improved by reducing the stimulus intensity. The runner will then be able to cover a longer distance in the same period of time or the same distance in a shorter time. For checking the running time or distance a measured circuit of 1.0 to 2.0 km length is recommended.

– Fartlek. Up to 30 minutes running at varying speeds depending on the runner's fitness and the character of terrain. Fartlek is a strenuous form of running and requires a relatively high endurance capacity.

Examples: 2 to 3 minutes of continuous running, acceleration runs over 100 m, 2 to 3 minutes continuous running, accelerating run uphill over 50 m, continuous run up to recovery, sharp run over 200 m, 2 to 5 minutes of continuous running etc.

– High speed races based on extensive interval work. Distances of 200 to 600 m at low speed and with a great number of repetitions. They can be var-ied by series, shuttle relays, "unlimited" relays, "Paarläufe" (running in pairs), etc.

– "Interval-Continuous-Runs" are also a good way for sprinters to develop basic endurance. Repeated running over 1.0 to 2.0 km distance with relatively short recovery intervals between runs, which can be taken up with jogging and some gymnastic exercises.

The appropriate length of intervals between two runs can be assessed by measuring pulse rates. A succeeding run may be started, when the runner's pulse has dropped to 120 beats per minute.

● Extensibility

For improving the extensibility of muscles and flexibility of joints involved in running, gymnastic exercises should be included in the programme (stretching exercises, limbering up, and relaxation exercises). The correct rotation of these two groups of exercises is essential for developing strength and extensibility of the sprinting muscles. They should therefore be included in every training session. We give here some examples from a multitude of exercises.

1. Forward and backward swings of one leg with gradual increase in height and intensity.

2. From a standing position: backward swing of one leg with simultaneous backward swinging of both arms overhead.

3. Alternate stretching and squatting. In squatting position heels touch the ground.

4. Wide straddle stand. Shift body weight to the extreme right with deep bending of right leg; repeat to the left.

5. Stretching and bending of both legs, with hands holding heels.

6. Sitting with slightly bent legs. Kickering of thigh to one side (knees to the ground).

7. Prone position with hands turned away at right angles. The left foot swings towards the right hand and vice versa.

Variation: the right heel swings towards the left hand and the left heel towards the right hand.

8. Hurdle seat with backward lean or half turn.

9. Lying on the side with arms on the ground, turned away from the trunk at right angles. Wide forward and backward swing of one leg.

10. Shoulder stand—wide straddling with legs.

Loosening exercises

1. Jogging and loosening of leg muscles in standing position.

2. Shoulder stand; legs directed upward; loosen and relax.

3. Squat or in horizontal position. Legs loosely bent, shaking leg muscles.

4. Standing with support; loose forward, backward or sideways swinging of one leg.

5. Lying face down, folding one or both lower legs to the buttocks or: vertical bending of lower legs and shaking of calf muscles.

Intensity of runs

For developing speed and endurance in workouts, it is very important to assess the performance level and to monitor loads by taking times.

In training for the sprints we distinguish between sprints up to 60 m at maximum (100 %) and sprints at sub-maximum (90 to 95 %) speed.

In training for endurance we distinguish between pace races of high, medium and low speed (100 m and more). Endurance runs are runs with an intensity of at least 95 % of the best possible performance.

Endurance runs at medium speed are

Table 19   Intensity Table (model)

100 m Perform.	30 m		60 m		100 m		200 m Perform.	200 m		400 m Perform.	400 m	
	max.	subm.	max.	subm.	h.	m.		h.	m.		h.	m.
10.0	3.6	4.0	6.3	7.1	10.5	11.1	20.0	21.1	22.2	45.0	47.4	50.0
10.5	3.8	4.2	6.6	7.4	11.0	11.7	21.0	22.1	23.3	46.5	48.9	51.7
11.0	4.0	4.4	6.9	7.7	11.6	12.2	22.0	23.2	24.5	48.0	50.5	53.3
11.5	4.2	4.6	7.3	8.1	12.1	12.8	23.0	24.2	25.6	49.5	52.1	55.0
12.0	4.3	4.8	7.6	8.4	12.6	13.3	24.0	25.3	26.7	51.0	53.7	56.7
12.5	4.5	5.0	7.9	8.7	13.2	13.9	25.0	26.3	27.8	52.5	55.3	58.3
13.0	4.7	5.2	8.2	9.0	13.7	14.4	26.0	27.4	28.9	54.0	56.8	60.0
13.5	4.9	5.4	8.5	9.3	14.2	15.0	27.0	28.4	30.0	55.5	58.4	61.7
14.0	5.1	5.6	8.8	9.6	14.7	15.5	28.0	29.5	31.1	57.0	60.0	63.3
14.5	5.3	5.8	9.1	9.9	15.2	16.0	29.0	30.5	32.2	58.5	61.6	65.0
15.0	5.5	6.0	9.4	10.2	15.7	16.5	30.0	31.6	33.4	60.0	63.2	66.7

Note: max.—maximum speed; subm.—sub-maximum speed; h.—high speed; m.—medium speed

runs at a minimum of 90 to 95 % of the best possible performance (cf. Tables 19, 20, 21). Endurance runs of low intensity are runs at a minimum of between 70 and 89 % of the best possible performance.

Examples:

1. A sprinter who covers 30 m at a minimum of 4.0 sec., or 60 m at 6.9 sec. in training is capable of about 11.0 sec. over the 100-m distance.
2. A sprinter whose best performance is 22.0 sec. over 200 m, is training at high intensity when his 200-m runs are faster than 23.2 sec. and at medium intensity, when they are faster than 24.5 sec.

3.3.5. Physical Requirements and Training Methods for Improving Performance in Middle- and Long-Distance Races

3.3.5.1. The Importance of Physical Condition

Top performances in middle- and long-distance races chiefly depend on the development level of the various forms of endurance. Consistent with the race distance, good performance in competition depends on a high level of physical condition and of coordinating abilities, such as speed, explosive power, strength endurance movability, supple-

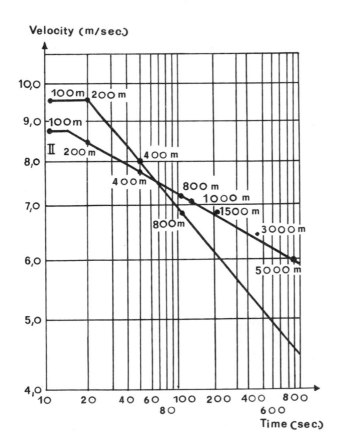

Fig. 26a The individual decrease in speed according to the running time and the different level of endurance capacity (according to Zatziorski, Volkov, Kulik)

Table 20   Distances and Sections of Relative Intensity (from Satziorski)

Partial section	Distances (m, km)	Max. work (min.) up to approx.	Relative Intensity
Short-Distance Race			Maximum
Short	100–200	0:22	(Minimum)
Long	400	0:45	
		0:50	(Maximum)
Middle-Distance Race			Sub-Maximum
Short	600–800	1:48	(Minimum)
		2:00	
Medium	1,000–1,600	3:58	
		4:10	
Long	2,000–3,000	7:55	(Maximum)
Long-Distance Race			High
Short	3,000–5,000	13:30	
Medium	10,000	29:00	
Long	15–30 km	90:00	
Extremely long	35–50 km	3:10:00	Moderate

ness, capacity to relax and agility. The quality of a 3000-m steeplechaser is mainly determined by strength, movability and agility. Slackness and ability to relax play a significant role in all middle- and long-distance races. During intermediate and final sprints or intense training stress, situations may arise when a low level of these qualities prevents the full utilization of competitive potential, notwithstanding frantic efforts to run well. This produces cramping which accelerates the build-up of fatigue and thus reduces proficiency. Finally anatomical, physiological and morphological factors such as the functioning of cardio-vascular circulatory and respiratory organs, balanced physical development (good proportions between trunk and legs, height and body weight — force load relation) may favourably influence performance in middle-distance and long-distance races.

● Endurance

Efficient running is expressed by the relation between speed and time (HILL). The capacity to sustain high speed during a planned period of time or over a given distance is therefore dependant on the endurance capacity. The longer the running time or distance, the more significant becomes endurance for the final result and the greater will be the permissible decrease in speed in relation to the maximum possible running speed over 60 or 100 m (Fig. 26a).

The demands placed on the runner's organism and endurance capacity vary according to the distance-time ratio, but are fairly constant for certain sections (FARFEL), particularly for sections in standard short-, middle- and long-distance races. Each section corresponds to a known requirement of relative intensity in regard to the demands imposed on the capacity of the body and on the endurance of the runner.

Table 21   Types of Endurance Training for Advanced and Beginners (Foundation Training)

	Advanced		Beginners	
	Duration (min.)	Distances (m, km)	Duration (min.)	Distances (m, km)
Sprinting speed endurance	below 0:15	100–150	0:15	70–100
Speed endurance	above 0:15 up to 0:50	150–400	0:15 0:40	100 200
Short-duration endurance	above 0:50 up to 2:00	400–800	0:40 2:00	200 600
Medium-duration endurance	above 2:00 up to 8:00	1,000–3,000	2:00 5:00	600 1,000
Long-duration endurance I	above 8:00 up to 30:00	3–10 km	5:00 40:00	1,000 8,000
II	above 30:00 up to 90:00	10–25/30 km	–	–
III	above 90:00 up to 240–300	25/30–50 km	–	–

HARRE [31] and PFEIFER [32] describe the endurance required over a typical section depending on the maximum time of a workout as follows (Table 21):

Sprint-speed endurance
Speed endurance
Short-duration endurance
Medium-duration endurance
Long-duration endurance.

These data characterize the various forms of endurance needed for competitions.

"The special (specific) endurance of an athlete is his capacity to perform a specific task as efficiently as is required by his particular event." [33]

In this the specific endurance capacity in middle- and long-distance races is not only characterized by the ability of a runner to cover the race distance at a relatively high and even average speed, but also to attain in intermediate spurts and final spurts over the respective sections speeds within the scope of his personal best performance. This implies that in a competition e.g.

– the 800-m runner aiming at 1:46 min. = 7.56 m/s must master a range of speeds over 200 m of up to approximately 8.50 m/s = 23.5 sec.

– the 1,500-m runner with a personal best result of 3:36 min. = 6.94 m/s must master a range of speeds over

31   D. Harre and others "Principles of Sports Training" (Translation from the German), Sportverlag, Berlin 1982.

32   H. Pfeifer "Zur Trainierbarkeit der Ausdauerfähigkeiten im Prozeß der körperlichen Vervollkommnung", in "Theorie und Praxis der Körperkultur", Sportverlag, Berlin 1968, Annex.

33   Gandelsmann/Nabatnikova/Matveyer/Farfel "Biologische und methodische Aspekte der Ausdauer" (Biological and Methodic Aspects of Endurance), in "Theorie und Praxis der Körperkultur", Moscow, Nr. 8/1972.

Table 22   Amount and Objectives of the Training in the Build-up Phase for Middle- and Long-Distance Races

Training month	Total weekly running km		General endurance per month %		Special endurance per month %		Maximum speed per month %	
	Middle-Dist.	Long-Dist.	Middle-Dist.	Long-Dist.	Middle-Dist.	Long-Dist.	Middle-Dist.	Long-Dist.
Preparatory Period								
November	60	80	100	100	–	–	–	–
December	80	100	100	100	–	–	–	–
January	100	130	100	100	–	–	–	–
February	100	130	99	100	–	–	–	–
March	120	150	94	100	5	–	0.5–1	–
April	100	130	94	95	5	5	0.5–1	–
Competitive Period								
May	60	80	88	90	10	10	1–2	–
June	40	60	83	95	15	15	1–2	–
July	30–50	40–80	85	85/90	15	10/15		
August	30–50	40–80	78–88	95–90	10–20	10–15	1–2	–

Mean values per week, respectively per month. Percentages refer to kilometres run.

200 m of up to approximately 8.33 m/s = 24.0 s.

– the 5,000-m runner with a personal best result of 13:20 min. = 6.25 m/s must master a range of speeds over 1,000 m of approximately 6.90 m/s = 2:25 min.

Because of the variable demands placed on the endurance required in competition and because of the wide range of pace it is evident that there must exist correlations between the different forms of the endurance for competition and that moreover correlations must exist also with other physical factors (speed, endurance etc.).

There are particularly close relations between the development of endurance for a particular distance race and the corresponding races over the nearest, shorter and longer distances. They ex-plain the dependence of the runner's proficiency over his special distance on his racing results in the over- and under-distance range.

It has been shown by investigations that long-term endurance has the greatest effect on all other aspects of the endurance in competition (VOLKOV, ZIMKIN, ASTRAND, MIES and others). They show that the level of short-duration and of medium-duration endurance is largely influenced by the level of long-duration endurance work. The explanation is that the level of the long-duration endurance work is in the main a function of the aerobic endurance capacity; in other words, the energy required for a sustained effort is supplied under aerobic conditions, i.e. sufficient oxygen is available for the absorption of nutrients. By training his capacity to bear a stress during a long period of time in the low, medium and high intensity range, the athlete must improve his maximum oxygen intake (the level of his aerobic endurance capacity), which is the basis of his particular proficiency. In all the endurance events (running, swimming, long-distance skiing etc.) athletes develop their basic endurance by specialized training with long-duration endurance stress. The various forms of continuous running are the most important training for runners. The development of basic endurance is assured by long-duration stress in the continuous running at medium speed undertaken under "steady state" conditions. The steady state is characterized by the balance between the organic functions of the human body and requires the economic functioning of the cardio-vascular circulatory and respiratory systems, the metabolism and a proper balance between oxygen intake and oxygen requirements. The level of the various aspects of endurance training for competition is not only determined by these relationships but affects also the level of the general endurance (i.e. not directed to a special event endurance).

"The general (non-specific) endurance of an athlete is reflected in his capacity to do physical work for a long period of time, involving many muscle groups of his body and having an indirect positive effect on his special discipline." (GANDELSMANN, NABATNIKOVA, MATVEYEV, FARFEL, 1972)

The general endurance for particular events of a runner can be improved by participation in sports outside his special event (swimming, skiing etc.) as part of developing endurance training.

The carry-over effect of general stamina training on the other forms of running depends on the kind of stress chosen for this purpose. This stress should be commensurate with or similar to the requirements for competition. The carry-over effect is based on the great versatility of the human organism, since the activity of the vegetative system is of relatively low specificity (ZIMKIN, 1956, MOTYLYANSKAYA and others, 1958, ZATZIORSKI, 1961). Training means which are not specialized for a particular sport or event pertain to the allround development of the runner's muscles, while the potential of his whole body is developed similarly.

● Speed

The quality of middle- and long-distance running is also influenced by the runners's speed level. One generally speaks of the basic speed level of a runner by indicating the maximum possible speed he achieves over a distance ranging between 30 to 80 m. But for the sake of simplicity the basic speed of a middle- and long-distance runner is also determined by his performance on the 100-m distance. According to OZOLIN (1959) it is useful for a middle- and long-distance runner to have a so-called speed reserve. The greater the speed reserve of a runner as compared to an opponent of the same qualities of endurance is, the greater his chance of succeeding in the final sprint. The speed reserve (SR) characterizes the difference between the athlete's average over the control distance (i.e. 100 m of the total distance) and his personal best performance over the same distance. According to OZOLIN the following formula holds:

Table 23

Race Distance	Amount of Basic Endurance Training	Maximum Amount of Special Endurance Training	
		Beginners grade III and II	Athletes with several years of training, grade I
800 m/1,500 m	8–30 km	3.0– 4.5 km	4.5– 6.0 km
800-m Women	6–15 km	2.4– 3.2 km	3.2– 4.0 km
3,000-m Steeplechase		4.5– 6.0 km	5.0– 8.0 km
5,000 m	10–40 km	5.0– 7.5 km	7.5–10.0 km
10,000 m		7.5–10.0 km	7.5–12.0 km

Figures based on one training unit in the phase of greatest load during preparatory period.

$$SR = \frac{t_d}{n} - t_{cd}$$

The speed reserve of an 800-m runner is calculated as follows:
– the time required for the total distance (t_d)
Example: 1:46 min. = 106 s
– the personal best performance over 100 m (t_{ed})
Example: 10.8 s
– the quotient n = length of race divided by check distance
Example: 800 m : 100 m = 8

$$SR = \frac{106\,s}{8} - 10.8\,s = 13.2\,s - 10.8\,s$$

$$= 2.4\,s$$

If another 800-m runner, due to his superior endurance capacity runs 1:46.0 with a personal best time of 11.5 s over 100 m, his speed reserve (SR) will only be 1.7 s.
The different values of SR can be explained as follows:
1. The runner with the greater SR has a greater chance of winning with the final spurt against the runner with equal endurance.
2. Since it is easier to improve endurance than speed, the runner with the greater SR has a greater potential.
3. In training beginners the emphasis must be on the development of a high level of basic speed.
The importance of a high level of basic speed for a long-distance runner is illustrated by the following example of calculating the SR.

Runner A: t_d = 5,000 m in 13:20 min. – 800 s
t_{ed} = 100 m in 11.8 s
n – 5,000 : 100 = 50

$$SR = \frac{800\,s}{50} - 11.8\,s = 16\,s - 11.8\,s$$

$$= 4.2\,s$$

Runner B: t_d = 5,000 m in 15:00 min. = 900 s
t_{ed} = 100 m in 11,8 s

$$SR = \frac{900\,s}{50} - 11.8\,s = 18\,s - 11.8\,s$$

$$= 6,2\,s$$

Runner C: t_d = 5,000 m in 15:00 min. = 900 s
t_{ed} = 100 m in 13.8 s

$$SR = \frac{900\,s}{50} - 13.8\,s = 18\,s - 13.8\,s$$

$$= 4.2\,s$$

The following conclusions can be drawn from the values for SR of runners A, B and C.

1. The absolute SR value does not give any clue as to the performance capacity over the particular race distance.

2. A greater SR value at equal performance over the 5,000-m competition distance reveals reserves for improving the endurance capacity.

3. A man with a higher SR has better chances of winning in a final spurt against an opponent with a similar time to his credit.

4. A low SR in conjunction with a poor competition result is the sign of a relatively high endurance level, but does not imply the chance of a marked improvement in performance if the runner is not capable of developing his basic speed (compare example C).

A high level of basic speed over 100 m is important for the long-distance runner for the very reason that victory or defeat are more and more decided over the last 400 metres. The best runners in the world cover the last lap in 52.5 to 56 sec. Runners with inferior basic speed over 100 m (say 13.0 s) can at best achieve 54.0 s over 400 m. So, in spite of a good endurance, their performance over the long distance is limited from the outset.

● Strength

Of the different qualities of strength it is explosive force and endurance which mainly determine performance over middle and long distances. Strength endurance is an integral part of the quantities of endurance specifically required for competition. Special strength endurance allied to speed ensures an optimal ratio between stride length and stride frequency for a given running speed. Special strength endurance is brought about by exercises developing the group of muscles used in the running action. The best methods for reaching this goal are those of extensive and intensive interval work. Special training means are exercises such as hopping and jumping runs, alternating jumps ets. In developing strength endurance through overall conditioning, exercises employed within the general build-up programme based on the duration method, the methods of extensive and intensive interval work, it is circuit training that appears particularly well-suited to the development of muscular strength required by the runner, because exercises can be organized in such a way that the respective groups of muscles are stressed alternately, while the cardio-vascular and respiratory systems, as well as metabolism, are submitted to a constant stress.

● Age, height and body weight

From analyses of data obtained at the 1972 Olympics on age, height and body weight of competitors, interesting conclusions have been derived. Data on the average age reveal that it increases in step with the distance or, in other words, the longer the racing distance, the higher the average age of performers. When looking at the minimum and maximum values, we find that top performances in middle- and long-distance races, as well as in race walking, are registered by relatively young sportsmen (between 20 and 23), but also by relatively old athletes. Although

164

Table 24   Mean Values of Age, Height and Weight of the 8 Best Performers at the Olympic Games 1972

	Age			Height			Body Weight		
	x̄	min.	max.	x̄	min.	max.	x̄	min.	max.
Men									
800 m	23.8	22	27	178	173	183	66.4	64	72
1,500 m	24.2	20	32	180	175	188	66.7	63	69
3,000-m Steeplechase	25.5	21	32	177	170	186	68	62	73
5,000 m	26.4	21	34	177	171	184	61.1	56	63
10,000 m	26.0	23	32	173	165	183	59.4	54	66
Marathon	32.1	23	40	173	165	183	58.7	53	64
20-km Walking	31.1	20	36	181	177	187	71.1	62	78
Women									
800 m	24.7	20	31	168	157	175	56	51	59
1,500 m	27	19	29	167	165	172	54	52	58

average values of the height showed that shorter men are most frequently found in longer race distances, the erratic values indicate that taller athletes are also among the best international long-distance and marathon runners.

Measures of the height should by all means be seen in relation to the body weight. It will then become evident that the runners will be the lighter the longer the race distance is. On the one hand this indicates the importance of a

Table 25   Training for Particular Distances

Race Distance	Under-Distance	Intensity	Over-Distance	Intensity
800 m	200/400/500/600/700 m	medium to high	1,000/1,200/1,500/1,600/2,000/3,000 m 8–18 km	medium to high low/medium/high
1,500 m	400/500/600/800 m 1,000/1,200 m	low/medium/high high	2,000/3,000 m 8–18 km	medium/high low/medium/high
5,000 m	1,000/1,500/1,600/2,000/3,000 m	medium till high	8–10–12–15–16–18–20 km	low/medium/high
10,000 m	1,000/1,500/1,600/2,000/3,000/5,000/7,500 m	medium till high	10–12–15–16–18–20–25–30 km	low/medium/high
Marathon	1,000/2,000/3,000/5,000/7,500/10,000 m	medium till high	50–60 km	low/medium
			Continuous runs: 10–15–16–18–20–25–30 km	low/medium/high

favourable weight-strength ratio but on the other hand shows that running performances depend mainly on the function of potentials and not so much on strength produced by actual muscle volume. The higher average values for the body weight of 3,000-m steeplechasers and middle-distance runners by comparison with long-distance runners prove the influence of muscular strength on the performance in these particular events.

3.3.5.2. Means for Developing Physical Properties of Middle- and Long-Distance Runners

The physical attributes of the middle- and long-distance runners are developed by general training or specific for competition means in accordance with the objectives of a given training session. Depending on the chosen racing distance, running speed, number of runs, recovery intervals between repetitions and activities during intervals, the particular training aims to develop a distinct component of the endurance. More particularity amog special training means all kinds of continuous runs, high-speed runs, pace-changing runs etc., over the usual under- and over-distance range depending on the length of the special distance (Table 25).

The physiological, educational and psychological effects of special training means can also be enhanced by using the right training methods. [34]

● Basic endurance

For the improvement of basic endur-

34 Training methods outlined in Section 2.7.2. are specified in detail for middle- and long-distance training.

ance, the following training is suggested: long-duration endurance stress by continuous runs or a great deal of tempo-running schedules using the extended interval method.

Duration method

Stimulus intensity: The stimulus intensity coincides with the average running speed in m/s in a continuous run over the complete distance. It is derived from the maximum possible speed over a controlled or race distance (5, 10, 15, 20, 42.2 km). Continuous runs are trained at low, medium and high speed in relation to the maximum possible speed. For the stimulus intensity we give three grades of relative intensity:

90–100 per cent = high
80– 90 per cent = medium
under 80 per cent = low

For developing basic endurance continuous runs at medium speed are particularly beneficial.

Continuous intensive running in relation to a particular distance improves long-duration endurance (I, II, III) (see Table 21) as a component of the endurance for a particular racing distance; this applies particularly to long-distance runners.

Stimulus volume. The stimulus volume in continuous runs is always related to the entire distance of the continuous run. It depends directly on the stimulus intensity, or on the running velocity resp. In general, the rule applies that the shorter the distance, the faster the run and vice versa. This rule is valid for continuous runs at all levels of relative intensity. The longest distances should be covered in the medium speed range. This is the best approach for im-

166

proving basic endurance. Long continuous runs at medium speed should therefore be given priority in training sessions. The length of training distances in continuous runs depends on the age, years of training, sex, fitness and special distance (see Table 25, column: over-distance, and Table 23 column of basic endurance training) of the particular athlete.

For possible forms of stress increase in work-rate see, Table 8, Variants 10–14.

Stimulus density: All forms of continuous runs act on the organism as an uninterrupted stress stimulus. This applies also to runs with significant changes in pace. Although the athlete recovers and restores his strength by running at a slower pace, he must keep his speed constant.

Stimulus duration: The stimulus duration is a crucial factor in the effect of continuous runs. Such runs must, invariably, represent long-duration endurance stress. How long a stimulus is applied depends on the age, training background, sex, fitness and special distance of the athlete. Stimulus duration and stimulus volume complement one another directly. The duration of a stimulus, measured in minutes or hours, certainly plays the dominant role in determining the stress for a beginner or the time for resuming the training after a break. The stimulus duration in a continuous run may therefore vary greatly and extend from about 5 minutes to 5 hours. Experience shows that continuous runs alternating between 30, 60 and 90 minutes at varying speed, may be advocated for experienced runners. Having managed these targets several times at medium speed and recorded the distances covered, the athlete will be guided by known distances in the next training phase (stimulus volume) and can thereby check the required running time (stimulus duration).

Training means:

1. Steady runs through woods and parkland, on roads and cross-country (flat and hilly terrain, at a relatively even low, medium and high speed);

2. Continuous runs—starting at a relatively slow pace, accelerating gradually and finishing strongly.

3. Continuous runs—with fast starting and finishing sections and at an easy pace in the middle section.

4. Continuous runs with pace acceleration uphill and medium to all-out effort.

5. Continuous runs—with fixed alternation between low and medium speed; low and high speed, medium and high speed over middle and long distances.

6. Fartlek—running an optional total distance with easy and fast sections; with fixed total distance and number of pace accelerations over certain sections, but optional speed pattern and length of intermediate sections at reduced speed.

7. Cross-country identical with continuous running but through difficult, changing terrain, mainly at an average high speed. Cross-country runs require will-power. Variations under foot and changes in the level of the land develop strength endurance.

Method of extended interval work

Basic endurance work with the character of a long-duration endurance workload can also be developed and improved by short-, middle- and long-distance races using extensive interval work. Load characteristics can be defined as follows:

Stimulus intensity: Runs at about 60 to 85 per cent of the maximum possible speed over the race distance. The stimulus intensity is calculated as follows:

Best performance over 400 m = 50 s = 100 per cent.

Speed runs over 400 m at 70 per cent:

$$100\% = 50\,s \quad 70\% = x\,s$$

$$\frac{50 \cdot 100}{70} = \frac{5\,000}{70} = 71.4\,s$$

The calculated time is the measure of the intensity of stimulus in each individual run and may, in this programme, vary naturally between 70 and 73 seconds.

Stimulus volume: With the aim of developing basic endurance at a higher speed level than can be applied in continuous runs, a great number of repetitions will be required. In relation to the chosen training distance the following schedules for experienced runners are in current use (Table 26).

Stimulus density: The interval has the real character of an "adequate interval". In accordance with the distance and training conditions it can vary between 30 seconds up to about 5 minutes, taken up by jogging over 100 to 1,000 m. The rule here is that the fitter the athlete the shorter should be the race run and the shorter the interval.

Stimulus duration: The speed work is interspersed with jogging. This creates the so-called interval continuous run; it is in fact very long when the runs at speed and jogging distances are added, although the stimulus duration in the individual run is relatively short.

Training means:

1. Pace runs, 100–1,000 m as interval continuous running.

– alone, in a group or with a partner, with definite tasks.

Examples: at each repetition another runner sets the pace;

– upon a given signal or on his own decision the last runner in a file moves up to a given position (1st, 2nd or 3rd position) etc.

2. Handicap runs–the handicaps should not be over-exacting, i.e. they should allow the athlete to keep within the proper speed range.

● Long-duration endurance work (I, II and III)

If the training target in a given session consists in developing long-duration endurance for a particular racing distance, the following training taken in conjunction with the respective methods are recommended:

Methods of continuous work

– Long-duration endurance III = 90 min. continuous run–at an even rate on relatively flat ground–at high speed– over 20 to 50 km;

– Long-duration endurance II = about 30 to 90 minutes.

1. Continuous run at relatively constant high speed over flat and hilly terrain (8 to 20 km);

Table 26

Distance	Number of Runs	Recovery Interval	Activities during Interval
200 m	20–40	30– 90 sec.	Jogging
400 m	20–40	60– 90 sec.	Jogging
800 m	10–20	60–120 sec.	Jogging
1,000 m	8–12	120–300 sec.	Jogging

2. Continuous run—with strong finish, over distances of 12 to 18 km;

3. Continuous run, with changing speeds—total distance 10 to 15 km, interspersed with 3 to 5 pace runs.

– Long-duration endurance I = 8 to 30 minutes.

Continuous run—at top speed over flat and hilly terrain (cross-country runs, competitive runs over 5 to 10 km).

Repetition work

High-speed races over 3,000, 5,000, 7,500, 10,000 m at more than 90 per cent of the maximum possible speed. These runs are usually employed only as test- or timed runs and, with the exception of the 3,000-m race, only once in a training session.

● Medium-duration endurance

The following training programme can and must be applied for the improvement of medium-duration endurance by the methods of extensive and intensive interval work and repetition work (Table 27). The examples are intended for experienced athletes of grades I/ II.

Extensive interval work

Stimulus intensity: about 80 to 85 per cent.

Stimulus volume: the total volume of the training programme consists of 6 to 16 km runs depending on the competition distance (typical programmes see Table 27).

Stimulus density: The recovery interval between the various runs is shorter than the running time, but it is the runner's pulse rate that decides the length of the rest. Pulse checks before every new run: not more than approx. 120 to 130 beats/min.

Stimulus duration: With regard to the duration, the length of the training distances should be within the range of medium-duration endurance. The physiological, educational and psychological effect of each single run develops the requirements of the medium-duration endurance load, but the overall programme has the character of a long-duration load.

Training Means:

Tempo runs—alone or in groups of athletes of a similar standard.

Intensive interval work

Stimulus intensity: approximately 85 to 90 per cent.

Stimulus volume: The distance in training should be within the range of medium-duration endurance. A middle-distance runner should therefore run

Table 27

Distance	Number of Runs	Recovery Interval (Recovery between Series)	Activities during Interval
800 m	8–12	90–120 sec.	Jogging/Walking
	(in series 2–3 × 4)	(3–5 min.)	Jogging/Walking
1,000 m	8–12	90–180 sec.	Jogging/Walking
	(in series 2–3 × 4)	(4–6 min.)	Jogging/Walking
2,000 m	6–8	120–180 sec.	Walking/Jogging
	(in series 2 × 3–4)	(5–10 min.)	Jogging/Walking

600, 800, 1,000 and 1,200 m, while long-distance runners will usually prefer distances of 1,000 to 2,000 m. The entire training programme of a middle-distance runner is about 3 to 6 km, that of the long-distance man about 5 to 12 km (see Table 28).

Repetition work

Medium-duration endurance is developed by repetition in training programmes approaching competition standards. The distances can also be in the under- or over-distance range. Runs under-distance should be at the racing speed of the special distance or faster. Over-distance runs should be performed with a reduction in speed typical of the next longer competition distance and permit 1 to 3 runs. Long-distance runners only run in the under-distance range (1,000, 2,000 and 3,000 m).
Stimulus intensity: Over 90 to 100 per cent of the maximum possible speed.
Stimulus volume: For middle-distance runners the distances of the various runs are $2/3$ to $1^1/_2$, for long-distance runners $1/_{10}$, $1/_5$ or $1/_3$ of the race distance (for typical schedules see Table 29).

Stimulus density: The length of recovery intervals depends on the target set by the training programme. If emphasis is on maintaining the planned high speed, cuts can be made in the planned total volume and the recovery interval should be of optimal length. The runner decides himself when he wishes to start the next run.
Stimulus duration: The length of the training distance together with the stimulus intensity produces a work load for a time which should lie within the range of the medium-duration endurance. If the potential of repetitions in this high intensity range is fully utilized, the overall duration of the programme will positively influence the long-duration capacity.

Training means

1. High-speed runs—alone or in groups of a similar standard—with and without tasks set by the trainer;
2. Handicap runs—with properly set handicaps and tasks set by the trainer;
3. Speed-changing runs—alone or in groups of the same standard—with and without tactical objectives—accelera-

Table 28

Distance	Number of Runs	Recovery Interval (Recovery between Series)	Activities during Interval
600 m	4–6	2–5 min.	Walking/Jogging
	(in series 2 × 2–3)	(5–10 min.)	Jogging/Walking
800 m	4–8	2–5 min.	Walking/Jogging
	(in series 2 × 2–4)	(5–10 min.)	Jogging/Walking
1,000 m	4–10	3–5 min.	Walking/Jogging
	(in series 2 × 2–5)	(5–10 min.)	Jogging/Walking
1,600 m	4–8	3–5 min.	Walking/Jogging
	(in series 2 × 2–4)	(5–10 min.)	Jogging/Walking
2,000 m	3–6	4–8 min.	Jogging/Walking
	(in series 2 × 3 or 3 × 2)	(5–10 min.)	Jogging/Walking

Table 29

Distance	Number of Runs	Recovery Interval	Activities during Recovery Interval
Middle-Distance Runners			
600 m	2–4	10–20 min.	Walking/Jogging
800 m	1–3	10–30 min.	Walking/Jogging
1,000 m	1–3	10–30 min.	Walking/Jogging
1,200 m	1–3	10–30 min.	Walking/Jogging
1,600 m	1–3	10–30 min.	Walking/Jogging
2,000 m	1–2	10–30 min.	Walking/Jogging
Long-Distance Runners			
1,000 m	1–3	10–20 min.	Jogging/Walking
	3–6	5–10 min.	Jogging/Walking
1,200 m	1–3	10–20 min.	Jogging/Walking
	3–6	5–10 min.	Jogging/Walking
1,600 m	1–3	10–20 min.	Jogging/Walking
	3–6	5–10 min.	Jogging/Walking
2,000 m	1–2	10–20 min.	Jogging/Walking
	3–5	5–10 min.	Jogging/Walking
3,000 m	1	–	–
	2–3	10–20 min.	Jogging/Walking

tions on oversections specified beforehand or upon an agreed signal at any time.

● Short-duration endurance

Top performances in middle-distance races are mainly determined by the level of short-duration endurance. Incentives for progress are derived from training programmes based on repetition work and intensive interval work. Since it is essential to reach in every single run the near maximum possible speed, training programmes should be arranged for groups of the same standard or for pairs at the same level. Top-class women can train together with men or with juniors. If no partner of the same standard is available, differences in performance must be levelled out in handicap runs in order to encourrage the best possible results. Such con-

tests can be used as a means of intensive training!

Intensive interval work

Stimulus intensity: 90 to 95 per cent of the maximum possible speed over the training distance.

*Stimulus volume:*The number of runs in a training session must be adapted to the planned stimulus intensity. If the runs are to be performed at 90 per cent of the best possible result, 6 to 8 runs would be adequate. If the best result (400 m) of a middle-distance runner is say 50 seconds, 55 seconds would represent 90 per cent. If the runner is to cover the 400-m speed-runs at 95 per cent of the maximum possible speed, only about 3 to 4 runs in a time of approximately 52.5 seconds would be reasonable.

Stimulus density: The rest interval between runs must be adapted to the training objectives. If the runner has to keep to a planned time, the interval is of secondary importance. But if the total volume of the programme is to be accomplished, a reduction in the planned speed can be allowed for in the last runs. Breaks of about 3 to 5 minutes are suggested.

Stimulus duration: If the training programme is carried out with a number of runs compatible with the particular intensity needed and with an interval of say 3 minutes, an improvement in the medium-duration endurance capacity may be anticipated.

Training means:

1. Runs at speed—alone or in groups of the same standard, with and without tasks set by the trainer;

2. Speed-changing runs—alone or in groups of the same standard, with accelerations over certain sections or at specified intervals of time or upon a signal given without preliminary warning;

3. Differential runs—alone or in groups of the same performance level; the target is e.g. a run over 400 m in 55 seconds. First half at 30 sec., second half at 25 sec. or vice versa;

4. Handicap runs—handicaps commensurate with the difference in performance and related to special tasks.

All runs should be started with an all-out effort (first 6 to 10 strides).

Repetition work

Training programmes based on repetition work are typical for the development of short-duration endurance of the middle-distance runner. In such a programme emphasis is on the need to attain the highest possible speed over the distances concerned. A measure of the training and fitness of the runner is his ability to keep up or even better his predicated speed even in the last run. The length of the recovery interval is therefore of secondary importance. All that counts is that the runner feels properly restored before taking up the next run.

Stimulus intensity: Speed is within the range of 95 to 97 per cent of the maximum possible speed over the various training distances. If the runner produces during training speeds in line with his previous best performances, a clear improvement in competition may be expected.

Stimulus volume: In schedules for short-duration endurance distances from 400 m up to and including 1,000 m. Depending on the distance length 1 to 2 or 2 to 3 runs should be undertaken. Schedules of 3×400 m, 3×600 m, 1 to 2×800 m, 1 to $2 \times 1,000$ m are customary for middle-distance runners and those of 1 to $3 \times 1,000$ m for long-distance runners.

Stimulus density: The rest should be of optimal duration throughout. It should be left to the runner to decide when he feels sufficiently rested for starting the next run. The rest should not be less than 10 min.

Stimulus duration: This should be within the range of short-duration endurance. The simultaneous and complex improvement of short-duration, medium-duration and speed endurance is to be expected.

Training means:

Speed runs, runs with changes in tempo, differential runs, handicap-runs—same as for intensive interval work.

Emphasis should be on the warm-up before the first run and on keeping

172

warm between runs. Specific objectives should stimulate the nervous energy of the runner. Competitions should be used as intensive training!

● Speed and sprint-speed endurance

For the development and improvement of speed endurance, the middle-distance runner must carry out a training programme which includes runs over relatively short distances (between 100 and 400 m) using repetition work and intensive interval work. Usually these training programmes are linked with the aim of developing basic speed at the same time. For this purpose the athlete will do short-distance runs after warming up, designed to develop e.g. acceleration capacity, maximum speed and sprint-speed endurance. These runs can also be used to prepare the athlete for the planned maximum speeds in runs for building up speed endurance.

Training means:
Speed and sprint-speed endurance

— Start, standing and crouch starts, run-ups from various positions over 20 to 100 m;
— acceleration runs at maximum speed, on middle and final sections, over 80 to 150 m;
— flying sprints, mixed with sections of optimal to maximal acceleration and final section in coasting over 20 to 100 m;
— high-speed runs from standing or crouch start or after some starting strides over 100 to 200 m;
— runs in a harness over 80 to 120 m;
— tug-runs with artificial traction over 80 to 120 m;
— downhill- and uphill-sprints

Speed endurance
Running at speed—runs with changes of tempo—differential runs—handicap runs—up-and downhill runs over 100—400 m.

● Strength—Strength endurance—Explosive strength

Runners require special strength in the group of muscles involved in running. Of particular importance is the push-off force from the ankle joint, requiring well developed calf muscles. Running and strength exercises are suggested for this purpose. Important for middle- and long-distance runners are knee-lift runs, running jumps and exercises for strengthening the ankle joints. Depending on whether extensive or intensive interval work is applied for these exercises, either strength endurance or explosive strength well be developed. Distances for the exercises are 20 to 50 m in 1 to 3 series, to develop explosive power. If emphasis is on the development of special strength endurance, the same exercises will be performed over distances of 50 to 60 m in series of 3 to 6 runs each or over distances in the 100 to 1,000-m range.

Jumping on the spot or slow advance, at and over obstacles are exercises of great importance. Jumps along the track, over 5 hurdles of some 70 to 90 cm height, with 1.5 to 2.5-m spacing between the hurdles, are popular. At least $5 \times 5 = 25$ jumps in 1 to 10 series can be made in one session, giving a total of 250 jumps.

Other exercises for developing strength-endurance are runs under difficult conditions, such as runs with harness-resistance (tyres, toboggans, with kettle-bell or sandbag), over sand-dunes (beach), in deep snow, running

Table 30   Weekly Schedule of Training during the Preparatory Period (Build-up Training/Middle–Distance Runners (CR = continuous run)

Day	Duration (min.)	Training Task	Training Means and Method	Distance (km, m)	Pace
Monday	60–70	A + B Basic endurance	CR through woods and parks	15	medium
	20–30	C Motor Loosening and stretching ex.	Gymnastics Acceleration runs	2–3 × 150	high
Tuesday	15	A Warm-up	CR	3	
	5	Gymnastics	Loosening and stretching exercises		
	5	Speed	Starts	3 × 30	high
			Acceleration runs	3 × 120	high
	45–60	B Basic endurance	Tempo runs (extensive) with 200-m jogging interval	20 × 200	low
	10–15	C Running-out	CR and loosening exercises	2–3	low
Wednesday	60–70	A + B Basic endurance	CR in hilly country (even pace)	15	low medium
	20–30	C Motor Loosening, Stretching	Gymnastics Gymnastics Acceleration runs	3–4 × 100	high
Thursday	30	A Warm-up	CR (even pace) Gymnastics, Running-ABC	15	low
	70	B Basic endurance	High-speed runs, extensive jogging	8–10 × 100 8–10 × 100	low
	20	C Running-out	CR Gymnastics, loosening, stretching	2	low
Friday	30	A Warm-up	CR and cross-country	3	low
	60	B General athletics	Basketball Circuit training CR and Gymnastics	5	low
	20	C Running-out			
Saturday	90	A + B Basic endurance	CR cross-country (tempo-changing runs)	15–18 × 100	low to high
		C Motor, loosening	Gymnastics, Slimming runs	3–4 × 100	high
Sunday	90	A + B + C Basic endurance	CR through woods and parks over relatively flat country (even pace)	20 × 120	medium

174

Table 31   Weekly Schedule of Training during the Competition Period (Build-up Training)

Day	Duration (min.)	Training Task	Training Means and Methods	Distance	Pace
Monday	90	A + B Basic endurance	CR through woods and parks (even pace)	10–15	medium
		Motor Loosening	Gymnastics Accelerations runs	4–6 × 100	
Tuesday	120	A Warm-up B Special strength	CR and Gymnastics Running-ABC	3–5	low
		Speed	"Wind-sprints"	3 × 100	high
		Short-duration endurance	High-speed runs Repetition method	3–4 × 400	high
		C Running-out Loosening	CR and Gymnastics	3–5	low
Wednesday	90	A + B + C Basic endurance Motor Loosening, Stretching	CR Acceleration runs Gymnastics	20 3 × 150	low
Thursday	120	A Limbering up B Speed	CR and Gymnastics High starts and run-ups	3–5 3 × 20	high
		Medium-duration endurance		3 × 40 3 × 60	
			High-speed runs Repetition method CR Gymnastics	3 × 600 3–5	
Friday	90	A + B Basic endurance	CR cross-country	15	medium
		C Motor, Loosening	Slimming runs	3 × 150	high
Saturday	45	A + B + C Preparation for Competition	CR, easy Gymnastics Acceleration runs High-speed run	3–5 3 × 100 1 × 400	low medium high
Sunday		Competition			

and jumping uphill (200 to 800 m), runs with weights (weight vest). The best way to develop general strength are exercises footed into a properly directed conditioning programme with special strength exercises and suitable gymnastic routines. Loosening and stretching exercises must be included in general conditioning schedules.

Table 33 Speed Schedules for Walking, Middle- and Long-Distance Running (according to F. Wilt)

m/s	100	200	300	400	600	800	1,000	1,200	1,500	2,000	5,000	10,000	15 km	20 km
8.70	11.5	23.0	34.5	46										
8.52	11.75	23.5	35.25	47										
8.33	12.0	24.0	36.0	48										
8.22	12.25	24.5	36.75	49	1:13.5									
8.00	12.5	25.0	37.5	50	1:15.0	1:40.0								
7.84	12.75	25.5	38.25	51	1:16.5	1:42.0								
7.69	13.0	26.0	39.0	52	1:18.0	1:44.0								
7.55	13.25	26.5	39.75	53	1:19.5	1:46.0	2:12.5							
7.41	13.5	27.0	40.5	54	1:21.0	1:48.0	2:15.0							
7.27	13.75	27.5	41.25	55	1:22.5	1:50.0	2:17.5	2:45.0						
7.14	14.0	28.0	42.0	56	1:24.0	1:52.0	2:20.0	2:48.0	3:30.0					
7.02	14.25	28.5	42.75	57	1:25.5	1:54.0	2:22.5	2:51.0	3:33.7					
6.90	14.5	29.0	43.5	58	1:27.0	1:56.0	2:25.0	2:54.0	3:37.5					
6.78	14.75	29.5	44.25	59	1:28.5	1:58.0	2:27.0	2:57.0	3:41.2	4:55.0				
6.67	15.0	30.0	45.0	60	1:30.0	2:00.0	2:30.0	3:00.0	3:45.0	5:00.0				
6.56	15.25	30.5	45.75	61	1:31.5	2:02.0	2:32.5	3:03.0	3:48.7	5:05.0				
6.45	15.5	31.0	46.5	62	1:33.0	2:04.0	2:35.0	3:06.0	3:52.5	5:10.0				
6.35	15.75	31.5	47.25	63	1:34.5	2:06.0	2:37.5	3:09.0	3:56.2	5:15.0	13:07.5			
6.25	16.0	32.0	48.0	64	1:36.0	2:08.0	2:40.0	3:12.0	4:00.0	5:20.0	13:20.0	26:40.0		
6.15	16.25	32.5	48.75	65	1:37.5	2:10.0	2:42.5	3:15.0	4:03.7	5:25.0	13:32.5	27:05.0		
6.06	16.5	33.0	49.5	66	1:39.0	2:12.0	2:45.0	3:18.0	4:07.5	5:30.0	13:45.0	27:30.0	41:15.0	55:00.0
5.97	16.75	33.5	50.25	67	1:40.5	2:14.0	2:47.5	3:21.0	4:11.2	5:35.0	13:57.5	27:55.0	41:52.0	55:50.0
5.88	17.0	34.0	51.0	68	1:42.0	2:16.0	2:50.0	3:24.0	4:15.0	5:40.0	14:10.0	28:20.0	42:30.0	56:40.0
5.80	17.25	34.5	51.75	69	1:43.5	2:18.0	2:52.5	3:27.0	4:18.7	5:45.0	14:22.5	28:45.0	43:07.0	57:30.0
5.71	17.5	35.0	52.5	70	1:45.0	2:20.0	2:55.0	3:30.0	4:22.5	5:50.0	14:35.0	29:10.0	43:45.0	58:20.0
5.56	18.0	36.0	54.0	72	1:48.0	2:24.0	3:00.0	3:36.0	4:30.0	6:00.0	15:00.0	30:00.0	45:00.0	60:00.0
5.41	18.5	37.0	55.5	74	1:51.0	2:28.0	3:05.0	3:42.0	4:37.5	6:10.0	15:25.0	30:50.0	46:15.0	61:40.0
5.26	19.0	38.0	57.0	76	1:54.0	2:32.0	3:10.0	3:48.0	4:45.0	6:20.0	15:50.0	31:40.0	47:30.0	63:20.0
5.13	19.5	39.0	58.5	78	1:57.0	2:36.0	3:15.0	3:54.0	4:52.5	6:30.0	16:15.0	32:30.0	48:45.0	65:00.0
5.00	20.0	40.0	60.0	80	2:00.0	2:40.0	3:20.0	4:00.0	5:00.0	6:40.0	16:40.0	33:20.0	50:00.0	66:40.0
4.88	20.5	41.0	61.5	82	2:03.0	2:44.0	3:25.0	4:06.0	5:07.5	6:50.0	17:05.0	34:10.0	51:15.0	68:20.0

m/s	100	200	300	400	600	800	1,000	1,200	1,500	2,000	5,000	10,000	15 km	20 km
4.76	21.0	42.0	63.0	84	2:06.0	2:48.0	3:30.0	4:12.0	5:15.0	7:00.0	17:30.0	35:00.0	52:30.0	70:00.0
4.65	21.5	43.0	64.5	86	2:09.0	2:52.0	3:35.0	4:18.0	5:22.5	7:10.0	17:55.0	35:50.0	53:45.0	71:40.0
4.55	22.0	44.0	66.0	88	2:12.0	2:56.0	3:40.0	4:24.0	5:30.0	7:20.0	18:20.0	36:40.0	55:00.0	73:20.0
4.44	22.5	45.0	67.5	90	2:15.0	3:00.0	3:45.0	4:30.0	5:37.5	7:30.0	18:45.0	37:30.0	56:15.0	75:00.0
4.35	23.0	46.0	69.0	92	2:18.0	3:04.0	3:50.0	4:36.0	5:45.0	7:40.0	19:10.0	38:20.0	57:30.0	76:40.0
4.17	24.0	48.0	72.0	96	2:24.0	3:12.0	4:00.0	4:48.0	6:00.0	8:00.0	20:00.0	40:00.0	60:00.0	80:00.0
4.00	25.0	50.0	75.0	100	2:30.0	3:20.0	4:10.0	5:00.0	6:15.0	8:20.0	20:50.0	41:40.0	62:30.0	83:20.0
3.85	26.0	52.0	78.0	104	2:36.0	3:28.0	4:20.0	5:12.0	6:30.0	8:40.0	21:40.0	43:20.0	65:00.0	86:40.0
3.70	27.0	54.0	81.0	108	2:42.0	3:36.0	4:30.0	5:24.0	6:45.0	9:00.0	22:30.0	45:00.0	67:30.0	90:00.0
3.57	28.0	–	–	1:52	–	3:44.0	4:40.0	5:36.0	7:00.0	9:20.0	23:20.0	46:40.0	70:00.0	93:20.0
3.45	29.0	–	–	1:56	–	3:52.0	4:50.0	5:48.0	7:15.0	9:40.0	24:10.0	48:20.0	72:30.0	96:40.0
3.33	30.0	–	–	2:00	–	4:00.0	5:00.0	6:00.0	7:30.0	10:00.0	25:00.0	50:00.0	75:00.0	100:00.0
3.23	31.0	–	–	2:04	–	4:08.0	5:10.0	6:12.0	7:45.0	10:20.0	25:50.0	51:40.0	77:30.0	103:20.0
3.12	32.0	–	–	2:08	–	4:16.0	5:20.0	6:24.0	8:00.0	10:40.0	26:40.0	53:20.0	80:00.0	106:40.0
3.03	33.0	–	–	2:12	–	4:24.0	5:30.0	–	–	11:00.0	27:30.0	55:00.0	82:30.0	110:00.0
2.94	34.0	–	–	2:16	–	4:32.0	5:40.0	–	–	11:20.0	28:20.0	56:40.0	85:00.0	113:20.0
2.86	35.0	–	–	2:20	–	4:40.0	5:50.0	–	–	11:40.0	29:10.0	58:20.0	87:30.0	116:40.0
2.78	36.0	–	–	2:24	–	4:48.0	6:00.0	–	–	12:00.0	30:00.0	60:00.0	90:00.0	120:00.0
2.70	37.0	–	–	2:28	–	4:56.0	6:10.0	–	–	12:20.0	30:50.0	61:40.0	92:30.0	123:20.0
2.63	38.0	–	–	–	–	–	6:20.0	–	–	12:40.0	31:40.0	63:20.0	95:00.0	126:40.0
2.56	39.0	–	–	–	–	–	6:30.0	–	–	13:00.0	32:30.0	65:00.0	97:30.0	130:00.0
2.50	40.0	–	–	–	–	–	6:40.0	–	–	13:20.0	33:20.0	66:40.0	100:00.0	133:20.0

Table 32 Weekly Schedule of Training during the Preparatory Period (Build-up Training—Distance Runner)

Day	Duration (min.)	Training Task	Training Means and Methods	Distance (km, m)	Pace
Monday	90	Basic endurance Motor Loosening	CR cross-country Gymnastics Acceleration runs	15 3—4 × 150	high
Tuesday	100	Basic endurance Loosening Stretching	CR through parks and along roads	20	medium
Wednesday	120	Basic endurance Stretching	CR through woods, parks and along roads Gymnastics	25	low medium
Thursday	120	Speed Strength endurance Basic endurance	CR Gymnastics Running-ABC Acceleration runs Slimming runs CR over hilly country	3—5 3 × 100 15	 low high
Friday	90	Basic endurance Loosening Stretching	CR with speed changes (flat country) Gymnastics	15	low medium
Saturday	100	Basic endurance Motor Loosening	CR cross-country Gymnastics Acceleration runs	20 3 × 150	medium
Sunday	120—130	Basic endurance	CR through parks, along roads (flat) Gymnastics	30	low

● General endurance

General endurance is developed by training methods which are not peculiar to running in relation to methods developing endurance. An important role in this take long-duration, medium-duration and short-duration weight workouts in circuit schedules, but also swimming, skiing and cycling, as well as games and light-hearted exercises. When dealing with novices such training methods should be applied in a wide variety of ways for the build-up of endurance. They should not overtax young sportsmen, and yet develop the capacity of the body in proportion to the demands placed on a specific form of endurance in a similar or the same way. They also render the training process more interesting and enjoyable. For more advanced athletes training methods which are not specifically concerned with running should

178

Table 34   Weekly Schedule of Training during the Competition Period in the Build-up Training (Long-Distance Runners)

Day	Duration (min.)	Training Task	Training Means and Method	Distance (km, m)	Pace
Monday	120	Basic endurance Loosening	CR through woods and parks, along roads (flat terrain)	20	medium
		Strength endurance	Gymnastics Running-ABC		
Tuesday	120	Basic endurance Motor	CR on flat terrain Gymnastics	3–5	low
			Acceleration runs	3 × 150	low
			High-speed runs (extens.)	20 × 400	low
			Running-out	3–5	
Wednesday	120	Basic endurance	CR on flat terrain	3–5	low/ medium
		Motor	Gymnastics		
		Loosening	Slimming runs	3 × 100	
Thursday	90 120	Basic endurance Medium-duration endurance	CR over flat terrain Running-in	3–5	low
			Gymnastics		
			Acceleration runs	3 × 150	high
			High-speed runs/ Repetition method	3 × 1,000	high
			Running-out	3–5	
Friday	90	Basic endurance Motor	CR on flat terrain Gymnastics Running-ABC	15	medium/ low
		Loosening	Acceleration runs	3 × 100	
			High-speed runs	1 × 400	
Saturday	45	Preparation for competition	CR through woods and parks Gymnastics	8–10	low
			Acceleration runs	3–4 × 150	
Sunday		Competition		5,000 or 10,000	high

be included in programmes for stabilizing general condition or for balancing high specific stress. All this is based on the condition that young athletes have received a good allround training in various sports events in conditioning or basic training or in compulsory sport at school and have acquired the techniques involved.

Introductory explanation concerning the speed schedules (Table 33)

The table gives intermediate times to be recorded in order to achieve a given performance over particular distances.

Example: if an intermediate time of 66 seconds is recorded over 400 m, running 4:07.5 at an easy pace on 1,500 m and 13:45 on 5,000 m are longer distance equivalents. The schedule can also be used for setting up schedules of planned competition performances and for assessing the average speed of continuous-run and pace-run workloads.

3.4.   The Hurdle Races

Every hurdle race is based on certain conditions laid down in the rules of the various Track and Field Associations and to which a hurdler must adhere (Table 35).

The 100-m hurdles for women, the 110-m and the 400-m hurdles for men are Olympic events. Their rules are fixed by the International Amateur Athletics Federation (IAAF), whereas the conditions for children and juniors depend on the individual countries.

3.4.1.   Technique

3.4.1.1.   The 110-m hurdles

The 110-m hurdle race for men is technically the most difficult. This technique will therefore be treated in the first place in full detail, while particulars of the 100-m and 400-m hurdles will be dealt with later. The track sections into which the race may be conveniently divided are: the start, the approach to the first hurdle, hurdle clearance, running between the hurdles and the finishing sprint to the tape. These sections must be technically mastered, if the sprinting abilities of a hurdler are to become fully realized.

● The start and the approach to the first hurdle

The hurdler has to cover a distance of 13.72 m (= 15 yards) for the first hurdle. In this rather short distance he must develop a fairly high speed. The initial speed at the first hurdle is of great importance for the final performance, since no essential speed acceleration is achieved between the hurdles.

The starting position and the take-off are not very different from that of the sprinter. The hurdler should, however, make it a principle to place his trailing foot on the front block, so that, having performed 8 strides, he can clear the hurdle. In order to develop high speed in the approach to the first hurdle, he must not only be an excellent sprinter but also keep a properly balanced stride. Most hurdlers take 8 strides to arrive 2 m short of the first hurdle. The stride length is progressively increased up to the last stride before clearance, which will be shorter than the previous one.

Taller men with good sprinting skills will find that the approach distance of 13.72 m is too short for 8 strides and that they achieve a better momentum by using only 7 strides. Whether a hurdler should approach the first hurdle with 7 or 8 strides can be determined

180

Table 35   Hurdles and Distances according to the Competition Regulations of the Athletics Association of the GDR (DVfL der DDR)

Age group	Distance (m)	Height of Hurdle (cm)	Distance to 1st Hurdle	Distance between Hurdles (m)	Distance from Final Hurdle to Finish (m)	Number of Hurdles
Male						
8/9	30	40.0	6.00	6.00	6.00	4
10	60	76.2	11.50	7.00	13.00	6
11	60	76.2	11.50	7.50	11.00	6
12	60	76.2	11.50	8.00	8.50	6
13	100	84.0	13.00	8.50	10.50	10
14	110	91.4	13.72	8.70	17.98	10
15	110	91.4	13.72	8.90	16.18	10
16/17	110	100.0	13.72	9.14	14.02	10
Men	110	106.7	13.72	9.14	14.02	10
15	300	91.4	42.00	33.00	27.00	8
16/17, Men	400	91.4	45.00	35.00	40.00	10
Female						
8/9	30	40.0	6.00	6.00	6.00	4
10	60	76.2	11.50	7.00	13.50	6
11	60	76.2	11.50	7.50	11.00	6
12	60	76.2	11.50	7.50	11.00	6
13	80	76.2	12.00	8.00	12.00	8
14	100	76.2	13.00	8.50	10.50	10
15	100	76.2	13.00	8.50	10.50	10
16/17	100	84.0	13.00	8.50	10.50	10
Women	100	84.0	13.00	8.50	10.50	10
Women	400	76.2	45.00	35.00	40.00	10

by recording times at the first, second and third hurdle. If the number of strides to the first hurdle is changed, the crouch-start technique must be adjusted accordingly. In the seven-stride approach the leading foot is placed on the front block.

During the approach the hurdler straightens up his body, viz. after the first 6 to 10 m he adopts his normal sprinting position to be ready in time for a good hurdle clearance. This is mainly due to the hurdler's aim of focusing his eyes on the hurdle ahead at an early stage, since this helps him to adopt the proper stride rhythm. Most hurdlers look up at the first hurdle as early as after the first or second stride.

● The clearance stride

Each hurdle must be cleared quickly and safely. The first prerequisite is keeping the proper distance for the so-called "tackling" of the hurdle. This distance should always be sufficiently long (generally 1.90 to 2.20 m) to allow the leading leg to sweep forward and upward in a straight line. Too short a distance for the take-off results in most cases in a "jump" over the hurdle. If, on the other hand, the distance is too long, the danger arises of striking or knocking down the hurdle bar. The stride across the hurdle must follow smoothly the ordinary sprinting strides. This requires a good training level and a really positive approach to the hurdle.

The component movements during hurdle clearance will be treated separately for a clearer understanding.

● The action of the leading leg

The complete action consists of a quick forward and upward thrust of the leading leg in the direction of the hurdle edge and the active downward pressing of the thigh immediately after clearance for the landing. The action of the leading leg introduces the sequence of movements much as in the ordinary running stride. In order to get over the hurdle, however, a more vigorous upward drive of the thigh and the lower leg are necessary. Therefore the thigh goes up beyond the horizontal. In this phase the lower leg points downward almost vertically and completes its drive by being projected vigorously towards the edge of the hurdle (Fig. 27/ Pos. 1—4).

This driving force results in a complete

but brief stretching at the knee joint before the foot crosses the hurdle. The downward movement of the leg sets in immediately afterwards. For this action the lead leg is slightly flexed at the knee joint, thus ensuring a *resilient impact* of the leading foot to the track beyond the hurdle. By pressing the thigh down and backward, the downward movement can be quickened. An active landing ensures the best get-away stride.

Variant of the leading leg action. With many hurdlers the leading leg is not fully stretched after the initial swing, but bent at the knee joint. If this flexion is only slight, no technical disadvantage will ensue. A strong flexion, however, impedes a low forward lean, so that the trajectory of the centre of gravity cannot take the most economic path over the hurdle. The excessive flexion is often caused by a too slow forward swing of the shank or by an insufficient flexibility at the hip joints.

● The action of the trailing leg

For a rational clearance of the hurdle, the trailing leg must be stretched away from the body when clearing the hurdle. This movement, if correctly performed, requires good mobility of the hip. The main function of the trailing leg consists in performing the get-away

Fig. 27

stride without unnecessary delay after clearance.

The sequence of the athlete's movements should be as follows: after a vigorous push-off from the ground follows a phase of relaxation for the take-off leg, i.e. the lower leg swings slightly upward in a relaxed manner. An active forward movement of the thigh should begin only when the foot of the leading leg has reached the edge of the hurdle. The proper timing of the relaxation phase is decisive for the coordination of the leg movements.

The vigorous thrust of the leading leg forward and upward and the initial lagging behind of the trailing leg in the relaxation phase ensures the accomplishment of a full extension of both legs (Fig. 27, Pos. 3 and 4). This phase brings about an expansion, mainly of the pelvic muscles, and a rapid pull-through of the trailing leg. The lateral bending of the thigh and the foot begins during the relaxation phase and ends just in front of the edge of the hurdle. The thigh is then bent away from the pelvis to almost a right angle and the lower leg points horizontally backwards. The next movement leads forward over the hurdle with a flat, slightly upward turned thigh (Fig. 27/ Pos. 6–10).

At the moment of landing of the leading leg, the trailing movement is not yet fully completed, since the thigh and the lower trailing leg are still laterally bent away from the body, viz. not yet in the running direction. In this phase the position of the thighs is approximately horizontal. The lower leg will go forward for the first stride after the hurdle, when the knee points in the running direction.

As already mentioned, the relaxation phase is extremely important for a good coordination of the leg movements. This phase is part and parcel of every running stride, only that it is somewhat longer in the hurdle stride. Therefore hurdles with an inadequately developed feel for the proper movement cannot always seize the right moment for the pull-through of the leg. If this movement is started too early, the trailing leg comes forward too quickly into the running direction, causing a "dead phase", meaning that the trailing leg must brake or interrupt the forward drive, because ther leading foot has not yet touched the ground. A delayed pull-through of the leg often leads to the striking or knocking down of the hurdle with the knee or the ankle.

● The action of the arms

The usual movements during running are also executed during hurdle clearance, with the sole difference that in the hurdle stride the arms perform additional functions. They must, for instance, contribute in a greater degree to maintaining body balance. The arm on the opposite side of the leading leg must, additionally, aid the realization of a proper forward lean of the trunk.

If during the approach to the hurdle the shank of the leading leg is thrust forward, the opposite arm comes forward simultaneously. It is suggested that the hand be brought into the proximity of the foot, thus assisting the forward lean of the trunk. When the trailing leg comes forward, the trailing arm swings backward to counterbalance this movement. It is either almost stretched (as in the backward arm movement of a breast-stroke swimmer) or flexed at the elbow, similar to the crawling motion in the water. It does not matter in which way the backward movement is performed, as long as the shoulder axis remains frontal and the arm is not swept backward too strongly. After landing, the arms give an immediate effective support to the get-away stride.

During the hurdle stride the leading arm is almost passive. It remains strongly flexed alongside or slightly ahead of the body and supports the forward movement only after the landing.

Variant of the arm action. One familiar variant of the arm action is the double arm action. During the last stride before clearance, at the latest, the hurdler brings both arms forward ahead of the body, in order to thrust them forward towards the hurdle together with the leading leg. This wide forward movement of the arms brings the centre of gravity into a favourable position above the hurdle. Nevertheless this variant of the arm action is hardly seen in top performers, because during a certain lapse of time the "amble" position is necessary, which is not conducive to a smooth running rhythm.

● Position of the upper body

A hurdler with a good technique keeps a low trajectory of the body's CG over the hurdle. This is achieved by a proper changing of position of the limbs in relation to the body's centre of gravity. Since the flight path of the centre of gravity is fixed after the take-off action, all movements during the supportless phase create countermovements for maintaining the body balance. A downward lean of the trunk (upper accompanying chart) automatically causes a lifting of the pelvis and of the trailing leg (lower accompanying chart). A pronounced forward lean of the body is therefore a preliminary condition for a flat trajectory of the body CG over the hurdle.

The forward lean of the trunk already begins during the approach to the hurdle, in order to achieve a flat take-off angle. After the take-off most good hurdlers accentuate the forward lean by further lowering the upper part of the body forward and downward, in order to achieve a marked lean before the body's centre of gravity passes the hurdle. A favourable forward lean implies that the hand of the leading arm reaches—or could reach—the foot of the leading leg. With most hurdlers the eyes are facing ahead during the hurdle stride (Fig. 27, Pos. 5).

The forward sweep of the trailing leg is

counterbalanced by an uplift of the trunk. A certain forward lean should, however, be maintained, to make sure that on landing the body's centre of gravity lies above the leading leg or slightly ahead of it. This is the only way to continue running without delay.

● Length of the hurdle stride

Athletes with good running qualities and physical condition will attempt to shorten the flight time over the hurdle. Since, for technical reasons, it is impossible to shorten the approach distance to the hurdle, time can be gained only by an active landing of the leading leg. Such a saving of time is equivalent to the shortening of the distance of landing behind the hurdle and a relative increase of the distance between the hurdles. For weaker or shorter hurdlers the active landing is not always recommended, since it tends to make them use longer strides between the hurdles, thus reducing the velocity of strides. A high stride frequency between the hurdles is, however, the basis for a good performance. In general the hurdle stride is of about 3.50 m length, of which 2.10 m (= 60 per cent) apply to the track distance before and 1.40 m (= 40 per cent) to the distance behind the hurdle.

● Judging of the hurdle stride

When observing a hurdle stride or appreciating its technical quality, the landing phase is most revealing, especially if the following points are taken into consideration:
1. Position of the centre of gravity of the body. The most suitable running position has been adopted if, after the landing, the centre of gravity lies over the lead leg or slightly ahead of it.
2. Position of the hip and shoulder axis. Both axes must possibly remain constantly square to the running direction, as a body twist in most cases leads to a deviation from the straight line.
3. Length of the hurdle stride. With due consideration of individual differences, the length of the hurdle stride and of the get-away stride should be in good proportion.

● The three-step rhythm between the hurdles

In the 110-m hurlde race the distance between hurdles is 9.14 m (= 10 yards). If we deduce from this the length of the hurdle stride, there remains for the three strides between the hurdles—sometimes called three-step rhythm—a distance of about 5.65 m, i.e. 1.88 m for each step. But practice shows clearly, that the three steps are not of equal length. Thus the first stride after the landing, which is of about 1.55 to 1.60 m, will always be the shortest, because the push-off force is reduced by the preceding hurdle stride. There follows a wide second stride measuring 2.00 to 2.20 m and this is the longest between the hurdles. The last stride before the hurdle is always slightly shorter than the previous one.

● The finishing sprint to the tape

The 110-m hurdle race will always end with a finishing sprint covering 14.02 m. On this section of the distance, the hurdler increases his speed by sprinting towards the tape with vigorous strides, increasing the stride length in line with speed. Measurement of strides has shown that not all hurdlers succeed in doing this. At first they use strides of similar length as between the hurdles. This means that with this pattern of striding they could clear eleven hurdles.

● An example of stride pattern

Table 36 gives guidance for a stride pattern over the most important track sections. These values are not necessarily applicable to all hurdlers, since individual conditions may greatly vary. But as all hurdlers have the same space at their disposal, the "latitude" for an individual stride pattern is limited. Considerable deviations would therefore have negative results.

3.4.1.2. The 100-m Hurdles for Women

The 100-m hurdles for women is one of the youngest events of track and field. It took the place of the 80-m hurdle race. This decision was taken in 1968 at the Olympic Games in Mexico-City. The conditions and requirements of this hurdles event take into consideration the improving performance level of women. It offers better opportunities to women who are excellent sprinters than the 80-m hurdles did.

A technical analysis of the hurdle race for women showed that here also many technical features of the 110-m hurdle race apply. We can therefore refer to the technique in this chapter. Particulars of the hurdle race for women are dealt with next.

● Running rhythm

Good hurdling depends on the sprinting qualities and technical skills of the hurdler. Compared with the 80-m hurdles the 100-m hurdle race requires superior running abilities. It is techni-cally more difficult to master the approach distance and the distances between hurdles than to clear the somewhat higher hurdles.

Experience has shown so far that only women who are top-class sprinters master sprint-hurdling.

● Approach to the first hurdle

After the start the maximum speed should be reached as quickly as possible. It is therefore of paramount importance that the 13 m approach distance is covered with the greatest possible acceleration. All runners use 8 strides before clearing the hurdle (cf. Table 37).

● Running between the hurdles

The distance between hurdles measures 8.5 m. After landing behind the hurdle (1.10 m)—at almost the same distance as in the 80-m hurdle race—and after the push-off in front of the hurdle (2.00 m) there remains a distance of 5.40 m for the three strides between the hurdles. In order to cover this distance like a sprinter, the quality of the first stride is of special importance. This stride should be close to 1.60 m in length to initiate the proper proportions between the three strides. A proper technique of hurdle clearance depends on the correct performance of the first stride.

● The hurdle stride

The technical details of the hurdle stride depend on the hurdle height and refer mainly to the action of the leading leg and the trailing leg as well as to the position of the upper body.

● Action of leading leg

There is hardly any difference between

Table 36 *An Example of Stride Pattern for the 110 Metres Hurdles*

		Length (m)	Distance (m)
Approach to the first hurdle	1st Stride	0.60	0.60
	2nd Stride	1.10	1.70
	3rd Stride	1.35	3.05
	4th Stride	1.50	4.55
	5th Stride	1.65	6.20
	6th Stride	1.80	8.00
	7th Stride	1.90	9.90
	8th Stride	1.80	11.70
Take-off distance to the first hurdle		2.02	13.72
Landing behind the hurdle		1.40	1.40
Three-stride rhythm	1st Stride	1.55	2.95
	2nd Stride	2.10	5.05
	3rd Stride	2.00	7.05
Take-off distance to the second hurdle		2.09	9.14

Table 37 *Comparison of Stride Pattern in the 100 Metres and 80 Metres Hurdle Races*

		100-m Hurdles (m)		80-m Hurdles (m)	
Approach to the 1st hurdle	1st Stride	0.65	0.65	0.45	0.45
	2nd Stride	1.05	1.70	1.00	1.45
	3rd Stride	1.35	3.05	1.15	2.60
	4th Stride	1.40	4.45	1.30	3.90
	5th Stride	1.50	5.95	1.45	5.35
	6th Stride	1.65	7.60	1.55	6.90
	7th Stride	1.75	9.35	1.70	8.10
	8th Stride	1.70	11.05	1.55	10.15
Take-off distance to the 1st hurdle		1.95	13.00	1.85	12.00
Landing behind the 1st hurdle		1.10	1.10	0.90	0.90
	1st Stride	1.60	2.70	1.50	2.40
	2nd Stride	1.95	4.65	1.90	4.30
	3rd Stride	1.85	6.50	1.75	6.05
Take-off distance to the 2nd hurdle		2.00	8.50	1.95	8.00

the action of the leading leg for the 100-m hurdles and that of the 80-m hurdles. At the take-off for the hurdle clearance, the thigh is brought up level with the horizontal. Then the lower leg swings forward and upward only to a point that must be attained for a safe clearance. The difficulty of the leading leg action consists in bracing the forward swing of the lower leg when the heel has reached the edge of the hurdle. If properly mastered, stretching at the knee joint will not be complete (Fig. 28, Pos. 1—5).

Good women sprinters should make it a point to land as quickly as possible behind the hurdle. This is achieved by an acceleration of the landing by a downward and backward push of the thigh as soon as the foot has passed the edge of the hurdle. Contact with the ground behind the hurdle should be on the front part of the ball of the foot with a slightly bent knee joint; good runners avoid the lowering of the heel towards the ground.

Variant of the leading leg action. Some top-class women hurdlers thrust their lower leg upward with such intensity that there is a complete stretching at the knee joint. In general this technique seems uneconomic, because the movement of the front leg leads so far upwards that landing is delayed. The action of the leading leg should, however, always be seen in connection with the individual height of the woman.

Most women hurdlers are so tall that it is wrong for them to stretch the leg at the knee joint. With shorter women hurdlers such an action of the leading leg hardly occurs or can be compensated by a fast swinging action.

● Trailing leg action

In order to keep a low trajectory of the body's centre of gravity, the hurdler must stretch the thigh of the trailing leg laterally away from the body. In a well executed trailing-leg action, a woman hurdler sweeps her trailing knee low over the top of the hurdle. In clearing the 84-cm hurdle the spread of the legs will be more pronounced than in crossing a hurdle of only 76.2 cm height. But all women hurdlers let the thigh hang downward when passing the hurdle; the degree of the downward sag depends on the height of the individual. Short women hurdlers will bend the trailing leg away more from the pelvis than taller women. As soon as the knee of the trailing leg comes over the top of the hurdle, the thigh has to be brought into position for a vigorous first stride after clearance. The whole

movement of the trailing leg is somewhat ascending, so that at the end of this action the thigh is slightly turned upward.

● Body position

A proper flight path over the 84-cm hurdle does not require an exaggerated downward dip. Women hurdlers adopt a lower lean than in normal sprinting mainly for the purpose of getting the centre of gravity into a sound position for the landing behind the hurdle. The degree of forward lean depends on the height of the athlete; short women hurdlers usually accentuate the forward lean.

3.4.1.3. The 400-m Hurdles

This is known as the most strenuous event of all hurdle races. Due to the degree of fatigue inherent in 400-m hurdling, the technique of the event is more difficult to learn.

● Running rhythm

After an appropriate number of strides, the 400-m hurdler must clear the hurdles without hesitation and make full use of his sprinting ability. Depending on the condition of the individual hurdler, the striding rhythm on the rela-

tively long running sections varies. Most hurdlers cover the 45-m distance of the approach to the first hurdle with 22, only few with 21 or 23 strides. When using an even number of strides, the trailing leg is placed on the front block in the starting position. For running between hurdles the principle applies that, once adopted, the rhythm should be held right through to the last hurdle, because changing the number of strides might entail an unnecessary loss of time. Hurdlers with poorly developed sprinting ability (lack of special endurance) may be forced to change the stride rhythm when premature fatigue has a deteriorating effect on speed and length of strides.

Every hurdler should, however, be prepared for the challenge of a change in the stride rhythm, since other factors, such as wind- and track-conditions, may also influence the stride pattern. It is therefore recommended that the leading leg action be trained with the left or the right leg alternately and that the necessary skill and adaptability for such a functional change of the leg action be acquired by appropriate running exercises (see section "Special Agility", page 204).

The stride rhythm between hurdles consists for most hurdlers of 13, 15 or

Fig. 28

189

17 strides. An uneven number has the advantage that no change of function of the legs in the hurdle stride must take place. Yet there are hurdlers who, from the very beginning—or after changing the rhythm—use 14 or 16 strides between hurdles and change the lead- and trailing-leg actions over every other hurdle. Every hurdler will have to adopt the stride plan best suited for him, depending on his stride length and sprinting ability. Most specialists, nowadays, use 15 strides between the hurdles, giving them an average stride length of some 2.12 m and of 3.20 m for the hurdle stride.

Up to now the 13-stride plan with an average stride length of about 2.45 m has rarely been adopted. For the majority of hurdlers it is too difficult to sustain and leads to premature fatigue. This is the reason why some of the top hurdlers of the world use this stride rhythm only over certain sections of the 400-m hurdles. With growing efficiency top hurdlers may give it more consideration in the future.

● Hurdle clearance

No particular technique is required for the hurdle stride in the 400-m hurdles; it is comprable to that of the 110- or 100-m technique. Which is the more rational depends mainly on the body height of the hurdler. Short men tend to use the 100-m technique, while taller ones prefer the technique of the 100-m hurdle race.

The stride length for clearing the hurdle is about 3.20 m. The take-off is about 2.0 m in front and the landing about 1.20 m behind the hurdle.

3.4.1.4. Timing in Hurdle Races

● 110-m hurdles

Analyses of times taken of hurdlers at each hurdle (distance 9.14 m) have shown [35] that after the start the approach and the clearance of the first hurdle, even over the first measured section (from landing behind the first up to the landing behind the second hurdle) all the athletes achieved the highest test results of the whole race. This same result can be achieved again

35 G. Schmolinsky "Untersuchungen über den Geschwindigkeitsverlauf im 100-m-Hürdenlauf der Männer", in "Theorie und Praxis der Körperkultur", Sportverlag, Berlin, 3/1959.

Fig. 29 Hurdle clearance in the bends

between other hurdle distances (Fig. 30).

The lowest values are generally measured between the 9th and the 10th hurdle. Only in the finishing sprint speed rises again and comes near to maximum. Each of the analysed hurdle races reveals that as far as speed is concerned, two typical sections stand out: a first section of approximately constant speed, also called the section of maximum speed, and a second section, characterized by a marked loss in speed (the approach to the first hurdle and the final spurt up to the tape are hereby not considered). The length of the respective sections depends on the performance level and abilities of the hurdler. The section of maximum speed ranges from the landing point behind the first to the landing point behind the sixth hurdle (five hurdle distances). The section of decreasing speed begins behind the sixth hurdle and ends after the landing point behind the 10th hurdle (four hurdle distances).

● 80-m and 100-m hurdle races

All the analyses given here refer to the 80-m hurdles for women. They revealed

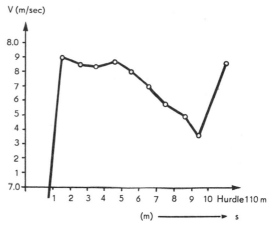

Fig. 30

that it is possible to increase the speed up to about the fifth hurdle. No similar data have so far come to our notice of the 100-m hurdles. They are most probably similar to those of the 110-m hurdles for men.

● 400-m hurdles

For good performances, the correct distribution is of vital importance, i.e. certain principles for the speed pattern must be adhered to.

In order to find out the optimal performance in the 400-m hurdles by calculation, the following empirical values may give some guidance:

1. The basis for the 400-m hurdles results is the best time clocked for the 400 m flat. A time difference between the two distances of about 2.5 to 3.0 seconds for top performers and of 3.0 to 3.5 seconds for beginners are to be looked for.

2. Important for the final result of the 400-m hurdles is the proper choice of the initial velocity up to 200 m. At this mark the intermediate time should be around 2.0 to 2.3 seconds slower than sprinting over 200 m flat. From a

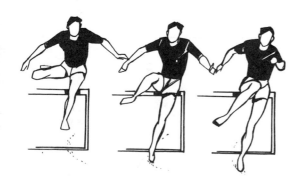

Table 38   Intermediate Times

80-m Hurdle Race

Performance (sec.)	10.6–11.2	11.7–12.2	12.4–12.8
1st Hurdle	2.1	2.2	2.3
2nd Hurdle	3.3	3.5	3.6
3rd Hurdle	4.4	4.7	4.9
4th Hurdle	5.5	5.9	6.1
5th Hurdle	6.5	7.1	7.3
6th Hurdle	7.5	8.3	8.6
7th Hurdle	8.5	9.5	9.9
8th Hurdle	9.5	10.7	11.2
Goal	1.3	1.3	1.4

100-m Hurdle Race

Performance (sec.)	12.5–13.0	13.0–13.5	13.5–14.0	14.0–14.5
1st Hurdle	1.9	1.9	2.0	2.1
2nd Hurdle	2.9	2.9	3.1	3.2
3rd Hurdle	3.9	4.0	4.2	4.4
4th Hurdle	5.0	5.2	5.3	5.6
5th Hurdle	6.1	6.3	6.5	6.8
6th Hurdle	7.1	7.4	7.7	8.0
7th Hurdle	8.2	8.5	8.9	9.2
8th Hurdle	9.3	9.7	10.1	10.5
9th Hurdle	10.4	10.9	11.3	11.8
10th Hurdle	11.6	12.1	12.5	13.1
Goal	1.2	1.2	1.3	1.5

110-m Hurdle Race

Performance (sec.)	13.0–13.5	13.5–14.0	14.0–14.5	14.5–15.0	15.0–15.5	15.5–16.0
1st Hurdle	2.3	2.5	2.5	2.6	2.6	2.7
2nd Hurdle	3.3	3.5	3.5	3.7	3.8	4.0
3rd Hurdle	4.3	4.5	4.6	4.9	5.0	5.2
4th Hurdle	5.3	5.5	5.7	6.0	6.2	6.4
5th Hurdle	6.4	6.6	6.8	7.2	7.4	7.7
6th Hurdle	7.4	7.7	7.9	8.3	8.6	8.9
7th Hurdle	8.5	8.8	9.0	9.5	9.8	10.1
8th Hurdle	9.5	9.9	10.2	10.7	11.0	11.4
9th Hurdle	10.6	11.0	11.4	11.9	12.3	12.7
10th Hurdle	11.8	12.2	12.6	13.1	13.6	14.1
Goal	1.4	1.5	1.6	1.6	1.6	1.7

400-m Hurdle Race

Performance (sec.)	49.0–50.0	50.0–51.0	51.0–52.0	52.0–53.0	53.0–54.0	54.0–55.0
1st Hurdle	5.9	6.0	6.1	6.2	6.3	6.3
2nd Hurdle	9.8	10.0	10.2	10.3	10.4	10.4
3rd Hurdle	13.8	14.0	14.3	14.4	14.5	14.6
4th Hurdle	17.8	18.0	18.4	18.6	18.7	18.9
5th Hurdle	21.9	22.1	22.6	33.9	23.1	23.4
6th Hurdle	26.2	26,4	26.9	27.2	27.6	27.9
7th Hurdle	30.6	30.9	31.4	31.7	32.1	32.6
8th Hurdle	35.0	35.5	36.1	36.5	37.0	37.5
9th Hurdle	39.6	40.2	40.9	41.5	42.1	42.8
10th Hurdle	44.3	45.0	45.8	46.5	47.2	48.0
Goal	5.2	5.5	5.6	6.0	6.3	6.5

chronological comparison of the two halves of a 400 m hurdle distance it should turn out that the hurdler was only about 2 to 3 seconds slower on the second half than on the first.
Example:
The best time of a hurdler over 200 m is 22.0 sec. Therefore his time distribution in a 400-m hurdle race should be as follows:
For the first
200 m (22.0 + 2.5 sec.) = 24.5 sec.
For the second
200 m (24.5 + 3.0 sec.) = 27.5 sec.
Final result = 52.0 sec.

3.4.1.5. Intermediate Times in Hurdle Races

For all hurdle distances the time recorded for a particular section (in training as well as in competitons) is a useful means of checking the fitness of the athlete. Intermediate times will also give the astute coach clues as to the effectiveness of his work. The figures in Table 38 show the time clocked at the instant the leading leg meets the ground after clearance of one hurdle and lands behind the next. In these values roughly 0.2 seconds are added for the time of reaction at the start.

3.4.2. Technical Training

Under easier conditions hurdling can be learnt comparatively quickly by children, adolescents and adults. The conditions should be related to the age and the efficiency level of the learners. Table 39 gives some practical guidance.
The object of the technical training should be to achieve harmony between the sprinting and the hurdling strides and to lead the learner step by step to competition level.

3.4.2.1. Special Preparatory Exercises

Special preparation should mainly include exercises which convey to the athlete under simplified conditions the idea of the rhythmic movement and the technique of hurdling. To this belong all the exercises in which running is interrupted rhythmically by hurdle strides and which are exacting with regard both to speed and agility.

Examples of exercises:

1. Runs over obstacles (small marked pits, bars placed on the ground, medicine balls, benches placed across the lane, etc.) with spacings that can be covered in a three-stride-rhythm.

2. "Pursuit Race"—two flights of low hurdles are placed in such a way that the athletes can run up and back.

Runners A and B start at the same time and chase each other (Fig. 31a).

Task: Who is faster? Who chases whom?

Patterns of competitions:

a) Clock the running time after a certain number of laps.

b) Measure length of distance covered at a pre-determined time.

c) Practise relay racing.

3. "Hurdle-Relays". Set up two flights of hurdles for each team. They should be placed in such a way that running up and back is possible. Each of the participating teams is split up in two groups. Runner A begins the run. As soon as his leading leg lands behind the last hurdle, A 1 dashes forward etc. (Fig. 31b).

4. Hurdle gymnastics. Exercises for developing special agility (cf. 3.4.3.2.). Conditions can be varied by increasing the space between the hurdles or the number and height of hurdles. The above exercises are particularly suited for children and juniors and can be carried out in various competitive forms.

3.4.2.2. Basic Exercises of Technical Training

The relatively small number of exercises given below concentrate on the main tasks. The hurdle conditions in the different exercises can be varied, since the training of technique is paramount and to which the hurdle conditions and the running pace must conform. Having gained confidence and perfected the hurdling technique, running at near to competition speed by hurdling at high and maximum speed gains more and more in importance.

Future 400-m hurdlers should train the right leg as the trailing leg, as this is useful in running round bends. But to

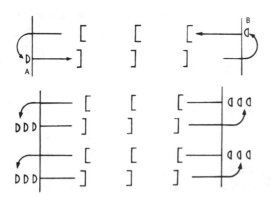

Fig. 31a,b

Fig. 32

Table 39 Lay-Out for Technical Training

Age (years)	Approach to the 1st Hurdle (m)	Hurdle Distances (m)	Hurdle Height (cm)
7–8	8.00	4.00	20–60
		4.50	
		5.00	
		5.50	
9–10		4.50	
	10.00	5.00	40–60
		5.50	
		5.00	
		5.50	
	11.00	6.00	50–76.2 (2 ft. 6 in.)
		6.50	
11–12		5.50	
	10.00	6.00	50–76.2 (2 ft. 6 in.)
		6.50	
		7.00	
	11.50	7.50	60–76.2 (2 ft. 6 in.)
13–14	10.00–12.00	6.50	76.2 (2 ft. 6 in.)
		7.00	
	12.00	7.50	76.2 (2 ft. 6 in.)
		8.00	
15–16		7.00	
	12.00	7.50	76.2 (2 ft. 6 in.)
		8.00	
		8.00	
	13.50	8.30	91.4 (1 yd.)
		8.50	
		8.90	
17–18		8.00	
	13.00–13.50	8.50	76.2
		8.90	91.4 (1 yd.)
		8.50	91.4 (1 yd.)–100
	13.72	8.90	
		9.14	100
		9.14	

be on the safe side, the potential 400-m hurdler should train both legs for trailing and leading actions (two-leg training).

The following set of exercises is recommended:

– Exercise 1: Run over 4 to 6 over- turned hurdles or over 40 to 60 cm high obstacles, using the three-stride-rhythm (Fig. 32).

Set up several hurdle flights with varying conditions. The performers will soon find out for themselves or through hints which conditions are best suited for them. Marking the distance to the first hurdle (length of approach), the take-off point in front of the hurdle and the landing point behind the hurdle facilitates the execution of the exercise.

Aim: Execute the complete movement of the hurdle-stride and get the "feel" for the three-stride-rhythm.

Points to note: Hurdles or obstacles must be sprinted over and not jumped over.

Hint: A very marked running rhythm is proper to the hurdle race. This can be rhythmically stressed by onlookers beating out the rhythm and helping the speed and pattern of strides. This sometimes assists beginners as well as advanced hurdlers in tackling particular technical problems. For this reason the technical training of the stride rhythm should not be confined to exercise 1. Such emphasis of the rhythm might be: ... and ... one ... two ... forward! The "and" refers to the first stride. The beating-out of the rhythm starts, when the leading foot touches the ground behind the hurdle, i.e. before the next new movement starts. If e.g. the first stride after the landing should be longer, this will be emphasized by accentuating the "and". The word "forward" invites the athlete to adopt a correct trunk posture during the hurdle stride.

Quicker beating-out of the rhythm can spur the hurdler on to increase his pace.

– Exercise 2: Special training of the

pull-through movement across the hurdle.

Several hurdles or obstacles are set up in a row. At first their height should not be more than 50 to 76.2 cm; later on it will be adapted to the training level of the individual. The athlete runs in the three-stride-rhythm alongside the hurdle, so that only the leading leg is swept over the hurdle.

A useful exercise, particularly for beginners, is to run up to the hurdle in a knee-lift run and sweep the leading leg over the hurdle. Use 5 or 7 strides between hurdles.

Aim: Emphasis must be on the accurate execution of the leading leg action.

Points to note: Active push-off in front of the hurdle. Bring the thigh of the leading leg up to the horizontal and thrust the shank towards the hurdle edge. Active landing on the ball of the foot. Swing the arm forward.

– Exercise 3: Special training of the trailing leg action over the hurdle.

Several hurdles are placed one behind the other. The athlete trails his leg *in walking* alongside a hurdle. The trailing action can be repeated after five, three strides or one. For stressing the necessity of bending the trailing leg away, use hurdles of 76.2 to 91.4 cm height even for beginners.

Performing the trailing leg action *in running* is more difficult. For this purpose the hurdles must be lowered again to 50 or 76.2 centimetres, so as to prevent jumping over the hurdles. Marking the take-off point in front of the hurdle and the landing point behind the hurdle for the trailing leg facilitates the technically correct execution. Start at low speed and increase speed gradually in line with technical improve-

ment. Use three or five strides between the hurdles. The leading leg action can be simulated on the side of the hurdle.

Aim: Concentrate on the correct execution of the trailing leg action.

Points to note: Watch landing point of the leading leg! The trailing action will only succeed if the leading leg touches the ground sideways behind the hurdle (in walking some 1 to 2, in running about 2 to 4 feet). Bend away the foot and the thigh after take-off. Negotiate the hurdle in walking, not in jumping. Pull through the thigh of the trailing leg in a flat sweep over the hurdle in running direction. Bring the body's centre of gravity in a favourable position on landing behind the hurdle; link up the trailing-leg movement smoothly with the getaway stride (important: length of get-away stride!). Train the forward and backward movement of the swinging arm.

Auxiliary Exercises

Training the swinging movements:
1. Swing leg up against wall bars or similar apparatus. The learner begins with standing, then continues with some approach strides bringing him 1 to 1.5 m short of the wall bars. From there he swings his leg up against the wall bars and at the same time brings forward his upper body and opposite arm.
2. Swinging movement in standing, walking and running.
Train the trailing leg movement: The trailing leg action can be repeated several times standing or walking, with and without hurdles.
When training standing, support by a partner or a tree etc. is helpful.

Fig. 33

– Exercise 4: Race across hurdles of different heights.
Use three strides between hurdles and 8 strides for approach run. The height increases from hurdle to hurdle; stop at 76.2-cm hurdles for beginners (Fig. 33).
Example:
1st hurdle = 50 cm or 76.2 cm
2nd hurdle = 65 cm or 84.0 cm
3rd hurdle = 76,2 cm or 91.4 cm
or similar variations.
Aim: Meet gradually increasing technical demands during the race.
Points to note: Speedy run-up to first hurdle and between hurdles. A hesitant running style impedes the execution of the three-strides-rhythm and of the hurdle stride. Checks should chiefly concentrate on leg movements and trunk posture during the hurdle stride. Watch the linearity of the forward movement, the coordination of the legs and a good forward body lean.
Hint: Increase number of higher hurdles in line with increasing skill. At the same time increase distances between hurdles, thus inducing the hurdler to run faster.
– Exercise 5: Clearance of hurdles of 76.2 cm (84.0 and 91.4 cm) height.
The distance between hurdles should be covered with three strides; its length will be related to the technical level and running ability of the hurdler.
Aim: Improvement and consolidation of technique of hurdle stride.
Points to note: Technical details specified above apply also to the hurdle

stride. The fast run-up to the first hurdle and stride proportions between hurdles are particularly important for advanced hurdlers.
Hint: Particular attention must be paid by 200-m and 400-m hurdlers to the special running rhythm.
– Exercise 6: Do the hurdle race under conditions as in a competition by using the crouch start.
Many hurdlers (men and women) who master exercise 5 continue to have difficulties negotiating their special hurdle heights and distances. In this case exercises 2 – 5 should be repeated but with correspondingly increased demands placed on the hurdlers, until these two factors are fully mastered for competition.
Aim: Have hurdle races with and without starting orders from crouch start, alone or with competitors, contests, timetaking.
Points to note: Crouch start and run-up to first hurdle. Hurdle stride and running rhythm. Harmonious style.

3.4.2.3.   Technical Training with Aids

The exercises outlined so far require hurdles. The next examples show that it is possible to train the hurdle technique also without hurdles. The same aims and remarks apply here.
– Exercise 1: Running over several benches placed across the lane. The distances between benches are covered in three strides.

197

– Exercise 2: Train the leading leg action (drive). For this purpose a soft ball—held in place by a rubber ring—or a small medicine ball are placed on each bench. Swing leg over the ball (Fig. 34a).

– Exercise 3: Train the trailing movement. Swing trailing leg over a medicine ball lying next to the ordinary ball. Since the trailing action must be executed alternately with the right and the left leg, another medicine ball should be placed on the other side of the ordinary ball (Fig. 34b).

– Exercise 4: Running a hurdle-like race. A provisional hurdle can be constructed by placing a bar over two medicine balls (use also jumping uprights with bar on top) (Fig. 34c).

– Exercise 5: Special training of leading and trailing leg action. A medicine ball placed at one end of the bench will allow practice of the leading and the trailing leg action.

3.4.2.4. Ancillary Exercises

The following exercises are only intended for runners who have carried out fully basic technical training. Exer-

cises for developing a higher running speed in hurdling:

1. Hurdling with longer approach and clearing of three hurdles. This exercise is only of value for the 100-m and 110-m hurdlers, because the development of speed under the given conditions is subject to certain limitations. A longer approach in training must lead to a speed increase at the first hurdle, in the hurdle stride and in the three-stride-rhythm. It is sufficient to lengthen the approach by two additional strides.

2. Approach and clearing 1st and 2nd hurdle. The first hurdle has been slightly lowered in order to allow for a faster take-off.

3. Clearing 3 to 12 slightly lower hurdles with normal hurdle distances by using the three-stride-rhythm.

4. Use shorter approach and shorter hurdle distances in clearing 3 to 5 hurdles. This exercise is recommended for the 400-m hurdler. Shorter distances will allow him to concentrate on the improvement of the hurdle-stride technique at high speed. Variations of the 3-, 4- and 5-stride rhythm increase the demands placed on the athlete.

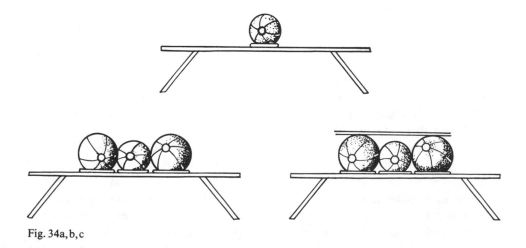

Fig. 34a,b,c

5. Clearing 3 to 5 hurdles, followed by a flat run over 100 to 200 metres with high and medium intensity. These runs are particularly beneficial to the 400-m hurdler.

6. Clearing 5 to 10 hurdles of 76.2, 84.0 or 91.4 cm height, using only one stride between hurdles. The hurdle distances are 3.0 to 3.5 m. This exercise may be applied in training the leading or rear leg movements by walking alongside the hurdles, as well as for practising the complete hurdle movement. It becomes a special strength exercise if many hurdles have to be cleared.

3.4.2.5. Fault-Reason-Correction

In the take-off clearance of the first hurdle

— Fault: The run to the first hurdle was not done with all-out-effort.

Reason: The runner is too awed by the hurdle; he raises his trunk too soon after the start or chops his stride.

Correction: Set the first hurdle lower or let the hurdler run with a partner (stimulus!). Practise the take-off and the flight over two hurdles.

In the running between the hurdles

— Fault: The athlete does not run in a straight line between the hurdles.

Reason: The fault lies generally in the wrong execution of the hurdle stride and is due to a lack of suppleness and agility.

Correction: Improve suppleness and agility

— Fault: Strides have "jumping" character.

Reason: Insufficient speed. The runner has difficulty in reaching the next hurdle with three strides. Watch proportion between strides.

Correction: Develop sprinting abilities, train rhythm first. Reduce hurdle distances.

In the hurdle stride

— Fault: The athlete "jumps" over the hurdles.

Reason: The hurdler is overawed by the hurdle or takes off too close to the hurdle, so that his body is propelled too much upwards.

Correction: Lower hurdles temporarily. Mark take-off point. Increase speed by clearing low hurdles.

— Fault: The stride of the trailing leg is not properly coordinated with get-away stride.

Reason:

a) The rear leg action has started too early. The knee of the rear leg points in running direction before the leading leg has touched down behind the hurdle.

b) The rear leg movement is too low, causing the knee or foot to knock down the hurdle.

Correction: In the first case the relaxation phase after the first take-off must be prolonged. In the second case the trailing leg action must be perfected by special exercises.

— Fault: The front leg does not come through straight over the hurdle. The shank points outward or inward.

Reason: Take-off is too close to the hurdle.

Correction: Mark point of take-off for clearing the hurdle. Do special exercises for leading leg action.

— Fault: Tarring effect on landing behind the hurdle.

Reason: Insufficient body lean in the landing phase, so that the body's centre of gravity is brought behind the leading leg on touching the ground.

Correction: Accentuate forward lean during the complete hurdle stride.

3.4.3. Physical Requirements and Training Methods for Improving Performance

3.4.3.1. The Importance of Physical Condition

Good results in hurdling are mainly related to the hurdler's running ability (speed and special endurance), to his special mobility and agility as well as to his body height. Sprinting abilities are the basis of the hurdling performance. Mobility, agility and height are important attributes for learning and improving the hurdle technique.

● Sprinting ability

Every hurdling performance is to a certain degree a function of the sprinting ability of the athlete over the corresponding flat distance. It is necessary to be a good 100-m or 200-m sprinter to become a good hurdler over the same distances. For good results in hurdling the following minimum results must be achieved over flat distances:
100-m women hurdlers –
100-m in appr. 11.5 sec.
110-m hurdlers (men) –
100-m in apr. 10.5 sec.
400-m hurdlers (women) –
400-m in appr. 53.5 sec.
400-m hurdlers (men) –
400-m in appr. 47.0 sec.
In order to make full use of sprinting ability in hurdling, corresponding technical skills are required. The extent of the practical application of sprinting abilities is measured by the difference between running times on flat and corresponding hurdling distances. If the time difference is small, the athlete has a technically correct style and fully utilizes his sprinting ability. A further improvement in performance can then hardly be expected without a corresponding progress in sprinting ability. If, however, the time difference is great, the hurdler does not correctly apply his sprinting ability because of technical shortcomings. In this case increased training of technique is of major importance.

● Time difference between the 100-m race and the 100-m hurdles of women

Experience shows that a time difference of 1.5 sec. can be considered as very good and up to 2.0 sec. as good.

Example:
100-m performance
= 11.5 sec. (+ 1.5 to 2.0 sec.)
= 100-m hurdling performance
= 13.0 sec. to 13.5 sec.

● Significance of the time difference between the 100-m flat and the 110-m hurdle race

The smaller the time difference between the performance over these two distances, the better the sprinting ability can be used in hurdling. A difference of 3.0 seconds is very good and up to 4.0 seconds is still good.

Example:
100-m performance
= 10.5 sec. (+ 3.0 to 4.0 sec.)
= 100-m hurdling performance
= 13.5 to 14.5 sec.

● Significance of the difference in time between the 400-m flat and the 400-m hurdle race

A time difference of 2.5 sec. between the 400-m result and the 400-m hurdle result is very good and up to 3.5 sec. is still good.

Example:
400-m result
= 47.0 sec. (+ 2.5 to 3.5 sec.)
= 400-m hurdling performance
= 49.5 sec. to 50.0 sec.
If the time difference is unsatisfactory, this is not always due to technical shortcomings in the 400-m hurdles. It is more frequently due to a change in the stride rhythm between the hurdles, by wich time is lost; the reason is mainly lack of special endurance.

3.4.3.2. Means for Developing Physical Properties

● The development of running ability
Every hurdler is at the same time a sprinter and should therefore not only do hurdling training but also sprint training. We shall here only deal with forms of running recommended for hurdle training. These forms are based on known speed patterns over the corresponding hurdle distances (see section 3.4.1.4.). In contrast to exercises which are chiefly aimed at improving technical skills, the forms of running outlined below help to develop and apply running in a hurdles race and serve at the same time to perfect technique. Their target is to improve or maintain the special proficiency of the hurdler. They take an important part in all training programmes from the spring right through to the end of the season. Experience has shown that during this period hurdle training is often practised only at wide intervals, e.g. once a week or even only once in two weeks. The reason for this is that hurdle training is frequently underestimated. But every hurdler should try to master his special distance, as this will give him self-confidence and reliable technique,

the two crucial factors for good results. He must therefore keep in close touch with the special features of his event. In order to stimulate interest in more frequent hurdle training, it may be found useful to couple hurdling with pure running in one training session. This avoids too much repetition of hurdling and makes the training more varied.
The hurdle training can naturally also include exercises for improving technique or hurdling agility, besides varied running routines. Usually a training session begins with such exercises before the running is started.

Running for 100-m women hurdlers and 110-m hurdlers (men)

The following running exercises are designed to develop speed and special endurance under hurdling conditions. They should therefore be carried out mainly at high or maximum speed. After each run there should be a rest, the length of which will depend on the preceding work load. It should be at least long enough to allow the hurdler to start the next hurdle run with full or just below full effort. Training will mainly follow the pattern of the repetition method. If, due to growing fatigue, speed drops off after several runs (timing), some repetitions may still be added for developing special endurance and will-power.
— Start and run over two hurdles
The idea is to develop the highest possible speed over this section, in order to achieve a good start. This is the most difficult part of the distance for all men and women hurdlers, because when coming off the first hurdle after a sharp take-off, they must immediately drop into the proper rhythm for the strides between the hurdles. All the adverse ef-

fects resulting from a defective stride pattern or the knocking down of a hurdle will detract from the final result.

— Start and run over three to five hurdles. This form of sprinting helps to develop the acceleration potential and the maximum speed capacity. With a sufficient number of repetitions it also contributes to special endurance. It is the most important form of running, because after a successful start and clearance of some hurdles, the technique of the hurdle stride and the three-stride rhythm become consolidated.

— Start and run over more than five hurdles. This exercise aims mainly at developing special endurance. High demands are placed on the running ability of the athlete. With less experienced runners (men or women) the stride frequency usually ebbs away after the fifth hurdle, so that an otherwise good run deteriorates. This routine is therefore particularly dependent on the development level of running quality.

Sprinting schedules for 400-m hurdlers

The schedules for 400-m hurdlers aim mainly at the development of special endurance. For this reason intensive interval and repetition work should be applied. The tempo of the runs is comparable to that of the tempo of competition. The use of the interval method is recommended. Several tempo runs up to about 200 m (= 5th hurdle) are suggested for the development of special endurance. The rest intervals should not be prolonged up to complete recovery, if the designed physiological effect is to be produced. A variant on the intensive interval method is a series of runs over relatively short hurdle distances, e.g. $2 \times (3 \times 3$ hurdles). This series of runs consists of three runs over three hurdles with a break of only 30 to 90 seconds between them. Due to the short break it is necessary to lay out two flights of hurdles, so as to allow the athletes to run up and back. After a series of runs, a break of about 10 minutes is normal.

In longer high-speed runs (up to 5 hurdles) smaller series e.g. $2 \times (2 \times 5$ hurdles) and longer breaks (about 4 to 6 minutes) should be arranged. After a longer break of about 15 minutes the next series of two runs over 5 hurdles may follow.

The repetition method must be emphasized when tempo running can induce marked fatigue. This, for instance, is the case in the run over 8 or 10 hurdles. Before doing a planned repetition, a rest for recovery of some 15 to 20 minutes should be allowed. In practice shorter hurdle distances may naturally be used for the repetition method, particularly when e.g. technical or rhythmical exercises or an increased amount of training are the main objectives.

The two methods can also be brought together in one training session.

The following forms of running are the most important in the training programme of the 400-m hurdler:

— Start and run over two to three hurdles. With this exercise the 400-m hurdler develops accuracy in the approach to the first hurdle over 45 m and trains the transition to the planned stride rhythm between the hurdles. At the same time, bearing in mind the scheduled intermediate time at 200 m, he must be careful to achieve the right starting speed.

— Start and run over 200 m with the 400-m hurdles (5 hurdles + 15 m) in mind.

This running form helps to develop

and consolidate the athlete's stride pattern and pace judgement.

– Start and run over 300 m with the 400-m hurdle race (8 hurdles + 10 m) in mind.

In contrast with running over shorter distances the typical fatigue effect many hurdlers experience after one run now appears only. The training run over 300 m represents stress that is often comparable to that of competition. This form of running gives the runner and his coach clues as to the level of efficiency he has reached (timing).

– Combination of hurdle and flat race

Start and run over 3 to 5 hurdles plus 100 to 200 m flat with high and medium speed.

Start and run over the 1st to 3rd and the 6th to 8th hurdle–flat race in between. This is a good means of training for bend running over hurdles.

● Special mobility

The mobility required for the hurdle race is mainly achieved by general and special gymnastic exercises. Only the most important of the special exercises are outlined below. The extent to which they should be applied depends on the mobility of the athlete. As a general principle gymnastic exercises should be part and parcel of every training programme.

Examples:

1. Quick and high forward and upward thrust of one leg. The trunk remains upright.

2. Alternating a straddle step.

3. In easy lateral bent position quick and wide trunk-bending. The head is swung through the straddled legs, the knees may be slightly bent.

4. Fast repeated execution of the leading and trailing leg movements in standing, walking or running.

5. In hurdle seat–bend trunk forward, sideways and backward (Fig. 35).

6. From extended seat backward drive of one leg into hurdle seat (Fig. 36).

7. Hurdle seat with half a turn: the athlete assumes the hurdle seat; he rises–usually by using his arms–in order to return to the hurdle seat after having performed half a turn in the direction of the trailing leg. Thus the two legs constantly exchange their functions (Fig. 37).

8. Exercise on the hurdle (hurdle height for men about 106 cm, for women about 91.4 cm). The shanks with the knees are lying on the rail bar of the hurdle. In this position the hurdler bends his trunk forward (head to knee) (Fig. 38).

9. Exercise on the hurdle (hurdle height as before). The foot of the extended leg lies on the hurdle. Rapid low trunk bending forward (Fig. 39).

Hints for developing special mobility:

It is widely thought that gymnastic exercises, and particularly those with a strong stretching effect, have a negative influence stretching effect, have a negative influence on the athlete's speed. This opinion is justified if the muscles

Fig. 35

and tendons are overstrained by incorrect effort so that, as with an overstretched rubber band, the take-off power is reduced. Many of the best hurdlers prove by their high sprinting capacity that intense straining during gymnastic exercises has not done them any harm. For avoiding injuries a thorough warm-up before the gymnastic routines is, of course, vital. The degree of difficulty of the exercises must be gradually increased. A gymnastic programme should therefore never be started with special exercises but with simpler routines.

Gymnastic exercises should, once well mastered, be mainly executed in spurts, in order to maintain or promote the sort of sprinting required. It is therefore not recommended that the athlete remains long in, say, the hurdle seat, because this static stretching is unnatural for the sprinter. A rapid change between stretching and loosening exercises is by far to be preferred.

Gymnastic schedules should be varied and interesting. This is the case when, apart from some standard routines, the basic programme is frequently varied.

● Special agility

To develop hurdling agility training with hurdlers is different from that of normal conditions and face the runner constantly with new but soluble problems.

Within the scope of the suggested examples new running conditions should be created by changing—with or without the athlete's knowledge—height of hurdles and distances between them.

Examples:

1. Hurdle race with varying heights of the hurdles and of distances between them. Make it a principle to fix an uneven number of strides between hurdles; this is not necessary for 400-m hurdlers if they are capable of doing training and leading leg movements alternately with both legs.

2. Set up a row of several staggered hurdles (Fig. 40). The athlete runs between the hurdles and alternately sweeps his right or left leg over the side of the hurdle. If he uses an even number of strides between hurdles, an alternate front- and rear-leg movement of both legs will follow. An uneven number of strides forces him to constantly change the front- and rear-leg function of legs at each hurdle. The variation from even to uneven numbers of strides in one run requires great agility! This exercise is therefore advocated for 400-m hurdlers.

3. Steeplechasing over hurdles of varying heights and distances between hurdles.

This run may be performed in a

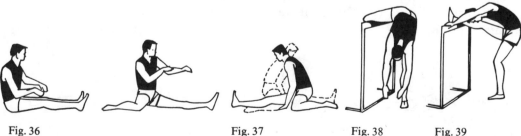

Fig. 36   Fig. 37   Fig. 38   Fig. 39

straight or a winding line and can acquire a competitive character by taking times (Fig. 41).

4. Run over 200 m or 300 m under conditions of the 400-m hurdle race. The athlete will be asked to use 15 strides between the first 3 hurdles and 16 strides between the remaining hurdles. The change-over from one stride rhythm to the other should not be visible.

3.4.4. Technique of the 3000-m Steeplechase

The international competition rules require that in the 3000-m steeplechase 28 barriers of 91.7 cm height and of 3.96 m width must be cleared 28 times. Additionally a water jump consisting of a 3.66 square sloping up from 76 cm depth at the near end to a point level with the ground at the far end, having a fixed beam (upper edge 91.1 to 91.7 cm above the ground) at the near end, has to be cleared in every lap. The distances between the obstacles and to the water jump have to be 78 m.

The obstacles force the hurdler to interrupt his normal running rhythm 35 times and require special technical skills.

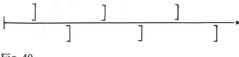

Fig. 40

Fig. 41

In the competition rules no special way of clearing the obstacles is laid down. The athlete may use his hands or place his feet on the obstacles but it saves time and energy to cross the obstacle without touching it.

For this purpose the athlete must learn a technique which is similar to that of the hurdle race in the 400-m distance. Over that distance the hurdles have the same height as the obstacles and the fatigue factor may strongly influence the technique in both these distances. A detailed description of the hurdle technique would at this point be an unnecessary repetition. Therefore only particular details will be emphasized. Generally speaking the steeplechase differs from the hurdle race in two respects: running does not take place in lanes and the distances between the obstacles are considerably longer. Due to these two factors a consistent stride rhythm cannot be sustained. This makes it necessary to train both legs for leading and trailing functions, in order to be prepared for a change in rhythm in competitions.

Other factors which may slightly influence the hurdle technique are the lower running pace and the crowding that occurs in the clearance of hurdles. The first requires a somewhat shorter hurdle stride and the second a good arm work.

3.4.4.1. Technique on the Water Jump

The water jump is the most time- and energy-consuming obstacle. A good technique for an economic clearance of the water jump is therefore necessary, but unfortunately often neglected. A technically poor water clearance jump

205

will have a strongly negative effect on the final result.

In Figure 42 we see a water jump technique which has proved satisfactory and is widely used.

● Approaching the obstacle and take-off

The average pace of a 3000-m steeplechase does usually not allow for an easy and smooth jump on to the obstacle beam. Therefore, the pace must be accelerated over the last 10 strides. The speed thus obtained must only be just sufficient to place the foot on the beam without special effort. The last stride should not be considerably longer than the previous ones in order to avoid a too steep trajectory of the body's centre of gravity. Running up on to the beam instead of jumping up is the crux of the matter.

The take-off from the ground should be part of the harmonious run without any braking effect. While the take-off leg completely stretches, the swinging leg assists the forward and upward movement of the body by driving the thigh up to the horizontal, while the shank is slightly bent away. The distance of the take-off point from the obstacle will depend on the speed and the size of the athlete. It is usually between 1.50 to 1.80 metres.

● Placing the foot on the beam and clearing the water jump

Before the foot of the slightly bent swinging leg is placed on the beam, the trunk is well bent forward in order to keep a low trajectory of the centre of gravity. When the foot has reached the beam, the knee-joint is almost at a right angle. The body's centre of gravity moves in a flattened curve over the beam. The foot should land on the beam with its metacarpal part, so that a safe take-off is guaranteed. This is best achieved by gripping the edge of the beam with the two front spikes, the little toe being level with the front edge of the beam. When the body's CG has passed the beam, the bent supporting leg is extended with full strength. The extension should be more forward than upward. The body should have a good forward lean and the arms help to keep balance. The swinging leg assists the forward jump by a powerful swing of the thigh almost to the horizontal with

Fig. 42

the shank hanging down loosely. The take-off from the beam must be properly controlled, i.e. the force applied and the body posture will be determined by the spot at which the jump is aimed. Energy can be saved by not clearing the water jump in its full length, but to land in shallow water at about 30 cm from its far end. The runner should concentrate on a safe landing and focus on the spot before he extends his leg on the beam for the jump.

● Flight-phase, touchdown and getaway stride

When the take-off leg has left the beam, it hangs backward loosely. This creates a sort of long striding jump in which the arms help to keep the balance. In the further course of the flight phase the thighs of both legs are lowered. The lower part of the trailing leg folds up loosely to the buttocks, while the leading leg moves in the direction of the next landing area, thus coming to an almost full extension at the knee joint. This leg action is very important, because the impact of the body weight after the jump could hardly be cush-

ioned by a strongly bent leg and an undesired buckling at the knee joint would result. The body's CG must, at this moment, be over the landing foot. Before it makes contact with the inclined surface inside the water jump, the lower part of the trailing leg drives forward, passes the pivoting foot and makes contact with the track surface in a short energetic downstep (Fig. 42, Pos. 9 and 10).

On account of the horizontal velocity, the body's CG is quickly shifted ahead of the supporting leg. The next stride must be adjusted to the usual stride pattern.

● Judging the Water Jump

The quality of the clearance of the water jump will be judged by the following characteristics:
1. The distance of the take-off point from the obstacle should allow "running-up".
2. The trajectory of the centre of gravity of the body should describe an even curve with only one peak and follow a flattened line over the beam (Fig. 42). On landing the body's CG must be

above or slightly ahead of the landing foot.

3. Position of the hip- and shoulder axes—transverse to running direction.

3.4.4.2. Running between the Obstacles

The running technique between the obstacles is basically the same as that of the long-distance race. It is influenced by the quality of the technique of obstacle clearance. The smoother the obstacle clearance, the more harmonious and technically correct will be the running between the obstacles. The stride length is not as consistent as in long-distance running. Before the obstacle the speed is slightly increased by lengthening the stride. The first two to three strides behind the obstacles are usually shortened, particularly with growing fatigue.

3.4.5. Technical Training for the 3000-m Steeplechase

3.4.5.1. Special Preparatory Exercises

It is recommended that in the special training for steeplechasing exercises be chosen which, under easier conditions, give a rough idea of the sequence of movement needed in clearing the obstacles so as to develop the necessary abilities and skills (see 3.4.2.1.).

3.4.5.2. Basic Exercises of Technical Training

For the much longer distances between the obstacles in steeplechasing, con-

trary to hurdling, the use of a consistent stride rhythm is not possible nor necessary (in a lap of 390 m, the distance between the obstacles is 78 m). The "two-leg" training for leading and trailing function is therefore recommended.

The most economic way of clearing the obstacles of 91.4 cm height is by using the hurdle stride of the 400-m hurdler. Jumping on to the beam should, although permitted, be avoided, since it results in a loss of time.

The main prerequisite for a technically correct clearance of the obstacles is proficiency in basic hurdling exercises (see also sets of exercises for the hurdle race—3.4.2.2.). Additional training is only required for the water jump.

For acquiring specialized technical skills the steeplechaser is advised to do the following exercises:

– Exercise 1: Run over several hurdles (76.2 to 91.4 cm height, spacing 20 to 30 m) at medium to moderate pace.

Purpose: Learn to coordinate (space and time!) the running movement with the hurdle stride with long distances between the hurdles.

Points to note: Harmonious coordination of the running with the hurdling stride. The take-off in front of the hurdle must be at the proper distance (about 1.50 to 1.70 m before the hurdle and landing of the leading leg 1.00 to 1.30 m behind it).

– Exercise 2: Run over two or more hurdles under conditions near or similar to those of competition.

Purpose: Perfecting the technique of steeplechasing under competition-like conditions.

Points to note: Constant speed between the obstacles. Good coordination of arm- and leg-movements. Good forward lean of trunk during hurdle stride.

– Exercise 3: Clearing the water jump under near-competition conditions.

Length of run-up—20 to 30 metres; length of getting away approximately 20 m. Provide a safe landing area by using a mat.

Purpose: Acquire a proper water-jump technique.

Points to note: Increase the speed up to the last 10 to 12 metres. Watch for good knee- and hip-flexion on the beam. Jump off when the centre of gravity of the body is above the supporting leg. Keep the body low at take-off. Cushion the body weight elastically on landing. Shift weight to leading leg.

Auxiliary Exercise: Clearing the water jump can be trained under easier conditions when taking off from an obstacle on to the pit.

– Exercise 4: Clearing the water jump under near-competition conditions.

Fill the pit with water. Increase the approach to 40 to 50 m. After clearing the water jump run 30 metres at racing speed.

Purpose: Harmonious coordination of run-up with take-off and get-away stride with as little effort as possible. Practise running under difficult conditions; landing in the water; continue to run with wet shoes.

Points to note: See exercise 3. Landing after wide jump—stride (3.20 to 3.40 m) in shallow water for saving energy. The get-away stride follows immediately after the water pit on firm ground. The next strides follow at reduced speed.

Hints: Most steeplechasers jump off the beam with the take-off leg. To be on the safe side, the jump off the beam should be practised with both (left and right) legs. Thus the runner need not check

his stride or proceed to a change before the pit.

Check marks on the ground are useful aids for beginners in training for the water jump clearance. Mark the 5th and 7th stride and the take-off point before the "run-up" to the beam.

Negotiating the water jump should also be trained for in conditions similar to competition. Two or more steeplechasers run simultaneously to the water jump. The direct confrontation with competitors forces the runner to apply tactical means (try to be on the beam before the opponent) and makes for the consolidation of the sequence of movement of the water jump clearance under pressure.

3.4.5.3. Fault–Reason–Correction

– Fault: The athlete jumps on to the beam.

Reason: Too close approach to the beam. He does not properly coordinate the last strides of the approach with the take-off from the beam.

Correction: Train the landing under easier conditions, e.g. jump on to a box and jump off to a landing area.

– Fault: The jump into the water was too short.

Reason: Lack of force. The "run-up" on to the beam was too slow. Weak push-off. Insufficient leg drive.

Correction: Develop sprinting ability which is an important prerequisite for a good clearance. Practise especially the approach to the obstacle and the jump off it (possibly under easier conditions).

– Fault: The jump over the water is too high. The impact cannot be absorbed by the runner and he sags into his knees on landing.

Reason: He jumps too high.

– Fault: Landing is on both legs as in the final jump.

Reason. He fails to prepare for the landing or concentrates on it too late.

Correction: Train the landing under easier conditions, e.g. jump on to a box and off it into a landing area.

– Fault: The running rhythm is disrupted, particularly before and after the obstacles.

Reason: Bad adaptation to space. The runner comes too close or not close enough to the obstacles and either chops down his strides or consciously lengthens them.

Correction: Train to approach the obstacle from varying distances.

3.5.   The Relays

This track event demands dedication and team spirit from each member. Because of its sustained excitement it arouses great interest and enthusiasm with spectators. In local and top competitive sport relays are highlights of any meeting, not least because of the large number of performers participating.

Table 40   Relay Competitions organized in the GDR

Events	Age Groups (Years)							Men/Women
	10	11	12	13	14	15	16/17	
4 × 50 m	×	×						
4 × 100 m			×	×	×	×	×	×
4 × 200 m						×	×	×
4 × 800 m	×	×	×	×	×	×	×	×
4 × 1,500 m								×
Swedish Relay 400/300/200/100 m				×	×	×	×	×
Olympic Relay 800/200/200/400 m					×	×	×	×

In some countries English distances in yards and miles are still commonly used for relays; they correspond basically to the distances mentioned in the following (e.g. 4 × 400 yards or 4 × 1 mile). In addition to the relays listed in Table 40 for which, with few exceptions, World, European and National Records may be set, relays can also be held as mass track competitions with stages corresponding to the distances current for different age-groups. In addition large-scale relays (usually Road Relay Races, as e.g. "Lauf der BZ am Abend"–Berlin Newspaper– and Cross-country Relays over varying distances) are organized. The length of the stages is generally related to the total racing distance and to the age and sex of participants. We are here only concerned with the 4 × 100-m relay, as this fast event places high demands on the technical skills of the athlete.

3.5.1.   Technique

Techniques employed in relay racing are largely dictated by competition rules. We shall therefore only make a few introductory remarks. The baton must be passed only within a 20 m take-over zone. This zone begins 10 metres before the scratch line (100-m marking) and ends 10 metres after it. The outgoing relay runner may commence running 10 metres outside the take-over zone. He therefore covers 30 m to the end of this zone (Fig. 43). This rule applies only to the 4×100-m relay.

After the baton-pass, the incoming sprinter must remain in his lane until all changes have been completed. If he deliberately impedes a member of another team by leaving his lane or his position, he is liable to cause the disqualification of his own team. A good baton-exchange needs to satisfy the following two conditions.:

1. The baton-exchange must take place after some 12 to 16 m running, measured from the beginning of the take-over zone.

2. The baton must be passed inside a short distance to be covered by some three to four strides and without unnecessary loss of time.

By an ideal exchange technique and an optimal utilization of the take-over zone a time can be recorded in the 4×100-m relay which is about 2.5 sec. better than the total of the individual times of the four sprinters (Table 41). This is feasible because the passes take place after a flying start, i.e. at the great-

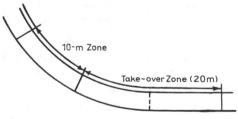

Fig. 43

Table 41   Finalists in the 4×100-Metres Relay Race for Men at the Olympic Games 1972

Country	Placing	Performance	Difference between the time scored at the relay race and the total of individual best results (sec.)
USA	1st	38.19	1.91
USSR	2nd	38.50	2.10
FRG	3rd	38.79	2.21
CSSR	4th	38.82	1.88
GDR	5th	38.90	1.60
Poland	6th	39.03	1.87

est possible speed by the receiving runner.

3.5.1.1.   Baton-Changing Methods

In practice three baton-exchange methods: the outside-, the inside- and the Frankfurt (or mixed) method are used. All three methods are practically equivalent. Not the type of exchange but, apart from sprinting skills, the mastery of the exchange technique used is important for achieving a good relay time.

– *The outside exchange*
The incoming runner holds the baton in his left hand. He approaches the receiving member from outside and passes the baton into his right (outer) hand. This type of exchange[1] is used preferably for beginners, because they are better at grasping the baton with the right than with the left hand (Fig. 44).

– *The inside exchange*
The incoming runner holds the baton in his right hand. He approaches the runner waiting for the baton from the

Fig. 44

inside and passes it to the outgoing runner's (inner) hand.

In outside as well as in inside baton-exchange methods the baton is, after receiving, immediately transferred from the receiving to the passing hand.

– *The Frankfurt exchange (mixed method)*

This type of exchange is a combination of the outside and the inside exchange methods: the first and third passes are on the inside and the second is on the outside. The runners in the bend hold the baton in the right hand, the runners on straightaways in the left hand. After receiving there is no change-over of the baton to the other hand.

All three exchange methods have their pros and cons, of which only major ones will be discussed here.

The outside exchange has the advantage that the receiving hand is, as a rule, more skilled than the left one. Its drawback is that at the first and third changes the baton is not moving the shortest possible way.

The advantage of the inside exchange is the economic use of space at the first

and third exchanges. Drawbacks are the relatively long distances of the receiving members.

The Frankfurt exchange also satisfies the demand of an economic use of space, but taking the baton often creates difficulties: as there is never a change-over of the baton from one hand to the other, the space for seizing it becomes ever smaller and the baton is frequently dropped.

3.5.1.2.   The Start

The start for the 4×100-m relay is basically the same as for the 400 m. The starting blocks are placed close to the outer line of the track. The baton lies between the forefinger and the thumb and is enclosed by the other fingers. After a successful start the runner quickly passes to the inside of his lane.

3.5.1.3.   The Markings for the Start

The second, third and fourth runners place a checkmark on their lanes just

213

behind their starting positions. It consists of one or several chalk lines across a cinder track. Coloured tape is used on Tartan lanes; it may be stuck or fastened on to the coating (placing marking objects on or alongside the track is not allowed). This is a check mark for the outgoing runner: his start begins when the incoming runner reaches him.

The distance between the check mark and the starting position depends on the speed of the incoming runner and on the acceleration of the outgoing runner. It should be sufficiently long to allow the baton to be passed without visible delay (if the second, third and fourth runners start 10 m before the take-over zone, a baton-pass between 22 and 26 m for men and between 19 and 22 m for women should be attempted).

Most relay runners find out in training the right distance for the check mark and control it in competitions. Small changes are naturally inevitable, due to the varied fitness of athletes and changes in training and competition conditions.

It has proved advantageous in practice if in all training in differing conditions attention is also paid to the feeling of the right moment of the start. This is where the runner learns to concentrate fully on his partner and to adapt to his speed.

3.5.1.4. Running inside the Take-Over Zone

In this zone a rapid and rational baton-exchange has to be prepared and executed at speed. The runners receiving the baton (runners No. 2, 3 and 4) start to sprint 10 m before the take-over zone. The outgoing runner must focus his attention on the check mark and the incoming runner. When preparing for the start, his head is turned round. In order to keep the body twist as small as possible, he will use the most favourable (narrowest) angle of vision backward. In the take-over zone the runners keep close to the inner or outer line of their lane (depending on the type of baton-exchange applied). The start of the outgoing runner must be at maximum speed. The runner passing the baton should slow down his speed as little as possible.

3.5.1.5. The Baton-Exchange

During the exchange the baton must be delivered firmly and safely into the hand of the receiving runner. The arm movement is basically the same as in running. A prolonged extension of the arm may gain ground but disturbs the stride rhythm and reduces speed. When the incoming runner has approached his partner (within 2 to 3 m) he indicates to him by a signal when to extend his receiving arm backwards. The arm fixed in this position serves as a point of orientation. If the signal comes too early or too late, this results in an unsteady baton-pass and consequently in a loss of time. The same thing occurs if the runner receiving the baton moves his arm up, down or to the side. In an action like an uppercut the baton is put firmly into the grasping hand between the spread thumb and the four locked fingers. In spite of his fixed arm, the outgoing runner must be able to continue accelerating during the take-over. In the outside or inside exchange it is useful to pass the baton from one hand to the other immediately after the exchange, because a later change will disturb the stride rhythm and is also frequently forgotten, so that there is uncertainty in the change-over.

In the past other methods of baton-changing were used. These will, however, not be discussed here.

3.5.2.   Tactics

The tactical order of running in relays serves the purpose of gaining any possible advantages over opposing teams by the applications of particular tactics.

Thus attention should be given to the following aspects:
a) Sprinting abilities
b) Starting abilities
c) Mastery of baton-changing
d) Competitive qualities
e) Physique.

Influence of sprinting abilities on running order

Performers:
The first and fourth runners cover roughly 110 m each, and the third and fourth about 120 m before a safe exchange is performed, resp. before the tape is reached (see Fig. 45). If the new Competition Rule of the I.A.A.F. is applied, the running distance to be covered by runners No. 2, 3 and 4 may be lengthened by 10 m. Runners with the best individual time should therefore be placed on the "long" distances.

Influence of starting abilities on running order

The best starter should be No. 1 in the relay, so as to gain ground from the onset over the first leg.

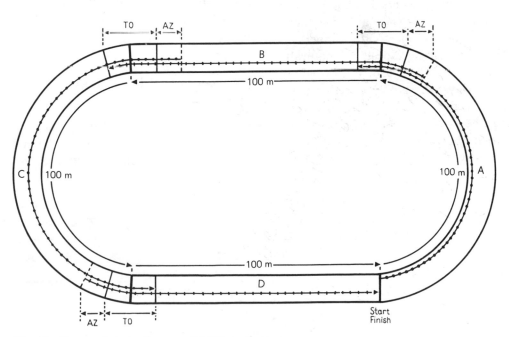

Fig. 45   Staggered starts diagram: 4 × 100-m relays

Mastery of baton-changing and running order

The first and last runners participate only in one phase of the baton-exchange. Thus the first runner only delivers the baton while the fourth only receives it. Runners with poor technical abilities in the baton-exchange may be placed in these positions.

Effect of competitive qualities on running order

It is often the last runner in closely matched relays who decides the victory over the last few metres. Combative and strong-willed sprinters are therefore best used on the last leg.

Effect of physique on running order

The two bends must be considered when deciding how the running order should be affected by this criterion. Because of the greater centrifugal force generated by tall runners, they are relatively slower in bends than shorter men. In positions No. 1 and 3 we therefore frequently find shorter runners.

All the foregoing aspects are naturally interlinked. They can be varied in many ways. If we do not find runners in the running order, proposed here, it may be sometimes due to the need to outwit the opponent's plans. Yet the best way to encounter the opposition is

to have one's own well-conceived tactics. The longer the legs, the more important tactical considerations become.

Harmonious cooperation between squad members is a further important aspect. For the baton-exchange partners should be chosen who are well suited to each other. Once a relay team has been well established, a change in position or a substitution should be considered only in urgent circumstances. Experience shows that the best sprinters are not always the best relay runners.

3.5.3. Technical Training

The aim of the training in technique in relays is a quick, economic and safe baton-exchange. All exercises should therefore be chiefly concentrated on these points. Hence it is suggested that practising the use of the baton be started without much preliminary work.

3.5.3.1. Special Preparatory Exercises

In the preparation for relay races a great variety of relay forms may be applied (e.g. medley relays, shuttle relays,

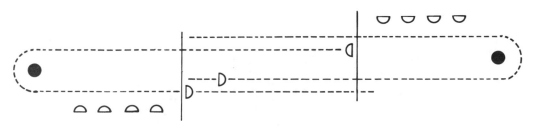

Fig. 46

circle relays—Fig. 46—etc.). We refer to the booklet: "Run, Jump, Throw" [36] containing a lot of exercises with examples for this phase of training. In choosing the forms to be used, the age of the athletes, their level of mental and physical development will have to be considered. The following is an example which has proved successful in training for relays.

Exercise: Tag with tapping zone. The athletes form two groups. Group A stands, ready to start, at a mark in front of the tapping zone, while group B, standing 30 metres further on start, upon a signal, sprint at full speed to the tapping zone.

Task: Without looking back, team A waits for the whistle of the trainer to run as fast as possible through the tapping zone in order to avoid the tap of the partner from group B. Another form: the members of team A withdraw to a line drawn 4 to 5 metres behind the starting line. When the approaching partner passes this line, the runner who is due to start dashes off (Fig. 47).

We regard this exercise as very useful, because the requirement of getting away from the opponent as quickly as possible helps avoid the typical mistake of beginners in the baton-exchange, namely the habit of looking back.

36 Team of Authors "Lauft, springt, werft" (Run, jump, throw), Sportverlag, Berlin 1961.

3.5.3.2. Basic Exercises of Technical Training

It has been pointed out that of the three suggested baton-exchange methods the outer exchange is the best suited for beginners (see section 3.5.1.1.). In the basic technical training acquirement of the outer exchange this should therefore be emphasized. But these exercises can naturally also be used for learning the two other exchange methods: the inside and the Frankfurt exchange.

Exercise 1: Baton-exchange at walking pace.

Two partners walk one behind the other in echelon at 80 cm distance. The partner at the rear holds the baton in his left hand and delivers it into the right hand of the man in front who, on hearing a signal, extends his arm back to receive the baton. The runner receiving the baton shifts the baton from the right into the left hand. Having delivered the baton he overtakes his partner and in turn receives the baton. After some repetitions the walking speed is increased.

Purpose: Practice in use of baton and in baton-exchange procedure.

Points to note: Correct backward extension of the arm. Maintenance of the baton-pass distance. The eyes of the runner with the baton are focused on the exchange area.

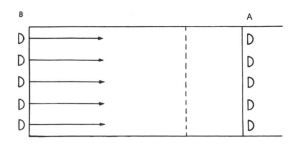

Fig. 47

217

– Exercise 2: Baton-exchange at running speed.
Repeat the same procedure as in exercise 1, but with jogging and running. Speed is increased with growing confidence.
Purpose: Correct the firm delivery of baton at higher speed.
Points to note: Keep the proper distance. The receiving runner must not look back. Correct baton-pass.

– Exercise 3: Baton-pass in the changer-over zone at medium and high speed.
a) Baton-exchange on straightaways.
b) Baton-exchange from the bend into the straightaway.
c) Baton-exchange from the straightaway into the bend.
These variations should be practised in the given order, to accustom the runner to varying conditions.
The starting position of the outgoing runner depends on the competitive pressure. If the race is of average intensity, the athlete may stand at the beginning of the exchange zone. It is not necessary to place a check-mark (train for the "feel" of the take-off). If training is at top intensity, the team members may commence running 10 m before the take-over zone, find out and fix the spot for the check-mark. The approach distance to be covered by the incoming runner is about 30 to 50 m.
Purpose: Safe and rational baton-pass at high speed.
Points to note: Correct understanding or assessment of the moment of departure by the outgoing member. Determine the marking for the start (the running speed should be adapted to the two exchanging partners). Economical baton-exchange.

– Exercise 4: Baton-exchange under competitive conditions.
The basic technical training must be aimed at producing relays in near competition conditions. It is designed to prepare the performers directly for the competition. The following rules must be applied: start with pistol or another starting device; run in lanes marked with chalk lines on the track; running with opposing teams; accurate timekeeping and use of finishing tape. If one team is definitely superior to the other, handicaps should be introduced.
Purpose: Checking training performances under competitive conditions.
Points to note: Quick, safe and economic baton-pass. Good utilization of the take-over zone. Optimal time gain, Check the time of exchange by taking times at 30 m. Method (Fig. 48): Measured area of 30 m, beginning 10 m before the take-over zone and ending with it. At the beginning and end of the measured course marking by a post. A third post should be placed at a distance of 20 to 25 m from the central point of the measured area and horizontally to it. Measure direction of the beginning and end of the measured area from this post. When the incoming

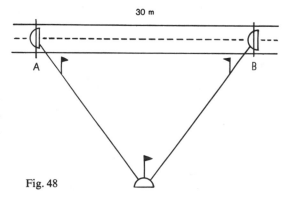

Fig. 48

218

runner passes point A (beginning of the measured area) he will be clocked. When the receiver passes point B (end of the measured area) he will also be clocked. The thus obtained "flying" 30-m time is an aid for assessing a proper exchange.

3.5.3.3. Ancillary Exercises

Ancillary exercises aim at making full use of the take-over zone and at the achievement of a safe baton-delivery.
– Exercise 1: Adjust the check mark according to a chart which gives velocity against time (Table 42).

Purpose: Use of index figures for the optimal utilization of the change-over zone.

Points to note: Appropriate length of the approach run by the incoming member (50 to 70 m). Time-coordination: when runner A reaches the check mark, runner B must start. Utilization of the take-over zone. Safe and firm baton-pass.
– Exercise 2: "Blind baton-exchange". The outgoing runner does not wait for

Table 42   *Adjusting of the Check Mark (see Tom Ecker in "Der Leichtathlet", No. 13/1969)*

		Time (in seconds) of the incoming sprinter over a 25-m distance									
		2.5	2.6	2.7	2.8	2.9	3.0	3.1	3.2	3.3	3.4
		m	m	m	m	m	m	m	m	m	m
Time (in seconds) of the outgoing runner over a distance of 26 m	3.5	10.0	8.7	7.4	6.3	5.2	4.2	3.2	2.3	1.5	0.7
	3.6	11.0	9.7	8.3	7.1	6.0	5.0	4.0	3.1	2.3	1.5
	3.7	12.0	10.6	9.3	8.0	6.9	5.8	4.8	3.9	3.0	2.2
	3.8	13.0	11.6	10.2	8.9	7.8	6.7	5.6	4.7	3.8	2.9
	3.9	14.0	12.5	11.2	9.8	8.6	7.5	6.4	5.5	4.6	3.7
	4.0	15.0	13.5	12.0	10.7	9.5	8.3	7.2	6.2	5.3	4.4
	4.1	16.0	14.4	13.0	11.6	10.3	9.2	8.0	7.0	6.1	5.1
	4.2	17.0	15.4	13.9	12.5	11.2	10.0	8.9	7.8	8.8	5.9
	4.3	18.0	16.4	14.8	13.4	12.1	10.6	9.7	8.6	7.8	6.6
	4.4	19.0	17.3	15.7	14.3	12.9	11.7	10.5	9.4	8.4	7.3
	4.5	20.0	18.3	16.7	15.2	13.8	12.5	11.3	10.1	9.1	8.1
	4.6	21.0	19.3	17.6	16.1	14.7	13.3	12.1	10.9	9.9	8.8
	4.7	22.0	20.2	18.5	17.0	15.5	14.2	12.9	11.7	10.6	9.5
	4.8	23.0	21.2	19.4	17.9	16.4	15.0	13.7	12.5	11.4	10.3
	4.9	24.0	22.1	20.4	18.8	17.2	15.8	14.5	13.3	12.1	11.0
	5.0	25.0	23.1	21.3	19.7	18.1	16.7	15.3	14.1	12.9	11.8

The given index figures are an aid to assessing with a fair degree of accuracy the spot for placing the starting mark after clocking the time of the runner with the baton on the last 25 m and of the receiving runner on the first 26 m.
Example: Time recorded by runner A over the last 25 m = 2.6 sec.
          Time recorded by runner B over the first 26 m = 3.6 sec.
The starting mark should therefore be placed at a distance of 9.70 m from the outgoing runner.
A further variant is the time check of the acceleration of the receiving runner from the start to the exchange zone (= 30 m).

an acoustic signal before extending his arm backwards but reaches back automatically when crossing a mark at some 8 to 6 m before the end of the take-over zone.

Purpose: Greater safety in baton-exchanging under competitive conditions. Having practised the baton-pass several times with acoustic signals, the outgoing runner should be able to assess precisely the spot at which the exchange must take place and reach back with his arm without waiting for a signal.

Points to note: Practise a safe and quick baton-exchange with optimal use of take-over zone.

– Exercise 3: Baton-exchange in the marked area.

The incoming member dove-tails with the outgoing sprinter. At a distance of about 30 to 60 metres there is a marked area of about 2 to 3 m. This represents the take-over zone. Both runners can accelerate as hard as they like.

Purpose: Baton-pass within a small area.

Points to note: Quick and safe delivery.

– Exercise 4: 4 × 25-m relay (2 × 50-m relay etc.)

The first runner stands at the start holding the baton; further runners stand at distances of 25 m between them, i.e. at 25 m, 50 m and 75 m. Every baton-receiving member of the team marks his starting point. The baton must be brought to the goal by the quickest possible means. Clocking at 100 m gives clues as to the exchange technique.

Purpose: Baton-exchange in near competition conditions.

Points to note: Baton-exchange technique (start, baton-pass and take-over).

3.5.3.4. Fault–Reason–Correction

Examples illustrating typical mistakes, especially those of beginners: Emphasis of controls should always be on runners receiving the baton, as they bear the main responsibility for a good exchange.

– Fault: The incoming runner does not reach the outgoing runner in time; he overruns the mark for the exchange.

Reason: The outgoing runner started too soon; the distance from the starting mark to the take-over zone is too long; the incoming runner overestimated his speed; nervousness of the starting runner.

Correction: Greater concentration at the start or reduction of the distance. Intensive practice of the baton-pass at medium and high speed in training races or training competitions; accurate assessment of the partner's speed and of one's own condition on the given day; attention to weather and track conditions (soft track and headwind are factors reducing speed, hard tracks and a following wind make for faster times).

– Fault: The take-over is missed.

Reason: The receiving member started too late. Under-estimation of the speed of the incoming athlete; over-estimation of the individual's starting ability; slow reaction (the time elapsing from the moment when the runner actually sees his partner reaching the starting line up to the point when he starts the running movement).

Correction: Improve concentration at the start or adjust distance of check-mark; for further possibilities see correction to preceding fault.

– Fault: The receiving runner turns round during the baton-exchange action.

Reason: Lack of self-confidence in baton-take-over; nervousness.

Correction: Practise baton-exchange at slower speed; look steadily ahead.

— Fault: The incoming runner extends his arm forward too early or the other runner stretches his arm back too soon, or perhaps starts running with arm extended backwards (most frequent fault in beginners).

Reason: The incoming runner is exhausted (he fears he cannot reach his partner) or the outgoing runner is afraid he will not receive the baton in time.

Correction: Drill baton-exchange and pay special attention to arm action.

— Fault: The baton is dropped

Reason: Too hasty delivery; the outgoing runner is mentally unprepared for accepting the baton, he is too nervous.

Correction: Change to "safety fist" at medium speed; pay attention to movement sequence in baton-changing; the incoming runner is responsible for a safe baton-pass; he must hold on the baton until the outgoing runner has firmly grasped it.

— Fault: The receiver's hips and legs are not pointing in running direction in the starting position.

Reason: Incorrect understanding of starting position. Nervousness.

Correction: Practise the high start. Find out the most favourable angle of vision backward to the mark and the incoming runner.

4. The Jump

4.1. Fundamental Mechanics of the Jumping Technique

All jumps consist of a cyclic motion, the approach, and an a-cyclic motion, the jump proper, and are characterized by different flight phases.

If we want to understand what happens in a jump and attempt to analyse it, we must first get acquainted with certain relationships. In every jump, as in all other track and field events, the athlete must tackle the physical laws of his environment. He must generate by forces within him a certain quantity of energy which will allow him to overcome external forces (friction, ground resistance), to counteract gravity and to move in the air for a given time.

Among the internal forces of the jumper are his muscular power, which allows him to bend and stretch at the joints (especially at the hip, knee and ankle joints).

From a mechanical point of view the jump, or more precisely the flight phase of a jump, is comparable to that of a throw, where the speed at release, the release angle and the height at release determine the so-called parabola of thrust, which air resistance changes into a ballistic curve in such a manner that the descending branch of the flight curve is modified to a greater extent than the ascending branch (Fig. 49).

4.1.1. The Take-Off

From a biomechanical point of view, the take-off in the jumps is a complicated process. During take-off (with respect to what we call the swinging movements) a constant interplay of forces (both in amount and direction) takes place.

Basically during the take-off phase the following interplay of forces can be observed. They will be described in the light of two characteristic positions (beginning and end) of the take-off action (Fig. 50 and Footnote [37]).

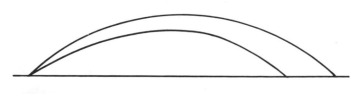

Fig. 49

P_M = resultant muscular power—its components P_{Mx}; P_{My}

$P_{\dot{M}}$ = ground reaction of the resultant muscular power

G = centre of gravity of the jumper ($G = m \cdot g$)

F = frictional force

R = required ground resistance force

$\left.\begin{array}{l} - mb_x \\ - mb_y \end{array}\right\}$ D'Alembert's auxiliary forces

During take-off checking, extending and centrifugal forces generate a muscular power (P_M). This muscular power produces in the support (take-off) area a reaction called ground reaction of muscular power ($P_{\dot{M}}$), which is equal in amount but opposite in direction.

At the same time there must be an equilibrium of forces in the support area, so that the ground reaction of the muscular power has to be compensated for by other forces. These are the ground resistance force (R) in the vertical direction and the frictional force (F) in the horizontal direction. In order to effect the take-off, the ground resistance force and the frictional force must be at least as much as the corresponding components of the ground reaction of muscular power. For instance, a sheet of ice can just about hold a man walking on it normally, but it will crack as soon as he starts running. In running the ground reaction of the muscular power increases, since the ground resistance is smaller than the y-component of the ground reaction of muscular power (P_{My}) according to HOCHMUTH.

From a mathematical equation of the conditions we have outlined, we obtain the following relations governing the acceleration potentials, which are thus generated:

$$b_x = \frac{P_{Mx}}{m} \text{ and } b_y = \frac{1}{m}(P_{My} - G)$$

37 In the above description due allowance must be made for the fact that the resultant muscular power (P_M) does not, as a rule, pass through the CG of the body and that therefore additional torque is produced which should not be ignored. But as only the most important power effects are dealt with in the above description, it has not been taken into account.

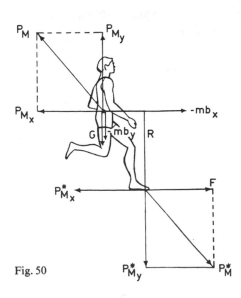

Fig. 50

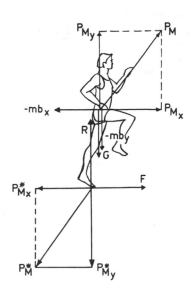

The inclination of the resultant acceleration vector with the horizontal is given by β; this angle is called the "take-off angle" [38] (cf. Fig. 51). We must, however, bear in mind that during the take-off action the resultant acceleration vector continuously changes in magnitude and direction, so that constantly changing values will result for the take-off angle.

It follows that the representation of the take-off angle by a line drawn from the jumper's toes to his centre of gravity on leaving the ground (which is still to be found in practice) is an incorrect interpretation.

4.1.2. The Flight

Through the acceleration force P, generated by the take-off, a velocity is imparted to the jumper, in which the vertical component predominates. One should, however, bear in mind that in the high jump the line of action of the forces of acceleration is entirely directed backwards and upwards, thus involving no positive horizontal component as appearing in the other jumping events in roughly the last third of the jump. The vectors of the vertical component of the take-off velocity combine during take-off with the run-up velocity [39] and the horizontal component of the take-off speed, so that at projection the centre of gravity of the body can be characterized by the following velocity parallelogram (Fig. 51):

v_0 = velocity of projection
α_0 = angle of projection
β_0 = "take-off angle"
v_a = take-off velocity, produced by the acceleration force P.

The ratio of the vertical to the horizontal speed has in the various jumping events the following approximate values:

Triple Jump   1 : (4.0–3.0)
Long Jump   1 : (3.0–2.5)
High Jump   1 : (0.6–0.5)

This ratio also determines the angle of projection of the CG of the body α_0; in the triple jump it is 14 to 18°, in the long jump 18 to 22° and in the high jump 60 to 65°. Therefore, the greater the horizontal velocity, the smaller the angle at projection and vice versa.

We give an example from the long jump:

Jumper A is assumed to have the following values

$v_a = 3.2 \, \text{m/s}$; $v_x = 8.2 \, \text{m/s}$; $\alpha_0 = 21°$.

---

38   Cf. G. Hochmuth "Biomechanik sportlicher Bewegung", 5th ed., Sportverlag, Berlin 1982. – English edition: G. Hochmuth "Biomechanics of Athletic Movement", Sportverlag, Berlin 1984, Section 5.3.

39   During take-off part of the velocity is, depending on the particular event, reduced by checking.

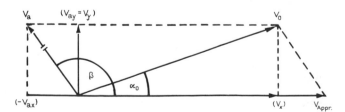

Fig. 51

Jumper B, however, can only develop a horizontal velocity of 8.0 m/s. If he wants to jump the same distance, he must build up a greater velocity at take-off, which he achieves to a certain degree by a somewhat longer take-off time. In this case he would have to reach a vertical projection velocity of 3.67 m/s. The angle at projection would then be 24.6°. The vertical projection velocity can, however, be increased only within certain limits, because the extremely short take-off time (0.12–0.14 sec.) simply does not allow for a maximum development of power. A limiting value would have to be assumed, which would probably be below 3.5 m/s. Higher values can only be achieved if the horizontal velocity is reduced. These would result in a longer take-off time, as is the case in the high jump.

Once the jumper has lost contact with the ground, the trajectory of his CG and hence the potential jumping distance (or height) has already been determined.

The trajectory, which is the resultant of the velocity at projection v_0, the projection angle α_0 and the height of projection of the body's CG, cannot be influenced anymore by internal forces (muscular forces) applied during the flight phase. It is only the path of the centre of gravity of different parts of the body that can be altered, and that only in relation to the trajectory of the body's CG.

When lowering one part of the body, another part will be raised in accordance with the formula:

$$x = \frac{m \cdot l}{m - m}$$

M = total mass of the body;
m = mass of the translated part of the body;
l = projection of the centre of gravity of the translated part of the body.

Example: According to FISCHER, the bulk of both arms is 0.13 of the total mass of the body. Assuming that a jumper weighing 80 kg, standing in a vertical position with raised arms, brings down his arms, there will be a downward shifting of the centre of gravity of both arms by about 60 cm. By this shifting the partial centre of gravity of the trunk with head and legs will according to the formula

$$x = \frac{m \cdot l}{M - m} = \frac{10.4 \cdot 60}{80 - 10.4},$$

be raised by 8.95 cm.

This means that in reaction to the downward movement of the arms all other parts of the body are raised by 9 cm to maintain stability of the trajectory.

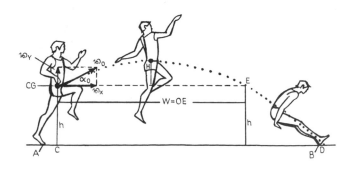

Fig. 52

This example shows that the athlete's movements during the flight phase have no influence on the length of the trajectory. In the long jump all movements in the air only help to put the jumper's body in the best position for landing.

In the high jump, the jumper's movements in the air have naturally greater significance. A jump will only be considered successful if all parts of the body have crossed the bar without knocking it down.

If we analyse the long jump, we obtain the following relations (Fig. 52):

Point A = take-off; point B = landing point; distance A–B = the measurable length of the jump. Points C and D designate the projection path of the body's CG and the point of intersection of the path of the body's CG with the ground level respectively; the distance C–D is therefore the flight distance proper of the CG of the body. The distance C–CG = h is the height at take-off, amounting to approximately 1.1–1.2 m in the long jump and 1.25 to 1.35 m in the high jump and is mainly a function of the size of the high jumper.

If we consider the variables in the parabola over the distance CG–E, the following relationships are obtained:

$$W = \frac{v_0^2 \cdot \sin 2\alpha_0}{g} = \frac{2v_y \cdot v_x}{g}$$

$$H = \frac{v_0^2 \cdot \sin^2 \alpha_0}{2g} = \frac{v^2}{2g}$$

These two equations show that the velocity at take-off v_0 has the greatest influence on the flight distance or jumping height, because it's square is large by comparison with $\sin 2\alpha_0$ or $\sin^2 \alpha_0$.

But these equations (2nd form) show also that for the height of take-off only the vertical speed component matters, while in the projection distance both velocity components, with the horizontal component predominating, are important. If the height h at take-off is taken into consideration, the equation for the flight distance assumes the following form:

$$W = \frac{v_0^2 \cdot \cos \alpha_0}{g}$$
$$\left(\sin \alpha_0 + \sqrt{\sin^2 \alpha_0 + \frac{2gh}{v_0^2}} \right)$$

In the height of flight only the height at take-off is added, so that

$$H = \frac{v_0^2 \cdot \sin^2 \alpha_0}{2g} + h.$$

Assuming the acceleration is constant, the equation for the velocity at take-off can be determined as follows:

$$v_0 - \frac{2h}{t}, \text{ wherein}$$

h = height through which the CG of the body is raised during take-off (Fig. 53) and

t = (time) duration of take-off.

Therefore the magnitude of the velocity at take-off depends on the length of the path of propulsion and the time required for take-off [40]. In practice both factors are taken into consideration. Important factors for achieving a long trajectory of the body's CG are a good backward lean in the initial position and an accentuated lifting of the leading leg, the arms, and the shoulders at the end of the take-off. In the long jump and triple jump the athlete attempts to achieve a rapid take-off by a

40 Power, which must of course be assumed, as it plays the most important role, is not considered here.

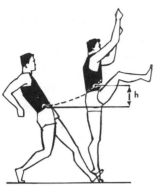

Fig. 53

flat, fast and active foot plant which reduces the braking effect to a minimum.

The driving leg action in the long and the triple jump as well as in pole vaulting is basically the same. In the high jump the leading leg can be bent or stretched. In using the latter form the jumper can take advantage of a greater amplitude of swing and of the bulk of the legs, so that in the final results between 25 and 30 per cent of the general vertical shifting of the body's CG is derived from the use of this pattern of movement. During the extension of the swinging leg a force is applied to the jumper's body which is greater than his body weight. This leg extension alone will lift the athlete off the ground. Whether, at the outset, to use a bent or an extended leading leg in the high jump and the assessment of its effectiveness should, however, always be seen in the context of the entire movement at take-off. It must be assumed that in bending the leading leg the distance between the partial mass of the swinging leg from the point of rotation (hip joint) is reduced, which leads to a higher velocity and hence to a shorter take-off time. Jumpers using the flop prefer this form, as more run-up speed

can be transferred to the take-off. In relation to an economical movement in the attack of the crossbar and the optimal transposition of the different parts of the body on top of the bar, the advantages of the extended leading leg action are mainly exploited by Western roll jumpers. Today one rarely sees top-class roll jumpers (men and women) using the bent leading leg action.

There are also differences in the arm movements. In the triple and high jump both the alternating and the double-arm technique are applied. In the triple jump this is possible only in the jump or in the step and jump.

During the flight through the air the jumper is involved in two forms of movement:

1. In a movement of translation which shifts the athlete's body along a parabolic arc and which is expressed by the pathway it covers.

2. In a rotatory movement which brings the jumper into an appropriate position in relation to the crossbar in the high jump or from the take-off position into the landing position (backward rotation) in the long jump, where it is the main rotation movement. Rotations assume greatest importance in high jumps of the roll or flop variety.

4.1.3.   The Landing

The landing is the concluding part of the jump and is of varying importance in the different events. In the high jump and pole vault, a soft springy landing of the jumper should be aimed at, in order to avoid body injuries or premature fatigue. The pole vaulter must, for example, absorb an impact of three or four times his body weight on landing.

227

In the long and triple jumps the measurable result depends essentially on an economical landing. The jumper must be endowed with agility and mobility to avoid falling back at landing, thus reducing the length of the jump. A particular drawback in this context is the backward rotation which we have already referred to. This tends to make the body fall back.

On the other hand, the landing exerts on the ground an equal unbalanced impact, which produces the "blocking" effect and, in combination with the horizontal component of the landing velocity, a forward rotation moment.

Finally, after the landing, muscular forces can be brought into action which will render the final phase of the landing more effective.

Giving at the knees has the advantage that in the subsequent pivoting of the body over the feet the moment of inertia becomes smaller as the body mass approaches the axis of rotation, i.e. the feet.

4.2.   The Long Jump

4.2.1.   Technique

The long-jump technique is viewed as an effective sequence of movements from approach, through take-off and flight, to landing.

The rules allow a variety of techniques for movements in mid-air. This is an outstanding feature of the long jump and distinguishes ist from most other events.

In practice and in the literature the long jump technique is highlighted by this part of the jump, which became known as float style, hang style and running-in-the-air style (also called hitch-kick). This should not, however, lead us to overestimate the flight phase in the long jump.

Essential factors for a good jump are the fast run-up with a change of rhythm and cadence during the last three strides and the quick, powerful and well coordinated take-off, permitting the jumper to maintain body balance while in the air.

The distance jumped is determined by the trajectory of the body's CG, which is a resultant of the take-off velocity, the take-off angle, and the height of projection. Once the jumper has lost contact with the ground, his body's CG will follow a predetermined flight curve which cannot be altered by any action while airborn.

During the flight the jumper should only be concerned with retaining body balance and preparing for an optimum landing. Just before landing he will concentrate on keeping the loss of momentum on landing as small as possible [41].

41 By loss on landing we mean the difference between the theoretically possible length of the jump (determined by the take-off velocity, take-off angle and height of projection) and the distance actually achieved. No gain is possible on landing, since, for mechanical reasons, the distance which is theoretically possible cannot be exceeded by bringing the legs further forward.

Basically the long jump is subdivided into two main sections:

a) the approach-run ending with the take-off,

b) the flight concluding with the landing.

During the initial phases the conditions for flight and landing are created; thus they are the most important in the long jump technique. In the air and on landing the forces developed during the run-up and take-off must become effective; consequently the importance of the two main sections is clearly decided in favour of the first.

When analysing jumping technique, one should always bear in mind that single movements are only parts of the complete movement and that they must therefore be considered in their relation to one another. Hence it is hardly possible to achieve a considerable improvement in the landing action without correcting the complete jump, including the last part of the run-up.

4.2.1.1. The Approach

The approach-run is of vital importance for the long jump. The greater the run-up velocity which a jumper can transfer at take-off without great loss of momentum, the better the final result will be. It is by no means fortuitous that world-class jumpers also have good performances over 100 m or in hurdle races (see Table 43). The 100-m times are, however, not directly comparable to the jumping results, since it is the speed achieved over the first 40 to 50 m which is decisive in the long jump.

The rhythm in the approach-run must allow the athlete to reach the take-off board at top speed and in the best position to bring the take-off foot square on the board with great precision. These are the main aspects of a good approach-run.

● Length and velocity of the run-up

It should be the aim of every long jump-

Table 43

Name	Country	Long Jump Performance	100-m time
Men			
Beamon	USA	8.90 m	10.3 sec.
Lewis	USA	8.79 m	10.0 sec.
Boston	USA	8.35 m	10.4 sec.
Ter-Ovanesian	USSR	8.35 m	10.4 sec.
Beer	GDR	8.19 m	10.4 sec.
Owens	USA	8.13 m	10.2 sec.
Women			
Cusmir	Roumania	7.43 m	11.7 sec.
Bardauskiene	USSR	7.09 m	11.5 sec.
Siegl	GDR	6.99 m	11.2 sec.
Voigt	GDR	6.92 m	11.6 sec.
Rand	Great Britain	6.76 m	11.6 sec.
Nygrinová	ČSSR	6.70 m	11.7 sec.

er to take off at the greatest possible speed.

H. GUNDLACH has found that fast sprinters reach their maximum speed at some 50 m. Yet the section in which near to maximum speed is reached begins at about 35 m (cf. also 3.1.4.).

If a long jumper was to take off at maximum speed, the length of his approach would have to be some 50—60 m. Such a long run would cost too much energy to permit an effective take-off.

A length of run-up permitting the jumper to reach near maximum speed would appear sufficient. This is confirmed by the following examples: in recent competitions world-class jumpers used an approach-run of some 40 to 45 m, involving some 22 to 24 strides.

An average of 17 to 20 strides was recorded for women. This corresponds to a run-up of 30 to 35 m. Boys and girls, youths and beginners use shorter approach-runs. These criteria can only serve as a rough guide, because the exact length of approach is obviously an individual matter which every jumper must decide for himself.

● Beginning of the approach and acceleration

The jumper begins his approach from a standing start. The first strides are similar to those of a sprinter in the starting section, only not as "hard" as sprinting strides, since the jumper must be cautious to maintain the spring in his muscles. With increasing speed the jumper gradually straightens up and the run becomes more upright. He continues with a smooth stride pattern; it is important that he runs on the ball of the feet.

The acceleration is assisted by synchronized relaxed arm movements.

● Precision of the approach-run

It is essential for every jumper to find out his own form of approach, adapted to his personal qualities. The exuberant jumper will start to increase his stride frequency sooner than the more calm and steady athlete, who will increase his speed almost evenly over the whole distance.

Every long jumper must work out his approach rhythm, i.e. in each approach increase his pace at the same rate, and take care to keep the degree of muscle contraction uniform.

If he satisfies these demands, his lengthening of strides will become standardized and precision in the stride pattern will be ensured. He will thus be able to perform the take-off under similar conditions. Also the approach-run should always begin from the same position. The more experience in movement the jumper has, the quicker he can establish his approach rhythm through practice. Under the stress of major competitions inexperienced jumpers tend to change their starting and acceleration pattern in the approach by applying more muscular strength. The result is often not the desired gain in speed but failure due to inaccuracy in the approach.

● Check-marks

Check-marks are valuable aids for training and controlling the run-up during work-outs and competitions. They help to achieve precision in the approach and can therefore be recommended to all jumpers. They should be placed in such a manner that they can be hit by the take-off foot. One check-mark at a distance which is the mid-point of the run is usually sufficient.

Hitting the mark should not be at the expense of concentration on the achievement of a high run-up speed. These orientation-marks will facilitate the development of a special distance awareness by a combination of the correct assessment of the distance to the board and of the effort required to reach it.

Experienced jumpers who have acquired this sense of distance through many years of training and have a well-established pattern of strides in the approach can do without such marks.

● Rhythm-changes during the last strides

During the last strides the jumper is preparing for the transition from the run-up to the jump itself.

Contrary to the old notion that in this section a certain coasting or "freewheeling" takes place, the jumper either accelerates or maintains the previously attained sprinting speed.

The physical preparation for the actual take-off includes some adjustments. In this phase the jumper will assume a more upright position, since the forward lean used in sprints would prevent a good take-off lift. Throughout the approach, but particularly during the last strides, the knees are picked up high in front in preparation for the energetic forward drive of the free leg. A visible change in the rhythm of strides is noticeable in some jumpers; this need, however, not be taught consciously. Most crucial of all is the fast and powerful execution of the last stride. Frequently the next-to-last stride is slightly lengthened in order to obtain a favourable low initial position and thereby a longer path of acceleration of the body's CG. The changes in the stride pattern are less marked in fast jumpers than in slower moving athletes. The reason is that it is easier to lower the body's CG at a low speed without producing drawbacks for the jumper. Fast sprinters tend to change the last stride slightly in order to win time for the complete extension of the free leg which is so important for an ideal take-off angle. This somewhat longer stride should not, however, become a marked "blocking" step, as this would offset the advantages of a fast run-up. The significance of the loss of time resulting from excessive "blocking" is specified by DIATCHKOV by the following values:

Forward velocity lost in relation to jumping height [42]

60 cm = 14.4 per cent
42 cm = 9.5 per cent
36 cm = 6.6 per cent

Hence the last stride must, in the first place, bring the flight phase rapidly to an end, so that the curve of the jumper's CG has no descending branch but moves only upwards after lowering in the penultimate stride. Even while changing rhythm the long jumper must strive to move on the ball of the foot.

4.2.1.2. The take-off

This is the most important and at the same time the most difficult single phase in the long jump. The whole action takes only 0.12–0.13 seconds. During this short time all take-off movements must be performed in the proper sequence and be well coordinated.

The take-off is usually subdivided into three major sections:

42 V. M. Diatchkov "Der Weitsprung" (The Long Jump), Moscow 1953.

1. The foot plant
2. The absorption of the impact (at the knee, hip and ankle joints)
3. The active extension at take-off.

The effective take-off is not only the result of a quick extension of the take-off leg, but also a result of the hip extension, of a powerful upward swinging of the free leg and the arms and of the lifting of the shoulders. All these movements should be well blended into one powerful action.

As outlined in the fundamentals of the jump, the take-off speed depends to a great extent on the height of the vertical shift of the body's CG and the duration of this shift. Applied to the long jump this means that the take-off must always be an explosive action in which the path of propulsion of the body's CG should achieve the optimum length.

Important factors are hence not only the lowering of the CG in the penultimate stride, but also the lifting of all parts of the body during take-off. Also a high propulsion of the body's CG will lead to a longer flight curve.

● Foot plant

In planting the take-off foot the action is similar to the actual movement in running. But in view of the fact that in the long jump the horizontal velocity must be transformed into a vertical momentum, which is directed forward and upward, the take-off foot should be set somewhat further forward. This should, however, not produce a "blocking" effect, as this would lead to a considerable loss in speed. This is followed by an active planting of the foot. The jumper does not wait until the foot has touched the ground, but places the leg, with a quick grabbing movement, back

and down; the foot plant must be vigorous but not hard. When hitting the board, the leg is almost fully extended (170°) at an angle of about 118 to 120° with the ground (according to V. M. DIATCHKOV). The jumper should attempt to land with the flat part of the foot. This can be achieved by pressing the tip of the foot slightly downward just before hitting the board.

Planting the foot with the heel first and rolling it up over the ball and toes is not practical in the long jump, since this would entail a loss in forward momentum and cause tension in the take-off leg.

● The absorption of the impact

The movements in this phase are usually not given sufficient attention, although the quality of the take-off largely depends on it.

The main task here is to prepare for an effective forward and upward push.

In this phase the forces resulting from the active planting of the take-off leg are absorbed by a slight flexing at the ankle, knee and hip joints. This puts a special strain on the knee joint (DIATCHKOV). The flexing at the knee joint of the take-off leg reaches an angle of 145 to 150 degrees. If this angle is lower or higher, two mistakes may occur at take-off:

1st Fault: Premature take-off

Reason: The take-off leg is not sufficiently flexed.

Consequence: Increased "blocking" effect; too much strain on the take-off leg.

2nd Fault: Delayed take-off

Reason: The take-off leg is flexed too much

Consequence: The extension of the leg is started too late; this reduces the height of projection and hence the length of the jump. During the absorption of the impact the extensors of the take-off leg are already tensed for the explosive straightening action. At the end of the absorption phase the jumper's take-off foot moves on to the ball of the foot, thus creating the preliminary tension of the foot extensors to conclude the lift off the board. This occurs when the swinging leg has reached the take-off leg, while the vertical projection line of the body's CG has not yet passed the support provided by the take-off leg. All movements at take-off are, beginning with the change-over to the ball of the foot, directed forwards and upwards.

● The active take-off

When favourable conditions for an active leap upward have been created in the absorption phase, the take-off action itself will be easy to perform.

The movements of the swinging leg also contribute to the effective take-off. Shortly after the foot has hit the board, the swinging leg starts a wide forward-upward drive. Important points are:

1. The swinging movement must begin from the hip, which is shifted forwards and upwards.

2. At the end of the swing the forward drive must be braced, so that the driving force can be transmitted to the body.

3. During the swing the leg remains well flexed at the knee joint. At the end of the take-off action the thigh reaches the horizontal.

4. A forward inclination of the line of force can be increased through an effective swing, thus creating favourable conditions for the backward rotation.

The extension of the take-off leg begins immediately (about 0.08 sec.) after the foot plant. At this juncture the thigh of the swinging leg has already finished half of its upward-forward drive. [43] The extension follows slowly at first, then becomes explosive when the angle of support is further lowered and the take-off leg is relieved of stress (among other factors), by the transference of movement from the swinging leg and the arms to the trunk. The arms are moved up but then quickly braced. The elbows are slightly turned out, so that the shoulders can be raised more easily and balance more easily maintained. When the jumper's toes have come off the ground, definite conditions for the subsequent flight have been created.

The jumping distance which is theoretically possible is mainly determined by the take-off velocity, the take-off height of the body's CG and the take-off angle. However, the position of the jumper's body at the end of the take-off phase will depend on the extent to which he can utilize the length of the flight and the magnitude of the loss on landing. The take-off velocity varies according to the age, sex and training level of the athlete, while the take-off angle is in all jumpers between 18 and 22°. Even at the end of the take-off the trunk must remain upright. A forward lean of the trunk at the end of the take-off would leave the body's CG outside the line of much of the take-off leg's vertical force of acceleration. The jump would become flat and, in the worst possible case, an angular momentum forward would be created, which would make it impossible to bring the legs well forward on landing.

43 Cf. R. Ballreich "Weitsprunganalyse", Bartel und Wernitz, Berlin 1970, p. 99.

A small backward rotation should, however, be introduced at take-off (the line of force is slightly ahead of the body's CG). This produces favourable conditions for a good flight with little backward lean of the trunk in the first part of the flight phase. An important prerequisite for producing a backward rotation is the upright position of the trunk combined with a powerful forward and upward swing of the free leg. The idea that at the end of the take-off the trunk should form a straight line with the take-off leg is erroneous. The take-off leg is at an angle of 76 to 80° with the track, while the trunk must be erect (Fig. 54).

4.2.1.3. The Flight and the Landing

Once the jumper has lost contact with the ground, he can no longer change the flight curve of the body's CG. His movements in the air can only have the purpose of keeping his balance and preparing for a good landing with the smallest possible loss on landing (cf. 4.1.2.). Whether the jumper uses the float, the hitch-kick or the hang style, is immaterial.

Today the hitch-kick is the most commonly employed mid-air action, because it ensures an efficient take-off and an early preparation for the landing. By the circling movements of the arms and legs during the flight, an apparent backward rotation is produced, which is important in a good preparation for the landing. In the hang style the following mistake may creep in during training: the jumper anticipates the hang movement, so that at take-off the swinging leg remains passive or is not fully brought into action. The hang style is therefore not recommended for beginners. The float style, in which all the separate masses of the body approximate to the body's CG, creates mechanically the most unfavourable conditions for the landing. In this style even the smallest forward rotation will detract from the result. The most economical sequence of movements appears to be that represented in Fig. 55 (according to DIATCHKOV). After the take-off the jumper performs a striding movement, in which his hip is brought forward. At the same time he assumes the backward lean which is characteristic of the first part of the flight (Fig. 55,

Fig. 54

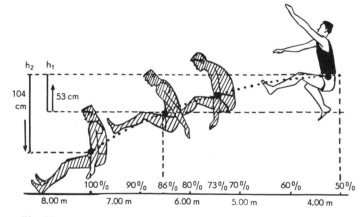

Fig. 55

234

Pos. 2/3). This backward lean should not be mistaken for a strong frontal arching (hollow-back position). Excessive bending backwards does not bring the body into a more advantageous position for the landing, because it forces the legs back too much (for balance), so that the conditions for lifting the legs for the landing remain unchanged.

When the jumper reaches the highest point of the flight curve, his trunk must have come upright again and the legs a little forward (Fig. 55/4).

From the highest point onwards, the jumper starts the preparation for the actual landing. The aim is, first, to bring his legs up to the horizontal—beyond the flight curve of his body's CG. In order to compensate, the trunk must bend forward (Fig. 55/5). When the jumper's CG has dropped to about its initial level at take-off, his trunk begins to rise again slightly. As a reaction the legs come down to a point where the feet are on the same level with the flight path of the body's CG. At the same time the hips are shifted forward. With these landing preparations the feet will meet the sand close to the point of landing which is theoretically possible

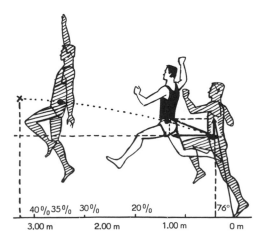

(Fig. 55/6, 7). Landing in the "sitting" position is better than allowing the body to fold up like a jackknife just before or during ground contact. But the jumper can only arrive in a "sitting" position, if he has lifted his legs to the horizontal in the last part of the flight (Fig. 56). If a jumper, due to inadequate movements in the first part of the flight, cannot arrive at this position, he will have to land in a crouched position to avoid a still greater loss on landing (Fig. 57).

After the feet have touched the sand in the pit, the jumper must strive for a good finish of the landing, i.e. he must prevent his body from falling back. In order to do so he bends his legs and shifts his knees and pelvis energetically forward above the landing point.

4.2.1.4. The Stride-Long Jump

Although the float style is the simplest jumping technique with respect to possible patterns of movement, a good execution of it seldom occurs because of the difficulty of keeping the body balanced. Those who wish to make real progress in this event should therefore choose another style. The float style (fast bunching up with feet and legs after take-off) in its old form should be omitted from sports lessons for pupils and beginners and replaced by the stride-long jump (Fig. 58). In this style the reaching striding position of the take-off phase is maintained for a long time (Pos. 1 to 3). Only just before landing the take-off leg comes forward to join the swinging leg (Pos. 4 and 5). The trunk is kept upright until this moment. Only when the jumper lifts his legs in preparation for the landing does the trunk bend forward.

Fig. 56

4.2.1.5. The Hang-Style

After the take-off the jumper allows his swinging leg to drop until it almost reaches the vertical line, where it is joined by the flexed take-off leg. The lower parts of both legs are close together at a right angle with the thighs (Fig. 59, Pos. 2—4). The arms continue their upward movement started at take-off and remain above the head during the first part of the flight (Pos. 4 and 5).

The jumper's body travels half the jumping distance in this position. For landing he lifts both legs upward and forward and lowers the trunk in a balancing movement (Pos. 5—7). Just before touching the ground, the jumper thrusts his calves well forward. Whether landing will be in a "sitting" or tucked position depends on the ability of the individual (Pos. 8 and 9).

With this style the performers are easily tempted to prolong the hang unneccessarily, which generally leads to a poor landing. Some jumpers also have difficulty in assuming the required backward lean in the first part of the flight.

The possibility of correcting this mistake is offered by a combination of the hitch-kick with the hang-style. In the

Fig. 58

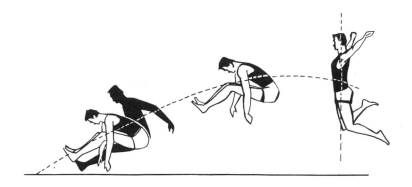

Fig. 57

first part of the jump the athlete performs a first complete scissoring movement with his legs, just as in the hitch-kick, providing for a good backward lean. After this stride the flexed legs are not parallel as in the hang-style, but the take-off leg is somewhat ahead of the swinging leg. All further movements correspond to those of the hang-style.

This combination allows for a better use of the swinging leg during take-off. This combination is not only conducive to a more powerful take-off, but also increases the forward inclination of the line of force.

4.2.1.6. The Hitch-Kick

In the hitch-kick (Fig. 60) the jumper actually continues to run in the air. He usually performs $2^1/_2$ strides in mid-air. Jumpers with outstanding results (around 8 m), such as Boston, Ter-Ovanesian, Long, Beer, have even been seen using $3^1/_2$ strides.

After take-off the long jumper actively lowers the extending swinging leg and moves it backward (1st stride), (Fig. 60, Pos. 1 and 2), at the same time bringing the strongly bent take-off leg forward. In this phase of the jump a slight backward lean is clearly apparent (slight angular momentum back-

ward). While the jumper completes his second stride with his swinging leg, bringing it up to the horizontal, his trunk comes forward in a counter-balancing movement (Pos. 6). The take-off leg remains in this position (requiring strong abdominal muscles), until the swinging leg is drawn up to the same level (Pos. 7 and 8). Up to this moment the trunk is leaning forward for balance. In the subsequent "uprighting" of the trunk the legs come down and the hips are shifted forward (the jumper assumes the landing position for the "sitting" landing, as outlined earlier) (Pos. 10). In the hitch-kick only a jumper who is able to lift his legs above the flight curve of his body's CG should attempt the "sitting" position for landing. The stride rhythm is assisted by synchronized rotating arm movements. Just before landing the arms are brought back slightly behind the body for landing and then swing vigorously forward when the heels have broken the sand.

4.2.2.   The Technical Training

4.2.2.1.   Special Preparatory Exercises

Apart from spring the following physical abilities must be developed for the main technical phases of the long jump:

a) the ability to take off with one leg from a fast run-up (springing ability);

b) the ability to keep balance and orientation during a long flight phase;

c) the ability to take off from a given check mark (development of a sense of distance). This indicates that the special preparatory exercises must in all cases be jumps with a take-off from one leg.

The basic forms of these exercises are:

Hop-ups: take-off with one leg from fast run—the swinging leg is strongly flexed at the knee joint, the upper body is erect; landing is on the swinging leg.

Bounces: each stride one jump—high knee pick-up of swinging leg after take-

Fig. 59

238

off; during the flight the take-off leg remains behind the body.

Hops: special form of the stride-hop in gymnastics, with accentuated swinging leg and arm action.

These three basic forms can be presented as games and easily adapted to the various demands placed on special preparation.

A few examples:

Basic form: Hop-up

1. Hop-ups over low but broad obstacles (e.g. two crossbars, rubber line, the long side of the cover of a box, and the like).
2. Hop-ups from check marks (e.g. zone jumping, jump on to a low box from increasingly distant marks, jumps from a take-off zone into a landing area etc.).
3. Hop-ups over several broad obstacles with one to three strides in between.
4. Hop-ups from the springboard (e.g. as high long jump over a rubber line, landing on a remote finishing circle etc.).
5. Hop-ups for clearing natural broad obstacles (e.g. ditches, brooks, hollows).

Basic form: Bouncing

1. Competitive jumping from checkmark (multiple jumps) (compare also triple jump, chapter 4.3.2.).
2. Jumping up stairs and steps.
3. Bouncing over low obstacles.
4. Jumping on marks (e.g. from hoop to hoop, from line to line).

Basic form: Hopping

1. Hopping with short step in between.
2. Competitive hopping (individual and team scoring) for time over a given distance and with a fixed number of hops.

4.2.2.2. Basic Exercises of Technical Training

The technique of the long jump has no particular difficulties for an athlete who has received a thorough preparation. The approach-run and the take-off are the same for the different techniques. It is quite easy to switch over to a new technique without learning fresh skills for the approach and the take-off.

The beginners should therefore start with the technique of the stride-long jump, which is simple. All the elements of an economical take-off, such as a fast take-off stride, powerful drive of the swinging leg, and erect upper body, are accentuated in this technique. Furthermore the learner is not distracted from the more essential aspects by complicated movements.

Building on this base, the hang-style or the hitch-kick can be developed at any time. The advanced jumper must be familiar with the various techniques and select the one best suited to him.

The sets of exercises should be applied in the proper sequence, with the idea of practising first the main phase, i.e. the take-off and its relationships with the approach, then working out the movements in the flight phase and landing from a gradually lengthened approach.

4.2.2.3. Basic Exercises for Learning the Stride-Long Jump (Squat Jump)

– Exercise 1: Hop-up with an approach of 3 to 5 strides over a broad obstacle into the pit.

Use as obstacles two upright, elastic lines and so on. To ensure a safe landing, the take-off leg must land shortly after the swinging leg and absorb the bodily impact.

Purpose: To learn the take-off and the first phases of the flight.

Points to note: After a vigorous extension at take-off with high pick-up of the swinging leg, attempt to keep the striding position as long as possible. The upper body is erect, with a slight backward lean, and the swinging leg remains behind the body.

– Exercise 2: Stride-long jump with 6 to 8 strides approach over a broad obstacle. The take-off leg drives forward and upward over the far rear side of the obstacle to join the swinging leg, the calf to which is also moving upwards. The so-called sitting position results in preparation for the landing. Landing is performed with both legs.

Purpose: To learn the movements during the flight and on landing.

Points to note: Maintain the stride position as long as possible. The two phases of the flight (coasting—landing preparation) must be clearly recognizable.

Fig. 60

240

– Exercise 3: Stride-long jump from the take-off zone of 60 cm with 6 to 10 strides approach.

For lengthening the approach-run use as a measure two walking strides as being equal to one running stride.

Purpose: Introduction of the take-off mark; practice of the complete movement without apparatus.

Points to note: Fast last take-off stride with body erect, followed by a vigorous swinging leg action.

– Exercise 4: Stride-long jump over a sand wall. In order to utilize to the full the flight curve of the CG, the heels should be lifted high. A sand wall near the landing point forces the learners into preparing properly for the landing.

Purpose: To learn an economical landing action.

Points to note: During the first part of the flight the upper body must have a slight backward lean. The legs can only come up to the sitting position if on take-off a slight backward rotation has been introduced.

– Exercise 5: Stride-long jump with longer approach and gradually reduced take-off zone (down to 20 cm). There is a simple method for determining the length of approach: run from the board until you reach maximum speed. A partner or trainer can mark the corresponding distance for the foot plant of the take-off leg. Care must always be taken to start the approach with the same leg.

Purpose: To train the approach: master the form of the stride-long jump.

Points to note: Do not stumble or overstride before taken-off.

4.2.2.4. Basic Exercises for Learning the Skills of the Hitch-Kick

– Exercise 1: Hop-up from a raised take-off area with 6 strides approach. The athlete either jumps into a deeper pit or places two box covers one behind the other to obtain a raised take-off area (Fig. 61).

Purpose: To lengthen the flight phase, thus creating better learning conditions for the movements in the air.

The hop-up is related to known movement patterns; at the same time the athlete gets used to new conditions.

Points to note: Rapid foot plant, upper body erect; during the flight the swing-

ing leg must be well behind the body (a leg brought forward too early is the result of an incomplete extension).

– Exercise 2: Jump from the raised take-off area with 2 strides in the air; continue to run in the pit.

Purpose: To learn the stride rhythm while in the air.

Points to note: The beginner tends only to simulate the strides with his lower legs. The fact that he must continue to run in the pit after landing forces him to bring his legs under him with a full striding movement. This is the only way he can run further in the pit.

Ancillary exercises: Since the beginner has no obious means of orientation, it is useful to use a substitute. The trainer holds a light bar at a height of 50 cm and at 2 m distance from the take-off board. The jumper tries to kick the bar away by vigorously moving his swinging leg downwards and backwards.

– Exercise 3: Stride-long jump from raised take-off area with 6 to 8 strides approach.

Purpose: To learn the complete movement.

Points to note: After a powerful take-off a clear striding pattern must become visible. Emphasis is on the second stride, as it leads directly to the landing.

Ancillary exercises:

a) Practise leg movements with the support of a bar or hanging on a high piece of apparatus.

b) Repeated jumps with the help of partners. Two partners run along, one on either side of the athlete, holding and supporting him by the upper arm. At each jump he is slightly lifted, so that the time he is in the air is prolonged. This helps to train striding movements in the air.

– Exercise 4: Hitch-kick from take-off board with 8 to 10 strides approach-run.

Purpose: Apply the skills already learned under normal take-off conditions.

Points to note: Sufficiently fast approach; short, energetic take-off stride with powerful foot plant. The hip and knee joints are only slightly flexed. Be careful that no blocking occurs in the attempt to jump high.

– Exercise 5: Hitch-kick from 10 to 16 strides approach; fix the point for placing a check mark for the approach.

4.2.2.5. Basic Exercises for Learning the Hang-Style Technique

– Exercise 1: Hop-up from raised take-off area (cf. exercise 1 of hitch-kick).

– Exercise 2: Do successive easy jumps, landing on both legs, using two or three connecting steps.

Purpose: Begin to learn the sequence of movements.

In order to learn the hang-style start with hop-ups; then do consecutive easy jumps, landing on both legs, with emphasis on the swinging leg action; lead them directly to the hang-style jump. Although the jumper should first execute it from a raised take-off area, with a short approach, quite soon he should concentrate on consolidating the complete movement from the approach through take-off to landing.

4.2.2.6. Ancillary Exercises

The special difficulty in the long jump is that the high speed developed during the approach-run must be kept up right

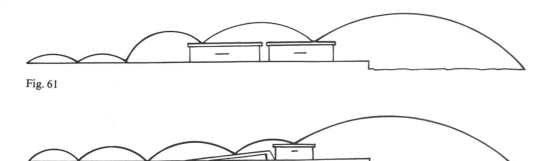

Fig. 61

Fig. 62

through the take-off. The rapid take-off movements require exceptional coordination. Additionally, the board must be hit with great precision if the jumper's ability to perform is to be completely utilized.

Complementary exercises for the long jump should therefore be concentrated mainly on the improvement of take-off movements and the precision of the approach. These exercises should be done in coordination with special strength exercises; frequently the two are identical.

— *Ancillary exercises for improving the approach:*

1. Development of precision in the approach by repeated approach-runs of varying length, but using the same number of strides (REWSON Method) [44].

This method, developed in the USSR and slightly changed here in organization, provides for the following course of exercises:

a) Fixing the starting mark (4 to 5 trials—from this point the approach will be lengthened or shortened in all subsequent exercises.

b) Lengthen the approach by two feet
(2 to 3 approach-runs)

c) Shorten the approach by two feet
(2 to 3 approach-runs)

d) Lengthen the approach by one foot
(2 to 3 approach-runs)

e) Shorten the approach-run by one foot
(2 to 3 approach-runs)

f) Start alternately a foot before and a foot behind the standard point (two run-throughs).

The jumper must attempt to hit the board, without shortening or lengthening his strides before reaching the board.

The object of this method is to improve the ability to judge distances, using a suitable stride pattern to a given point (connecting optic analysor with motor system).

Similarly, the following variations should be carried out: run-ups with the wind—against the wind—with a crosswind; run-ups on Tartan and cinder track. Through these, then, the same distance should always be covered in the same number of steps.

44 A. Rewson "Wie entgeht man dem Übertreten beim Weitsprung?" (How to avoid stepping over in the Long Jump), in "Der Leichtathlet", Nr. 14/1960, Appendix "Der Leichtathletik-Trainer".

2. Development of approach rhythm using check-marks. Short approach-run of only 10 to 11 double strides. Place a check-mark for the 5th and 6th double stride.

— *Ancillary exercises for improving the take-off:*

1. Take-off from springboard and box cover (Fig. 62). The last stride must be very short.

2. Take-off on the ball of the foot from 4 to 6 strides approach. This is the best exercise for eliminating the tendency of beginners to check with the heel.

3. Take-off from balance beam. To prevent the beam from slipping because of a wrong foot plant (checking), a partner or coach should sit on the beam (Fig. 63).

4. Jumps from short approach, clearing a very low obstacle (bar, rubber line) with take-off stride.

5. Jumps from low take-off area with medium or full-length approach. The object is to improve speed and coordination of take-off movements. M. and D. BATCHVAROV [45] have developed an aid for this exercise—a box with removable parts.

6. Take-off from approach on a downhill runway.

The increase in speed thus obtained has the same effect as the routines of exercises 5. This exercise serves to develop special strength for take-off.

— *Ancillary exercises for training the flight phase:*

1. Long jumps from springboard. The artificially lengthened flight path places higher demands on the jumper's

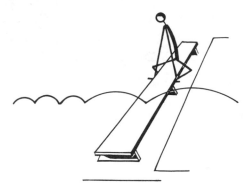

Fig. 63

balancing ability (not to be used too frequently because of possible detriment to the active take-off).

2. Long jumps into the deep pit.

3. Jump with accentuated 2nd stride in the air, landing on take-off leg.

— *Ancillary exercises for training the landing:*

1. Long jumps over a rubber line of 20 cm height, placed near the limit of performance.

2. Take-off from swinging leg and, after active landing of legs, landing in sitting position on a heap of sand (high-jump layout).

3. Standing long jump over a heap of sand or rubber line.

In these three exercises the jumper is forced to lift his legs up high to get across the obstacles.

4.2.2.7. Fault—Reason—Correction

In the approach-run

— Fault: Slowing down over last strides.

Reason: The approach-run is too long or the jumpers reach high speed too soon. Insufficient preparation to take off at high speed.

Correction: Acceleration runs without

45 M. and D. Batchvarov. "Etwas Neues in der Trainingsmethodik des Weitspringers" (Something New in the Training Methodics of the Long Jumper) in "Der Leichtathlet", Nr. 4/1961, Appendix "Der Leichtathletik-Trainer".

jump. The jumper lacks a proper sense of speed and rhythm. Shorten approach and improve take-off technique at gradually increased speed.

In the take-off

— Fault: Too long stride with pronounced landing on heel.

Reason: The jumper tries to jump too high.

Correction: Cover the whole approach distance by striding on the ball of the foot. Train rhythm on the last strides. Repeated jumps from full approach speed. Watch proper foot plant, particularly at take-off from short approach. Jumps over broad flat obstacles.

— Fault: Forward lean of the trunk.

Reason: The jumper does not change his stride pattern over the last strides. Wrong understanding of take-off and position in the air. Wrong head carriage. The eyes are not focussing ahead but on the take-off board.

Correction: Explain the fault; change of rhythm on last strides. Even in jumps from short approach, the eyes should not be focussed on the take-off board.

— Fault: The swinging movements are not powerful enough.

Reason: The jumper concentrates too much on the subsequent movements in mid-air.

Correction: Jumps from short approach with accentuated swinging movement. Jumps in which the athlete attempts to hit an object with the knee of the swinging leg.

— Fault: The hips are not properly extended.

Reasons: Slow last stride and insufficient explosive strength.

Correction: Train rhythm and do special strength exercises

During the flight

— Fault: The jumper loses balance. Mistake in the take-off.

Reasons: Poor agility or the take-off board is uneven.

Correction: Special training of take-off. Improve agility by using springboard or jumping pit.

— Fault: The jumper does not lift his legs properly before landing.

Reasons: a) no backward lean in the first part of the flight; b) poorly developed calf muscles, so that the jumper is unable to lift his legs high enough.

Correction: Train landing—jump over apparatus in sitting position. Special training of take-off, with special concentration on correct trunk position, strengthen abdominal muscles.

On Landing

— Fault: Too early touchdown of legs; the full length of flight is not fully utilized.

Reasons: The jumper is afraid of falling backwards. Poor preparation for landing.

Correction: Standing long jumps. Jumps over low obstacles placed near the landing spot.

— Fault: The jumper falls back into the pit on landing.

Reasons: Stiffness at knee joints on landing. No positive clawing movement with the feet.

Correction: Train the active landing action on sand heap (high-jump layout).

4.2.3. Physical Requirements and Training Methods for Improving Performance in the Long and Triple Jumps

4.2.3.1. The Importance of Physical Condition

The physical abilities required for the long and triple jump are:
1. Speed
2. Rapid force (explosive force)
3. Endurance
4. Special coordination ability
5. Special agility.

Body size does not seem to be a determining factor. Long jumpers are, next to triple jumpers and pole vaulters, generally the shortest athletes among performers in technical events.

● Speed

In this context speed must be understood as the ability to develop the highest possible run-up speed over a distance of 40 to 50 m (approach distance).

As is generally known, the horizontal velocity at take-off is mainly a function of momentum, built up during the approach and maintained right up to the take-off board. The athlete's results in

the 100-m sprint cannot serve as an absolute criterion here, because it is only the maximum speed achieved on the last few strides before take-off that counts. More precise clues to the special speed of the long and triple jumper are supplied by the speed developed over the last 20 m before the board. over this section top-class athletes managed some 9.6 to 10.5 m/s. (20 m "flying" in 2.1 to 1.9 sec.). Beginners should manage 8.0 bis 8.5 sec. (20 m "flying" in 2.5 to 2.4 sec.). Good sprinting results indicate that an athlete has the potential for reaching a high maximum speed. A 50-m run from crouch start also can serve as a test distance for this special speed. Very good jumpers should do this in approximately 5.6 to 6.0 sec.

● *Explosive strength (Spring strength)*

The resolution of the most important task in the long and triple jump, performing a powerful take-off from a fast run-up, depends on the speed and strength of push-off. In the past there have, unfortunately, been far too few good sprinters with sufficient spring to do outstanding long jumps. Not only the force applied at take-off, but also the acceleration in the starting section, depend on spring. A good acceleration permits a shorter approach-run, thus saving energy and offering greater likelihood of hitting the board.

Explosive power is generally measured by the height the jumper reaches with a single vertical jump. By attaching a measuring tape to the jumper's belt one can measure the difference between the belt height in standing and at the highest point in the jump.

Explosive power is well developed if there is a difference of 65 to 70 cm in

Table 44 Mean Values of Age, Height and Weight of the 6 best Performers at the Olympic Games 1972

	Men		Women
	Long Jump	Triple Jump	Long Jump
Age (years)	24.6	26.2	26.0
Height (cm)	186	187	169
Weight (kg)	76.5	78.0	59.2

men and of 45 to 55 cm in women and very well developed with a difference of 80 cm or 60 cm respectively. A second test, which is particularly recommended for long- and triple jumpers, is to perform ten one-leg jumps from a short approach (involving 5 or 6 strides). The beginner should attempt to cover 30 m in this way. Very good jumpers can do 40 m and more.

● Endurance

Endurance is important during workouts, where sustaining high work loads require endurance, but it also plays a role in competition. A good general jumping endurance is needed when training for spring, if the athlete is to get through a large number of repetitions. During competitions the jumper requires special endurance, enabling him to do at least six jumps from a full approach without showing signs of fatigue. To this must be added in every competition 2 to 4 trial runups. The jumper who reaches a final must complete a total of 8 to 10 runs over 35 to 40 m with take-off. If there is a big pool of competitors, the competition time may be so long that a special warm-up becomes necessary. This also costs energy! High special endurance levels are in such cases important prerequisites for good results.

Jumpers with a well developed special endurance can increase their performance even in the last round.

● Special coordination abilities

In the long jump and triple jump this factor may be considered as the jumper's ability to adapt to varying competition layouts, weather conditions, and situations. Particularly important is the skill to hit the board under all circumstances (cf. 4.2.2.). Balance in mid-air and a reaching landing depend on orientation during the flight, which also is a mark of coordination. These play an important role in competition.

● Special mobility

At first glance it would appear unimportant in the long and triple jump. Apart from a good general mobility, which is required for an easy relaxed approach, the long jumper, as well as the triple jumper, must possess outstanding mobility at the hip joints and in the vertebral column. Whether the jumper will be able to bring his legs well up and forward before landing, is not only a question of strength and balance, but also a question of how close he can bring his trunk to his thighs. In good jumpers (Beamon, Boston) the head is between the knees when preparing for the landing. The landing itself requires great mobility in the hips for quickly shifting the pelvis forward. This frequently produces a strong backward arching.

4.2.3.2.   Means for Developing Physical Properties

● Speed

The long jumper and the triple jumper use in the preparation phase almost the same training programme as the short-distance runner.

In the spring and during the season proper the main part of workouts must be devoted to the development of speed over short sprinting distances. Frequent approaches on the track or on the runway, serving at the same time to consolidate precision in the approach, are especially recommended. One of the most effective training means are also 30 to 50-m sprints from a crouch start. Frequent timing for checking the development of speed is well worthwhile.

Seven to nine approach-runs at maximum speed and with the greatest possible precision should be performed. At the end of these runs the take-off can be simulated to drive home the take-off rhythm. Dashes over 30 to 50 m should be done with the same frequency.

● Strength

General Strength Exercises: Before doing special strength work, a general foundation must have been laid by training. The following groups of exercises can be applied.

1. Hopping and jumping exercises without apparatus, as e.g. hopping in a tucked position, squat vaults from the tuck position, rope skipping, cossacks' dance, alone or with partner, holding hands etc.

2. Jumping exercises with apparatus and for clearing obstacles; jumps over hurdles with strides between, final jumps over 4 to 5 hurdles with and without a hop between the hurdles, jumps on one leg with and without a hop between the obstacles, over hurdles, benches, parts of the box etc.

3. Jumps with sandbag, kettle bell or weight vest (all exercises mentioned under 1 and 2).

4. Exercises with barbell (80 to 150 kg), particularly knee bending, jumps from half-tucked position, feathering jumps and jumps for strengthening the ankles (50 to 60 kg) (cf. also training high jump).

Special strength exercises:

Special strength exercises are composed of jumping and swinging exercises with movements corresponding to those of the take-off for the long jump. They are usually executed without or with only a slight additional load. The following exercises can be applied:

1. Jumping practice:

a) Take-off in forward and upward direction from long straddle stride

b) Take-off from standing from a knee-high box (only the take-off leg is on the box)

c) Bounding over box covers

d) Bounding uphill or in sand

e) Jumps on sand with pronounced stretching of hips

f) Take-off, at the same time pushing a medicine ball upwards with both arms.

2. Swinging exercises:

a) Swings with swinging leg, on sand; this exercise is particularly effective if executed with weights

b) Jumps up a wall-ladder

c) Repeated take-offs with pronounced shoulder action (shrugging shoulders).

d) Take-off jumps on to rings or horizontal bar or branch of a tree

e) Pushing off medicine ball with the knee

f) Hanging on wall-bars-push off medicine ball which has been passed to, with legs.

All exercises are performed in series of 6 to 8 repetitions with active recovery (gymnastics, jogging).

● Endurance

Development of endurance through running: In this respect the jumper's training is much like that of the sprinter, except that the amount of running in training is lower to allow for the development of strength and the learning of skills.

Development of endurance by jumps: The jumper acquires special endurance in jumping by systematically increasing the volume of jumping loads, particularly in the preparation phase. This is naturally somewhat to the detriment of the explosiveness of muscular contraction. Loads must therefore be reduced before the beginning of the competition phase. After some time for recovery the jumper regains his maximum speed.

● Special coordination

For developing a sense of distance which enables the ˙jumper to hit the take-off board with great accuracy, the most important exercises have been listed under "Ancillary Exercises" (see 4.2.2.6.).

Jumping agility is best developed by using the most varied forms of jumping. Particularly suitable are jumps with new patterns of movement or varied successive jumps or jumps which require clearance of unusual obstacles. For long and triple jumpers the following jumping forms are recommended:

Table 45   Weekly Schedule of Training during the Preparatory Period (Foundation Training)

Day	Duration (min.)	Training Task A = Preparation B = Main Part C = Closing		Training Means
Monday	60		Endurance	Runs through woods (Fartlek) During breaks various jumping exercises
Wednesday	15	A	Warm-up	Easy run or basketball
	25	B	Technique	Ancillary exercises for training the take-off
	15		Development of general strength and coordination	shot-put from standing
	30		Development of general jumping strength	One- and two-leg jumping exercises over hurdles (5)
	5	C	Loosening	Easy run on the ball of the foot-three laps around the gymnasium
Thursday	15	A	Warm-up	Slow run and gymnastics
	60	B	Development of strength	Exercises with barbell. Between series gymnastic exercises and easy run
	10	C	Running down	Jogging
Saturday	20	A	Warm-up and improvement of agility	Slow run, general and special gymnastics
	20	B	Development of jumping force	Jumping exercises on box covers (100–200 jumps)
	10		Development of trunk muscles	Exercises on wall bars
	30	C	Development of coordination ability and endurance	Basketball

Table 46   *Weekly Schedule of Training during the Competition Period (Foundation Training)*

Day	Duration (min.)	Training Task A = Preparation B = Main Part C = Closing		Training Means
Tuesday	15 20	A	Warm-up and improvement of special mobility	800–1,000 m easy jogging, general and special gymnastics, 2 to 3 acceleration runs
	30	B	Technique Development of speed	6 to 7 approach runs on runway, if possible three with head and three with following wind, 8 to 10 jumps from medium approach run
	12		Development of speed endurance	2 to 3 times 100 m at sub-maximum speed
	20		Development of maximum strength	Exercises with barbell (three exercises in 2 to 3 series)
		C	Running down	Jogging or game
Wednesday	20	A	Warm-up	Same as Tuesday
	30	B	Development of speed	4 to 5 flying starts over 30 m (timing) 5 to 6 starts over 50 m (timing)
	20		Improvement of versatility	30 to 40 shot puts or other throwing exercises
	20		Development of jumping strength	Jumping exercises (jumping up steps and stairs, jumps on one leg, bounding)
		C	Running down	Jogging
Friday	20	A	Warm-up	Same as Tuesday
	20	B	Take-off drills	Long jumps from short run-up
	15		Development of coordination ability	Hurdling-run over 4 to 5 hurdles
	15		Improvement of speed	30 to 40 runs in form of relays
	5	C	Loosening	400 m easy jogging
Sunday (if no competition)	30	A	Warm-up similar to that for competition	Running up to 1,000 m, gymnastics (great volume), four to five acceleration runs, two to three take-offs from short run-up
	30	B	Technique	8–10 Jumps with full-length run-up under different conditions
	15	C	Loosening	Warming down or game

1. Long jumps, sideways and backwards from standing;
2. Long jump from kneeling position on a box;
3. Jumps from springboard with turns and other movements in the air;
4. Jumps from springboard to springboard;

5. Take-off from various take-off areas (boards, track, grass, sand);
6. Every kind of high jump;
7. Long jumps with the less agile leg;
8. Long jumps with different movements in mid-air, which the coach indicates a few strides before take-off.

250

● Mobility

Particularly important are active movements for the mobility of the hips and the trunk. The following exercises are recommended:

1. Trunk bending forward in standing straddle position, swing arms and head between legs;
2. Trunk bending forward in sitting straddle position, touch the ground with the head and arms as far forward as possible;
3. Horizontal position on back; lift and join trunk and legs. The legs are slightly straddled to allow head and hands to come through;
4. Quick circling of trunk left and right, $1^1/_2$ circle each;
5. Straddle vaults;
6. Uphold—forward, upward and backward swinging of legs;
7. Trunk bending forward in sitting (hurdle seat);
8. Trunk bending backwards, kneeling, until the head touches the ground;
9. From horizontal position on back quickly bridge body. Trunk bending forward and backward should always be alternated.

4.3.   The Triple Jump

The triple jump consists of an approach, three successive jumps, and a landing. The sequence of jumps is laid down by International Competition Rules. According to these rules the hop and step must be made with the same leg, and the jump proper with the other leg. From this results the three-jump-rhythm: right-right-left or left-left-right respectively, which gives to each jump a special character. This is clearly expressed by the commonly used English words:

Hop   = first jump
Step   = second jump
Jump   = third jump.

The single jumps differ in their length, in their take-off angles, in their decreasing take-off speed and in their height of flight.
The triple jumper must be a versatile athlete, possessing jumping strength, jumping agility, and endurance, but also spring.
Spring must be evenly developd in both legs. For maintaining balance during the triple jump, agility is an important prerequisite.

4.3.1.   The Technique

The aim in a triple jump is to jump as far as possible with three successive jumps. The difficulty is to maintain a high horizontal speed throughout the three jumps. An effective technique is characterized by the following features:

4.3.1.1.   The Approach

The approach has the task:
1. to produce a high (optimum) horizontal velocity

2. to prepare for an effective first take-off from the board.

Accordingly, the approach is subdivided into sections: the acceleration section, in which two thirds of the distance are covered, and the preparatory rhythm section, involving 5 to 6 strides.

Jumpers do not all use the same length of approach; it varies between 35 and 42, involving an average of 18 to 22 strides. Jumpers with good acceleration will naturally require a shorter approach than those who must run longer distances to achieve the necessary speed.

As a rule triple jumpers place checkmarks some 12 to 14, and 5 to 6 strides before the first jump. These marks give the jumper orientation for the precise execution of the approach. They are especially important for beginners. Should, during competitions, a change in approach be required (because of head or following wind, soft track and the like), the marks should be shifted in the appropriate direction.

The approach should be executed so that the acceleration section is not disturbed at the marks.

Once the athlete has acquired precision in his approach, the check-marks can be disregarded.

● Beginning and first section of the approach

Almost every jumper has his own way of beginning the approach. Some jumpers do a few preliminary strides, others start standing, trying to reach maximum speed quickly.

What is important is to begin each time at the same speed, as this creates the basis for hitting the board precisely.

In the first section of the approach the jumper must develop a relatively high speed. This is best achieved by a rapidly accelerated run.

Jumpers who have difficulty in achieving an approach in a smooth relaxed manner, should increase the length of their approach, which makes smooth running easier.

● Second section of the run-up

This section is of special importance in the preparation for the first take-off. The transition from acceleration to a higher pace rate and a slightly reduced stride length takes place over this section. This causes a change in the rhythm of the approach.

The first take-off is flatter and faster than that in the long jump. To achieve this the take-off leg must be slightly flexed and hit the board in a fast, firm movement. By this the time for the first take-off can be reduced and the loss of horizontal momentum kept low. The jumper must strive to bring his CG into a favourable (high) position before the first take-off.

4.3.1.2. The Hop (First Jump)

The jumper's efforts are concentrated on:

1. Keeping the loss in speed as low as possible;
2. Reaching an optimum jumping length which still permits a controlled landing and beginning of the step;
3. Preparing the landing and take-off for the step;
4. Maintaining balance.

Like the other jumps the hop consists of a take-off, flight phase and landing, with a take-off angle of some 14 to 16°. The take-off must be executed rapidly and drive the body well forward. The right leg lands on the take-off board on the flat part of the foot (Fig. 64, Pos. 1). The body's CG must not be lowered, as this would increase the flexing of the take-off leg in absorbing the impact. The explosive extension of the right leg at take-off is assisted by the powerful drive of the free leg and arms (Pos. 2). The thigh of the free leg swings up to the horizontal. The knee is flexed to an acute angle. This flexion at the knee joint makes the leg into a short pendulum, allowing it to rapidly swing forward. Some triple jumpers have been seen flexing the knee of the swinging leg only slightly, so that their thigh forms an obtuse angle with the lower part of the leg. Like a long pendulum the swinging leg can be moved forward only relatively slowly; the jumper must therefore try to make his leg act like a short pendulum. The swinging movement of the arms is adapted to the running rhythm. The upper body is erect (Fig. 64, Pos. 4) and the counter-acting movements of the arms serve to maintain balance.

During the flight the jumper performs the so-called "reverse" of the legs which corresponds to the first part of the flight phase in the hitch-kick (Pos. 4–7). By reversing the legs he is preparing an effective landing and take-off for the step. The thigh of the take-off leg should thereby be lifted as high as possible into a reaching position (Pos. 6), from which the landing can be initiated by an energetic striking movement down and back.

Landing is on the flat part of the foot about 1 to $1^1/_2$ feet in front of the vertical projection of the body's CG. The flat-footed landing is necessary to distribute the high pressure load over a relatively large surface.

The movement of the take-off leg has a "pawing" or "shuffling" character in the sense that just before landing the foot performs a backward movement in relation to the body. This keeps the braking and rotating impulses as low as possible.

The stretching and swinging movements are started just before making contact with the ground. Under the impact of the body weight the extension movement is interrupted just when the foot touches the ground. This produces an excellent pretension of the leg extensors and triggers the reactive muscular forces. An early beginning of the swinging movements ensures their well-timed cooperation for the take-off. At the moment of landing the body is erect to avoid undesirable rotation.

The length of the hop depends, first, on the technical mastery of the athlete. Beginners should not take off for the hop with full strength. Once they master the technique and can support greater strain at the ankle joints, they may apply more force at take-off.

The advanced athlete should strive for optimum length, which is usually one metre below what he can do in the long jump.

4.3.1.3.   The Step (Second Jump)

The specifications outlined for the hop are basically the same for the step. This is the shortest of the three jumps and takes place under difficult conditions, as the same leg must absorb the body mass and accelerate it again. The pressure load in jumps of 16 m and more is six times the load of the jumper's weight.

The weight absorption phase is very short, but takes longer than in the hop.

Fig. 64

The take-off must be an explosive action; the better the stretching and swinging movements are coordinated, the more effective the take-off will be.

The free leg swings up to the horizontal, the upper and the lower leg bend at an acute angle (Fig. 64, Pos. 11). The upper body and the head are erect. The movements of the arms are synchronized with those of the legs and serve chiefly to maintain balance. Positions 11 and 12 show the position in the air which is typical in the triple jump.

The thigh of the swinging leg is tensed in advance by a reaching movement forward and upward and then brought down for the active landing.

Landing is on the flat part of the foot and ahead of the vertical line of projection of the body's CG. The higher the horizontal speed is achieved, the further forward of this vertical projection line will the contact with the foot be. Otherwise the body will pass the support point too quickly and thus not receive the full benefit of the take-off extension, which would begin too late. If the landing has been firm and positive, the jarring effect will be small. Positions 9–15 illustrate the step.

4.3.1.4.   The Jump (Third Jump)

In the final jump the athlete will focus his attention on:
1. Keeping the loss of horizontal mo-

254

mentum as low as possible by an active take-off;

2. Preparing for the landing.

During the third take-off the loss of horizontal velocity wil be greatest, because it comes after two jumps with long flight phases.

In executing the jump all the variations used in mid-air in the long jump can be applied, as the structure of this jump is similar in a number of respects to that of the long jump. The only difference is a lower horizontal velocity, so that the jumper will not be able to bring his legs as far to the front as in the long jump.

Positions 16—19 show one of the technical variations for the jump. The ratio of the jumping phases in relation to one another and to the total length is one of the factors determining the success of the triple jump. On this will depend whether a jumper can use his potential to the fullest.

The different ratios have also a certain influence on the execution of single technical elements, e.g. utilization of weights of different parts of the body or the position of the body at take-off and during the flight. The distance ratio mainly depends on how the hop was executed. More precisely: in the hop the jumper must combine two contradictory requirements:

a) produce as long a flight curve of the body's CG as possible and

b) keep the loss of horizontal momentum as low as possible.

The first demand requires a speed ratio of the horizontal and vertical components at take-off of $v_h : v_v = 2.5 : 1$. This ratio results in a relatively high angle at take-off and therefore also at landing and thus in a relatively great loss in horizontal velocity.

The second demand can be satisfied by a speed ratio of $V_h : v_v = 3.5 : 1$. This, however, results in a low take-off angle and a short distance of flight of the body's CG.

It is therefore essential to find the speed ratio that combines both requirements (a and b) optimally.

In the past there have been jumpers, who sought as long a flight curve as possible in the hop and others who consciously sacrificed a maximum length of the hop in favour of a high horizontal speed right through to the jump. Typical exponents of the two tendencies were:

a) Fyodesseiev (USSR), who used the following ratios:

Hop 6.50 m = 38.9 per cent
Step 4.82 m = 28.9 per cent
Jump 5.38 m = 38.2 per cent
     16.70 m

b) Schmidt (Poland) with

Hop 5.99 m = 35.2 per cent
Step 5.02 m = 29.5 per cent
Jump 6.02 m = 35.3 per cent
     17.03 m

Both ratio patterns proved successful; the choice of a particular rhythm was determined by the physical and mental make-up of the jumpers. Very fast jumpers should tend to the second variant, while athletes with plenty of spring should be more inclined to the first.

On the whole the question of ratios is more a matter of method.

The beginner should start with flatter hops and not do them with full effort.

This will allow him to conserve much of the horizontal momentum for the final leap and to create easier conditions during the other phases. Some suggest that the most economical relationship is about 35 : 30 : 35 per cent. With increasing skill and fitness, the athlete should try to make the length of the hop approach that of his long jump, without permitting much loss of horizontal momentum. This would change the relationship to about 37 : 28 : 35 per cent. It can thus be seen that no overall pattern for the form of the relationship in the triple jump exists; one can only set targets for better results. On the way to this level of accomplishment, the optimum relationship of the single jumps changes gradually, according to the level of fitness and technical skills of each jumper. The main criterion for an efficient ratio between the different phases should be the length of the step in relation to the hop. The step should have about 80 to 85% of the length of the hop; this value may be lower in beginners (75 to 80%).

4.3.2. Technical Training

The high demands placed on strength and agility in this event require a particularly thorough preparation, which should start early, if possible in childhood. Therefore exercises for the special preparation should be given ample time.

4.3.2.1. Special Preparatory Exercises

In selecting the exercises for special preparation allowance must be made for the special facets of the technique. These are in the triple jump:

Fig. 65

a) Take-off after a long flight phase (active landing)

b) Maintain balance and conserve speed over several successive jumps.

As basic forms for the special preparatory exercises we suggest: bounding runs, successive hop-ups; a combination of jumps on one leg and bounding runs.

1. Jumps through parts of a box (Fig. 65). The parts of the box are placed one behind the other. The pupils jump either with hop-ups and one linking step or with jumps on one leg and an intermediate hop from one part of the box into the other.

2. Hop-ups and jumps on one leg over obstacles (medicine balls, clubs, gymnastic benches, and so on), which are arranged to form several lines. The distance between the lines can increase from line to line. As an incentive the various exercises can be done in teams and for the shortest time.

3. Jumps over bars, skipping ropes, gymnastic hoops or chalk marks. The athletes jump from space to space with a bounding run or jumps on one leg. The distances between pieces of apparatus or check-marks can be varied according to age and proficiency.

4. Marked jumps on upper parts of boxes. For the bounding run the upper parts of the box are placed directly one behind the other 1.00 to 1.50 m apart; if using jumps on one leg, they are placed diagonally at distances of 2.00 to 2.50 m.

5. Competitive jumping with run-up. The learners stand in several lines behind a take-off mark from which they will perform 3 or more consecutive jumps after a short run-up. Each pupil remains on the spot where he landed after the last jump. The winner is the one who is ahead of the others. The winners of each line then compete in a final.

6. Cover a given distance with as few jumps as possible. Jumping will be executed with and without a run-up, by bounding or by jumps on one leg.

7. Lattice-jumping. Draw 5 to 6 lines at intervals of 1.80 to 2.00 m in a rectangular field of 10×20 m, parallel with the 20-m side. Place clubs 1.00 m apart, marking out one long side of the field. From the opposite right or left corner of the field the athletes jump first between the pair of clubs opposite them, by touching each section of the field only once. At the next passage they jump from the same starting point

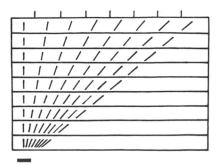

Fig. 66

257

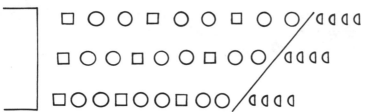

Fig. 67

towards the second pair of clubs etc. The winner is the first to the last club.

8. Jumps from mat to mat. Gymnastic mats are placed on the ground one behind the other at distances of 1.50 to 1.80 m (depending on the age of the participants). The pupils do only one stride on the mat, then jump across the interval to the next.

9. Jump over a double ditch. Two parallel ditches (width 1.50 and 1.00 m) are drawn on the ground with chalk, 30 cm apart. The pupils jump from a short approach by two consecutive jumps (double-jump), using a bounding run or jumps on one leg, over both obstacles. For safety reasons the rear edge of the second ditch should be in the jumping pit.

10. Marked jumps with a hop-step-and jump-rhythm. Small circles, one behind the other, are drawn on the ground at distances of 2.00 to 2.50 m. The athletes must jump, using the hop-step-and-jump rhythm, from circle to circle. For a better orientation, the circles can be drawn in two colours or instead of every third circle draw a square (Fig. 67). This exercise gives preparation for the basic method and can be used long before practising the triple jump proper.

4.3.2.2. Basic Exercises of Technical Training

Experience shows that the "complex method" is the best way of teaching the triple jump in all phases of training, as the single jumps can be executed correctly only as part of the complete movement, i.e. by learning the jumping rhythm. The aim of the basic technical training must be:

a) to understand the correct sequence of movements

b) to arrive at a nearly exact jumping rhythm

c) to master jumps from a short run-up without great effort.

The following series of exercises is recommended:

– Exercise 1: Successive triple jumps, short distances, from walking.

Purpose: Getting familiar with the sequence of movements and the jumping rhythm.

Points to note: Accentuated swinging leg action; constant rhythm.

–• Exercise 2: Triple jump, from walking, into a pit.

Purpose: Same as in exercise 1: get accustomed to the competition layout.

Points to note: Proper ratio of jumps (in duration, not yet in distance). Fluent movement of take-off leg after the first take-off. Powerful action of the swinging leg in the step.

– Exercise 3: Triple jump from take-off zone, using 4 to 6 approach strides.

Purpose: Learning to do movements at greater speed.

Points to note: Ratio of strides, and distances; fluent movement of the swinging leg during the hop.

— Exercise 4: Triple jump with marks for the single jumps, with approach of 6 to 8 strides.

Purpose: Make learners use maximum strength, particularly in the step and jump.

Points to note: Special accent on the step by an active landing. Foot plant on the sole of the foot.

— Exercise 5: Triple jump from board, or marks the width of a board, from 6 to 10 strides approach (move the take-off zone back from the pit).

Purpose: Introduce conditions similar to those of competition.

Points to note: Rotation on landing will now increase. Their reason is easily explained. Point out that the active landing and the position of the upper body at take-off are the best way of preventing undesirable rotation on landing. Gradually increase approach. Every new length of approach creates new and greater difficulties on landing between jumps.

4.3.2.3. Ancillary Exercises

A further technical improvement can only be achieved when it is closely allied to a special development of force, required for the virtually complete utilization of speed and spring by the jumper. A series of ancillary exercises serve this purpose. The improvement of particular phases of the jump is obtained either by making conditions difficult or by practising parts only of the rhythmic movements.

● Ancillary exercises for training the run-up and the hop

All special exercises for training the approach and take-off in the long jump serve this purpose (see 4.2.2.6.). The only difference is in practising the rhythm. The triple jumper needs, because of his different rhythm, a checkmark placed about 10 m from the board, giving him the signal for immediate preparation for the take-off.

● Ancillary exercises for training the flight phase of the hop and the execution of the step

1. Jumps on one leg over low obstacles with and without a linking hop. The obstacles can be made progressively higher (Fig. 68). The obstacles force the jumper to reverse the legs in the air and to execute the active landing properly.
2. Several successive jumps on one leg from a fast approach (multiple jumps). The jumper must try to lose as little initial speed as possible. This exercise can also be performed competitively for time and distance.
3. Triple jump from the cover of a box after short approach. The flight curve of the hop will obviously be higher and longer because of the raised take-off platform. This influences the direction of the hop as well as the movements at landing and take-off, making them more difficult and requiring more attention (Fig. 69).
4. Same as 3, but also doing the jump from the cover of a box (Fig. 70).
5. Same as 3, but doing the step over a box cover (Fig. 71).

259

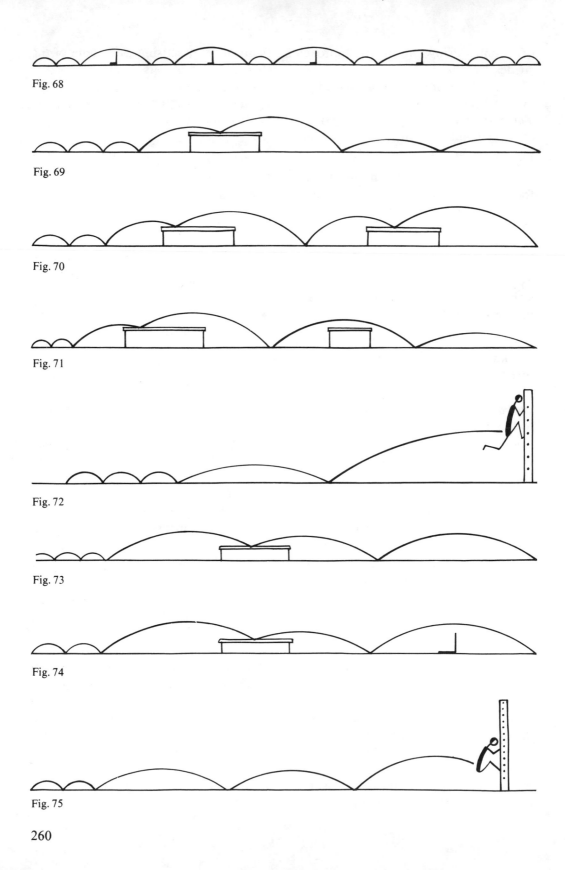

Fig. 68

Fig. 69

Fig. 70

Fig. 71

Fig. 72

Fig. 73

Fig. 74

Fig. 75

6. Successive hop-ups, driving the swinging leg up high.

7. Hop and step from short approach, landing on wall bars (the hands grab an accessible bar). The jumper must attempt to land as high as possible on the wall-bars with his swinging leg.

8. Same as 7, but landing on a box of medium height or on heaped mats.

● Ancillary exercises for training the jump

1. Long jumps with a weaker leg.

2. Triple jump from short approach; hop on to a box cover (Fig. 73).

3. Same as 2, but doing the jump over an obstacle of 30 to 50 cm height and at a distance of 1.50 m from the take-off area (Fig. 74).

4. Triple jump from short approach, landing with both legs on wall-bars (Fig. 75).

5. Same as 4, but landing from the jump on a heap of mats or a jumping hill (pole vault facility).

4.3.2.4.   Fault–Reason–Correction

In the hop

– Fault: The take-off leg lands too far away from the body ("blocking" step).

Reason: Attempting a hop that is too high.

Correction: Run on the ball of the foot until take-off. Acceleration on the last strides. Do all ancillary exercises of the long jumper for improving the take-off.

– Fault: Premature movement of legs in the air.

Reason: Too slow take-off and short duration of flight.

Correction: Train take-off with good swinging leg action; start leg movements in the air upon command.

– Fault: The jumping leg lands too far away from the body's CG.

Reason: Passive landing.

Correction: Do jumps with active foot plant; do series of jumps on soft ground.

In the Step

– Fault: Flight curve too flat.

Reason: a) poor muscular strength; b) delayed take-off and weak swinging leg action; c) too much forward lean of the upper body.

Correction: a) Special strength exercises; b) from fast run-up jumping step, then drive swinging leg up high (also over low obstacles); c) conscious training of position of the upper body.

In the jump

– Fault: Flight curve too flat

Reason: Poor take-off with inadequate coordination of arms and swinging leg.

Correction: Clear obstacles or jump on a box for final leap.

– Fault: Lowering legs too soon for landing.

Reason: The position of the upper body on take-off is not correct.

Correction: Practise the final leap with upper body erect: jumps on to the wall bars and jumps landing on sand in sitting position.

The physical requirements and training of the triple jumper are basically the same as those for the long jumper. No specifications are therefore given and we refer to the section 4.2.3. on the "Long Jump".

4.4.   The High Jump

The high jump consists of a sequence of movements aimed at clearing a vertical obstacle. In this action gravity is off-set by a powerful push-off, which sends the jumper "flying" across the obstacle. In this flight his body's CG follows a steep, relatively short parabolic flight curve, which is predetermined by the take-off speed (v_0), the take-off angle (a_0) and the take-off height (h_0) and cannot be altered by any kind of movement on the part of the jumper in the air. Some special points of technical interest are:
1. that every movement in the air causes a reaction movement in the opposite direction;
2. that certain phases in the jump, particularly with the straddle and flop style, require rotating moments, which must be generated during take-off and
3. that the rotation movements generated at take-off can be accelerated or delayed by corresponding movements of parts of the body in the air.
For a better understanding of some difficult aspects of the high jump, essential points of a more general nature will be dealt with in detail in various paragraphs referring to the Straddle.

4.4.1.   The Technique

For analysis the complete movement is subdivided into several phases: the run-up, the take-off, bar clearance and landing.
All the phases are so closely interrelated, that it is only theoretically possible to define the end of one and the be-ginning of the next. Thus an effective take-off will chiefly depend on the approach pattern and the rhythm and speed built up during the approach. All the subsequent explanations refer to a jumper who takes off from the left leg.

4.4.1.1.   The Approach

The purpose of the approach is:
1. to produce an optimum convertible horizontal momentum, permitting the jumper to achieve a favourable take-off angle ($\alpha_0 = 60$ to $65°$) at the greatest take-off velocity possible;
2. to prepare for the take-off by a proper rhythm of approach in relation to the structural change of the last strides;
3. to obtain an advantageous angle of flight to the bar (angle between the bar and the projection line of the flight curve), which is roughly determined by the angle of approach in relation with the style of jump used.
This purpose can be achieved by using the following approach pattern:
The approach-run must be in a straight line—usually some seven to nine hard running strides, frequently after two to three strides of easy walking.
The speed at the end of the approach must be controllable, permitting the jumper to convert the horizontal plane of motion into an almost vertical one. An approach velocity of some 7 m/s has been recorded for top jumpers.
The amount of speed developed depends on the training level of the athlete. High jumpers should attempt to convert a horizontal speed that is as

high as possible, because the vertical take-off speed, which is the chief determining factor for the height of the jump, depends on it.

The direction of the approach, i.e. the approach angle, will vary according to the jumping style and the leg the athlete uses for the take-off. In the Western Roll, in which the different parts of the body cross the bar almost simultaneously, the flight path across the bar will be kept short. In this case steep approach angles are more advantageous than flat ones. The approach to the bar on a diagonal line serves only to provide a favourable position for the swinging leg action. As a rule the approach angle in the Western Roll is between 40 to 60°.

In the Straddle different parts of the body clear the bar one after the other. Near to the bar the flight path must therefore be longer to avoid the last parts of the body, and particularly the swinging leg, touching the bar. For this style a flatter angle of approach should be chosen. It varies, as a rule, between 25 and 45°.

In these two kinds of jump the approach is performed from the side of the take-off leg; in the Eastern cut-off and Scissors, from the right side. This means that the left-footed jumper does the approach from the left side in the Straddle and Western Roll and from the right side in the Eastern Cut-Off and Scissors. For the Scissors we recommend approach angles between 25 and 45°.

A few remarks regarding the speed pattern and approach rhythm:

Investigations have shown that there is no uniform acceleration in the approach. The rate of acceleration varies in all cases. It has been further found that in all successful jumps acceleration stops at the penultimate stride, while any further acceleration invariably results in failure. What is the reason for this?

The approach has two parts. In the first part emphasis is on the development of speed, while the second part, e.g. the last two or three strides, serve the preparation of the take-off. These different tasks are also clearly reflected in the structure of the strides. A distinct rhythm is generated which shows itself in different applications of power and hence in different lengths and durations of the strides. The preparation for take-off is upset if the jumper, in place of a smooth rhythm, suddenly accelerates his movements.

There are different ways of achieving an effective approach rhythm in which, however, the following demands must be satisfied:

1. The body's CG must be low before take-off in order to obtain a longer path of acceleration.

2. Favourable conditions for the best possible utilization of the swinging masses (swinging leg and arms) must be created, so that the velocity and amplitude of movements can be increased to the maximum.

3. The reacting forces developed in the muscles and ligaments must be fully utilized for increasing the take-off velocity. V. M. DIATCHKOV [46] has studied the pattern of rhythm in the approach for the high jump, and has substantiated six variations, of which the one outlined below is known by experience to be the best.

46 V. M. Diatchkov "Zur Anlaufgestaltung im Hochsprung" (The Approach for the High Jump), in "Der Leichtathlet", Nr. 29/1960, Appendix "Der Leichtathletik-Trainer").

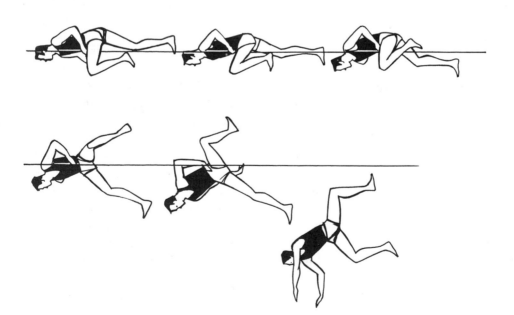

Fig. 76

"The fluent increase of velocity and length of strides in the approach-run is replaced by a marked push-off and greater amplitude of motion in the penultimate stride; this stride is hence the longest. Simultaneously a gradual lowering of the body's CG, as the jumper approaches the take-off, leads to a reduction in time, as well as to a shortening of the length of the last stride in spite of the advanced position of the take-off leg. Because of this during the last stride the foot dwells longer on the support. As has been shown by an analysis of the structure of the last approach strides, the prolongation of the support phase over the last strides has a positive influence on increasing the amplitude of the swing with the free leg in the take-off proper."

4.4.1.2. The Take-Off

The beginning of the take-off is marked by the foot plant of the jumping leg on the take-off point. This point can only be fixed theoretically, because practically it begins with the last strides.
In the section 4.4.1.1. ("The Approach") we stated that the last strides prepare the take-off and that they are subject to a change in structure, speed and length. Normally the jumper performs the last two strides over a relatively deeply bent knee (Fig. 76, Pos. 1 and 3) and reduces the flight phase in favour of the support phase. According to the most recent findings the penultimate stride should be about 1 foot longer than the last stride, which blends with the take-off proper. The swinging leg is now pushing more in the forward-upward plane, thus accelerating the pelvis considerably, so that it gets ahead of the shoulder girdle, giv-

ing the jumper the extended backward lean before take-off which is typical of the high jump. (Fig. 76, Pos. 4 and 5). Just one point concerning the arm action in the high jump. Two forms of arm movement are known in the high jump: the normal alternating arm movement and the double-arm technique. On the last step the arm of the free-leg side is kept behind the trunk, while the arm of the take-off side is brought back to join it. In this position both arms are behind the trunk.
Purpose of the take-off:
1. Check the horizontal run-up speed and convert the horizontal direction of movement into a relatively steep vertical plane.
2. Develop a high take-off speed and optimal take-off angle.
3. Produce the rotating moments required for clearing the bar.
Although take-off is an action which occurs in a very short time (0.15 to 0.25 sec.), it has two fundamental phases: the checking and the acceleration phase.
The checking phase. It begins with the foot plant of the jumping leg, which is in the Straddle at about 70 cm (an arm's length) from the bar. The foot of the jumping leg, landing heel first, is immediately slapped down, which renders the ankle joint into a lever mechanism that will become effective subsequently. At the same time the knee is straightened, while the hips continue their forward and upward movement, thus increasing the backward lean of the body to its maximum (120 to 127°). The thigh and the upper body now form almost a straight line (Fig. 76, Pos. 5).
The knee extension which we have just mentioned is vital. The jumping leg

acts first as a lever, which immediately introduces the conversion from the horizontal movement. By this extension the leg extensors are pre-tensed. Through their elasticity they react positively against the forces of inertia produced by the body weight and the swinging masses which force the knee to bend. This triggers the reaction forces of the muscles which are attempting to regain the former position.

These forces will then assist the conscious stretching movement and are one of the determining factors for achieving a high take-off and hence projection speed. If the two first phases merge, i.e. if the knee bends immediately after the heel plant, the desired effect cannot be obtained.

During the slapping down of the foot, the arms and the swinging leg continue their previously started forward movement. The swinging leg is still well bent at the knee-joint. The bracing phase is ended, as soon as the curve of the body's CG has reached its lowest position. Now the positive acceleration phase begins.

The acceleration phase. The jumping leg reacts to the forces exerting power on the support by an increasing tension of the muscles, especially of the free-leg extensors. This tension produces the levering effect which we have already mentioned, causing a bending of the body's flight path upwards. In this phase the strongest locking of the knee is not yet concluded. The knee joint opens, i.e. the jumping leg straightens only when the swinging masses (swinging leg and arms) have passed their maximum acceleration, in fact when pressure on the support leg is released. At this point the angle at the knee joint is of about 135 to 140°.

This line of force must not be interrupted by bending at the hip joint. The pelvis must continue to press forward and upward. The upper part of the body must be brought out of its lean through a bending of the upper part of the spine, resulting in the typical crouched position of the high jumper before the actual take-off (Fig. 76, Pos. 6 and 7).

During this phase the body's CG moves in a vertical line and favourable conditions are created for the subsequent bar clearance by introducing angular momenta which vary according to the form of bar clearance used.

It is difficult for the jumper to generate these angular momenta, as his body must, for this purpose, assume positions which work against the logical application of force. Good jumpers therefore attempt to delay this moment as long as possible, thus keeping impulse losses small. In contrast with this, bad jumpers try to prepare for the rotation during the approach and in the transition to the take-off by stepping out of the line of the run-up. In doing this the body weight is shifted too much and too early over the jumping leg, and this, as we have already mentioned, leads to the loss of a great part of the force impulses during lift.

In the final take-off phase the body must be completely extended from the toes upwards, reaching an angle of 90° to the horizontal.

In the Straddle (Fig. 76) the heel, after coming off the ground, is pressed inwards, so that the foot turns out. This movement is introduced by the swinging leg but involves the whole body. The leg swings upward and forward in the running direction and draws, in the final phase of the take-off, the hip of the free side of the body into the movement. This brings the jumper, at the end of the jump and at the beginning of the bar clearance phase, into a position which will allow the various parts of his body to drift across the bar in a flattened arc (Fig. 76, Pos. 10 and 11). The arms also swing upwards in the Straddle in an analogous movement to that of the legs, in which the arm and shoulders of the free-leg side swing higher than those of the other side.

Beginners, but some top-class jumpers as well, frequently make the mistake of introducing the rotation by angling the swinging leg towards the bar. This leads to an excessive "laying" and to considerable loss of height.

We now briefly explain the action of the swinging leg. The movements of the swinging leg have great importance for the performance and the success of the take-off. This action has the following aims and characteristics:

1. The swinging leg action creates a movement, which is transmitted to the body as soon as this action is braced. The faster the movement of the swinging leg, the more energy can be drawn from it at the end for the take-off.

2. Because of the considerable acceleration of the swinging leg during absorption of the impact, the pressure on the take-off leg is increased and engenders reaction forces in the calf muscles. This is why the velocity of the swinging leg has such a great influence on the speed of take-off.

3. The height of the swinging leg at the end of the push-off is one of the determining factors for the take-off height of the body's CG.

4. The angular momentum produced by the strong one-sided pull of the swinging leg in a forward-upward direction is particularly important for the Western Roll and Straddle.

Actually two techniques can be applied for the swinging leg action: one in which the leg is bent at the knee joint and one in which it is straight. On the whole the straight leg technique is more advantageous for the Parallel Straddle (also with final diving, cf. 4.4.1.3.), so much so that the majority of the world-best jumpers use it. Short analysis of the extended swinging leg action:

The action of the swinging leg is introduced by the hips, which move forward and upward before and during touchdown of the take-off leg. The leg is still strongly bent at the knee joint and the point of the foot is cocked to prevent hitting the ground. The jumper must now endeavour to get his swinging leg past the take-off leg as rapidly as possible. When this has occurred, the jumper will thrust the lower part of his leg vigorously forward and upward with a whip-like movement, so that his swinging leg is now completely extended in a horizontal position (Fig. 76, Pos. 8). This movement is of the greatest importance, because the kinetic energy produced by the lower part of the leg is transmitted to the whole leg at the moment of extension, so that it experiences an additional acceleration. In order to maintain this extended position all muscles of the swinging leg must be tensed so as to avoid the lower leg lagging behind the complete movement. The idea that after this movement the leg should bend again is erroneous. It can often be seen in jumpers, but is only a sign of lack of suppleness.

The swinging movement of the arms and of the free leg are halted just before the end of the take-off. In the Straddle the hip side must be drawn into the forward-upward movement of the swinging leg to produce the required rotation impulses.

4.4.1.3. Bar Clearance and Landing

The highlights of the jump are the techniques used in crossing the bar; the different jumping styles are named accordingly. Basically five jumping techniques are known: Straddle, Western Roll, Eastern Cut-Off with and without trunk layout, Scissors and Fosbury Flop (cf. 4.4.1.4.).

All these forms have naturally variations which will not be discussed here.

The movements during bar clearance have as their purpose:

1. to bring the parts of the body into the most favourable relation to one another so as to prevent the bar being knocked down and to enable the jumper to utilize, as best he can, the rotating movement through acceleration or deceleration, in order to cross the bar;

2. to create favourable conditions for a safe landing.

In both Roll and Straddle, at the end of the take-off, the air-born body is brought from an almost vertical position to a near horizontal one for clearing the bar. In fact the only difference is that the rotation is more marked in one style than in the other, so that shifting of the various parts of the body naturally varies.

These differences become evident only during bar clearance and in preparation for the landing; in the first phase, i.e. during the approach to the bar, the differences between the Roll and Straddle style are only slight. In preparation for the bar clearance the straddle jumper, particularly through the unilateral pull of the swinging leg, begins to rotate with front of the body to the bar, almost flying on to it in this position. Then begins the so-called shifting work. The swinging leg, which reaches the bar first, together with the arm of the same side, and is initially almost at right angles to the trunk, is now stretched along the bar. At the same time the jumping leg is drawn up close to the hollow of the knee of the swinging leg and pressed outwards. As a result the parts of the body are grouped around the longitudinal axis of the body and the jumper experiences an acceleration of angular momentum about this axis. The jumper now turns his face and chest completely to the bar and is lying almost parallel to it. The head should be pressed to the chest. The arms, which at first were in front of the body, are now on the side and close to the trunk; frequently the inside arm is curled up on the chest.

In this phase the turning outwards of the jumping leg is started, one of the most important movements in crossing the bar. The thigh is turned outwards in a pronounced manner from the hip joint, at which point the knee and tip of the foot (also turned outwards!) assume the leading role in the movement. It is not necessary to straighten the knee simultaneously; it is far better to keep the leg bent. If the turning outwards is limited by a lack of mobility at the hip joint, it is continued by an additional torque about the spine.

The jumper is now moving away from the bar and preparing for landing. Since the rotation of his body about the long axis would force him to land on his back, he must now strive to delay this rotation. This is achieved by allow-

Fig. 77

ing the trunk, arms and swinging leg to move downwards, away from the longitudinal axis, by extending the jumping leg upwards and backwards. This makes for a soft landing. The free leg and arm usually touch the ground first, thus reducing the impact. The body then rolls over the shoulder or the hips to the back.

This technique can be further improved by diving over the bar (Fig. 77). This should not, however, be confused with the "Dive Straddle", a technique which shall be discussed separately.

From the position of the body on top of the bar described above, the trunk and the swinging leg fold together, so to speak, with the pelvis as a turning point (Pos. 2). Through this diving movement the pelvis, and with it the joint of the jumping leg, is shifted upwards, permitting the jumper better to turn this leg away from the bar. This, of course, requires excellent judgement, which can only be acquired after long experience. A jumper should therefore attempt this technique only when he masters the Parallel Straddle perfectly. Often these two forms more or less merge into each other, or else one form is more pronounced than the other.

The Dive Straddle differs from the Parallel Straddle in that the body makes a greater angle (sloping more) with the bar. In this style it is not a rolling movement but rather a tipping movement that predominates. It requires considerable angular momentum and a corresponding amount of strength to produce it, so that this technique is not as efficient as might be expected, considering the different phases of bar clearance separately. If we mention it here briefly, it is because it has a certain amount of importance in college sports and in the training of beginners (see also 4.4.6.). Fundamental requirements for the approach and take-off: cf. sections 4.4.1.1. and 4.4.1.2.

4.4.2.   Technical Training for the Straddle Jump

Since the Straddle is still taught today—mainly in schools—this jumping technique merits discussion here.

But we should first make clear when to begin with the training of the Straddle style. Generally one may say that an important prerequisite is a fair amount of explosive force, jumping ability and jumping experience. This means that the push-off in an upward direction must be thoroughly mastered. If these demands are not satisfied, various mistakes may creep in during training of the Straddle jump over low heights which will hinder further development.

As a rule, therefore, one should not start with special training of the straddle before the age of 13 or 14, whereas learning the crude or simplified form can be started by boys and by girls, at the age of 9 or 10 years, mainly with the object of building up versatility and agility.

The straddle jump should be learned in two stages, with different objectives. The first stage serves the training of beginners and for practice on a mass basis; it includes the foundation training (also some special training) and should lead the jumper to the mastery of a satisfactory straddle jump technique.

The second training stage is characterized by the systematic training of different elements and their various relationships and may be regarded as special training, which should result in the coordinated execution of the sequence of movements.

This training system should chiefly be used by the high-jump specialist and provides the foundation for the special technical training.

4.4.2.1. Special Preparatory Exercises

Before starting to train a particular sequence of movements, a more general preparation for the high jump is required. Because of its special requirements, the following points must be taken into account:

a) The jumper must take off with one leg from a forward movement (walking or running) and clear a high obstacle in a free jump.

b) To achieve a steep and high flight curve, the action of the swinging masses (swinging leg and arms) must be smoothly linked with the take-off movement.

c) In modern high jumping (straddle style) the rotation of the body plays an important role. This requires a special technique for producing angular momentum at the end of the take-off.

In the light of these points three basic forms emerge for the special preparation of the high jump:

1. Jumps over various obstacles with a take-off from one leg, putting special emphasis on a relatively long take-off stride and adequate backward lean in the jumping position.

2. Jumps with a longer flight phase than usual, requiring special agility, in which considerable demands are placed on the jumper's sense of orientation by turns and obstacles.

3. Gymnastic exercises requiring jumping power, jumping agility and mobility (handsprings, somersaults, stretching exercises) but also a "feel" for the cushioning function of the roll-off movements (rolls in various forms). In the preparation for the Fosbury Flop take-off from a curved run-up (oblique position), followed by rotation around the longitudinal axis, should be practised in addition to exercises of the foundation programme.

4.4.2.2. Foundation Programme of Technical Training

The technical foundation should lead to a relatively rapid success and familiarization of the athlete with the chief elements of the sequence of movements. This stage should be reached in a short time without too much splitting up and drilling of parts of the complete movement. It should provide the learner with an understanding of the movement which must be consolidated and ingrained by practice. If in this process

Fig. 78

the athlete shows aptitude for the high jump he should (not too late!) turn to corresponding ancillary exercises for acquiring precision in the execution of the different parts of the technique.

– Exercise 1: From one-stride approach–jump with half turn, landing on the leading leg. The approach angle should be about 30 to 40°, the height of the bar 60 to 80 cm (Fig. 78).

Purpose: Learn the take-off with synchronized swinging leg and arm movements and rotation about the longitudinal axis of the athlete.

Points to note: Extend the swinging leg, drive it up quickly and precisely in line with the running direction; swing both arms forward and upward simultaneously from a retracted position (double-arm swing). After take-off the lower part of the take-off leg is brought close to the hollow of the knee of the swinging leg; at the same time the knee and the toes of the foot are turned outwards. After crossing the bar the loosely extended swinging leg is dropped, so that the body assumes an almost vertical position during bar clearance. While rotating his body the jumper's eyes are focussed on the bar. By pressing the chin to the chest, a hollow back can be avoided.

– Exercise 2: Same as exercise 1, but with three strides approach.

– Exercise 3: Same as exercise 2, but with ¾ rotation.

Purpose: Push-off in vertical direction, at the same time increasing the angular momentum by swinging the leading leg upwards.

Points to note: In the execution of these movements special attention should be given to a fast take-off stride and the conscious and accentuated forward drive of the hips, particularly on the free-leg side. This exercise should be repeated many times, raising the bar in accordance with the jumper's skill, but only to a point where the jump can be executed easily. It should be stressed from the outset, that during take-off the swing of the leading leg must be very vigorous, since the rotation moment produced chiefly depends on this swing.

These exercises lay the foundation for a correct take-off technique and for learning an important element of the straddle jump in the flight phase, i.e. the rotation about the body's long axis. Since the jumper clears the bar in an almost erect position, the serious mistake of bending over the bar can be avoided by the athlete, who is forced to push off in an upward direction.

– Exercise 4: Same approach and take-off as in exercise 3. Landing is now on the swinging leg and immedi-

271

Fig. 79

ately afterwards on the hand of the same side; it concludes by a roll-off over the hips or the shoulder. At the beginning the bar should have a height of some 70 to 80 cm, but it should soon be raised (Fig. 79).

Purpose: The vertical position of the body during take-off must be reversed into an almost horizontal one, so that the jumper crosses the bar with the front part of his body turned towards the bar.

Points to note: The jumper must focus the bar as in the other exercises. The foot and hand should land at approximately the same distance from the projection line of the bar and close to it.

It is advisable to execute these and all other exercises on to a jumping hill or on to a sufficiently high heap of mats.

Ancillary exercise: In the front leaning rest the jumper brings the foot of the jumping leg (as at the beginning of bar clearance) to the hollow of the knee of the swinging leg and turns the knee

and toes well outwards. The pelvis is then consciously introduced into this movement, so that now a rotation and body torque around the spine takes place. Straightening of the jumping leg is not required in this (Fig. 80).

– Exercise 5: Same as 4, only with longer approach (5, 7 or 9 strides) and jumping over higher heights.

Purpose: Training the complete sequence of movements.

These exercises will provide the athlete with the main skills of the straddle jump. They require relatively little time. Learners endowed with natural ability learn it in one lesson.

An athlete who satisfies all requirements for this event and wishes to specialize, should start immediately with the special technical training, before faults become ingrained and prevent further progress.

– Ancillary exercises for straddle jump technique

Decisive factors for proficiency in the high jump are, above all, the take-off

Fig. 80

272

Fig. 81   Fig. 82

technique and the coordination of the approach with the take-off. Therefore the exercises for learning the take-off in connection with a rhythmic approach have priority in the learning process.

In the next chapter the ancillary exercises are dealt with in complex groups, representing the methodical sequence, so that the whole training complex forms a closed system for learning the straddle jump.

● Exercises for Perfecting the Free-Leg-Action in Relation with Take-Off and for Training the Coordination of Approach with Take-Off

1. Improving the jumping stance:
The jumper stands on his flexed swinging leg next to a support (high-jump upright, wall bars, tree), which he holds on to at chest level; the swinging leg is set back. He now rapidly brings his jumping leg forward to the jumping position. It must be stressed that the hips are brought forward and that the flexed jumping leg lands with the heel first. The swinging leg is bent at an angle of about 90° (Fig. 81).
2. Practising the action of the swinging leg on the spot: The jumper stands on his take-off leg and holds on to a support (to the left of left-foot jumpers); his upper body is slightly bent forward. The free leg now swings back and with it the pelvis. Then the jumper immediately drives his hips forward and swings the free leg forward and upward in a fast pendulum-like movement. Before passing the horizontal the leg is completely extended in the knee; the toes are kept back and point towards the shin. This swinging movement must be so powerful that it lifts the jumper off the ground.
3. Same as 2, but without support, from one-stride approach, marked forward drive of the hips to speed up the swing of the free leg. This exercise should be combined with an active take-off; landing is on the free leg.
4. The same exercise, only with three strides approach. Once the take-off technique is acquired, the approach may be lengthened and the speed increased. At the same time the action of the leading leg can be executed more rapidly. This requires a fast take-off and contributes to a higher pressure on the take-off leg and hence to the development of jumping power (Fig. 82).

273

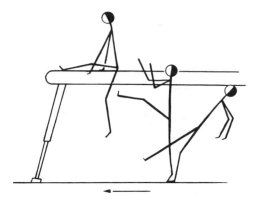

Fig. 83

Table 47 Length of the Last Approach Strides

	Approach Strides	
	penultimate	last
Schawlakadse	2.30–2.35	1.95–1.97
Brumel	2.25–2.30	1.90–1.92
Beilschmidt	2.05–2.10	1.65–1.70
Ackermann	1.95–2.00	1.90–1.95

This exercise can be performed without interruption (about 60 to 70 times). Mistakes should be detected and corrected immediately. Not having to concentrate on clearing the bar, the jumper can perform many more jumps during the same time.

To drive these movements home, they can be done in series over several hurdles (height according to the athlete's proficiency). For the same purpose use jumps to hit a suitable object with the swinging leg, the head or the hand, as well as jumps on to a table, box, vaulting horse, boards, walls and so on (Fig. 83).

5. Learning the approach rhythm:

Once the jumper can do the above exercises from three or more approach strides, he should immediately start to train the approach rhythm. The penultimate stride must be stressed and lengthened but the last stride must be short. The following forms are recommended for imparting the rhythm:

a) Instructions on the execution of the movement

b) Vocal encouragement and help by counting, clapping hands, etc.

c) Visual assistance by markings

d) Compel the athlete to use a certain stride pattern by placing obstacles (broken bars etc.) on the track (Fig. 84) [47].

When beginning to use an approach involving seven and more strides, attention must be paid to the continuous increase of speed and to a flowing transition to the last two strides. The stride pattern specified in Table 47 will give some guidance.

6. Learning the take-off technique with a rhythmical full-length approach and bar clearance in an erect position.

a) Clearing a low jumping height from the front in such a manner that after take-off the foot of the jumping leg comes near the hollow of the knee of the swinging leg and the knee of the

47 Cf. H. G. Rabe "Der Rhythmus der letzten Anlaufschritte beim Weitsprung" (Rhythm of the Last Approach Strides in the Long Jump), in "Der Leichtathlet", Nr. 13/1959, Appendix "Der Leichtathletik-Trainer".

Fig. 84

274

Fig. 85

jumping leg is turned outwards. The body remains upright. At the moment of clearing the bar, the swinging leg is dropped for landing (Fig. 85).

Execute first with 3 approach strides. Having gained confidence, the bar will be raised and the approach lengthened to competition length (involving 7 to 9 strides); watch stride rhythm.

The purpose of this exercise is to approach the take-off spot with the body's CG in a low position and to proceed firmly to the take-off. The dominant movement in this must be the powerful forward and upward drive of the hips, as the development of speed by the swing of the free leg and hence the effectiveness of the take-off depend on it.

b) In order to learn how to move in a straight line in the approach and in the take-off, the same exercise is repeated with an approach-angle of some 30 to 40°. The take-off point should not be more than 60 to 70 cm (an arm's length) away from the projection line of the bar. In clearing the bar the trunk must not lean towards the bar; the bar must be crossed in an upright position and in line with the direction of the run-up. For better control it is useful to draw a lane in the sand, marking the take-off and landing points. Landing is on a line drawn out from the running direction.

● Exercises for Appropriating the Take-Off Technique of the Straddle Jump

As a result of the swinging movement of the free leg and the arm of the same side, the jumper begins to turn about his long axis (left-foot jumpers to the left). Care must be taken that the swinging movement of the free leg is exactly in the direction of the run-up and that the jumping leg forms an extended line with the body. An inward turn of the swinging leg or the toes or an inclination of the body in the direction of turning are serious mistakes which should be corrected from the outset.

1. Imitation and arm movement:

In the jumping stance both arms have retreated behind the trunk and now swing forward and upward in such a manner that the arm of the free-leg side swings slightly inwards and sweeps higher than the other arm.

2. Jump with ¾ rotation from 3 to 5 strides approach: During take-off the hip of the free-leg side must be included in the swinging movement, so that the jumper begins to turn about his long axis to the side of the take-off leg while concluding the push-off. This rotation, if properly executed, will be about 90°. The jumper lands on the take-off leg (Fig. 86).

3. Jump with rotation of 180 to 360° (Pirouette):

a) Same approach and take-off as in preceding exercises. A greater rotation can be obtained if, after take-off, which provides a first rotating impulse, the jumper lowers his free leg to the plant leg. By bringing the weight of the free

275

Fig. 86

Fig. 87

leg towards the axis of rotation (the jumper's long axis), the moment of inertia in relation to this axis is reduced and the rotation accelerated. This will enable the jumper to do an initial turn of 180°. By applying greater force against the ground and by the better control, the rotation can be increased to 360°.

If the movement is to be successful, the jumper's body must remain completely extended. He may later drop his arms alongside the body, thus further increasing the speed of rotation.

b) Same as exercise 3a: After the approach and take-off the free leg is lowered and the plant foot brought close to the hollow of the knee of the free leg. This again increases the angular velocity, so that a rotation of 180° and later of 360° can be achieved. The landing follows, beginning on the free leg, however the jumping leg is immediately brought forward for a soft landing in stride position (Fig. 87).

● Exercises for training the bar clearance

1. Pirouette with inclined axis of rotation over the crossbar: The movements of the pirouette described in exercise 3b are executed on a high-jump lay-out from a full approach and at an angle of approach of 30 to 40°. To obtain a pronounced inclination of the body's long axis, the hips and the swinging leg must be pushed forward more actively than the upper body, so that the pelvis reaches the bar sooner than the shoulders, thus giving the body an inclined position. After push-off and with his push-off leg drawn up to his trunk, the jumper turns his chest to the bar and clears it in this position. He lands on the leading leg first and then on the hands, precisely along the extended run-up line. By gradually raising the crossbar, the inclination of the body's long axis can be increased.

2. Simulation of the trunk position on top of the bar for clearance:

a) The jumper assumes on a horse without pommels the position which is typical of this phase of the jump. His trunk and free leg are lying on the horse, bent at a slight angle to each other. The head, the right shoulder and the right arm, as well as the foot of the free leg, are behind the horse. The jumping leg is drawn up and points upwards with the heel (cf. Fig. 76, Pos. 13).

276

b) From a shorter approach at an angle of some 30 to 40°, the jumper leaps up to the horse, landing in the position described above. The precise execution of the movements is important. If mistakes are made in this phase, they should be corrected immediately. The height of the horse is between the shoulder and body height of the jumper.

3. Simulation of the take-off leg movement in clearing the bar: see Fig. 80. The same exercise can be repeated on a horse, beam or steeplechase hurdle.

4. Straddle jump with appraoch—complete movement:

Having acquired the skills of the take-off, rotation, upward lift and jumping-leg action in clearing the bar, the complete movement of the straddle jump can be trained. Special attention must be given to the proper execution of the take-off (hip movement and explosive free-leg action!) and the position of the body in the upward lift.

In the course of time the crossbar may be gradually raised and technique perfected with emphasis on essential points. It can best be achieved by a frequent repetition of the different phases, which will be fixed in performing the complete jump. Some time will have to be devoted to the improvement and perfection of the coordination of the complete movement. This can be done at gradually increased speed, at the same time defining the best balance and direction of the application of force during take-off; the jumping rhythm as a whole must be perfected and fixed; and, finally, the acquired skills must be made constant and automatic.

4.4.2.3. Fault—Reason—Correction

In the approach

— Fault: The approach is too fast, so that the jumper misses the take-off point.

Reason: He does not master the approach rhythm; the jumper applies too much effort; incorrect understanding of the jump.

Correction: The jumper must gain the right understanding of the jump and of the approach rhythm; only the last strides should be performed aggressively and rapidly.

— Fault: The jumper stumbles or over-strides in the approach.

Reason: No precision in the length of approach, no approach rhythm.

Correction: Establish with perseverence the approach rhythm over 3—5—7 strides. Do at first only jumps from the front and from the side in erect position by drawing the take-off foot to the hollow of the free-leg knee. Only when the approach rhythm is well under control take up practising straddle jumps again.

— Fault: Loss of momentum before take-off.

Reason: Wrong understanding of movement. The jumper's muscles are not loose but tensed too soon, trying to assume backward lean before reaching the last stride.

Correction: Train the approach and sequence of movements without clearing the bar. Do jumps with full approach for kicking objects.

In the take-off

— Fault: In the take-off the jumper leans too much to the side of the take-off leg and does not get up high enough.

Reason: Wrong understanding of

277

movement: the last stride is not in line with the running direction but toward the free-leg side; this occurs particularly when the foot of the free leg has already been set too far to the right (with the left-footed jumper). The same when the take-off foot points to the bar. The turning impulse produced is too great; it will bring the jumper rapidly up to the horizontal but not provide the optimal lift, as the body's CG is not well placed in the line of force.

Correction: Do jumps in the Squat-, Scissors and Eastern Cut-Off style for getting the proper feeling of lifting the body. Additionally, do jumps with a marked free-leg action, one after the other, and finally straddle jumps from an approach on a drawn line with markings for the foot plant.

– Fault: A long flat flight curve.

Reason: a) Too fast approach, speed cannot be converted. b) Too short last stride. During the take-off extension the body's CG is not in the line of extension but too far ahead of it.

Correction: a) Practice continually the last run-up strides with take-off on grass or track; the same over several hurdles in a row. Put check-marks on take-off and landing spots. b) Do jumps from short approach, with emphasis on the correct jumping position. Lengthen approach only very gradually.

– Fault: The jumper exhibits a poor extension at take-off.

Reason: Lack of coordination between the approach and take-off, poorly developed jumping power.

Correction: Develop the muscles involved in the jumping action by special jumping exercises: do jumps one after another over hurdles with 5 or 7 approach strides. Train the approach

rhythm with fluent transition to the jumping stance.

In clearing the bar:

– Fault: The bar is not cleared in a horizontal position but sideways.

Reason: Incorrect understanding of the movement. This is a mistake often exhibited by jumpers who master the roll jump quite well.

Correction: Demonstrate and explain what is common between and what is different in the Roll and Straddle style jumps. Develop once again the Straddle style jump from the Pirouette. See that during bar clearance the crossbar is always in the jumper's field of vision.

– Fault: The swinging leg knocks down the bar during clearance.

Reason: Incorrect understanding of movement: the swinging leg is lowered too soon, because the straddle movement was begun too soon.

Correction: Endeavour to obtain a correct understanding of the movement. Jump on a horse with immediate correction of wrong movements.

– Fault: The crossbar is knocked down by the jumping leg.

Reason: a) The consequence of a sideways clearance of the bar. The jumper lacks angular velocity about his longitudinal axis. The mistake may also be in the take-off when the rotation impulse produced was too small, or on top of the bar, when the different limbs are shifted unfavourably with respect to the axis of rotation. b) On top of the bar the head is tilted back; this forces the hips and consequently the jumping leg down. This position of the head also hinders diving. c) The flight curve is too flat or too steep. The body floats across the bar too quickly and the work of the jumping leg sets in too late or, on the other hand, the body does not come away from the bar quick enough.

Correction: a) Practise the pirouette with complete rotation without bar and over the bar, landing on the free leg.

b) Pirouette with complete rotation over the bar, pressing consciously the chin to the chest and keeping the bar in the field of vision.

c) Find out the exact take-off spot (about 70 cm from the projection line of the bar = an arm's length). During training emphasize the coordination of the approach and take-off.

— Fault: The jumper lowers his inner arm too soon towards the pit, thus twisting his body.

Reason: Usually nervousness about the landing (particularly girls and women).

Correction: Frequent repetitions of the roll for consolidating the landing movement and conquering the fear of landing.

4.4.3. Technique of the Flop Jump

The following description of the Flop Jump is mainly based on an analysis of competitive jumps of Fosbury, the Olympic high-jump champion of 1968 and originator of this new style. The form of bar clearance is not the only new feature in this technique; it represents, in fact, a completely new approach to the high jump, from run-up to landing, and may be regarded as a great improvement.

The experience in the years after 1968 have shown that this technique can be used successfully by a great number of athletes, particularly boys, girls and women. Not as complicated as was ori-

ginally believed, it has become a widely used high-jump style.

4.4.3.1. The Approach

In the Flop the approach must fulfil the same tasks as in the Straddle jump (see 4.4.1.1.). In contrast to other jumps, however, the approach is characterized by a curve in the last strides, at minimum the final 3 or 4. Here the immediate preparation for take-off brings the jumper into the best possible position.

Current observation of top-class jumpers yields the following criteria for a suitable approach (Figg. 88):

— The approach involves some 9 to 13 strides. The starting point is about 15 to 20 m from the bar and along a perpendicular line to the bar, beginning 3 to 5 m outside the near upright. This depends on whether the jumper begins the approach on an almost straight line (with the starting point offset to the side), or whether the complete run-up is curved.

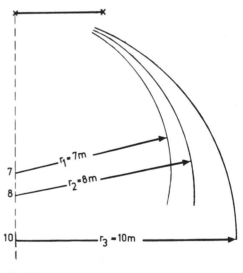

Fig. 88

– The radius of the curve is a function of the speed of approach. It becomes greater as speed increases and is some 6 to 8 m for boys, girls and beginners, and between 8 and 10 m for good jumpers.

– The distance of the take-off point from the bar is, as a rule, longer than in the Straddle jump: approximately 1 m for jumps of 2 m and higher.

In the first part of the approach speed is rapidly increased. In this part it appears better to run almost straight, as on a curve centrifugal forces increase with speed, placing an additional load on the jumper and fatiguing his jumping leg, at least during training.

The jumper should attempt to pick up speed on the subsequent strides (Fosbury has been timed at almost 8.0 m/s). As the bend increases, the jumper counteracts the increasing centrifugal force by leaning in at some 20 to 30°. In the Straddle jump this position, good for the take-off, can only be achieved through much more complicated movements. Here, most probably, resides the advantage of the Flop technique.

In this stance the support of the jumping leg is between the vertical projection line of the bar and that of the body's CG, an advantage which the Straddle jump does not offer. As the jumper takes off, the trajectory of his body's CG must intersect the line of extension of the jumping leg, thus permitting a fuller utilization of the vertical impulses.

The Straddle jumper is not in such an advantageous position at take-off, having to lean towards the bar to produce the required rotation impulse about his longitudinal axis. This induces the beginner to commit the cardinal error of clearing the bar "like a pike".

In the transition to the last stride, where the centrifugal force reaches its maximum, absorption of this force by the jumper is clearly visible. At the same time the body's CG is lowered, although not to the same extent as in the Straddle jump (see Fig. 89, Pos. 1).

In the foot plant of this stride the foot of the jumping leg is slightly set out of the curved approach toward the bar. Since the body's CG does not continue to move in an arc, but leaves the arc tangentially in the direction of the bar, the jumping leg, due to the lateral deviation from the initial radius, bends on a spot which is almost exactly below the trajectory of the body's CG. With

Fig. 89

the beginning of the last stride (see Fig. 89, Pos. 2), the jumper's trunk begins to straighten. Further biomechanical studies will have to be conducted for a better understanding of this feature which occupies a key position in the entire movement. The last stride will always be very fast and is, in this respect, similar to the last stride of the long jump; however, the high jumper's pronounced layout at take-off must be attempted in the Fosbury Flop. In this phase the upper body should not show the later leaning toward the bar; the trunk should maintain almost completely its lean toward the centre of the curve, so that a near vertical lift can be achieved at take-off (Fig. 89, Pos. 2).

4.4.3.2. The Take-off

Take-off is similar to that of the Scissor's jump. It is introduced by the leg that is remote from the bar and is a very explosive movement. While the jumping leg extends, the trunk comes up to an almost vertical position in preparation of bar clearance. Since the main extension line runs slightly outward, e.g. away from the bar, some of the power impetus passes outside the

body's CG and produces the torque required for revolving the body into a horizontal position, with the back facing the bar (Fig. 89, Pos. 4).

These movements are assisted by the arm swing and by the shoulders. To favour the inclination of the shoulder axis to the bar, the two arms should not be allowed to swing up simultaneously. The right arm swings energetically upward, while the left arm remains down. The fixed arm prevents the left shoulder from making a wide compensatory movement backward and thus helps to introduce the body's rotation around the long axis. If this element is exaggerated, as is sometimes the case in beginners, the jumper's back turns to the bar too soon, particularly when using the double-arm swing. An alternating arm swing should therefore be given preference. Rotation around the long axis must be produced mainly by turning the bent swinging leg slightly inward, about 15 to 20° off the running direction of the last stride. The head is turned toward the bar in a compensatory movement, allowing the jumper to keep his eyes on the bar while executing these movements (Fig. 89, Pos. 4 to 6).

Thus the jumper can constantly check his position in relation to the bar and adjust his movements accordingly. Just before the foot comes off the ground, the trunk is in almost vertical position above the take-off foot. Through arched tensioning of the trunk, the extension line of the jumping leg passes outside the body's CG (rotation impulse) just before take-off.

4.4.3.3. Clearing the Bar and Landing

The first phase of the flight after take-off is marked by a visible relaxation of the whole body. The swinging leg falls back loosely to join the loosely down-hanging jumping leg. The arms are kept close to the body. This extended position of the body favours rotation around the longitudinal axis. The jumper is literally whirled up and into suppine position with his shoulder axis almost parallel to the bar (Fig. 89, Pos. 5–8).

Immediately after the shoulders have crossed the bar, the second phase of bar clearance begins. It is introduced by a forceful forward pressing of the hips. Since the jumper's shoulders and legs come astride of the bar in a compensatory movement, his body forms a kind of bridge over the bar (Pos. 9 and 10). This is a critical moment when the jumper must succeed in bringing his pelvis across the bar. When this is achieved, the counter-movement in the way of a fast bending of the hips must follow quickly. This movement is clearly geared by the head with the chin pressed down to the chest (Pos. 11).

The pelvis is thus lowered just behind the bar, while the legs counteract by coming up and the upper body brakes the uncomfortable—at least for beginners—back- and downward movement (Pos. 11 and 12). As soon as the calves get into proximity of the bar which, due to the high horizontal speed happens rather rapidly, they are lifted up vertically through a fast extension at the knee joints, to bring them out of the danger zone as quickly as possible. On the whole this second phase is much like revolving around the bar in gymnastics and is a most elegant movement. The jumper's body then assumes the L-position, which is fixed by muscle contraction in preparation of the landing. This tensioning of the whole body is necessary for a safe landing, even when falling onto soft mats. The outspread arms touch the landing surface first and thus absorb the shock and direct the body into the proper position for landing (Pos. 13).

Since no differences have been found so far with regard to super-elevation of the body's CG above the bar in valid jumps between the Fosbury Flop and the world-best Straddle jumpers, we must presume that this kind of bar clearance is just as rational as the straddle movements. We believe that the great mobility of the hips in bending forward is more advantageous for shifting te legs than the splitting and sideward twisting of the legs. Further potentials lie in a consequent improvement of the hip mobility for the backward bend, thus forming a yet higher bridge above the bar and bringing the body's CG in a more favourable position for crossing.

4.4.4. Technical Training for the Flop

Learning the Flop technique is usually not complicated. With good physical preparation and the employment of suitable learning stages, a rough form of the technique is, as a rule, quickly achieved.

The current development and further perfection of the Flop is very much dependent on the availability of good facilities. Without overemphasizing the problem of landing on the back, the need to create safe landing conditions must be stressed, particularly when training beginners.

A sufficiently high and soft landing area is an absolute necessity. The use of foamrubber pads or chips, permitting "deep plunging" of the body, is recommended. When using foam-rubber padded mats, the distance from the bar to the mat should not be more than 60 to 70 cm for beginners. If necessary, the landing area should be raised by placing special supports under the mats. In the gymnasium one can use benches, boxes or a low jumping table as makeshifts. To avoid back injuries from falls to splintered bars, let the athlete jump over rubber lines and the like.

The provision of safe landing conditions means also that the athlete must be well prepared for the landing action. He must have gained wide experience through a great variety of practice, complemented by special falling and landing exercises.

4.4.5. Basic Exercises of Technical Training

– Exercise 1: Backward Flop from standing two-leg take-off "Standing Flop" (Fig. 90a).

Purpose: Learning the typical movements in mid-air and on landing.

Points to note: After a vigorous push-off upwards the typical flight position is achieved by consciously pushing the pelvis forward (arching). This position should be changed as late as possible through hip flexion with a fast whip-like forward thrust of the calves which, until then, are hanging loosely. Landing should be active and with tensed muscles, possibly on the whole back. Folding of the legs beyond the vertical (L-position) should be avoided, as well as somersaulting backwards.

To lengthen the time of flight this exercise can be performed from a take-off area raised by 30 to 50 cm (low box, bench).

The Standing Flop should not be practised for an unduly long time, as this would mean neglecting the upward directed push-off and inducing a too early layout on the back. This exercise is, however, necessary to get acquainted with the mid-air movement which typifies the Flop.

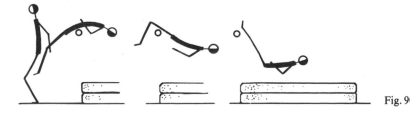

Fig. 90a

Fig. 90b

– Exercise 2: Steep Scissors (with the help of height marks) with $^3/_4$ rotation from 1, 3 or 5 strides approach, landing on both legs (Fig. 90b).

Purpose: Learning the take-off movement from an approach in a curved line and rotation about the long axis.

Points to note: Rotation is introduced by driving the swinging leg round energetically, with the knee coming across to the mid-line. Both shoulders are lifted in a jerky movement, the arm and the shoulder of the leading leg coming up head high. After lowering the swinging leg, landing is on both legs.

For safety reasons the jumper should practise without, or at a sufficient distance from the jumping area. This exercise is useful in preparing for the lift; after some repetitions experience may be gained in producing the required rotation impulse. The need to land on both legs forces the jumper to lower the swinging leg. Thus, together with the conscious forward pushing of the hip, the faulty sitting posture in the first part of the flight can be avoided.

– Exercise 3: Flop jump from 1, 3 and 5 strides approach (with supplementary height mark) (Fig. 90c and d).

Fig. 90c

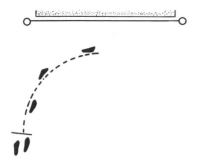

Fig. 90d

Purpose: Learning the complete movement with emphasis on a good lift.

Points to note: The movement drilled in exercise 2 merges into the complete movement, in which the jumper pushes off more strongly in the direction of the jumping pad. As he rises the jumper gets more and more into the horizontal position. In order to control this impulse, which is often overemphasized by beginners, the use of height indicators is recommended.

During the first jumps special attention must be focussed on the correct execution of the movement in the first part of the jump, i.e. during take-off and in the rising phase. It is better not to keep the height too low; the use of an elastic line instead of a bar makes failures less critical. The jumping pad should, at the beginning, be only a little lower than the jumping height. Once a good lift is assured and further movements during flight can be trained, the jumping pad can and must again be lowered to the jumping height. However, height indicators should be retained. They may prevent a too rapid drawing up of the legs, resulting in premature abandonment of the flight position.

Auxiliary exercises: Jumps on to a jumping table or a high pile of mats. From standing or after take-off on one leg from curved approach—jumps backward on to an obstacle (of the height of the jump) in such a manner that the upper body (shoulders) come to lie on it. The legs are hanging down loosely and the body is arched over the obstacle.

– Exercise 4: Flop jump from 7 to 9 strides approach.

Purpose: Learning the complete movement.

Points to note: With higher speed the radius of the approach curve may be increased (from 6 to 10 m). The take-off spot is shifted further away from the bar and placed nearer the upright.

– *Ancillary exercises:*

For a more intensive training of individual parts of the movement the following exercises are recommended:

Running with best possible style on a curved runway.

Take-off from fast run-up on curved runway with small radius.

Scissors with more than one quarter rotation towards the side of the jumping leg.

Practising take-off from one stride approach (simulation of take-off movement).

Jumps on to a table or a pile of mats (see auxiliary exercise); Standing Flop from mini-trampoline on to a soft jumping hill; take-off from raised take-off area (e.g. take-off stride from box cover).

Take-off balance board, persistently maintaining the take-off position.

4.4.6. Technique of the Scissors Style

The Scissors Style (Fig. 91) is simple to learn but a rather uneconomic jumping technique.

285

Fig. 91

The approach is from the swinging leg side; the take-off spot is about 70 to 80 cm from the bar. The initial swinging leg action can be chosen freely. Having been raised as far as the bar, this leg is pressed down behind the bar. The jumping leg which has been hanging down loosely during the lift is now drawn over the bar in a slightly bent position; the body is leaning forward towards the bar. Landing is on the swinging leg.

4.4.7. Basic Exercises of Technical Training

The Scissors style, which is the most uncomplicated high jump technique, is useful for initiating the novice high jumper into this event or for learning the take-off movement. It is, however, not recommended in training for quality athletic performance. Sports teachers, trainers and coaches are therefore well advised to use the Scissors style only for the above mentioned purpose and to quickly proceed to the technique of the Straddle or Fosbury Flop for competitive work.

Before beginning with the Scissors style, one should start with the Squat jump.

– Exercise 1: Squat jump from front with first 3, later 5 strides approach; bar height first 60 to 80 cm, then according to standards.

Purpose: Learning and "sensing" the take-off from medium approach speed.

Points to note: The jumper should approach the marked take-off spot at an easy relaxed pace. The last stride will be faster and more energetic, with a marked heel-first contact of the jumping leg. At take-off attention should be paid to the active extension and powerful action of the swinging leg and arms. After take-off the jumping leg is quickly tucked in, so that the jumper crosses the bar with the knees of both legs about chest high. The legs then come down loosely to absorb the impact of the weight of the body smoothly.

– Exercise 2: Scissors style from standing and with one stride approach; the bar is at a height of 60 to 80 cm. Reduce approach angle to the bar gradu-

286

ally from about 80° down to about 45°.

Purpose: Getting acquainted with the new movement rhythm in the flight phase. Learn the approach from the side.

Points to note: The jumper takes up a position with the swinging side turned to the bar, so that take-off may be executed with the leg which is further away from the bar. After a powerful take-off the swinging leg, having cleared the bar, is lowered, while the jumping leg which is slightly bent is brought across the bar in a swift movement. Landing is on the swinging leg.

— Exercise 3: Scissors style from 3 to 4 strides approach and with backward leaning trunk on crossing the bar; bar height according to level of efficiency, but not higher than can be mastered without great effort.

Purpose: Training the coordination of approach and take-off as well as improvement of bar clearance.

Points to note: Same as in exercise 2; on crossing the bar the upper body is markedly bent backwards, so that the flight curve of the body's CG is lowered. When the movement pattern is fixed to a certain extent, the task of landing on the buttocks and back may be set. This particular part of the movement is often grasped at first attempt by young athletes.

— Exercise 4: Scissors style with longer rhythmical approach (5 to 7 strides), until the length best suited to the individual has been determined; bar height according to efficiency level.

Purpose: Training the movement rhythm with higher speed on the approach; fix the jumping rhythm.

Points to note: Great importance must be given to a swift, accelerated, rhythmical approach and explosive take-off by making full use of the swinging forces. All the rest is of secondary importance! (For training the approach rhythm we refer to the description for the Straddle jump). Make it a point to swing the leading leg exactly in the direction of the run-up. If the movement is off this line, use a bit of cloth towards which the leg must be swung.

4.4.8.   Physical Requirements and Training Methods for Improving Performance

4.4.8.1.   The Importance of Physical Condition

Proficiency in the high jump is mainly a function of the following factors:
1. Jumping ability
2. Jumping agility and mobility
3. Body size.
Jumping ability and body size are plainly the basis for superior performance in this event, while jumping agility and mobility are important for mastering an economic technique in the flight and landing phases.

● Jumping ability

As mentioned above, the jumping ability, which must be regarded as a unity of ability and technique, is the basis and an absolute necessity for quality performance in this event. In the following considerations, the demands placed on the neuro-muscular and locomotion systems for executing this special take-off procedure will serve as a point of departure. Thus, the high jumper must be in a position to check the inertia generated by the jumping leg on meeting the ground after an approach-run, he must change the horizontal motion plane into a vertical one and, by an explosive straightening of the jumping leg in the last phase of the take-off, add a maximum to his positive acceleration impulse. This means that the jumper must develop great muscular forces (maximum strength ability) and perform a rapid and powerful extension through strong muscular contraction (explosive power ability).

Next to these demands, placed mainly on the jumping leg, the action of the swinging leg must be considered, which likewise involves an explosive movement, as it controls the timing of the take-off. These complex demands on jumping ability include also a high functional capacity of nervous processes triggering the excitation of the muscles. Apart from this, the ratio of the forces to be applied and the body weight, e.g. the load ratio, is of some importance (aptitude–selection). As the jumping ability is so complex, its level cannot be measured by one only parameter, as happened earlier with the propulsion height of the take-off jump. The assessment of jumping ability must take into account several factors corresponding to a number of different requirements. The test exercises can be of complex or relatively simple character.

● Jumping agility and mobility

Jumping agility plays an important role in learning and consolidating a complicated sequence of movements. Without systematically improving jumping agility there will be no improvement in technique. The high jumper must acquire the ability to orientate himself in every phase of the jump, to coordinate his different movements precisely and to adapt to varying conditions (jumping layout, weather). In the jump itself moments may arise, which require an immediate correction of the movement to "save" the jump. Only an agile jumper can master such situations.

Mobility is equally of great importance for the high jumper, especially for the effective action of the extended swinging leg and for the movements of the jumping leg in clearing the bar. As mobility depends on the elasticity of muscles, ligaments and joints, they should be developed slowly and systematically.

● Body weight and body size

Certain physical requirements, particularly body height and body size, must be satisfied for achieving top performances in the high jump. If an athlete is tall, the take-off height will be higher, independent of other physical qualities. Tall, slender jumpers with relatively low body weight are therefore ideal for the high jump.

As a guide we quote average values of body size and body weight of the six best high jumpers (men and women) at the 1972 Olympic Games (Table 48).

4.4.8.2.   Means for Developing Physical Properties

● Jumping ability

With respect to the abilities outlined in section 4.4.8.1., which the high jumper must acquire through training, especially through general and special strength and jumping exercises, we particularly stress the qualities necessary for developing checking and accelera-

Table 48 *Mean Values of Age, Height and Weight of the 6 best Performers at the Olympic Games 1972*

	Men	Women
Age (years)	22.9	21.7
Height (cm)	190	179
Weight (kg)	80.1	66.0

tion forces. Apart from technical skills, he must develop the muscles of his jumping leg, together with general body fitness.

Physical fitness is a necessity for developing jumping ability (maximum and explosive force ability for the jumping leg). This aspect must be taken into consideration when training with a large number of repetitions and with weights. The training programme of the high jumper must also include a series of general strength exercises, with particular emphasis on the snatch and clean and jerk. This develops general strength and extension force in the legs, while contributing to the capacity to relax in the clean phase.

In practising jumps some systematic principles must be heeded, of which only the essential ones are mentioned below:

– from general to special
– from two-leg to one-leg jumps
– from jumps without to jumps with weights
– from exercises from a position of relative rest to exercises in which the kinetic energy of the body, or the body with weights, is utilized for loading the groups of muscles of the lower extremities.

These principles are valid for annual plans as well as for those for several years ahead.

General strength exercises:
1. Snatch and clean and jerk the barbell
2. Exercises on apparatus (wall bars, parallel bars) or with implements (medicine ball, kettle bell, sandbag) as well as floor gymnastics.
3. Wrestling, resistance exercises.

General jumping programme:
It includes the following basic training means:
1. Jumping exercises without weights.
To this group belong all jumping exercises with take-off from one or both legs, e.g. jumps on one leg on the spot and in movement; squat vaults over hurdles with and without a linking hop; take-off from the bench (the jumping leg is placed on an apparatus of some 30 to 40 cm height (usually a balance beam); bounding runs; scissors style jumps; jumping run; skipping with variations; cossack dance; squat and stretch on one leg; hopping forward in tucked position, and other exercises.
2. Jumping exercises with low or medium weights (5 to 50 kg). To this group belong all the above mentioned exercises with the corresponding load (sandbag, weight vest or barbell).
3. Exercises for developping leg-extension power with heavy weights.
a) Knee-bending with barbell up to maximum load
b) Knee-bends with partner on the shoulders
c) Jumps from half squat with barbell; load 60 to 70 per cent of the maximum weight of exercise a)
d) Feathering jumps with barbell, load 40 to 50 per cent of the maximum weight of exercise a)
e) Jumps from ankle joints and other extension exercises for the ankle joints with barbell, weight up to maximum

load (this maximum weight is much higher than that achievable by exercise a).

Special jumping exercises

These are jumping exercises emphasizing technical characteristics of the take-off in high jumps. The main exercises are:

a) Consecutive take-offs with extended swinging leg, with 1, 3 and 5 intermediate strides.

b) Same as above, but over hurdles with 3 and 5 intermediate strides.

c) Take-off from approach, with swinging leg touching a suspended object.

In this connection the muscles participating in the swinging movement

Table 49   Weekly Schedule of Training during the Preparatory Period (Foundation Training)

Day	Duration (min.)	Training task A = Preparation B = Main Part C = Closing		Training Means
Monday	20–25	A	Warm-up and development of abdominal, back and arm muscles	Limbering up, exercises with medicine ball
	10		Special gymnastics	Exercises for extensibility and flexibility at hip joint
	30	B	Technique	Exercises for learning extended swing-leg action; take-offs with accentuated swing-leg action on the spot and with 1 to 3 strides approach; simulated movements on horse for improving certain jumping elements; jumps on to and over the horse
	20		Learning the shot put	Standing shot put and with glide
	30		Jumping training	General jumping exercises without and with weights (100–200 jumps)
	5	C	Running down	Jogging
Tuesday	30–40	A	Game	Basketball
	10–15	B	Exercising long or triple jumps	Long jump or triple jump with short approach (10 to 12 jumps)
	30–40		Training agility and mobility	Floor gymnastics (acrobatics) Gymnastic exercises for the development of extensibility and mobility
Thursday	20	A	Warm-up	Jogging, ankle work, ankle-jumps, acceleration runs
	20	B	Development of speed	Runs with knee pick-up, dribbling, acceleration runs, starts; runs over 3 to 4 hurdles
	15		Agility training	Jumps with springboard High jump with set task (among others jumps with swinging leg and different techniques)

Day	Duration (min.)	Training task A = Preparation B = Main Part C = Closing	Training Means
	30	Technical Training	Exercises for learning extended swing-leg action; squat jumps from front and from diagonal approach (10–12); straddle jumps (15–20) with simulated movements on horse or jumping table for training elements of bar clearance
	30	Training jumps and strength	Snatch, jerk and clean barbell of low weight (25–50 kg), especially for learning technically correct motion rhythm; general jumping exercises with and without weights (100 to 200 jumps); Knee-bends with partner (2×4–5)
	5	C Running down	Jogging
Saturday	60–90	Endurance and jumping strength	Runs through woods; Fartlek with gymnastics and special jumping exercises (consecutive take-offs, 5×4–5 and with touching branches with swinging leg, 8 to 10 times)

should be strengthened, e.g. abdominal muscles, the iliopsoas muscle, and the femoral extensors, using all respective gymnastic exercises and partial exercises corresponding to the sequence of movements with/without light weights (also with pulling resistance).

● Speed

For the high jumper all the fast jumps and jumping exercises are at the same time speed exercises. Great value should be attached to jumps over maximum heights, as this requires particularly rapid and intensive movements. Suitable forms as well are sprints and starts. Speed developing exercises should not be repeated too frequently; due to the high intensity the extent of training should be reduced.

● Jumping agility

For developing jumping agility a certain level of general coordination is required. Gaining jumping experience of all kinds, i.e. mastering a great number of different jumps and jumping styles is the key. The following exercises are suggested:
1. Jumps on open land, e.g.
a) Scissors over an inclined tree trunk with support on a hand.
b) Roll and Straddle jumps over an inclined tree trunk
c) Take-off with extended swinging leg; the foot of the swinging leg must touch the branches of the tree.
d) Same as above, with hands grasping a branch, hanging on it and then jumping down.

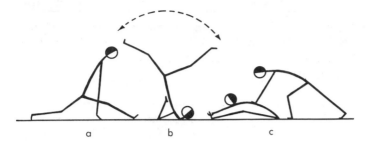

Fig. 92

e) Different exercises over obstacles or with tasks depending on the surroundings, as outlined in the technical training.

2. Technical jumps under various take-off conditions (take-off from sand, from the springboard and so on), as well as take-off with extended swinging leg.

It must be stressed that agility exercises place great demands on the nervous system of the athlete and tend to be exhausting. It is preferable, therefore, to do them at the beginning of the training session.

Certain exercises of this group, e.g. 1a, 1b and 3—take-off with swinging leg— can be used for recovery. They should be done at the end of the training session.

● Mobility

The high jumper must possess good hip mobility (spreading movement of swinging leg) and extensibility of calf muscles (extended swinging leg).

For developing these abilities gymnastic exercises, but also different special exercises of the hurdler, are ideal. Such exercises should be included in the daily schedules of the high jumper.

The most important are:

a) A reaching straddle stride with feathering, alternating legs (semi-rotation of upper body) (Fig. 92a).

b) Squat seat with the soles of the feet against each other. The hands press the knees down with a springy movement.

c) Press-ups with feet touching the ground over inner edge of the foot, lifting and lowering the pelvis.

d) Hurdle seat, one hand holds the spread leg by the knee and lifts it in a spring-like movement.

e) In hurdle seat (alternately rotating the trunk through 180°). During rotation the hands press the trunk upward.

f) With one leg lying with knee and foot on the edge of the hurdle, bend trunk forward.

g) Uphold, wide alternating spreading of legs (Fig. 92b).

h) Uphold, both extended legs are folded over the head, so that the toes touch the ground.

i) Squat seat, trunk bending forward and feathering, also with straddled legs.

k) Different splits (Fig. 92a, b, c).

● Jumping endurance

The high jumper requires more endurance than often believed. Only if he has endurance will he stand the training with high loads and the intensity of training during the main phase. One should start with general endurance exercises (e.g. runs along forest trails). The advanced jumper will develop endurance by a great number of repetitions of jumps and jumping exercises. The increase in the number of these exercises leads to some deterioration in speed and explosive force, so that, after some time, particularly prior to competitions, the loads should be reduced and recovery breaks inserted.

Table 50 Weekly Schedule of Training during the Competition Period (Foundation Training)

Day	Duration (min.)	Training task A = Preparation B = Main Part C = Closing		Training Means
Monday	15	A	Warm-up	Jogging, ankle work, acceleration runs, gymnastics;
	10		Special gymnastics	Exercises for stretched legs and hip flexibility
	45	B	Technique	Squat jumps from front and from the side (10–12), pay attention to approach rhythm; straddle jumps (25–40), 10 to 15 cm below best results
	20–30		Shot puts or discus throws	
	5	C	Warming down	Jogging
Tuesday	15	A	Warm-up	Game
		B	Long jump	5–6 jumps with full length approach
			Strength, jumping strength and speed development	Exercises with medicine ball, kettle bell or snatch and jerk and clean barbell; general jumping strength exercises with and without light weights (100); consecutive take-offs (5 × 4–5); acceleration runs and starts or hurdles
		C	Running down	Jogging
Thursday			same as Monday	
Friday			same as Tuesday (1)	
Saturday/Sunday			Rest or competition	

If there are competitions on Saturday or Sunday long jump exercises as well as exercises for strength and jumping strength are omitted.

4.5. The Pole Vault

The introduction of new, highly elastic poles has revolutionized the technique and coaching methods of pole vaulting. But even with older techniques, e.g. in metal-pole vaulting, there was a marked tendency of making better use of the elasticity of the pole by a higher grip, and to render the whole vaulting action more dynamic. A greater bend was achieved in metal poles by reducing the

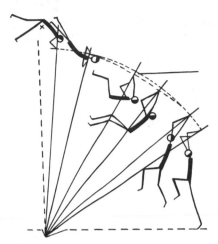

Fig. 93a

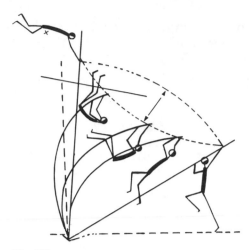

Fig. 93b

distance between the hands on the pole (from grip to fulcrum) by some 6 to 20 cm (Fig. 93a).

Greater bending than specified by the manufacturer became critical, because the light metal used did not straighten out after deformation by heavy bends, and the more elastic material (e.g. bamboo rods) was always loaded near the breaking point and did not stand up to such high loads. The fibre-glass poles, introduced in the USA between 1958 and 1961 by Brewer, Dolley, David and Uelses and in 1962 by Nikula in Finnland, began a new development in the pole vault. The use of elastic fibre-glass poles permitted a closer hand-hold, reducing the distance between the hands by 60 to 100 cm, and greater bending (Fig. 93b). Jumping with greater pole bending, through the use of highly elastic poles, led to a different utilization of the kinetic energy produced during approach and take-off.

1. In metal-pole vaulting the rigid implement acts as a lever with its support in the box and becoming upright in the direction of the vaulter.

2. In fibre-glass vaulting the kinetic energy produced by the pole plant in the first phase of the vault is partly transferred to the implement and stored in the bent pole as potential energy. Subsequently, in the recoiling phase of the pole, this energy is retransformed into kinetic energy to be used for the further upward drive of the vaulter.

These changes in the technique will be discussed in detail in the following chapters; they permitted a considerably higher grip on the pole and have greatly improved the results of pole vaulting in recent years. Some measured values, outlined in Table 51, illustrate these changes.

4.5.1. Technique

World-class vaulters are mainly oriented towards the "Pennel-Technique" [48]. We shall therefore not

48 This mechanical variety, called "Pennel-Technique" in sport practice, was first applied with success by the jumper J. Pennel, USA (5.35 m). World records were: 5.10, 5.13, 5.30 and 5.35 m.

Table 51   Hand-hold and Extra Height achieved in Pole Vaulting

Name	Country	Performance	Grip Height	Extra Height
Performance with Metal Pole				
Bragg	USA	4.80 m	3.95 m	0.85 m
Gutowski	USA	4.82 m	3.97 m	0.85 m
Richards	USA	4.73 m	3.93 m	0.80 m
Preussger	GDR	4.70 m	3.85 m	0.85 m
Performance with Glass-Fibre Pole				
Nordwig	GDR	5.50 m	4.67 m	0.93 m
Kozakiewicz	Poland	5.50 m	4.60 m	0.90 m
Kishkun	USSR	5.45 m	4.55 m	0.90 m
Seagren	USA	5.40 m	4.55 m	0.85 m
Pennel	USA	5.40 m	4.35 m	1.02 m

The hand-hold on the pole is measured from the grip point (thumb-index finger) of the upper hand to the top of the pole. From this value 20 cm (depth of the planting box) are deducted.

dwell on vaulting variations, which consist mainly of different take-off positions (corresponding to different handholds), but only refer to the most up-to-date and economic technique.

Although the following material is divided into several separate phases, following the main mechanical principles (bending and recoiling of the pole), it must be continually stressed that this is for purely theoretical considerations; the vaulting action itself is a single movement, in which all phases are closely interlinked and interdependent.

The analysis of the approach and vaulting movements will be described for the vaulter who carries the pole on his right side and takes off with the left foot.

4.5.1.1.   The Grip

A special feature of fibre-glass vaulting is the wide handspread in carrying the pole. The hands on the pole are about 90 to 120 cm (more than shoulders width) apart. The right hand grips the pole underneath at the upper end while the left hand holds it above at the fixed distance. When the vaulter faces straight ahead, with the pole pointing in the running direction, the handspread changes slightly. The right hand is rotated so that its back shows to the vaulter, while the index and middle fingers press down on the top of the pole to bring the planting end of the pole to about eye level. The thumb of the right hand rests on the side of the pole, away from the vaulter. In the grip of the left hand, the thumb serves as a fulcrum to the pole, while the other fingers grasp it from above. Both hands should grip the pole firmly but not tightly. The pole is carried on the right side of the vaulter at hip level. Both arms are bent at a right angle at the elbows (Fig. 94).

4.5.1.2.   The Approach

An efficient approach is an important prerequisite for a successful perform-

Fig. 94

ance in pole vaulting. The form and speed of approach determine whether the fibre-glass pole can be bent with the grip assumed and how quickly the momentum of the vaulter can be transferred to the pole. The approach is usually started in a striding position. Some vaulters prefer to do some preliminary walking steps before beginning the approach proper. The length of the approach depends on the acceleration capacity and acceleration pattern of the vaulter; it is determined by the number of strides the individual vaulter requires to reach optimum speed. The length of approach ascertained in this way is then expressed in metres and, mostly, transcribed to the runway in pole lengths. Generally the length of the run-up measures some 20 to 22 strides.

The approach is an acceleration run in which the vaulter reaches the highest speed at take-off. An effective vault with an adequate bending of the pole also depends on a suitable approach rhythm, which must ensure high speed at take-off. During the planting movement and preparation for the take-off a definite rhythm is established over the last three strides, the length of which (in feet) is: the last stride = $5^1/_2$ to 6, the penultimate stride = $7^1/_2$ to 8, and the third-to-last stride = $6^1/_2$ to 7.

Because of the additional weight of the pole, the position of the vaulter's centre of gravity slightly varies from that of jumpers without a pole. The vaulter reacts against the pull of the pole by pressure of the upper right hand and by a more upright position of the trunk than in sprinting. The closer the vaulter gets to the box and the more the pole is lowered, the more upright he becomes in order to counteract the weight of the pole and its lowering, without, however, leaning back. Over the last 3 to 5 strides the vaulter's body is almost erect. How much forward lean the vaulter has at the beginning of the approach and how much he becomes upright during the approach depends on the speed, the carry and the position of the pole. How should one carry the pole?

1. The most commonly used way of carrying the pole, which is also the most suitable for beginners, is with the forward end of the pole pointing forwards and upwards at about head level, with the pole in a vertical plane with the left shoulder. During the approach the pole gradually descends and points towards the back of the box on the last five or three strides from take-off. If the pole is carried in this way during the first half of the approach, its tendency to reduce speed will be minimized and a swift and safe pole plant achieved.

2. In another style the pole is carried parallel or almost parallel to the runway right from the start and the tip of the pole points straight ahead. This carry also ensures a swift and safe planting, but requires greater effort on the part of the vaulter, right from the outset, to resist the pull of the pole, which increases with the height of the grip. A "punching" forward and back-

Fig. 95

ward of the pole is uneconomic because it forces the vaulter to adapt his stride frequency to the swinging frequency of the pole and hinders the build-up of speed and of a constant stride rhythm during the approach. Such an unsteady carry also hinders the safe planting of the pole.

No significant assistance can be given to the stride rhythm by the shoulder and arm action, as would be the case in a normal run, since the pole must move as steadily as possible. But in the wide hand spread on the fibre-glass pole the shoulders and arms can assist the running movement without influencing the pole carry. This applies mainly to the right elbow which follows the movement by swinging outward.

4.5.1.3. The Pole Plant

The movements of a vaulter using a fibre-glass pole when planting the pole in the box must ensure transfer of the run-up and take-off energy to the pole for an effective bending of the pole. The movements over the last two strides and during the pole plant should be performed without loss of speed. The handspread on the pole is not changed during this action. The wide handspread is an advantage in bending the pole and helps adjustments while hanging on to the unsteady object in the course of the vault. The pole plant is started some 3 to 5 strides from the take-off, when the pole is directed forwards and downwards toward the box. On the third-to-last stride (Fig. 95, Pos. 1) the pole is slightly shifted forward by bringing the right hand close to the right hip. During the penultimate stride (Fig. 95, Pos. 2 and 3), when the right leg swings upwards and forwards, the right hand leads the pole back and upward close to the body. This hand rotates the pole counterclockwise about its long axis, while the grip of the front hand is loosened to allow the pole to rotate. In the transition to the last stride, and during the last stride, the upward rotating movement of both hands, but particularly the extension of the right arm, is continued. Just before the left (jumping) leg comes to the ground (Fig. 95, Pos. 4), the tip of the pole is planted in the box, at the edge between the back and the bottom. It is undesirable to hit

Fig. 96

the bottom first with the tip of the pole, letting it glide back to the wall, as this makes the pole plant insecure. When the impact of the pole plant in the box encounters resistance, the arm movements must be concluded and the arms ready to transfer the run-up and approach energy to the pole (Fig. 95, Pos. 5).

The beginning of the transfer takes place in the transition from the shock absorption of the take-off extension, when kinetic energy is imparted to the pole, causing the first slight bending of the pole.

4.5.1.4. The Take-Off

With fibre-glass vaulting the action of the legs at take-off is forward and up-ward, simulating the dynamics of the take-off in the long jump. Leading the action is the swinging leg, which is driven forward vigorously in flexed po-sition, bringing the thigh almost up to the horizontal, wit the lower part of the leg loosely hanging down, thus giving strong assistance to the extension of the take-off leg. During this action the up-per body is erect. The run-up and take-off energy is transmitted to the pole through the right arm, which is almost fully extended, and through the left arm, which forms a fixed right angle

299

with the body (Fig. 96, Pos. 1). This arm is acting as a strut, exerting pressure against the pole, while the upper arm exerts a pull, causing the pole to bend (Fig. 103b). An effective transfer of the run-up and take-off energy to the pole is achieved by the position of the take-off point directly under the right hand grip on the pole. In the Pennel technique the take-off point could be directly beneath the mid-point between the wide hand-spread or beneath the right hand grip on the pole. But this is a matter for each individual vaulter to decide.

For achieving a maximum bend with an optimally rigid pole, this take-off technique is the most effective and should be learned.

4.5.1.5. The L-Position

● Movements during the swing-up to the L-position

With fibre-glass vaulting the lowering of the swinging leg is of no or little importance, while the hang and swing-up of the legs to the L-position play an important part in the bending of the pole, leading quickly to its maximum bend.

As soon as the jumper has left the ground after take-off, his body is thrown forward by the impetus of the forward swing, while the left arm, still acting as a strut, prevents the vaulter's body, hanging on the pole by the extended right arm, from being driven towards the pole (Fig. 96, Pos. 2). The forward-upward swing is begun by the vigorous forward swinging of the extended left leg (Fig. 96, Pos. 2–4). The forward swing of the leg is accompanied by a layback of the upper body. The right arm is extended, the left arm noticeably flexed, to ensure a level posi-

tion of the shoulders. In this "hang" position of the body beneath the pole, the vaulter lifts both legs, flexed at the knee joints, vigorously, thus rapidly increasing the bend in the pole (Fig. 96, Pos. 5). From this phase onwards both legs work together. The vaulter's body is still hanging beneath the pole and the pelvis has not yet passed the pole; here the greatest bend is achieved. During the swing-up of the legs the left arm "gives", bringing the forearm close to the pole. The change between the fixed position in the phase of the greatest load, i.e. during take-off, and the transition from this position in the phase described above, is one of the most critical points in the dynamics of the swing-up to the L-position.

● The L-position

As the body swings powerfully upwards, the legs and then the hips drive past the pole. The vaulter's body now assumes a position simulating an "L", if viewed from the side of the vault. Characteristics of this position are the upper body rolled back, bending at the hips, and the hang from the extended right arm. The pelvis is first level with the head, lower than the hands, but in front of the pole. The thighs of the flexed legs are close to the pole. This L-position is typical and necessary in the phase prior to the recoil of the pole (Fig. 96, Pos. 6). The pole, which in the phases of maximum bending was pointing directly forward, now moves slightly left as the pole straightens out, since the body, hanging on its right side, comes now more over the pole's support in the box.

● The extended L-position

With the start of the recoil of the pole

and the assumption of the L-position, all movements of the vaulter must be in the vertical direction as the pole straightens out further. This must, however, not be a passive movement, allowing the body to be "lifted" from the L-position, but a continuation of the lifting of the pelvis out of the lowest position level with the head, up to the grip of the left hand (Fig. 96, Pos. 6) and further to a sort of bent inverted hang with the pelvis close to the right hand grip (Fig. 96, Pos. 7).

This upward movement of the pelvis and extension of the initial position during the time of the recoil of the pole is assisted by the straightening of the hitherto flexed legs. The upper body is still hanging (now in vertical position) on the extended right arm. The left arm is pulled up, bringing the forearm alongside the bent pole (Fig. 97). The fixed position of this arm, assumed during take-off, is finally abandoned in this phase. Due to this and to the lifting of the pelvis, the shoulder axis becomes the axis of rotation of the vertically upward swinging body.

The difficulty of the movements leaving the L-position is that they must take place in time with the pole's recoil. Any premature reverse, while the pole is still bent, obstructs the complete straightening out of the pole, preventing it from making available the potential energy stored for the following movements. These movements, if well synchronized with the recoil of the pole, are an important phase for the utilization of the advantages offered by the fibre-glass pole and a determining factor for a successful vault.

4.5.1.6.   The Turn and Reverse

The pull with the upper arm and leftward turn of the body about its longitudinal axis takes place during the last phase of the pole's recoil, while the hips are high up and close to the grip of the upper hand. It brings the vaulter into a good position for clearing the bar face downward (Fig. 96, Pos. 8). This turning movement is introduced by rotating the hips with the legs close together. During the turn and reverse the body is almost completely in front of the pole. The reverse involves a reversal of the position of head and hands, the turn a rotation of the body about its long axis (see Fig. 96, Pos. 8–10). In 10 the head is below the hands and in 12 above.

In fibre-glass vaulting the phases of the reverse are usually not made with the body in contact with the pole. In fact the reverse does not take place "on the pole" but "in front of the pole". There is still sufficient momentum left from the straightening out of the pole for the further ascent of the body, so that in completion of the turning movement with the right shoulder the vaulter's body is well up above the grip. The reverse is completed with the ending of the turn. In a dynamic vault with a high grip the pole stands up almost ver-

Fig. 97

301

tically (near 90°). From this follows a substantial distance of the uprights from the box and a late final point of bar clearance.

4.5.1.7. The Push-Off from the Pole

The reverse is followed very quickly by the push-up, so that these actions actually merge into each other. Many vaulters delay the push-up, but this deprives them of the shift forward momentum required for getting away from the crossbar and not falling on to it. Due to the wide handspread the vaulter must withdraw his lower hand from the pole soon after the reverse (Fig. 96, Pos. 10). The fast push-up from the pole is brought about exclusively by the extension of the right arm; this is the last impulse imparted to the body which is still moving upwards. The complete extension of the right arm is important, as the full length of the arm is needed for achieving the extra height above the bar (Pos. 11). Competition rules permit the pole to fall under the bar, but the vaulter who uses poles longer than the jumping height should take care to throw the pole back in take-off direction by the thrust of the right hand.

4.5.1.8. Bar Clearance

The most appropriate form of the bar clearance is the fly-away arch (Fig. 96, Pos. 12). It allows, through a favourable distribution of the various parts of the body, a low position of the body's CG and a sufficient distance for all parts of the body to clear the crossbar. If speed is lacking, the clearance will have to be performed purely by the supporting phase of the right arm. But if the as-

cending body is in the line of force of the push-up, it receives sufficient momentum through the transfer of potential energy from the last part of the pole's recoil to achieve a fly-away clearance, which is characterized by the additional height achieved above the crossbar (Fig. 98). While this form is considered to be the best for metal-pole vaulting, the fly-away clearance comes more naturally in fibre-glass vaulting, simply as the result of a perfect vault, and is easily learned.

In spite of the higher grip the transfer of potential energy into kinetic energy during the pole's recoil supplies sufficient momentum if the movements during these phases are properly mastered. This force drives mostly forward and gives the movements amplitude. With fibre-glass vaulting it is therefore difficult during the phases of the pole's recoil and during bar clearance to direct all the movements in the vertical direction. When the culminating point of bar clearance is reached, the proper distance of the crossbar, i.e. the proper distance between the uprights, determines the further success of the vault. The distance between the uprights is therefore of the greatest importance in pole vaulting. It must be checked and adjusted before every attempt.

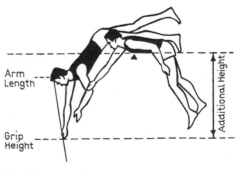

Fig. 98

302

When the chest reaches the bar, a strong rotation impulse, caused by the falling legs, draws the body away from the bar without changing its arched form (Fig. 96, Pos. 15). Through this rotation about the bar a new form of landing is introduced. By snatching the arms up and throwing the lower parts of the legs back to produce a hollow back, the body can also be drawn away from the bar.

4.5.1.9. The Landing

The ever increasing heights which are being vaulted increase the height of falling and hence the impact on landing which is several times the body weight. By piling soft elastic material such as foam rubber, sponge rubber or Motopren to create a jumping hill, the landing becomes safe and conserves energy. The vaulter will no more attempt to land on his feet but in a sitting position (Fig. 96, Pos. 15/16) and then roll back. Such soft material saves the vaulter from injuries on landing, removes fears about the vaulting height, and gives some assurance that even in the event of a broken pole or uncontrolled landings no serious injuries will result.

4.5.1.10. Pole Material and Choice of the Proper Pole

The fibre-glass pole is a tube wound from alkali-free glass-fibre material and bonded with synthetic resin (epoxyde and phenolic resin). The resin serves as a binding material and has high elastic properties. The 8—16 layers of fibre-glass material give the pole its stability and high bending strength needed to cope with high loads. Differences in elasticity are determined by the glass-fibre layers and the wall thickness of the material. The poles are classified by measuring the sag at a certain length. The pole types are designated by the specifications of length and peak load with the body weight of the vaulter at a certain grip height.

In choosing the proper pole different factors must be considered:
1. Weight of the jumper
2. Height of the grip on the fibre-glass pole: This depends on the approach and take-off energy, body size and the height of the grip of the jumper.
3. Technical perfection of the vaulter's movements on the pole, particularly during the phases of pole bending.

In choosing a pole it is important to know the upper limit at which the pole can be gripped without the risk of a break. It is also necessary to know the lower point at which the pole can be gripped to bend at all. The coach will have to find out the proper pole for his athlete by experimenting with different types of pole. Only thus can the magnitude of the bending be judged and the vaulter be protected from overbending and breaking it. The growing physical strength of vaulters in general and the fatigue of the material by frequent use requires the direction of the vaulter to optimally stiff poles and the change to increasingly stiffer types. In order to be equipped for the varied training and competitive conditions (quality of the runway, head or following wind, weather conditions, standard of performers), the advanced vaulters must possess several fibre-glass poles of the same type but of various grades of elasticity and must master the techniques required for them. Fibre-glass performers should have in competitions a selection of poles of varying elasticity in order to be prepared for different conditions.

It hardly needs stressing that such a thin and elastic tube should be handled with care and protected from cracks, dents and other exterior damage.

4.5.2.   Technical Training

As outlined in the "Technique of the Pole Vault" the flawless and dynamic performance of a pole vault at competitive level is quite complicated. But any talented boy can learn vaulting, even with fibre-glass poles, if he receives the proper instruction. If the preparatory exercises and part of the complementary exercises are started at the best age (according to MEINEL between 9 and 13 years), vaulting can be learned relatively quickly. [49] This has been confirmed by experiences in our country and abroad.

The fact that the pattern of movement is fairly complicated and difficult to learn, should not lead one to conclude that a great number of complicated preliminary exercises must be included in the training schedules. On the contrary, a relatively small number of preparatory and basic exercises, clearly explained and demonstrated and frequently repeated, usually leads to early success.

The learning process is subdivided into three segments: During the first segment the novice pole vaulter gets acquainted with the lifting and bearing function of the pole: he learns to mas-

49 Cf. Team of Authors "Leichtathletik – ein Buch für Lehrer, Trainer und Übungsleiter im Kindersport", 3rd ed., Volk und Wissen, Berlin 1966.

ter its lability and to overcome initial fears (it is boys between 9 and 13 years who best manage this).

The second segment is characterized by the transition from simple pole jumping to pole vaulting proper. The objectives are to master the competitive jump over the crossbar (best age between 14 and 16 years). Beginning with this segment fibre-glass vaulting should be included in the technical training programme.

The third segment covers the systematic training of different sections but also of the complete movement, including proper timing, coordination and dynamics. It is in this phase that the learning of skills and the build-up of definite physical and psychological qualities fuse into a whole. This process takes place during a properly directed special training lasting several years.

4.5.2.1.   Special Preparatory Exercises

Before learning the technique proper, a certain amount of preparation is required. The learner must first grasp how to manipulate the pole and understand its lifting functions.

It may be difficult in some areas to obtain the required pole material. For training boys, wooden poles (ash, cedar, spruce) or bamboo rods and light metal tubes can be used. Fibre-glass vaulting should only be started with boys who show aptitude and inclination for the event. For the choice of the appropriate fibre-glass pole see section 4.5.1.10.

In all preparatory exercises the pole should be planted in the sand pit (not yet in the planting box). The sand in

304

Fig. 99

the jumping pit should always be loose.

Three basic forms of jumps can be applied during the special preparation: the "witch-ride"; "the pole long jump" and the open air jump.

The "witch-ride" (Fig. 99)

By this form the jumper learns quickly and effectively to have confidence in the strength and capacity of the pole and to overcome fears often present in beginners. This process is accompanied by an exciting jumping sensation, which delights the youngster.

After an approach of 5 to 7 strides the jumper plants his pole in the pit, takes off and hangs on an outstretched upper arm. The legs are straddled and astride the pole. In this position the jumper is carried by the pole and lands on both legs in a straddled position.

Order of exercises:

1. "Passive jump L".

The tip of the pole is in the pit; the jumper stands one step behind a verti-

Fig. 100   Fig. 101

cal line drawn down from the grip point and holds the pole above his head. After a first stride he takes off firmly with the left leg. The coach or trainer gives him a push from behind, so that with his chest against the pole he is carried by it past the vertical line (Fig. 100). This exercise must be repeated several times, each time raising the grip. This will give the jumper a feeling of being carried by the pole.

2. "Witch-ride" with 5 to 7 strides approach.
This jump must fulfil a kinetic function. At the beginning the grip is about 30 cm above reaching height. With growing skill it is raised by a further 60 to 80 cm. During the planting of the pole the lower (left) hand must not get closer to the top hand than by 40 cm. This is important in view of the future learning of the fibre-glass technique.

3. Same as 2, but with 7 to 9 strides approach. Running speed and grip height increase, allowing the jumper to move past the vertical (jumping sensation).

The pole long jump (Fig. 101)
The pole long jump with a half turn has certain elements of pole vaulting. Apart from the pole plant and take-off it serves to develop the swinging of the legs on the side of the pole, the pull up and the turn.
Carry out exercises in the following order:

1. Create a right sense of movement. The movement is started with 3 to 5 running strides. The pole is gripped as high as the jumper can reach; after take-off the jumper swings past the pole, leaving it on his left (the upper body is slightly leaning leftwards). In the last part of the jump he does the pull-up, combined with a half turn, and finally lands.

2. Pole jump with half turn from 5 to 7 strides.

3. Same as 2, but using a marked "pit". For this, place a bar 1 m from the pit edge and a second one 1.5–2 m further on. The jumper is asked to plant the pole in front of the first bar and to land behind the second one when the turn is completed.

4. Same as 3; just before landing, the pole must be taken to the right shoulder. The marking of such an improvised pit has proved useful for a dynamic and correlated execution of the jump (emotional motivation, better orientation and checking opportunity). With growing confidence the pit can be widened to 3 m. In all pole long jumps, unlike the "witch-ride", the grip should be higher (start at reaching height and increase gradually). If the grip is too high, the jump will be a failure from the outset. The pole long jump should be constantly improved, as it helps to perfect the time-space-coordination which is so important for pole vaulting.
Success in pole jumps—of any kind—will come sooner if the planting zone is some 40 to 50 cm lower than the take-off area. By using the same approach rhythm it allows for a much higher grip on the pole. This higher grip produces a longer levering effect of the pole. It gives the jumper more time for the movements on the pole. When the jumper has acquired sufficient skill the depth of the pole plant can be reduced and the approach lengthened (2 to 4 running strides).

Jumps in open areas
Jumps in other suitable surroundings

(sand or gravel pits with a steep slope, natural pits etc.) help to develop courage and reactions, as well as general and special jumping agility, but have no direct connection with the learning of the fibre-glass technique. Jumps in other open areas should be started only when the "witch-ride" and the pole long jump with half turn are properly mastered.

4.5.2.2. Basic Exercises of Technical Training

Experience shows that after a thorough special preparation and drilling of basic exercises the jumper can, after 25 to 35 training sessions, clear heights which are near the gripping point on the pole (2.80 to 3.50 m). The specialized training of this event has not yet started. The figures therefore refer merely to an ordinary track and field foundation training.

When the jumper has accomplished all the preparatory exercises and masters the pole long jump, pole vaulting can be developed by a large number of jumps over the bar. The bar is actually the most important point of orientation for the jumper, without which he could hardly learn, if at all, the proper pattern of movement for pole vaulting. But it would be asking too much from the beginner to jump under competitive conditions right from the outset. He would have to concentrate on too many factors. Easier jumping conditions in the beginning usually give better results.

– Exercise 1: Simplified vault with 7 to 9 approach strides

The pole should be planted in the sand pit (mark clearly planting zone). The crossbar is held by two persons at chest or head level or at reaching height. In the event of obvious failures the bar is lowered. This avoids "panicky" jumps and saves time and broken bars. The jumpers can clear the bar many times in short intervals and thus soon establish rhythmical movements (up to 25 jumps in a training session is a suitable number).

Points to note: The take-off should take place vertically under the grip and with the left leg. Find optimal grip point by trial and error and stick to it. When the jumper has done about 50 jumps in this way (two training sessions) and when the trainer feels confident that he does them without fear, the next basic exercise can be started.

– Exercise 2: same as exercise 1

Here the crossbar should be placed on pegs of the uprights. The distance of the bar from the pole plant zone should be some 40 to 60 cm. The planting zone should be a diagonal hole of about 50 cm depth.

Points to note: During pole plant the handspread should be some 40 to 50 cm. Active take-off with accentuated swinging leg action.

Good use should also be made of the swinging of the left leg, i.e., the swing must come from below and not be interrupted by a premature arm-pull. Furthermore, during bar clearance, the turn should be no less than 180° with subsequent push-off from the pole.

This form of jumping for bar clearance should be given preference during five to ten further workouts. As the jumper acquires more skill, the approach can be lengthened to 10 strides.

In the last and in the following basic exercises fibre-glass vaulting can be effectively started. The more or less pronounced fibre-glass bending results, at first, from the 40 to 50 cm handspread, the optimum grip height and the jumper's weight. It is hence not yet the result of "international" bending, which will be only sought later on. In accordance with the standard of the jumper a relatively soft type of pole should be chosen.

The jumps under competitive conditions (with planting box), which now follow, require a precise stride length, a fixed approach distance and stride pattern, a skilled pole carry and pole plant. All these elements must be perfected simultaneously with jumps over bars.

– Exercise 3: Accelerating with pole over 40 to 50 m

Purpose: Learning to sprint with the pole and with the proper pole carry. Determine the best stride pattern for the individual and the right moment for pole descent.

Points to note: Continuous increase in speed, technically correct sprinting (running on the ball of the foot, knee pick-up, full extension of the take-off leg, accentuated upright trunk position). The latter is a special feature of the pole vaulter and conditioned by the pole carry and planting. During carry the tip of the pole should not go beyond head level and should, after the first 20 m, be gradually lowered to knee level.

– Exercise 4: Determining the approach length. The jumper marks a take-off spot on the runway. After some 2 to 4 walking steps this spot is hit with the left (jumping) leg. The jumper now begins an acceleration run (cf. Exercise 3). The coach watches the stride pattern and marks the landing points of the jumping leg at the desired number of strides (8, 10, 12, 14, 16).

This exercise is repeated several times. The take-off spot so determined, on which the vaulter takes up his position, is vertically under the upper grip. Now the vaulter can mark the imaginary back wall of the planting box with the tip of the pole. From this mark backward the length of the run-up can be measured either in pole lengths or with a measuring tape and transferred to the runway.

Over this distance he will now drill the approach in relation with the most appropriate acceleration, well timed pole descent, pole plant and take-off. Corrections to comply with the texture of the track and with wind conditions may become necessary.

Fixing the approach in this manner has to be repeated every year, even by advanced vaulters. In this individual requirements must be taken into account (cf. 4.5.1.4.).

– Exercise 5: Pole plant with "intentional" pole bending (Fig. 102)

Purpose: The planting move is a decisive phase for the subsequent vault. It must bring the vaulter into a favourable position in relation to the pole (just below or behind the pole) before take-off. It also marks the beginning of the pole bend.

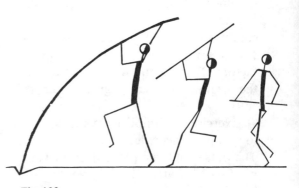

Fig. 102

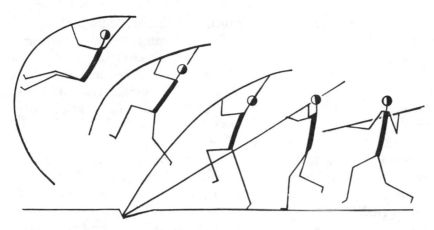

Fig. 103a

Sequence of movements (Fig. 103a):
It can be seen from this drawing that the pole plant begins on the penultimate stride. The handspread is the width of the shoulders. Directly before the take-off extension the right arm is straightened. The left arm is at a fixed angle to the trunk. This levering action of the arms causes the pole to bend immediately the vaulter leaves the ground (Fig. 103b).
Sequence of exercises:
a) Having clearly demonstrated and explained the pole plant, the athlete can practise the pole plant repeatedly with a two-stride rhythm.
Points to note: The right hand is brought forwards and upwards as the right leg touches the ground (cf. Fig. 102). The hands on the pole are the width of the shoulders apart. The left

hand does not glide upwards but remains fixed after the pole plant.
b) Same as a), but as a separate move in the planting box (or against a wall or some other resisting object); the vaulter stands about 4 m from the planting box in striding position, with the left leg set forward; he then walks into take-off with two strides. Pole-plant move as under a). The take-off is simulated by the pick-up of the right knee. The hip is thereby vigorously pushed forward. By the pull of the right arm and the fixed position of the left arm the pole is made to bend if the grip is high enough (about 10 to 20 cm higher than the competition grip).
c) Same as b), but with several approach strides and more powerful movements. A check-mark has been placed at about 5 m from the planting

Fig. 103b

Fig. 104a

box and must be hit with the left foot after the preliminary walking strides.

d) Pole plant and take-off on to a lower pole plant zone from 7 strides approach (Fig. 104a).

Points to note: Powerful striding, well timed pole plant, fixed left arm. Active take-off with marked forward tendency. The grip should be so high that the pole gets beyond the vertical line after bending. In this exercise either the planting zone is lowered by 30 cm or the take-off area raised correspondingly (Fig. 104a and b). This permits grasping the pole at a much higher point, normally possible only after a long approach.

– Exercise 6: Vaults for basic performance under easier conditions

To arrive at an automatic and reliable performance of all parts of the vaulting movement, the regular and repeated successful interplay of all the forces and factors involved in the vault must be brought about. The jumps for basic performance are an excellent means of consolidating pole vaulting technique. They should be performed under conditions requiring the full concentration of the vaulter but without great effort (the bar should be at a height corresponding to 90 per cent of the actual performance capacity of the athlete).

Two forms of vaults for basic performance have proved effective:

a) Vaults under easier conditions

b) Vaults under competitive conditions after medium or full length approach.

For the vaults under a), easier conditions are provided by placing the planting box 10 to 20 cm deeper than usual. Thus the vaulter, after an approach of only 10 running strides, arrives at a handhold which could otherwise only be achieved by a long approach run (some 14 to 16 strides). With this shorter approach the number of vaults made in the same time can be doubled. This allows for a large number of vaults with a relatively high handhold and the desired pole bending. These conditions are obtained by sinking the box or by raising the take-off area some 20 to 30 cm; for this purpose several box covers or similar apparatus are placed one behind the other to serve as a run-up and take-off area (Fig. 104b)

Points to note: Depending on the standard of the vaulter, he will, together with his coach, concentrate on the coordination of the various vaulting phases and the dynamic course of the complete vault.

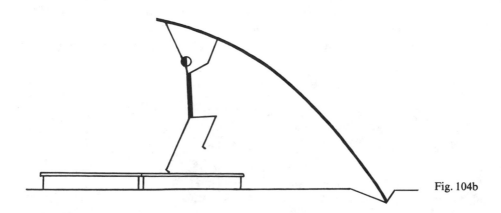

Fig. 104b

A point to be stressed right from the outset is the achievement of the optimal bending of the pole. If the correct execution of the approach, pole plant and take-off does not lead to sufficient bending of the pole, softer poles will have to be used. On the other hand a stiffer pole should be chosen if the bend is too pronounced.

It goes without saying that not all mistakes and shortcomings in the execution of the vault can be corrected simultaneously. Through close cooperation between the coach and the athlete the proper "point of attack" must be sought after and found. There is no ready-made formula for this. Experience has shown, however, that the main source of error lies either in the approach, pole plant or swing-up to the L-position; the consequences will be reflected only in the second half of the vault (cf. 4.5.2.4.).

These vaults for basic performance under easier conditions are to be repeated over and over again by the beginner or by the advanced vaulter for improving technique.

Exercise 7: Jumps for basic performance under competitive conditions

Once the course of vaulting movements has been thoroughly absorbed through the 6th basic exercise and the required technique has been acquired, the vaults for basic performance can be done under ordinary competitive conditions and should now stand in the foreground of technical training. For correcting mistakes, the methods of exercise 6 may, as a matter of principle, be applied. Additionally all phases contributing to the dynamics of the vault, such as approach rhythm, take-off speed, action of the left leg, must be given special attention. The best height

of grip should be found out by trial and error and kept to.

In doing vaults with short approach-runs softer poles can be used than when doing longer approach-runs (the best approach length for youths is between 12 and 16 strides and for advanced adults between 18 and 20 strides).

4.5.2.3. Ancillary Exercises

When an athlete displays special aptitude (constitutionally and physically) for pole vaulting and shows a personal inclination for the event, he should be encouraged by intensifying the technical training through ancillary exercises.

The complex of ancillary exercises is an integral part of the specialized training process. Some 4 to 6 years of hard fibre-glass training are required in order to, through an effective utilization of the approach (18 to 20 approach strides) and a grip height of some 4.00 to 4.40 m, achieve an increase in the height of the grip. Raising the optimum handhold 60 to 100 cm is a true criterion of mastery in vaulting.

The technical training will be adapted to the general and special physical skills and character of the athlete.

The objectives outlined for the improvement of technical skills call for a special methodical approach. In the analytical method different parts, such as the approach, pole plant, take-off and pole bending, swing to the L-position, reverse and bar clearance have first to be perfected separately; simultaneously or consecutively the coordination of the complete vault should be brought to perfection.

For the sake of clarity the different

complementary exercises have been subdivided into complexes forming a well organized whole. This sequence need not necessarily be applied in practice. The athlete and his coach must find out by intelligent and creative cooperation the most appropriate routines and determine how long and how often they should be practised. It must also be determined which variations in style are required by the constitution and temperament of the athlete and which are dependent on his athletic and technical training level.

The exercises for improving the approach are outlined in the section "Means for Developing Physical Properties" (4.5.3.2.).

● Exercises for perfecting a well timed pole plant and take-off

The correct combination of pole plant and take-off movements is of vital importance for the dynamics of the vault and the optimum grip height. This is a key point in the phase in which horizontal forces must be transferred into vertical ones. The more secure this transition is, the better will be the final result. This is why the transition from run-up to take-off in relation to the bending of the pole and swing-up on the pole should be trained constantly with great precision.

The sequence of movements of the pole plant and the methodical approach for inculcating it are outlined in the 5th basic exercise (4.5.2.2.).

1. Gaining understanding of the take-off as a Scissors jump on a 60 to 80 cm high gymnastic box.

Do 5 or 7 running strides to reach the box at a distance of 2.0 to 2.5 m. After take-off and swing-up of the thigh to the horizontal, relaxed touch-down with the swinging leg on the box—no take-off from the box. Landing in the sand pit on jumping leg (Fig. 105).

2. Same as exercise 1, but with 9 to 10 approach strides. The box is cleared without the swinging leg landing, but with the same sequence of movements.

3. Jumps with hanging on rope, balancing rings, football-goal frame and so on (Fig. 106).

The sequence of movements corresponds to that of exercise 1. After take-off, at the highest point of the flight curve (at about 1.0 to 1.5 m before the rope), the jumper grips the rope. He thus jumps into the hang. The hand-spread on the towrope should be 50 cm.

Fig. 105

Fig. 106

4. Having thus obtained the feel of the take-off, he will now start to practise with the pole. In doing so care should be taken
a) that the take-off is in the forward direction "into the pole";
b) that at the take-off a bending of the pole is achieved.
The execution of this movement is illustrated in Fig. 103a.
Points to note: A clear knee-pick-up must become visible over the last strides ("grow"). During the pole plant the stride pattern must remain straight (no deviations right or left). Well timed beginning and consistent execution of the pole planting move. After pole plant and take-off a clear bending of the pole must become visible. The upper body must hang "freely" on the pole, the legs are slightly straddled. When the pole has straightened out again and moved past the vertical line, the vaulter lands on both legs in the jumping pit. Warning! The pole must not be released by either hand. The resulting explosive extension is dangerous and may cause injuries.
This exercise should be practised with short and medium approach, under normal and artificial conditions, over and over again, for years, until perfection is reached.

● Exercises for learning and perfecting the swing-up to the L-position

The correct and effective swing-up to the L-position is crucially important for the subsequent utilization of the pole bend and recoil, as well as for achieving the desired extra height in the handhold. The dynamics on the pole are also greatly influenced by it. In fact, at the moment of the onset of the upward swing the pole is subject to an enormous load and displays the greatest bend.
The execution of the movement is illustrated in Fig. 107. In this phase of the vault the take-off leg has a special function to fulfil. On leaving the ground it changes its function to become the swinging leg for the rest of the vault. After leaving the ground it comes up to the horizontal in an extended position. As in the swinging action in the high jump, this effectively enhances the amplitude of swing and causes a direct utilization of the approach and take-off speed for the vaulter's movements on the pole.
It must be stressed that the action of

Fig. 107

the swinging leg after leaving the ground is not a personal matter to be solved by the individual. The same technical and methodical circumstances arise as in the high jump, where the extended swinging-leg action in the straddle jump has to be trained consciously.

Follow-on exercises:

1. Acquire the feel of the movement on the rope, gymnastic rings and so on.

Initial position: The right leg set forward, left back. The rope is gripped as high as the right hand can reach, the left hand grips shoulder width below. Upward swinging of the extended left leg, while rolling back the trunk. Thus the left knee reaches the right hand. Meanwhile the right arm remains completely extended. Any pulling of the arms must be avoided.

2. Same as 1, but with 5 strides approach and take-off (Fig. 108). The

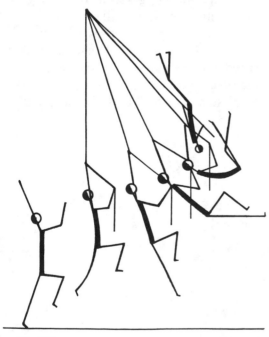

Fig. 108

take-off spot is at 1.0 to 1.5 m from the towrope.

Points to note: Consistent take-off; then, with a relaxed upper body, easy forward swing of the left leg. After some time this forward swinging movement will become active, with the upper body lying back for balance. Any pulling movement of the arms would destroy the flow of movement and the swing-round.

Proceeding in this manner, exercises 1 and 2 will be grasped after only a few work-outs.

3. Pole long jumping without a turn from 5 to 7 strides run-up. The pole will first be planted in a hole of about 40 cm depth in the sand and later on in the planting box.

Points to note: Consistent pole plant and take-off with initial forward swing of the left leg. The leg is at first brought up to about the horizontal. With growing confidence the swing of the left leg and the counter-balancing roll-back of the trunk is intensified to a point where, momentarily, the thigh of the left leg touches the pole. Only just before landing the upper body is brought upright again and the legs are brought down for a safe landing.

4. With growing confidence the pole can be gripped higher and the approach lengthened. This should lead to a greater bending of the pole and thus the pole long jump without a turn develops into a swing into the L-position. This exercise may create some difficulties at the beginning. During the jump the jumper usually turns leftwards. The reason is that the right leg is leading the movement and that the jumper pulls up his arms. Both mistakes must be corrected.

Fig. 109   Fig. 110

It takes about 14 to 20 sessions to learn this exercise. Once exercise 4 is well mastered, the run-up should be gradually—over months—be lengthened to competition distance. The pole is now planted in the box. The points to be watched are the same as in exercise 3. As this exercise belongs to the core of fibre-glass vaulting, an exact and confident execution of the movements and high-jump dynamics should be pursued.

5. Extension of the L-position with free reverse (Fig. 109). This exercise has as its purpose the use of the energy released by the pole for properly directed movements of the vaulter.
Description of the movement and points to note:
When the jumper has assumed the L-position with a corresponding substan-

tial bending of the pole, this position will be changed by bringing the legs further up towards the pole. This moves the pelvis, which in the L-position was approximately at the height of the lower hand, towards the upper hand, in line with the recoil of the pole but without any pulling by the arm. Only then the jumper begins to reverse by an explosive pull of the arm. The reverse takes place without the jumper's body touching the pole (thus the term "free reverse").

Perfecting the swing-up to the L-position and its extension will now be constantly on the training programme of the pole vaulter. Together with the pole plant and take-off such exercises occupy a key position in the acquisition of technique. They must be drilled to perfection!

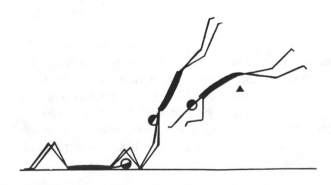

Fig. 111

● Exercises for improving the reverse and bar clearance

During the vault such phases as the swing-up and L-position as well as its extension, the pull-up with turn and the push-off from the pole form a continuous chain of actions. The coordination of different parts of the total movement should be trained through the jumps for basic performance preferably as a whole. In line with his level of technical training each vaulter will be given definite tasks in which special points are stressed for the vaulting phases he has to perfect. Regular practice and intelligent corrections are the most important means of achieving the desired improvement in technique.

The following exercises should be included in the technical training:

1. Acquire the proper feel for the reverse. The complete movement in its different parts is illustrated in Fig. 94, Pos. 10 to 12.

Points to note: The exercise begins with a backward lean of the upper body to give the pole, which should be gripped at the competitive height, an initial bend. The subsequent recoil will be used to perform a "springing reverse" by a jump-like push-off with the left leg and the pull-up of the arms (Fig. 110). It should be noted that during the reverse the right forearm and later also the right upper arm remain against the pole. This ensures an effective push-off.

2. Pole long jump with flying push-off from the pole (cf. Fig. 101). This exercise is basically the same as the pole long jump with a half turn, only the approach and also the movements on the pole are more explosive. After the turn a vigorous push-off from the pole in the clearly visible left-right order sets in. The jumper pushes off from the pole before landing on both legs.

3. Roll-back from a momentary handstand. This movement is repeated several times without interruption. A vigorous consecutive left-right push-off is a point to be watched. Landing is always on the left leg.

4. Same as in exercise 3, but as separate movement over a 50 to 70 cm high crossbar (Fig. 111).

5. The so-called "horse-bar-exercise" (Fig. 112).

From 5 to 7 approach strides-take-off with the left leg (the direction of approach is from the right side); the beginning of the jump is very much similar to that of the handspring or the cartwheel). After take-off the jumper swings into a momentary handstand. While the right hand acts as a support, the left hand pushes off. The jumper then endeavours to clear the bar in an arch-fly-away position. A bar of 60 to 100 cm height—measured from the push-off point of the right hand—must be cleared.

4.5.2.4.   Fault–Reason–Correction

In the approach:

– Fault: Uneconomic acceleration, so that there is an inevitable slowing down on the last strides.

Reason: Too much speed on the first half of the approach, or the approach is too long.

Correction: Place a check-mark at about 10 to 12 m from the planting box and set the task of running at optimum speed only from this mark onwards; or reduce the approach by 2 to 4 strides.

– Fault: The pole is being carried too tensely; the upper body is not facing straight ahead.

Fig. 112

Reason: The vaulter does not master the approach with the pole.

Correction: Repeat a great number of acceleration runs with pole up to 50 m.

— Fault: The last strides before the pole plant are off the line of run (turned to the right) (Fig. 113).

Reason: The jumper is mentally preparing the subsequent vaulting movements or is shaky during pole plant.

Correction: Place an orientation line (a skipping rope or something similar) to mark the direction of approach. Do a great number of pole plants from a medium approach.

During pole plant and take-off:

— Fault: Late descent of the pole.

Reason: The vaulter has not mastered the run-up with the pole carry for the pole plant.

Correction: Train the approach technique separately; focus the attention on

an early and gradual pole descent. Practise the pole descent first without and later with pole plant.

— Fault: Pole plant was too late—a classical mistake!

Reason: This specific pattern of movement is not yet fully automatic (or the jumper is "running under the pole").

Correction: Depending on how serious

Fig. 113

Fig. 114a

Fig. 114b

4. The left arm is not firm enough at the joints.

Corrections: Exercises for achieving a better pole bend (cf. 4.5.2.2., exercise 5). Find the most suitable pole by trial and error, same for grip height and length of approach.

– Fault: During the pole plant and take-off the right hand glides down.

Reason: 1. The right hand is unconsciously loosened. 2. Too high hand grip. 3. The jumper takes off before reaching the mark.

Correction: If necessary, readjust the length of the approach and grip height. Put an adhesive tape binding on the spots where the hands grip the pole, or, if the hands are sweaty, rub magnesia on the pole.

– Fault: Too early pull-up of the arm; interrupts movement.

Reason: Either incorrect understanding of the vault or too late pole plant.

Correction: Practise the swing-up to the L-position to correct faults. Attempt to achieve a consistent pole plant.

In the swing-up to the L-position:

– Fault: The vaulter swings away from the pole.

Reason: Incorrect understanding of the vault—insufficient backward lean—the left leg does not swing up to the pole, but in the direction of the crossbar.

Correction: Keep working at the swing-up to the L-position. Practise "free reverse" with extension of the L-position. This should be practised as a complementary exercise or as part of the vault for performance!

– Fault: The vaulter gets quite well into the L-position but lacks the drive to swing up further.

Reason: The grip on the pole is too

the mistake is, repeat the pole plant systematically (see 4.5.2.2., exercise 5). Permit no sloppiness in the execution of the movements.

– Fault: No swinging-leg action during take-off

Reason: Wrong understanding of take-off. This is usually found in vaulters who take off with the right leg.

Correction: See "Take-off exercises" (cf. 9.5.2.3.). Attention! This mistake can be very persistent. Spare no effort to get rid of it!

– Fault: The jumper misses the right moment for take-off (he starts the jump either behind or ahead of the take-off mark, as is shown in Figs. 114a and 114b).

Reason: Inaccuracy in the approach.

Correction: Adjust the beginning of the approach (lengthen or shorten the approach). At each jump the take-off point should be checked, because this mistake, if frequently repeated, may lead to injuries in the lumbar region.

– Fault: Insufficient bending of the pole.

Reason: 1. Unsuitable pole.
2. Poor technique in planting action.
3. Too narrow handspread or too low grip.

high. The role of the left arm has not been established.

Correction: Practise improving the extended L-position by turning the left forearm in simultaneously.

In bar clearance:

— Fault: The pole does not straighten out, e.g. the bar is knocked down by the body in falling because of a premature ending of the vaulting movement.

Reasons: 1. Wrong approach rhythm. 2. Grip too high. 3. Jumper takes off before the correct take-off point. 4. Arm pull-up too early. 5. The uprights are too far away from the box.

Correction: Eliminate the particular source of error.

— Fault: The pole is not pushed away or only weakly so.

Reason: Incorrect understanding of mechanics of vault.

Correction: Drill push off left-right in succession. Sometimes a shout will do, If this does not help, practise the bar clearance systematically (see p. 316).

4.5.3.   Physical Requirements and Training Methods for Improving Performance

Fibre-glass vaulting requires a many-sided physical development, strong will, courage and excellent coordination to master a tricky implement. The pole vaulter must possess sprinting speed and explosive force to give the pole maximum bend from a high hand grip through the transfer of great horizontal and vertical momentum. The arm and back muscles must be strengthened by intensive work to swing the hanging body up far beyond where the right hand has its grip. But the vaulter also requires plenty of special endurance, permitting him, during competitions, to make several successive vaults or to cope with competitions lasting several hours. He requires a sense of direction in the various positions of his body and presence of mind to react in a flash to failures or occasional pole breaks. Last but not least the coordination of movements decides the success of a vault. To satisfy all these demands, pole vault training must be considerable and manysided.

Essentially the following tasks must be solved:

1. The development and perfection of basic physical qualities.

2. The learning and improvement of the vaulting technique at the same time as steadily improving physical qualities.

3. The inculcation and development of special qualities of will-power for the vault as part of the general socialist education of the sportsman.

4.5.3.1.   The Importance of Physical Condition

The achievements of the world-class vaulters are the result of hard and regular training extending over many years. No natural talents for pole vaulting are required; all the physical requirements can be developed by training.

● Height and weight

A factor which is not dominant in the consideration of physical requirements for pole vaulting, but should also not be overlooked, is the vaulter's height or, more precisely, the height that can be reached by the vaulter during the take-off extension. The vaulter who can grip the pole at a height of 2.35 m during the take-off extension (own height

Age (years)	24.3
Height (cm)	181
Weight (kg)	73.5

1.80 m), assuming a handhold of 4 m, will gain some 25 cm in the grip height of the upper hand over a smaller man of only 1.70 m and a height he can reach of 2.20 m

Given the same physique and technique, a higher grip is conducive to better vaulting results (see Table 51). His own height and the height he can reach are therefore the determining factors for the assessment of the grip height on the pole and by no means a negligible physical prerequisite. Physical demands for pole vaulting have not changed appreciably in spite of the greater heights and the new fibre-glass technique.

But the decisive conditions for success are the physical qualities, which must be developed. In the pole vault the performance is determined by the following factors:

1. Speed of approach
2. Take-off strength
3. Body and arm strength
4. Agility and dexterity
5. Special condition

● Speed of approach and take-off strength

The maximum vaulting height in the pole vault can be achieved with a maximum grip height and an optimum transfer relationship. This can only be reached in fibre-glass vaulting by managing a good bend with an optimally stiff pole. A world-class vaulter reaches a handhold on the pole of 4.40 m; only through the highest possible horizontal and vertical speed in the run-up and take-off can a pole be bent with such a handhold. The vaulter himself must have so much acceleration that the further movements on the pole can be executed correctly. The speed of the run-up determines the general acceleration of the body for movements on the pole and the amplitude of the pole bend. The take-off should impart the last acceleration impulse. Hence the take-off in fibre-glass vaulting is actively and powerfully executed. In contrast to other jumping events, the take-off action in the pole vault includes other movements which are necessary for the further course of the vault (pole plant and beginning of transfer of the run-up and take-off energy to the pole). The slightest uncertainty or delay of the

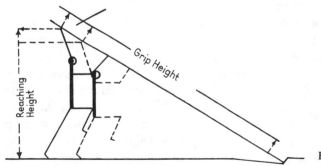

Fig. 115

movement as a whole decreases the approach speed or delays the take-off. Thus excellent timing and a good balance of the following factors are imperative:

1. Increase speed of run-up and preparation for take-off and pole plant.
2. Well timed coordination of the pole plant movement in the last two strides with a further increase of speed.
3. Strong take-off at top speed.
4. During take-off extension, transfer of run-up and take-off energy to the pole for bending through the proper arm work in the phases.

● Trunk and Arm Strength

In the further course of the vault the movements on the pole contain gymnastic elements. Individual and very different complicated movements, following in quick succession, must be executed powerfully and—determined by the total process of the vault-very quickly. So the special body and arm strength of the pole vaulter corresponds to the dynamic effort of some gymnastic elements. Without a systematic and comprehensive development of strength the learning and perfection of the vaulting technique, because of these many demands, is hardly possible. This is why trunk and arm strength has such a great importance for the vaulter's actions on the pole. Training should concentrate on the development of the following elements:

1. Firm grip of the hands; on the maintenance of the grip depends the success of the vault. If the grip slips during the vault, then the grip height changes, and the entire force of the vault is changed. Result: failures.
2. A good strengthening of the shoulder girdle; with the beginning of the swing-up the shoulders become the turning point of the swing.
3. Strong back and abdominal muscles. An effective swing up into the L-position requires active assistance; in this the back and abdominal muscles are of decisive importance.
4. Great arm strength to carry through the reverse into the support position and the push-off from the pole with the achievement of extra height.

These requirements alone show the versatility demanded of the vaulter.

● Agility and dexterity

The mastery of difficult movements such as those on the pole demand a great amount of coordination. Good vaulters stand out by their highly developed general coordination, which they have acquired mainly through their gymnastic and highly varied work. Building on these abilities, on the experience gained in gymnastic exercises, the vaulter must constantly develop special agility and dexterity. These are the abilities needed to tackle difficult movements involving the coordination of complicated fast movements, in the phase of learning as well as in the perfection of skills or when competing under a variety of vaulting conditions. The agility and dexterity further promote the capability of the vaulter to orient himself exactly in each phase of the movement and in any given position of the body. Without the further development of agility and dexterity, the jumper will not achieve technical perfection and his potentially best performance.

● Special endurance

Special endurance is a crucial requirement for a high training load in techni-

Table 53 *Time Distribution at the Pole Vault Competitions in Tokyo 1964*

Qualifying Competition	Final
Beginning: 4.20 m − 13 : 20 h	Beginning: 13 : 15 h
	4.20 m − 13 : 20 h
	4.60 m − 14 : 00 h
	4.70 m − 15 : 30 h
	4.80 m − 16 : 45 h
	4.85 m − 18 : 00 h
	4.90 m − 19 : 00 h
	4.95 m − 19 : 40 h
	5.00 m − 20 : 10 h
	5.05 m − 20 : 40 h
	5.10 m − 21 : 35 h
End: 4.60 m − 16 : 38 h	End: 22 : 08 h

cal training. Only with excellent special endurance is the vaulter in a position to carry through, in training, the great number of vaults over the bar, which are necessary for improvement and consolidation of the technique.

A special form of endurance is necessary for the vaulter if the competition lasts for several hours (3 to 5) (Table 53). The often relatively long periods of time between two attempts of a vaulter require optimal relaxation in the pauses and the full concentration and mobilization of mental and physical forces before each vault.

4.5.3.2. Means for Developing Physical Properties

In the previous section the highly varied demands placed on the pole vaulter were set out. The selection of the best means of developing the physical capabilities must correspond to these demands. The all-round instruction of a vaulter is a principal task of the training process, and forms the basis and prerequisite for a complete develop-

ment of an individual's physical abilities.

● Sprinting speed

Running takes up a great part of the total volume of pole vault training. The exercises set out here extend from fartlek over endurance running to the special run-up rhythm. Thus in running the means of training and routines already vary considerably; in the selection of the training pattern the phases of the training year, and the current routines of running work-outs, particularly, should be taken into consideration. The basic training for pole vaulting must be directed to the running pattern and the development of sprinting speed over 30 to 40 m. So the running training of the vaulter takes something from that of the sprinter. The most important training means for developing sprinting speed follow.

1. Speed and strength development through running and exercises
a) Runs with accentuated ankle work of 30 m at medium and high speed and with short strides;
b) Knee pick-ups in a slow run with and without weights (weight shoes, weight leggings);
c) Knee pick-up runs of 30 m with short strides;
d) Runs of 40 m with high knee pick-up in longer strides;
e) Uphill runs of 50 m;
f) Runs of 10 to 30 m against pulling resistance.
2. Speed development through runs
a) Standing and crouch starts, running up to 30 m;
b) Flying sprints over 30 to 60 m;
c) Acceleration runs of 40 to 100 m.
3. Speed development through running with the pole

a) Acceleration runs of 30 to 60 m with the pole;

b) Flying sprints with the pole from 20 to 30 m;

c) Approach runs with the pole without take-off (use the currently determined length of run-up, with and without check-marks).

The exercises are part of the special running programme of the pole vaulter and contribute to the good formation of the running movement and the carrying of the pole during a run at high speed. The execution of these runs requires that the vaulter has become used to running with the pole and exhibits no further mistakes of a technical nature.

● Running endurance

Especially in the foundation period and in the preparation phase of the training year, endurance runs contribute to the improvement of the general and special running endurance. They provide an important basis for runs to develop speed. In pole vault training tempo runs of 100 to 300 m and runs with changes in speed up to 150 m are included to improve running endurance. One carries through the runs according to the interval and repetition methods.

● Jumping strength

The general jumping strength exercises:

In pole vault training the development of explosive force shows a strong resemblance to the training of the long jumper and high jumper. The same general explosive force exercises are applied as specified in the training of the long and high jumper. The total volume of training of the pole vaulter re-quires a selection of the most effective explosive force exercises, so one can be limited to the following exercises:

1. Explosive force exercises without weights

The scope of the training programme includes in the main progression exercises, such as jump-runs, hop-runs, jumping up stairs, jumps on one leg and successive scissors jumps with an approach of several strides.

2. Explosive force exercises with higher weights

Among these are included: knee-bends of all kinds (quarter and half knee-bends to deep knee-bends) with dumbbells as well as ankle jumps and ankle-extension exercises with weights up to maximum.

The special explosive force exercises:

In special explosive force schedules the explosive force exercises are organized similarly to the mechanics of the vault take-off:

1. Long jumps with different lengths of run-up with the same take-off leg as in pole vault.

2. Long jumps from short to middle distance with movements of the arm as in the pole plant and take-off.

3. Take-offs with the pole from short to long approaches with poles of varying rigidity (pole bending exercises, see Fig. 103a).

● Trunk and arm strength

The manysided development of all the muscles should focus on the development of strength in the trunk and arm muscles. For that, chiefly strength exercises with a dynamic explosive character are used together with difficult movement coordination (back-roll into handstands, free circling of hips to a handstand, swing-ups to a handstand etc.), but fewer strength exercises of a static character (as e.g. horizontal position on parallel bars forwards or backwards etc.).

The general trunk and arm strengthening exercises:

1. General trunk and arm strengthening exercises without weights:

The most important methods of this category of preparation for a pole vaulter are gymnastics. These exercises involve the entire muscular system of the body in many ways and combine complicated movements; the exercises are taught along with strength development, agility, body control and coordination. Initially exercises on the horizontal bar, the rings and the parallel bars, as well as on the climbing pole and wall bars are carried out.

a) Supporting, gripping, bounding and climbing exercises, e.g. supported bounces on the bars; running and bouncing in handstand; somersaults forward, sideways and backward; hanging and climbing on a rope and on the climbing pole etc.

b) Swings, e.g. swings on the horizontal bar, parallel bar and rings; swinging in a hanging position on a rope; swinging into a handstand on the parallel bars; upward swings; giant swings on a horizontal bar; upward swings on the rings, and so on.

c) Coming into an upright position from a hang into the support position. All sorts of kips, backstands, upstands from a forward swing.

d) Uprights out of a hang or support position to a handstand, e.g. kips into a handstand, hip circle upswings into a handstand, back-roll into a handstand, giant swing, etc.

e) Exercises turning the body around the long axis, e.g. underswing with a half turn, somersaults with a half turn, high front vault etc.

2. General trunk and arm strengthening exercises with weights:

Training with dumbbells for improvement of the fitness of the wole body belongs to the group of general strength exercises with weights. Great emphasis is laid on the training of the arm and trunk muscles, especially on exercises of snatch and clean and jerk which additionally strengthen the leg muscles. The press is to be preferred for general strength building.

Special trunk and arm strength exercises:

Special strength exercises differ from the general exercises in that their execution approximates to the actual sequence of movements in the vault. Through the special strength exercises, the muscles involved in the pole vault are subjected to particular strain and thereby strengthened.

1. The special trunk and arm strengthening exercises without weights:

a) Swinging up on the towrope or on the wall bars out of a hang, with both arms in the L-position (see Fig. 108).

b) Swinging up on the wall bars out of a hang with one arm from the right hand.

c) Roll-back through a handstand, crossing a bar (see Fig. 111).

d) From front support bouncing on to

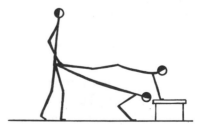

Fig. 116

324

Fig. 117

a box with the help of a partner (Fig. 116).

e) A short run-up and take-off through a sideways somersault on to a box or horse into a handstand. Through a powerful push-up out of this position of support into a handstand, then crossing a bar (Fig. 112). In order to achieve an alternating hand-push from the apparatus and to simulate the wide handspread in fibre-glass pole vaulting, a greater height for the right hand (by a sandbag or part of a box) must be created.

2. The special trunk and arm strengthening exercises with weights:

a) Hanging on a rope or on the climbing pole with weights (weight vest, weight shoes, weight leggings).

b) Pull-ups out of a hang on a rope or on a hanging pole with weights.

In order to increase the efficiency of the special strength exercises, a special apparatus for a few movements, e.g. for the arm push-up from the pole should be developed. Efficient combinations of exercises can be put together for practising on a strength apparatus (e.g. friction-pull apparatus).

c) Upward swinging out of a hanging position with weight shoes or weight leggings.

d) Presses lying on a bench—up to the maximum weight.

e) The special arm strength and the push-off action from the pole can be developed on an apparatus in which the vaulter, lying on a board on wheels, can push himself away from the pole. The board with the jumper must be moved upward on a fixed inclined plane. Through the adjustable height of the inclined plane the amount of stress on the arm action can be regulated (Fig. 117).

f) A special strengthening of the muscles involved in the turn during the reverse may be achieved through the combined exercise on the friction-pull apparatus [50]. The reverse into the support can be against the resistance of the pull apparatus; with a slight resistance the reverse may be made in a jump. The movement is then executed from a standing position but with higher resistance (Fig. 118).

● Agility and dexterity

A great amount of general dexterity and agility creates the basis for development of springing agility and dexterity. Thus in pole vault training many methods for advancing general agility and dexterity are applied. The development of vaulting agility and dexterity is worked at through a large number of different vaults and types of vault. Through these the vaulter can gain experience for the transition to the elastic

50 H. Gundlach/K. Hüttel "Ein neues Trainingsgerät für die Kraftentwicklung" (A new Training Implement for Developing Strength), in "Theorie und Praxis der Körperkultur", Nr. 7/1959.

Fig. 118

Table 54   Weekly Schedule of Training during the Preparatory Period (Foundation Training)

Day	Duration (min.)	Training Task	Training Means
Monday	15	Limbering up and special gymnastics for hurdling	Jogging; ankle work; acceleration runs up to 60—80 m; Exercises (sitting and standing) for increasing hip flexibility
	30—45	Speed training a) Running b) Exercises and runs for developing strength	a) Sprints up to 150 m; low starts with sprints up to 30 m; b) Runs with knee-pick-up, short strides; runs against pulling resistance or uphill; runs with knee pick-up and long strides;
	30	Exercises for developing special strength	Hanging; pull-ups with and without weight; Swings without and with half turn on horizontal bar
	20—25	Training coordination ability and endurance	Game: Basketball
Tuesday		Rest	
Wednesday	15	Warm-up	Jogging: runs combined with jumping exercises (bouncing, running jump, triple jump, one-leg jumps)
	15	Coordination	Floor gymnastics: rolls, somersaults, handstands
		Technique	Practice pole plant with take-off
	50	Improvement of pole plant and take-off	from short approach (if necessary walking); same but with medium approach; pole vaults with and without turn
	15	Throwing and putting exercises with shells	Standing put; shot put with glide; shot put; throws over back
	5	Running down	

Day	Duration (min.)	Training Task	Training Means
Thursday	15	Warm-up	Limbering up; ankle jumps; knee-pick-up runs
	15	Training strength and coordination	Gymnastics-apparatus work: parallel bars, horizontal bar
	60–80	Development of general and special strength	Standing press with low weight. Snatch with low weight (technical training!) Jerk with low and maximum load (3–4 trials of weight lifting) Snatch with high weight (80–90 % of maximum weight) 3 × 5 trials) Strengthening ob abdominal muscles through exercises on wall bars Press in lying position up to maximum load (2–3 trials of single weight height); half knee bends with medium to high load (3 × 6 exercises)
	10–20	Running down or game	Jogging or game with low weight (soccer tennis, punching the ball)
Friday		Rest	
Saturday	20	Warm-up and special preparation for technical training	Acceleration runs with and without pole; take-off and bending exercise from approach-run
	50	Technical Training Repetition of Wednesday's work and learning the swing-up to L-position on the pole	Repetition: pole plant and take-off from short and medium approach with slight bending of pole; learning the swing-up to L-position through driving action of left leg with backward laying of trunk (if necessary learn swing-up on rope)
	5	Running down	
Sunday	20	Warm-up and general gymnastics	Jogging: gymnastics (exercise with partner)
	90	Running training: General endurance Development of speed and strength (jumping strength)	Running through woods: acceleration runs up to 170 m continuous run-up to 1,500 m tempo-changing runs up to 200 m Development of general jumping strength without weights (one-leg jumps left and right, continuous jumps with 2 strides approach)
	5	Running down	

Table 55   Weekly Schedule of Training during the Competition Period (Foundation Training)

Day	Duration (min.)	Training Task	Training Means
Monday	15	Run-in	Jogging; acceleration runs; general stretching and loosening exercises
	50	Development of speed	Acceleration runs up to 60 m Crouch starts with sprints up to 30 m Flying sprints up to 40 m
	30	Special exercises for developing trunk- and arm-muscles Run-out	Uprises on wall-bars with load; handstands
Tuesday	15	Warm-up, preparation for technical training	Jogging; acceleration runs with pole; run-up controls with take-off and bending of pole
	35	Technical training; improving various elements	Jumps with short and medium approach Runs with particularly soft poles, giving special attention to elements requiring improvement
	20	Training explosive strength	Long jumps with medium approach runs; general exercises for developing explosive strength with light additional load
	15	Throwing and putting exercises	Standing throws (discus); Shot-put (standing and with glide)
	5	Run-out	
Wednesday		Rest	
Thursday	15	Run-up	Running; gymnastics; run-up controls; take-off and bending exercises
	40	Technical training; improving the whole course	Jumps with medium and long approach Runs over the cross-bar under facilitated conditions
	35	Training the run-up	Training and grooving the run-up through runs with pole, without take-off, giving special attention to the lowering of the pole
	15	Run-out or game	
Friday		Rest	
Saturday		Rest	
Sunday		Competition	

If no competition takes place on Sunday, the Monday programme can be repeated on Friday. In such cases technical training with competition character can be arranged on Sunday.

pole under various and quite different situations.

The following are the most important methods for developing the general and special jumping agility and dexterity:

— Methods of developing general coordination: All games but preferably basketball; general gymnastic exercises on apparatus; gymnastic jumps over box and horse, springboard jumps; dives; trampoline jumps; acrobatics; skiing and skating.

— Methods of developing special coordination. Gymnastic elements with special set tasks, e.g. underswings with a half turn, rolls backward into a handstand, among others; trampoline jumps with special set tasks, e.g. falls into the kip position and flight to a stand; falls into the kip position and half turn into flight to a stand.

These exercises correspond to the phases of the recoil of the pole; through the energy stored by the fall the trampoline makes possible movements in mid-air in the phases of energy release.

All forms of vaulting with the pole under special conditions and with special set tasks, such as bending exercises, with swing-up to the L-position, jumps under easier conditions with poles of varying rigidity.

● Special endurance

The training of special endurance is a part of the immediate competition preparation. Through a large number of vaults in technical training and through a high level of technical preparation, competition endurance is developed and advanced. A pole vaulter reaches his final competition height with the 8th to 12th attempt, on average. Through the development and training of special endurance in technical training twice this number of attemps, at least, should be made.

5. The Throwing Events

5.1. Fundamentals of Throwing Mechanics

Movements in field throws serve to throw or put the implement over as long a distance as possible. In doing this the athlete must observe physical laws (e.g. biological and mechanical laws) and general regulations laid down in the International Competition Rules. Hence the athlete's performance depends on his ability to tackle environmental factors and on his knowledge of their inherent laws. The better he is familiar with them, the more his movements will be properly directed and efficient.

Throws can be performed from a stationary position or using preliminary movements. When analysing the sequences of movement of the various throwing events, four major phases emerge (see Schedule).

If the major phases are ranked according to their importance for the final performance, the following order results:

1. Main phase
2. Wind-up phase
3. Preparation phase
4. Recovery phase.

This evaluation of the phases according to their importance for the end result is further emphasized if we consider the difference between a standing throw and a normal throw.

Shot put	1.5– 2.0 m
Discus throw	8.0–12.0 m
Javelin throw	25.0–30.0 m
Hammer throw	15.0–22.0 m

The *preparation phase* serves to get the

Schedule

Major Phases	Shot Put	Discus Throw	Hammer Throw	Javelin Throw
Preparation Phase	Initial Position	The Swings	The Pull-up and Swings	The Run-up
Wind-up Phase	The Glide	The Turns	The Turns	The Withdrawal and Impulse Stride
Main Phase	The Put	The Release	The Release	The Delivery
Final Phase	The Recovery	The Reverse	The Recovery	The Recovery

implement into an initial position which allows it to travel on a long and purposeful trajectory. In the *wind-up phase* the legs must get ahead of the implement and produce a preliminary tension which is transmitted from the legs via the trunk and arms to the implement. During *the main phase* the thrower imparts force to the implement, while in the *recovery phase* it is necessary to absorb the weight of the body which is moving in the throwing direction, if fouling is to be avoided.

In all throwing events three major sections of acceleration may be distinguished.

During the first section the body and the implement are accelerated together and move with the same velocity.

The distance between body and implement obtained during the preparation phase should be maintained or only slightly reduced. After this phase the body outpaces the implement and there is at most a slight acceleration. The thrower should therefore strive to keep this section as short as possible. In the shot put, for example, the speed drops to some 0.4 m/s during the gliding phase.

This is due to the fact that in this section the right leg (the pushing leg) has no contact with the ground.

Changes of velocity in the shot put

Initial position until the beginning of the glide
2.0–2.2 m/s
The glide
− 0.2–0.4 m/s
The put
+ 10–12.5 m/s
During the last section of the throw or the put respectively, all the muscles are acting in a concerted movement in order to produce the speed of release, which is the most important factor in increasing the distance. In order to transmit the maximum speed of release to the implement, the slower groups of muscles in the athlete's body must be brought into play first, followed by the smaller, faster groups of muscles (of the hands and feet) as the implement approaches maximum speed prior to release (cf. principle of coordination).

The range of a projectile depends on
the speed of release v_0
the angle of release α_0
the height of release h_0
the air resistance k
the gravity g

Since the parameter of gravity can be assumed to be constant (9.81 m/s²) and the air resistance may be neglected in shot putting and hammer throwing, the athlete will direct his efforts chiefly to the speed of release, angle of release and height of release; in discus and javelin throwing the conditions are different.

The effect of these factors on the range (R) is given by the following equation:

$$R = \frac{v_0^2 \cdot \cos \alpha_0}{g} \left(\sin \alpha_0 + \sqrt{\sin^2 \alpha_0 + \frac{2gh_0}{v_0^2}} \right) \quad [1]$$

From this mathematical equation, in which air resistance is neglected, we see each of the three factors has a different role to play.

5.1.1.   Speed of Release

In all throwing events the speed of release (v_0) is undoubtedly the most important factor since, from equation [1], distance is proportional to its square. We illustrate the extent to which an increase in the speed of release influences the throwing distance in the table below which refers to hammer throwing. It has been calculated from the above equation, where h_0 and α_0 were assumed to be constant.

			$h_0 = 2.0$ m	$\alpha_0 = 44°$				
v_0 (m/s)	19	20	21	22	23	24	25	26
R (m)	38.73	42.71	46.90	51.29	55.87	60.66	65.65	70.84

The athlete can increase the length of his throw on the average by 4.59 m (between 3.98 and 5.19 m) if he increases the speed of release by 1 m/s.

5.1.2.   Angle of Release

Less important is the angle of release of the implement. Since the magnitude of its influence cannot be seen at first glance from the equation, some values have been calculated and set out in a table below.

We assumed $v_0 = 24.0$ m/s and $h_0 = 2.0$ m for the calculation using equation (1).

If we look at the range of α_0 that is of practical interest to us (between 40° and 45°), the lesser significance of α_0 by

			$v_0 = 24$ m/s;	$h_0 = 2.0$ m				
α_0 (°)	20	25	30	35	40	45	50	55
R (m)	42.60	48.92	54.10	57.89	60.13	60.52	59.42	56.56

comparison with v_0 becomes apparent. A considerable deviation from the optimum angle of release would naturally be highly significant. The laws of ballistics tell us that in theory the optimum angle of release of the implement (α_{opt}) is 45°, if the point of landing is at the same level as the height of release. In field throws and puts the height of release is between 1.5 m and 2.3 m above the landing area. Hence the optimum angle of release must necessarily be less than 45° and depends on the height of release h_0 and the speed of release v_0. The relevant mathematical formula is:

$$\cos 2\alpha_{opt} = \frac{gh_0}{v_0^2 + gh_0} \qquad [2]$$

If we assume a constant height, the optimum angle of release increases as the speed increases.

Shot Put ($h_0 = 2.2$ m)

v_0 (m/s)	10	11	12	13
α_{opt} (°)	39.9	40.6	41.2	41.7

Hammer Throw ($h_0 = 2.0$ m)

v_0 (m/s)	20	22	24	26
α_{opt} (°)	43.6	43.9	44.05	44.2

In hammer and club throwing ($v_0 = 20$ to 26 m/s) α_{opt} may be taken as about 44°, while in the shot ($v_0 = 10-13$ m/s) it will be around 41°.

332

There are instances where an athlete cannot attain his maximum speed of release at the optimal calculated angles. This may be due to the hammer thrower being short (danger of touching the ground at the low point during turns) or to general biological factors in javelin throwing.

In the javelin and discus throw aerodynamic laws play an important role. In general the forces of air resistance reduce the horizontal velocity and hence the range. In order to minimize the effects of air resistance implements with smoothly polished surfaces and favourable aerodynamic forms should be used. The implement will remain in the air longer than might be calculated if it has a low horizontal resistance compared with a high air resistance acting against the vertical component of velocity. This ratio of K_x to K_y depends on the type and nature of the implement as well as on its stability in the air. The latter factor is again closely related to the angle of release. In all of this the influence of air flows (head or following wind) is of major importance.

The optimum angle of release in the javelin and discus throw will vary approximately between 30 and 37°.

5.1.3. Height of Release

The height of release (h_0) has the least influence on the throwing or putting distance. Nevertheless this factor must not be ignored, because a difference of

Table 56 *Survey of the competition weights for equipment for the relevant age groups*

Age Group (years)	Shot (kg)	Discus (kg)	Javelin (gm)	Hammer (gm)	Ball (gm)
Male					
8	3	–	–	–	80
9	3	–	–	–	80
10	4	–	600	–	150
11	4	–	600	–	150
12	4	1	600	4	150
13	4	1	600	4	150
14	5	1.500	600	5	150
15	5	1.500	800	5	150
16/17	6.250	1.750	800	6.250	150
Men	7.250	2	800	7.250	–
Female					
8	3	–	–	–	80
9	3	–	–	–	80
10	3	–	500	–	150
11	3	–	500	–	150
12	3	1	500	–	150
13	3	1	500	–	150
14	4	1	600	–	150
15	4	1	600	–	150
16/17	4	1	600	–	150
Women	4	1	600	–	–

a few centimetres can mean victory or defeat. A tall athlete is here at an advantage. From these calculations it follows that the height increment can be added to the length of flight.

Shot Put ($\alpha_0 = 41°$; $v_0 = 13$ m/s)

h_0 (m)	1.8	2.0	2.2	2.4	2.6
R (m)	18.93	19.11	19.29	19.48	19.66

Hammer Throw ($\alpha_0 = 44°$; $v_0 = 24$ m/s)

h_0 (m)	1.4	1.6	1.8	2.0	2.2
R (m)	60.07	60.28	60.45	60.66	60.87

It is clear that influence of the release height on the distance thrown diminishes as the velocity of the implement is increased. Thus while in the shot put an increase of h_0 by 0.2 m increases the distance of the throw by 1 %, the same increment would produce in the hammer throw only an increase of 0.3 % in distance. An athlete looking for first-class performances must continually attempt to increase the speed of release of the implement.

For the increase of kinetic energy the following equation holds:

$$E_{kin} = \frac{m}{2} v_0^2 = \int_{s_1}^{s_2} P(s)\, ds \qquad [3]$$

This shows that the speed of release is at its maximum, when the two factors: power P (in this case the athlete's muscular strength is the force producing the acceleration) and the path of acceleration are increased to a maximum, e.g. when maximal muscular forces become effective over a long acceleration path.

A thorough study of the technical development in throwing events over the last 30 years has revealed that it was always the improvement of these two factors which produced the best results.

Since the amount of power is hardly measurable in practice, the time of acceleration is frequently used as a criterion. This depends on P and s. A given acceleration path can be covered the faster, the greater the acceleration power available. An athlete should therefore try to combine the longest possible propulsion path with the shortest possible time of movement.

We stress at this point the relationship between muscular power and path of acceleration (e.g. in the shot).

A poorly developed athlete is not capable of accelerating powerfully from a low initial position. The demand for a longer acceleration path highlights the value and need to generate a powerful acceleration, which is of prime importance in this context. Not only the length of the acceleration path, but also its linearity is very important for the performance. [51] If the athlete accelerates the implement in a straight line (viewed from above and from the side in the shot put and javelin throw and in the plane of motion in discus and hammer throw), the forces of acceleration will become effective without any loss in the direction of projection.

When different components of the total impulse are to be transmitted to the implement (e.g. body extension and arm action in the shot put), these impulses must be well coordinated for reaching the maximum velocity of release. [52]

51 Cf. G. Hochmuth "Das biomechanische Prinzip des langen und gradlinigen Beschleunigungsweges" (The Biomechanical Principle of the Long and Straight Acceleration Path), in "Theorie und Praxis der Körperkultur", Nr. 4/1960.

52 Cf. G. Hochmuth "Das biomechanische Prinzip der Koordination von Teilimpulsen" (The Biomechanical Principle of the Coordination of Partial Impulses), in "Theorie und Praxis der Körperkultur", Nr. 5/1960.

The maximum velocity is achieved, when component velocities reach their maximum individual values simultaneously. For the application of strength this means that all the separate impulses must be completed at the same time. If, for instance, an athlete took off with the shot and stretched the putting arm when in mid-air, the velocity of the shot at the moment of release would be lower, because after completion of its power impulse the speed of his body begins to be reduced, so that less speed is transmitted to the implement. Furthermore the reaction force for the arm movement meets with no resistance from the ground. The shot and the body repell each other, so that the impulse for the arm extension is reduced.

If the left leg continues developing forces of acceleration in the line of action, the right foot will come off the ground or be dragged along the ground as is the case with club and javelin throwing.

In the rotary movements in the hammer and discus throw, the velocity of release is developed on a circular path. The acceleration path is analogous to the angular path. To reach a high velocity (v) along this path, and at the same time give rise to a high angular velocity (av), the radius of rotation (r) will also play a part ($v = av \cdot r$).

We define the radius of rotation as the distance from the axis about which the man-implement system rotates to the CG of the implement. In discus throwing the length of the throwing arm influences the magnitude of the radius. In hammer throwing (apart from the body position in the turns and its relation to arm length) the length of the wire and the position of the CG of the hammer head have yet to be taken into account. The greater the angular velocity and the radius, the greater will be the velocity at which the implement travels on its path and hence the further the distance of the throw.

5.2.   The Shot Put

The shot is put from a circle of 2.135 m (7 feet) in diameter.

A curved stopboard is fixed in the middle of the circumference of the front half of the circle.

The shot has to be put from the shoulder with one hand. When the athlete has taken a stance in the ring for starting his put, the shot has to be in the proximity of the chin. During the put the arm must not be lowered and the shot not be brought behind the shoulder line.

5.2.1.   Technique

The technique in shot putting is the same for men and women. In the initial position the putter stands erect, facing away from the direction of the put. This ensures a continuous acceleration of the implement along a straight line. The transition from the glide to the actual put can thus be accomplished with little loss of momentum. The angle of release should be between 41 and 45°.

335

5.2.1.1. Holding of the Shot

The putter holds the shot in his right hand, where it rests on the "base" of the fingers. The three middle fingers are only slightly splayed, while the thumb and the little finger give the shot lateral support, securing a safe position of the shot (Fig. 119a). The shot should not be firmly gripped nor be allowed to roll into the palm of the hand. The hand holding the shot will then be placed into the hollow of the collar bone in such a manner that it does not rest on the shoulders but against the right side of the neck and under the jaw. The elbow of the right arm is slightly raised and pressed forward. The upper arm points forward and downward. The head remains in its normal position. The right arm assumes a position which will not be changed for the subsequent forward dip in the initial stance. The elbow and forearm are then exactly below the shot. This position will be maintained until after the glide.

5.2.1.2. The Starting Position

The putter stands erect on the rear edge of the circle with the back turned to the stopboard. The right leg is on the midline of the circle. The left leg is set back slightly in the direction of the put. The implement is in the position described (Fig. 119b).

Fig. 119a

Fig. 119b

5.2.1.3. The Glide

With the glide the athlete moves across the circle and gives the shot the first impulse in the direction of the put. The glide should bring the putter into a sound position for the delivery of the shot. In the state of rest a rather high degree of inertia is inherent in the athlete's body with the shot. The actual movement must therefore be started with a preliminary action.

The most commonly used preliminary movements are:

a) The athlete stands erect. He then allows the trunk to drop over a well flexed right leg and moves the left leg towards the right leg.

b) Same initial stance. The putter is bending his trunk forward while the left leg swings backwards and upwards in a counter-balancing movement. When the trunk and the swinging leg are almost parallel to the ground, the supporting leg bends and the swinging leg is brought towards it (Fig. 120a, Pos. 1—4).

As the putter begins his glide across the circle, his left foot swings back and out across the circle, while the right foot pushes off in the putting direction. Thus he gets a position at the centre of

Fig. 120a

the circle, landing on the right leg (ball), with the upper body still square to the opposite side of the direction of the throw and with the left leg extended slightly towards the left side of the centre-line. The shot must remain over the rear edge of the circle as long as possible. Specialists tend to pivot the right leg over the heel. The swing of the left leg acts in a flat forward direction. The swinging foot must not be allowed to go up beyond the axis of the hip in any phase of the gliding action. Thus the athlete's body is drawn low into the circle by more a shifting than lifting motion. The swinging and the pushing leg

Fig. 120b

conclude their action simultaneously. While the swinging leg starts its downward movement, the foot of the supporting leg is dragged flat over the ground under the athlete's body in the direction of the mid-line of the circle. It is turned inward at an angle of about 120° the putting direction. The left leg must strike downward with a positive movement from the hip joint, so that it grounds over the inner edge of the foot against the stopboard. The shot putter should endeavour to conclude the movement of both legs almost simultaneously (Fig. 120a, Positions 5–9).

At the end of the glide the athlete must brace his forward movement and apply further force in the throwing direction.

Experience shows that between the hor-izontal gliding movement and the delivery of the shot there is an intermediate phase which contributes essentially to the success or failure of the put. This intermediate phase begins when the right leg meets the ground after its shift and ends when the left leg lands and starts to be braced.

If, when the right leg meets the ground, the centre of gravity of the body is still behind the area of support, it will move across the right leg until the left leg lands. This has a beneficial effect on the performance, since it allows full use to be made of the work of the right leg. But if, when the right leg lands, the body's centre of gravity is already above this leg, it will continue to move in the putting direction until the left leg has landed, thus moving away from the area of support of the right leg. When the driving leg begins to extend, the impetus of the force reaches the centre of gravity not from below but only from behind. This results in a pushing movement which reduces the distance of the throw, since the strength of the right leg cannot be fully used and therefore the body is not properly tensed.

We conclude therefore that the gliding and landing actions contribute essentially to the quality of the put. The athlete must take care to keep the arms and shoulders in a fixed position and not allow the trunk to come up too high during the glide. The acceleration must be initiated by the leg action alone and not by jerky movements of the trunk and arms.

5.2.1.4.   The Delivery Position

A sound delivery position is the primary condition for a successful performance in shot putting. Immediately after the glide, when both legs are on the ground, a phase we call the delivery position is achieved (Fig. 120a, Pos. 9). In this position the body weight is well over the flexed right leg in the centre of the circle. The left leg has landed with its inner edge against the stopboard. The landing area of the foot is only a few centimetres to the left of the mid-line, so that the feet stand almost one behind the other.

During the glide the upper body is slightly raised and the back is still facing in the direction of the put. The position of the trunk in relation to the legs is correct when the back, the left buttock and the left leg form a straight line (Fig. 120a, Pos. 9). This means that for the delivery the body dip is not fortuitous but depends on the degree of

flexion at the right knee. In this position the right side of the body must remain "open". The right hip is therefore somewhat ahead fo the putting shoulder.

5.2.1.5.   The Put

In the putting action force is imparted to the shot by a fast straightening of the legs, the raising and rotation of the trunk and the drive of the arm. This is the phase in which the greatest acceleration of the shot is achieved. The velocity with which the shot leaves the hand is thereby determined. The angle and height of release are determined by the driving movement of the arm. Several most important points for a good result arise at this stage. The final drive with the arm is initiated by the straightening of the right leg from the ankle joint and the accompanying upward movement of the trunk. In continuation of this movement the right side of the body, which is still extended, now swings forward and upward in the direction of the put. At the beginning of the leg extension and when bringing the body upright the shot is still resting against the neck. Once the chest faces in the putting direction, the right arm comes into action. Care must be taken that the elbow remains always behind the shot. In this phase this is possible only by allowing the shot to come away from the neck.

The slightly bent left leg has at first a bracing and levering function. This leg, as well as the entire left side of the body, must remain fixed at the joints and not give in to the pressure of the right leg at the hip or knee joints. When the straightening right leg has extended almost to the same degree as the left, both legs continue to extend together. The great force produced by the powerful extension of the legs has a strong bearing on the result. Effort at the ankle joints is of primary importance for a full extension of the legs. Towards the end of the extension movement, both feet are turned into putting direction, so that the legs and feet are then in the right position for the delivery phase.

The shot is propelled by a final simultaneous straightening of the legs, the trunk and the putting arm. A final acceleration can be imparted to the shot by an accentuated wrist movement and flick of the fingers.

Due to the explosive straightening of the legs and trunk it is only natural that in the last phase the thrower should come on to the tips of his toes or leave the ground for a split second.

The left arm has also a definite function to fulfil in the putting action. It assists the forward rotation of the trunk in the putting direction. Thereby the swinging arm is drawn into the put and expands the chest for a powerful release. When the chest is square to the direction of the put, the pulling action of the swinging arm must be checked prior to the push-off, thus preventing the body from being drawn into the put. This work of the left arm is conducive to a long put.

5.2.1.6.   The Recovery

After delivery stepping outside the circle is prevented by the recovery. It is best managed by a springing reversal of the feet. If the athlete's legs have been well extended by a fast explosive movement in the putting action, a floating phase will ensue. In this phase the

reverse takes place by approaching the right leg to the left and allowing the left leg to move backwards. On landing after this turn-jump the impact of the body weight is absorbed by a slightly bent right knee.

5.2.2.   Technical Training

Shot putting can be learnt relatively quickly if the athlete has the proper understanding of the correct technical exection of the various movements. The development of strength, speed and agility will facilitate the learning process and assist in the attainment of a good performance in a relatively short time. In the following chapters we outline only exercises for the special preparation and the acquisition of the technique of shot putting.

5.2.2.1.   Special Preparatory Exercises

In putting the shot primarily the shoulder-, trunk- and leg-muscles (extensors) are involved. The special preparatory exercises are needed to develop and strengthen these particular groups of muscles.

● Exercises for preparing the putting action

Exercises with the medicine-ball:
1. One-handed throwing, right and left
2. Two-handed throwing from the chest.
These exercises can be executed from various initial positions. Throwing from a sitting position is useful, as it compels the athlete to throw the medicine-ball with his arms only, without

involving other parts of the body.

Training can be made more interesting if it is interspersed with various forms of relays or games, e.g.

a) Two teams facing each other form a "lane"; they push one or several medicine balls towards each other in such a manner that the balls have to travel the whole lane. The ball is brought to the beginning of the lane by the member of the team who is the last to receive it. The winners are the team which does this a given number of times in the shortest time.

b) Driving the ball away. [53] Two teams face each other, each standing behind a marked line. Each member holds a medicine ball. A football or a volleyball lying on a centre line must be rolled of the line by the medicine ball. If the ball is driven across the marked line of the opposition, a point is scored. The team wins which scores the greatest number of points in a given time.

Exercises with the shot:

1. Push the shot up from the squat position by extending the legs and arms—then catch it again.
2. Push the shot up and forward from a low squatting position. These exercises can be performed with the right or the left arm or with both arms.

Exercises in support position:

1. "Lying face down"—bend and stretch the arms and legs. The points of support of the arms and legs are either on the same level or the legs are raised.
2. Bend and stretch the arms in inclined plane against the wall.

In this exercise stress is on a vigorous push against the wall until the fingertips come off the wall.

53 Other games see S. Rauchmaul "100 kleine Spiele", 13rd ed., Sportverlag, Berlin 1967.

● Exercises for developing the glide

Practise the glide in a row

The athletes stand in a row; each one of them seizes the flexed leg of the man in front, at the same time putting his hands on his shoulders. The whole group now moves backward in a low gliding movement. This exercise can also be executed alone; the athlete seizes his right lower leg with both hands and glides backward on his right leg, assisted by rapid movements of the left leg.

● Exercises for learning the push-off

1. Hopping backwards in a low squat position.
2. Cossack's dance: from a low squat the legs are extended and quickly withdrawn again under the body.

● Exercises for training the swinging leg movement

A medicine ball is placed behind the athlete at a distance of about 80 cm from the starting position. During the glide the ball is pushed back with the left leg in gliding direction.

The following exercises help the athlete to become familiar with the shot.

1. With the arms flexed and held in front of the body the shot is pushed from one hand to the other by a vigorous flick with the fingers.
2. With the body in an upright position the shot is pushed from the right to the left hand, accompanied by an easy movement of the legs.
3. For strengthening the finger and hand muscles, the shot is allowed to fall but gripped from above before reaching the ground.

5.2.2.2. Basic Exercises of Technical Training

The most rational and widely accepted technique in shot putting has the athlete's back initially facing in the direction of putting. The beginner should themfore not practise the shot put from a sideways initial position but immediately start with the back in the direction of putting. In learning the technique it is easier first to concentrate on single phases (the glide, the delivery stance, the put and the recovery) and to practise them separately. We recommend the following set of exercises, which are outlined for the right-handed putter.

– Exercise 1: Assuming the delivery stance

The athlete stands in a relaxed sideways straddle position. The left side of his body points in the putting direction. The right hand with the shot is held against the right side of the neck. The slightly bent left arm is held in front of the trunk. The upper body is turned 90° to face with the back in putting direction. Since the hips do not change position, a body torque is produced. In this position the right leg must be flexed, allowing the entire body weight to come over it. The delivery stance should be trained with and without the implement.

Purpose: To develop a keen sense of rhythm.

Points to note: Watch the correct position of the feet; the back must be facing in the putting direction!; shift the body weight on to the right leg.

Hint: It helps to draw a line in putting direction, as this will help the athlete to understand the correct position of the feet. The right foot is on the line and the left foot only just touches it with the toes.

– Exercise 2: Training the standing put

The shot is propelled in a forward and upward direction by extending the legs at the joints in the right order (ankle-, knee- and hip-joints), involving the right shoulder and putting arm in the movement.

Purpose: To learn the putting action from the position at the moment of release.

Points to note: Correct leg extension; the shot must be put and not thrown! (the elbow must be at shoulder height, behind the hand and the shot); powerful drive with a follow-up movement of the hand after delivery; the left shoulder must not be turned downwards or backwards, the left side of the body must form a lever; correct angle of release.

1st auxiliary exercise to exercise 2: This exercise is recommended for athletes who have not yet developed the right sense of rhythm.

The athlete stands in the release position. A partner holds his hand and makes him "sense" the proper putting direction by pressing his hand and leading his arm.

2nd auxiliary exercise to exercise 2: If the delivery is too low, set up two uprights for correction. The athlete must try to put the shot over the crossbar or tape (height mark).

3rd auxiliary exercise to exercise 2: In oder to prevent the athlete from throwing the shot, it helps to use heavy shots for practice.

– *Exercise 3:* Practising the glide

After a short preliminary movement, the athlete moves backward by lifting and kicking the left leg backward in putting direction and extending the right leg towards the centre of the circle. As the left leg moves downwards to make contact with the ground, the putter snatches the right leg under his body and lands in the release position.

Purpose: To lengthen the path of impulse.

Points to note: Space-gaining movement (marking); after the glide the body weight must remain over the right leg; watch the linearity of the put (the shot must be accelerated by the leg movements alone and not by jerky movements of the trunk).

Auxiliary exercise to exercise 3: Two partners train the glide together. During the glide one partner holds the other's trunk back by pulling his hand. This compels the athlete to work with the legs only.

– Exercise 4: Practising the complete movement.

The complete movement consists of the glide combined with the standing throw.

Purpose: To train the shot put under competitive conditions.

Points to note: The complete movement must be fluent and without any jerky movements; watch the smooth landing rhythm and the correct position of the feet; gradually increasing acceleration of the body and the shot; linearity of the driving movement.

5.2.2.3. Ancillary Exercises

The following exercises should only be used for athletes who have carried through basic technical training.

Exercises for perfecting the putting and extending movements:

1. The putting action (without jump-turn) is repeated several times by emphasizing the right leg extension. In this action the heel is deliberately lifted off the ground to feel the pressure on the ball of the foot. This exercise can be practised with resistance from a partner for greater efficiency.

2. Do series of puts using above-weight shots or medicine balls; every single technical element should receive attention.

Exercise for perfecting the gliding movement:

1. Continuous training of the gliding movement with weights: with weight cuffs on the right or the left leg or with a sandbag on the shoulder. Pay attention to a vigorous push-off and fast snatching of the right leg under the body's CG.

2. Practising the glide on an inclined plane (upward and downward) for learning the landing rhythm (right/left).

Simulation exercises:

The athlete repeats the movement with or without an implement under the control of a coach or a trainer; he can also check his movements in a mirror.

5.2.2.4. Fault–Reason–Correction

In the gliding movement:

– Fault: "Jumping" into the putting stance.

Reason: The force applied during the push-off is directed too much upwards; wrong direction of swinging leg movement.

Correction:

a) The glide must be started by the body's CG shifting towards the centre of the circle; for this purpose the right foot must be kept down at the rear edge of the circle as long as possible. The

343

last part of the push should be over the heel and not over the toes of the right foot.

b) Change the action of the swinging leg; only a low backward striking of the swinging leg on a straight line across the circle will produce a flat glide.

– Fault: Too short glide

Reason: Poor leg work; the extension of the right leg and the driving of the left leg are not powerful enough.

Correction: Put marks where the feet should land.

In the delivery position:

– Fault: After the glide the body's weight is not over the right leg.

Reason: The right leg is not drawn completely or not fast enough under the body. The left foot lands too late.

Correction: Train the correct landing rhythm. After the glide the legs should land almost simultaneously.

In the putting action:

– Fault: The leg is not fully extended prior to delivery.

Reason: Lack of coordination; poor physical condition.

Correction: Improve the standing put.

– Fault: The athlete lifts the right shoulder and lowers the left.

Reason: The right leg extends in the wrong direction.

Correction: The extension of the right leg must start from the ankle joint and proceed via the knee to the hip. At the same time the hip is pressed forward and torque produced at the shoulder girdle.

– Fault: The left side of the body does not form a lever, the athlete "gives" at the knee and hip joints.

Reason: The movement is not understood correctly.

Correction: Learn the correct movement pattern; develop sense of rhythm; fix the left leg and the left side of the body.

– Fault: The shot is thrown.

Reason: The putting arm starts too late with the delivery. The athlete has not mastered the sequence of movements.

Correction: Repeat movement slowly and, if possible, use overweight shots; imitate the putting action with a partner to sense the right direction of movement (see exercise 2: The standing put).

In the overall movement:

– Fault: The glide does not link up smoothly with the put–so there is checking.

Reason: The leg muscles are not properly tensed; delayed landing of the left foot after the glide.

Correction: Immediately after landing in the centre of the circle the right leg must be extended from the ankle joint upward. Active "touchdown" of the left leg.

– Fault: The flight path of the shot does not follow a straight line.

Reason: Additional backward swing of the right shoulder in the putting stance.

Correction: The shoulders must be kept fixed at the joints from the beginning of the glide through to the delivery stance.

5.2.3. Physical Requirements and Training Methods for Improving Performance

Any active sportsman, independent of his age, size and weight can learn shot putting. The importance of age, size, and weight for achieving high perform-ance should not, however, be under-rated. Many high-class shot putters are tall and bulky men or women who have strength and great speed. While the foregoing physical qualities can be de-veloped and perfected by training, the height cannot be changed and the weight only to a certain extent. Young athletes should take all these factors into consideration before deciding to go in for shot putting.

Some examples of the world best shot putters emphasize the influence of height and weight on the putting result (Table 57). The mean values of age, body height and body weight of the six best performers at the 1972 Olympic Games are revealing (Table 58).

Shot putting is an event in which top performances are often achieved only after a long career in the sport. It is therefore not unusual to find that shot putters who started training at the age of 15 or 16 reach their top level only af-ter some 8 to 12 years of hard regular training. Among the world best shot putters (men and women) there are

Table 57

	Per-form-ance (m)	Height (cm)	Weight (kg)
Men			
Matson (USA)	21.78	200	120
Rothenburg (GDR)	21.32	185	118
Briesenick (GDR)	21.67	191	116
Komar (Poland)	21.18	195	125
Women			
Chishova (USSR)	21.45	173	90
Gummel (GDR)	20.22	176	90
Ivanova (USSR)	19.39	168	84
Lange (GDR)	19.25	182	85

Table 58 Mean Values of Age, Height and Weight of the 6 best Performers at the Olympic Games 1972

	Men	Women
Age (years)	26.7	27.8
Height (cm)	192	177
Weight (kg)	120.2	86.8

some who are 25 or more years old. P. O'Brien (USA) set a world record at the age of 28 (19.33 m) and G. Zybina (USSR) improved her best result to 16.95 m when she was 31 years old.

5.2.3.1. The Importance of Physical Condition

The most important physical attributes of a shot putter are strength and speed.

● Strength

Strength is the main physical attribute of the shot putter. It is a primary condi-tion for putting the shot over a long dis-tance.

Considering the course of movements of the put, the long extensors of the legs and arms and the muscles of the trunk (especially of the back) must be well developed. All good shot putters (men and women) possess more than average strength. O'Brien pressed a barbell of 135 kg weight standing. He pressed three times 165 kg consecutively lying on a bench and made deep knee-bends with a barbell of more than 220 kg on his shoulders.

Taking the example of two successful GDR shot putters, Table 59 shows the influence of strength training with the dumb-bell on shot putting perform-ance.

Table 59   Significance and Influence of Dumb-bell Exercises in Shot Putting

Name	Hartmut Briesenick		Marianne Adam
Year	1970	1973	1976
Performance	22.55 m	21.67 m	21.67 m
Press lying on a bench (kg)	190	240	120
Jerk (kg)	165	170	125
Clean (kg)	165	170	105
Snatch	130	140	80

● Speed

Maximum strength alone does not, however, lead to success in shot putting. The shot putter must also have great speed or, more precisely, be able to apply force rapidly. Speed is therefore a vital factor for good results in shot putting. This is mainly due to the fact that inside a small circle (2.13 m) a high speed of release of the shot must be achieved. For putting the shot 19.00 m and more the release speed of the shot must be about 12.5 to 13 m/s. Practical experience shows that best results are achieved by athletes who can combine much strength with great speed.

5.2.3.2.   Means for Developing Physical Properties

● Strength

General strength exercises
Implement: Barbell
With the barbell on the neck—deep kneebends, half knee-bends with and without raised heel, on tiptoes; straddle-stride forward, trunk bending sideways; snatching with and without straddle stride, snatching the barbell to the chin, reversing hands; pull in the arms to the front and to the rear of the body; trunk circling.
Implement: Medicine-ball   /   kettle bell/ sandbag
Perform various throwing, pushing and lifting gymnastic exercises with these or similar implements, e.g. throws backward overhead; push te medicine-ball forward and upward, lift kettle bells sideways, trunk circling and "uprighting" from lying face downwards and flat on the back. Exercises for the development of strength of other events recommended for the thrower: gymnastics with apparatus, floor gymnastics, games, swimming, skiing and skating, hockey and wrestling.
For the development of explosive power
Triple-jumps from standing, right-right-right and left-left-left, triple-jumps from run-up, high jumps, jumps over obstacles, jumping up stairs, rope skipping, jumps on one leg over 25 to 50 m; running jumps over 30 to 100 m; jumps with additional load (sandbag or barbell).
Special strength exercises
Implement: Barbell
One- and two-arm pushing with and without a turn-jump; pushing from the chest in lying position (on a bench), from standing and sitting, to the front and to the rear of the head; arm-extension from putting stance with barbell on the shoulder.
Implement: Kettle bell/small barbell
In leaning support against wall bars—push up small barbell; "uprighting" from position of lying on back with alternating extension of arms.
Implement: Shells
Pushing with heavy shells (5 to 10 kg for women, 8 to 20 kg for men); use

346

Table 60   Weekly Schedule of Training during the Preparatory Period (Foundation Training)

Day	Duration (min.)	Training Task A = Preparation B = Main Part C = Closing		Training Means
Monday	15	A	Warm-up	Game (Basketball)
	60	B	Development of strength	General strength exercises (barbell, kettle bell, wall bars etc.)
	5	C	Loosening	Jogging, easy gymnastics
Wednesday	15	A	Warm-up	Running and gymnastics
	45	B	Development of speed and take-off strength	20–50-m sprints from high and flying start Jumping exercises: one-leg jumps, squat jumps, jump-run etc.
	5	C	Limbering down	Jogging
Thursday	15	A	Warm-up	Game
	30	B	Development of strength and explosive strength	General strength exercises Shelf jumps, jumps over obstacles, hurdles, uprights etc.)
	10	C	Loosening	Jogging, special preparatory exercises for shot putting
Saturday or Sunday	15	A	Warm-up	Jogging, special preparatory exercises for shot putting
	30	B	Technical training	Basic exercises of the technical training
	30		Development of strength	General strength exercises Special strength exercises Throws with heavy implements (kettle bell)
	10	C	Improving general endurance	Continuous run over several kilometres

various forms of puts, e.g. from low squat upward, alternate puts right and left, standing put, put from glide.
A series of puts as special form of strength development—put several shots (having the same or different weights) one after the other, then fetch them all together; shell-throwing above the head.
Implement: Sandbag
Gliding exercise with sandbag on shoulders.
Push-ups against the wall with sandbag on the shoulder.

● Speed

Running exercises
Sprints from crouch start, falling or flying start, up to 40 m, runs with changes of speed over 50 to 200 m.
Acceleration runs.
Runs at an easy pace with sudden bursts upon a signal (whistle), occasionally with the command to change direction.
Exercises for training quick response
The basic idea of these exercises is to perform a task quickly upon an optic

347

Table 61 Weekly Schedule of Training during the Competition Period (Foundation Training)

Day	Duration (min.)	Training Task A = Preparation B = Main Part C = Closing		Training Means
Monday	10	A	Warm-up	Running and gymnastics
	40	B	Development of strength	General strength exercises, mainly with barbell
	5	C	Limbering down	Jogging
Wednesday	10	A	Warm-up	Running, gymnastics, special preparatory exercises for shot put
	30	B	Technique	Basic exercises of technical training, special exercises
	30		Development of strength	Special strength exercises Series of throws with overweight and usual shot
	10		Development of running speed	Sprints up to 50 m
	10	C	Limbering down	Jogging
Thursday	10	A	Warm-up	Running
	15	B	Development of throwing speed	Shot puts with all-out effort
			Development of explosive strength	Jumps with all-out effort (one-leg squat jumps)
	10	C	Limbering down	Easy run through woods
Friday			Rest if athletes take part in competition on Saturday, otherwise easy speed and explosive strength-training	
Sunday			Competition (Shot Put, 100-m Sprint, Long Jump, High Jump)	

or acoustic signal; quick response to a signal (whistle): from various initial positions (lying, prone or supine, sitting etc.) execute an exercise or run over a given distance at considerable speed. Another exercise: pushing a certain number of medicine balls, shots etc. one after the other quickly and sharply into a goal. Measure the time required for pushing e.g. ten balls and the number of hits. Goalkeeper game.

5.3.   The Discus Throw

The discus throw is a slinging throw. The implement has to be thrown from a circle of 2.5 m in diameter. By rotation inside the circle the greatest possible acceleration is imparted to the discus.

5.3.1.   Technique

A rational technique in the discus throw has the following characteristics:

1. In the initial position the thrower has his back towards the direction of the throw.
2. There follows a long, flat jump-turn with a flight phase.
3. The slinging movement, called the release, takes place with a springlike push-off by both feet.

5.3.1.1.   Handhold

The hand is placed flat against the discus surface; the upper joints of the fingers grasp the rim of the discus. Its CG lies between the index and the middle finger. Due to a slight bending at the wrist the upper face of the discus touches the arm. This gives the required looseness of the muscles and prevents the discus from falling out of the hand in the subsequent movements (Fig. 121).

5.3.1.2.   The Initial Position

The thrower assumes a position at the rear edge of the circle, with the back facing in the direction of throwing. The feet are about shoulder width apart

Fig. 121

with the toes turned outwards. The athlete is in a relaxed "sitting-down" position. The body weight is evenly distributed over both feet. The right arm is hanging loosely by the right side, holding the discus.

5.3.1.3.   The Preliminary Swing

The purpose of the preliminary swing is to create the longest possible acceleration path of the implement. The width of the preliminary swing, which is important for an optimum radius of the initial path of the discus, depends on the position of the legs and the athlete's flexibility at the hip and shoulder joints.

The swinging movement is introduced by bringing the arm with the implement at hip or shoulder level across to the left side of the body (see Fig. 122, Pos. 2). The body weight is thereby easily moved from the right to the left leg. Almost without any interruption there follows the actual preliminary swing in which the discus is brought far back to the right behind the right shoulder. The body weight is now slightly transferred to the right. This swing is performed in an easy relaxed manner. The upper body with the left arm curled across the chest move along in the direction of the swing, producing at this stage a good torque or "wind-up" between the hip and the shoulder axes. The left heel is slightly raised from the ground.

The novice discus thrower should not turn the toes of the left foot into the swinging direction, since this would prevent the optimum wind-up and unnecessarily lengthen the path of the left foot at the beginning of the turn. The upper body is kept upright (Fig. 122, Pos. 1—3).

Fig. 122

5.3.1.4.   The Turn in the Circle

The purpose of the turn is to accelerate the discus continuously on the longest possible path.

At the beginning of the drive across the circle the thrower's body and the implement are accelerated simultaneously, but during the turn the legs are allowed to move ahead of the trunk and the arm with the discus, thus creating torque or "wind-up" between the hip and the shoulder axes as a result of the two different acceleration phases.

The thrower leads the turn with his legs. The left leg begins to spin around on the ball of the foot in the throwing direction. During this turning inwards movement the weight of the body is transferred and is supported by both legs. When the left leg has reached an angle of about 120° to the throwing direction, the right foot pushes off from the ground. Through this push-off action the weight is transferred to the left leg which swings in the throwing direction. The foot of the slightly bent right leg moves on an optimal radius towards the front edge of the circle. The relatively great distance thus brought about between the right foot and the throwing arm increases the wind-up

during the turn. When the chest faces in the throwing direction, the left foot pushes off to the front, starting the extension at the ankle joint. This produces the flight phase in the turn. The thrower is propelled forward and performs at the same time a rotation movement, assisted by the inward turning of the right foot.

During push-off the left leg must not be extended at the knee, as this extension usually acts in a vertical direction and produces an excessive lifting of the body's CG, which should move, if possible, in a plane. When the bent right leg has landed over the ball of the foot near the centre of the circle, the left leg is brought forward on the shortest possible path and planted actively over the inner edge of the foot in front of the right foot and almost parallel to it.

On landing the right knee assumes the same angular position it had at the beginning of the turn and before the snatching movement of the thigh.

"Giving" at the right knee joint must be avoided, since this prevents the fluent transition from the throwing to the releasing action. The legs land in quick succession. During the turn the shoulder follows a line parallel to the ground. The back of the throwing hand is turned upwards throughout.

350

5.3.1.5. The Throwing Position

After the turn the thrower must be in a well balanced position, permitting him to apply a fully effective force to the discus. The body weight is well over a bent right leg. The right foot lands at the centre of the circle at an angle ranging between 100 and 150° to the direction of the throw. The left leg which is slightly flexed has been set on the ground over the inner edge of the foot. In the throwing position the feet should be about 70 to 80 cm apart. The left foot meets the ground about 10 cm from the edge of the circle and at about 10 to 15 cm left of the direction of throwing (Fig. 122, Pos. 8). The angle between the throwing direction and the left foot is about 90°.

The arm holding the discus is still well back to the right to allow a maximum pull of the implement. In the throwing position the implement still has an arc of about 270° to traverse. The right hip is ahead of the right shoulder. This leads to a drive-in of the right side of the body (Fig. 122, Pos. 9).

The trunk is erect and the left side of the body is in a fixed position, forming a straight line from the foot to the shoulder. The torque or "wind-up" of the right side of the body is 70 to 90° between the axes of the shoulder and the hip and with about 45 to 60° between the shoulder and the throwing arm. The torque thus obtained is started at the end of the preliminary swing and is maintained right through to the final throwing action, when unwinding takes place during the release. If the torque is reduced while still in the throwing position, this is usually due to a delayed landing of the left foot.

5.3.1.6. The Release

The release is the most important phase in the entire movement of discus throwing. It determines the most significant angles: the angle of release and the angle of incidence of the airborne implement as well as the speed and height of release. This action is introduced by turning the right side of the body around (foot, knee, hip). The left side of the body forms a lever which counteracts the pressure of the right leg. During this swivelling movement of the right side of the body, the body weight remains over the right leg. When the axis of the hip has reached an angle of about 125° to the direction of the throw, the unwinding of the right side of the body begins. At this juncture the rotating motion goes over into a stretching movement, which is so powerful in its final phase, that the feet come off the ground momentarily. The chest faces in the throwing direction. The right arm is still retracted well behind the right side of the body and describes a wide radius in coming forward. The release is accompanied by a springy push-off with both feet from the ground. The discus is released at about shoulder height with the back of the hand turned upwards. A rotating movement is imparted to the implement in its clockwise spin by a strong tangential pull with the index finger. This will give it stability during flight.

The swivelling or rotation axis in the release is not the diagonal of the left foot and right shoulder, but the left side of the body.

5.3.1.7.   The Reserve

As the result of the powerful stretching of both legs, the feet lose contact with the ground for a split second in an upward and forward springing action. Immediately the discus has left the thrower's hand, he will reverse his feet to prevent himself from fouling at the front of the circle and to regain balance. He brings his right foot forward close to the edge of the circle and absorbs the body's impact by "giving" at the knee-joint.

5.3.2.   Technical Training

The method of teaching the discus throw has been considerably changed during recent years. It is now generally accepted that the phase influencing the whole sequence of movements is the re-

lease. Therefore the strictly analytical procedure has been abandoned to a great extent, so that when basic skills have been acquired, teaching of the overall movement is started relatively early. The KRUSTEV method frequently described in earlier publications is nowadays taught in a simplified form. A splitting up of the whole rotation movement into quarter turns has been discarded.

5.3.2.1.   Special Preparatory Exercises

In the special preparatory exercises for the discus emphasis is given to the preparation for the slinging throw, combined with strengthening of the muscles involved in the throwing action. The slinging movement is the main phase in the discus throw and should therefore be thoroughly drilled. Additionally various turn-jumps, throws from turns etc. serve to develop orientation in circular movements.

The following exercises are recommended:

1.. Long throws on a competitive basis using a sling ball or a small rubber ring.

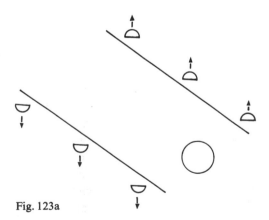

Fig. 123a

2. Various games involving the sling throw (using a sling ball or rubber ring).

3. Gymnastic routines for developing mobility.

4. Jumps with a turn over low obstacles or markings (the stress should be on space-gaining movements).

5. A sequence of jumps with turns on a line.

Exercises for accustoming the thrower with the discus:

1. Forward and backward swinging of the throwing arm which hangs loosely at the side of the body (for handhold of the implement see section 5.3.1.). The purpose of this exercise is to develop the "feel" for an easy relaxed movement of the throwing arm and to get accustomed to holding the discus while moving.

2. Rolling the discus over the index finger. After forward swinging of the throwing arm the discus is allowed to roll over the index finger along the ground, helped by a throwing movement of the hand. This rolling over the index finger (tangential finger flip) is an important condition for a stable spinning of the discus in flight.

Game: Two teams are lined up with their backs turned to each other (distance between about 5 m). Upon a given signal they all roll their discus forward as far as possible. Team 1 fetches the disci of team 2 and vice versa. The team wins which is first back to the line of the opposing team.

3. Figure of eight. The arm holding the discus swings in front of the body describing the path of an imaginary figure of eight; the back of the hand must be turned upwards throughout. Because of the centrifugal force the discus remains in the hand.

5.3.2.2. Basic Exercises of Technical Training

First some technical hints for avoiding possible injuries during group exercises. For reasons of safety and for the best use of available time, we recommend formations as shown in Fig. 123a, b and c. The coach or trainer must stand in a safe place where he has a good view of the whole group. We suggest the following series of exercises (described for right-handers):

– Exercise 1: Standing throw
The standing throw is executed after some forward and backward swings or a preliminary swing. Starting with backward and forward swings permits the athlete to concentrate fully on the essential parts of the exercise. The initial position is similar to the throwing

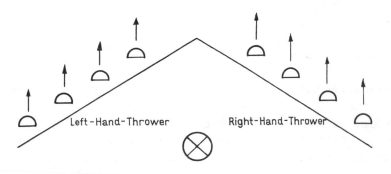
Left-Hand-Thrower   Right-Hand-Thrower

Fig. 123b

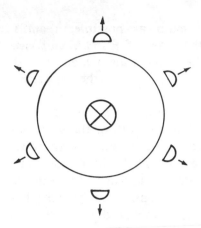

Fig. 123c

position described in the section "The Technique" (see 5.3.1.2.). After some swings the release action is started at the end of the backward swing.

Purpose: Learn the release from the throwing stance; learn to coordinate throwing movements.

Points to note: The backward swing reaches its lowest point at the end of this movement.

Hint: Begin with a series of preliminary swings in the throwing stance in an easy relaxed manner, without using the implement.

– Exercise 2: Throw from a $^4/_4$ turn

The thrower stands erect, facing in the direction of the throw. The feet are shoulder width apart, the left foot is about a foot ahead of the right one in the throwing direction. After a backward swing of the right arm the left leg pushes off forward in a firm and positive movement from the ankle joint. He then performs a wide jump-turn, the right leg landing in the centre of the circle (cf. Fig. 122, Pos. 6–11).

Purpose: Lengthening the drive path by a turn of 360°.

Points to note: The thrower must be in a sound position for the throw, with plenty of body torque; emphasis is on

the push-off forward with the left foot from the ankle joint without extension of the knee; concentrate on the landing rhythm of the legs. The left leg lands immediately after the right one in a positive and firm movement.

Hint: If the jump-turn is not wide enough, the following auxiliary exercises should be used: draw two lines at right angles to the direction of throwing and 1.25 m apart. During the turn the thrower must get across this "ditch". If movement is not on a straight line, it will be helpful to draw a chalk-line of 3 m long on the ground. The thrower stands with his feet astride it. After the turn he must land with the heel of the right foot and with the toes of the left foot touching this line.

– Exercise 3: Throw from a $^6/_4$ turn—over-all movement

Once the athlete has learnt to take up a sound throwing position and to balance his body weight well over the right foot before beginning the turn, he may start practising the complete movement.

Purpose: Learning the technique under competitive conditions.

Points to note: Avoid reversing the legs too soon.

Hint: If the legs are reversed too soon, this leads to an incomplete extension of the legs and to their premature lifting from the ground. Include special exercises for mastering the reverse.

5.3.2.3.   Ancillary Exercises

The following exercises are recommended for developing the final form:

1. Standing throws with preliminary movements; emphasis is on a positive extension of the leg and contact of both

legs with the ground for the required length of time.

2. Imitate the release with moderate resistance from a partner.

3. A series of throws with bars and shots from a standing position. Workout of complete movement with emphasis on specific technical tasks, especially for the leg movements.

4. Practise the turn from the initial position to the delivery stance with a strap discus.

5. Throws within a throwing sector reduced to a range of 20°.

6. Throws under varying wind conditions; throw as often as possible against head wind or with following wind.

7. Throw from ³/₄ turn with the right side of the body facing the throwing direction. During the backward swing the body weight is shifted to the right leg and absorbed by flexion at the knee joint. The right side of the body now swivels around in the throwing direction by pivoting on the right foot. Then the left foot is drawn low above the ground in the throwing direction by describing a semicircle and planted in front of the right foot. The athlete is now in a sound position for the throw (Fig. 124). For a quicker understanding of this exercise it is advisable to use a

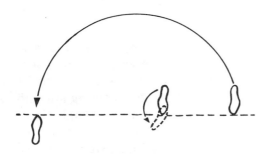

Fig. 124

club or a short iron bar before practising with the discus. This creates easier conditions and allows the thrower to fully concentrate on the swivelling movement.

Auxiliary exercise:
If an athlete has difficulties in understanding this movement, he should do the exercise with a partner: simulate the swivelling movement slowly about the right leg. He assumes the initial position described in exercise 3. The partner leads him by the left hand. After shifting the body weight to the right leg, he swivels around until he is in the throwing position. By a pull of the hand the partner can guide him into the correct position for the throw, allowing him to feel the torque between the axes of the shoulder and the hip, at the same time correcting mistakes in the trunk posture.

Posture: Lengthen the drive path by a turn of 270°.

Points to note: Avoid shifting the body weight to the left leg. The throwing arm and shoulder must remain well behind the hip.

5.3.2.4. Fault—Reason—Correction

In the preliminary swing:
— Fault: The preliminary swing is too high.

Reason: Too pronounced bending and stretching of legs.

Correction: Practise the preliminary swing; the strongest flexion of the leg is achieved when the discus is well back behind the right side of the body.

In the turn:
— Fault: "falling" into the turn.

Reason: The turn is introduced by turning the upper body (left shoulder) around. Insufficient weight transference to the left leg at the beginning of the turn.

Correction: Lead the turn with the legs.

– Fault: Too high jump-turn.

Reason: Pushing with the left leg is not from the ankle joint but by extending the knee—upward lifting too pronounced.

Correction: In stretching the left leg the knee must be slightly bent forward.

– Fault: Too short jump-turn.

Reason: The turning movement is too hasty, the forward push with the left leg is not powerful enough.

Correction: Practise the turn at lower speed. Use marks on the ground (see "Hint" to exercise 2).

– Fault: Progression is not in a straight line.

Reason: The weight is not properly transferred to the left leg or take-off with the left leg is delayed.

Correction: During the turn the chest must be facing in the throwing direction as long as possible. If the movement is not wide enough, use an auxiliary exercise (see "Hint", exercise 2).

In the throwing position:

– Fault: The body weight is not properly over the right leg.

Reason: Delayed landing of the left leg after the turn.

Correction: Bring the left leg forward in throwing direction, passing close to the right leg; fast and positive foot plant.

In the throw:

– Fault: The left side of the body does not form a straight line but "gives" at the knee and hip joints to the pressure of the right leg.

Reason: The left leg is not properly extended or starts straightening too late.

Correction: Attempt to "sense" the levering action of the left body side by fixing a pole to this side.

– Fault: The body is not fully extended during the throw.

Reason: Mistakes are being made in the throwing position. The thrower does not sufficiently extend his legs; he also does not extend both legs together but one after the other.

Correction: Practise standing throws with emphasis on leg extension.

In the reverse:

– Fault: The right leg leaves the ground too soon.

Reason: Inaccurate throwing position; the throwing arm is brought into action too soon.

Correction: During the release both legs remain on the ground and the body weight is evenly distributed between the legs.

5.3.3. Physical Requirements and Training Methods for Improving Performance

5.3.3.1. The Importance of Physical Condition

The main physical attributes for discus throwing are strength and speed; but mobility, agility, height, weight and age also play an important role.

● Strength

Strength in the leg, trunk, and arm muscles is an important prerequisite for discus throwing. They should be given special attention during strength work-outs in training. Although discus throwing requires a high degree of explosive force, maximum strength is just as critical for the result of the throw.

Table 62   *Performances with a Barbell by World-class Throwers*

Name	Length of Throw (m)	Pressing in Horizontal Position (kg)	Two-arm Thrust (kg)	Deep Knee-Bend (kg)
Schmidt (GDR)	71.16	215	–	230
Milde (GDR)	64.16	105	95	–
Thorith (GDR)	62.26	190	145	215

The greater the force a discus thrower can transmit to the implement, the further will be the throw.

A good criterion for the strength of the thrower is his performance with a barbell (Table 62).

● Speed

Good throwers achieve an initial velocity (v_0) of about 22 m/sec. To attain this high velocity, the thrower must be able to transmit force to the implement at the greatest possible speed. He should therefore be able to sprint (over 30 m) and jump well.

● Agility and mobility

The movement pattern in the discus requires a high degree of ability, enabling the athlete to accomplish this technically complicated exercise quickly and correctly under exacting competitive conditions. Good flexibility at the hip and shoulder joints are required for the important body twist.

Table 63   *Mean Values of Height and Weight of the 6 best Performers at the Olympic Games 1972*

	Men	Women
Age	28.7	27.8
Height (cm)	192	174
Weight (kg)	110.5	84.4

● Height, weight and age

These are important physical attributes for the discus thrower who whishes to excel. The same is true for the shot putter and hammer thrower. A potential world-class thrower should be at least 1.85 m tall when he begins to approach his top class training. Women who go in for discus throwing should have a minimum height of 1.75 m. Given this height and the increase in muscular bulk and strength achieved through training, the minimum weight of a discus thrower will be 95 to 100 kg (women 70 to 75 kg).

Experience shows that a thrower can maintain good form and performance over a relatively long period and that he is usually at his best between 26 and 30.

In the following summary we give the mean values of height and weight of the six best performers at the 1972 Olympic Games (Table 63).

5.3.3.2.   Means for Developing Physical Properties

● Strength

General strength exercises
Implement: Barbell
With the barbell on the neck—deep knee-bends, half knee-bends with and

357

Table 64 *Weekly Schedule of Training during the Preparatory Period (Foundation Training)*

Day	Duration (min.)	Training Task A = Preparation B = Main Part C = Closing		Training Means
Tuesday	20	A	Warm-up	Game
	30	B	Development of strength	General strength exercises
	10	C	Development of take-off strength	Jumps with and without additional weight
	10		Loosening exercises	Jogging-gymnastics
Wednesday	15	A	Warm-up	Gymnastics
	45	B	Improvement of the technique	Throws with competitive implement
	10	C	Development of speed and endurance	Runs over 50–200 m
	15		Development of mobility	Loosening and stretching exercises
Friday	15	A	Warm-up	Relay games
	30	B	Development of strength	General strength exercises with various implements
	15	C	Development of take-off strength and speed	Sprint from crouch start over 30 m
Saturday	15	A	Warm-up	Limbering up/Gymnastics
	30	B	Technique	Training with competitive implement
	60	C	Development of agility and speed	Running-gymnastics Training with competitive implement Games

without raised heels. On tiptoe– straddle forward and sideways, trunk bending forward and sideways, snatching the barbell with and without straddle stride, snatching the barbell to the chin; clean, push and press the barbell; press the barbell in horizontal position on a bench; pull the arms in at the front and rear of the body; lift the arms to the front and to the rear of the body.

Implement: Medicine ball, kettle bell, sandbag

Various forms of throws and gymnastic exercises can be done for the development of general strength with these implements, e.g. throwing the kettle bell, throwing the medicine ball backwards through the legs, trunk circling in sitting position with sandbag on the neck, etc.

Exercises for the development of take-off strength:

Triple jumps from standing and with approach run, high jumps, jumps over a box or skipping rope, jumps over obstacles; jumps on one or both legs for length etc. All jumps can also be executed with additional weight (sandbag, weight-vest).

Special strength exercises

Implement: Barbell

With barbell on the shoulders: trunk

Table 65   Weekly Schedule of Training during the Competition Period (Foundation Training)

Day	Duration (min.)	Training Task A = Preparation B = Main Part C = Closing		Training Means
Monday	15	A	Warm-up	Running, gymnastics
	60	B	Technique	Throws with competitive implement
	20		Development of strength	General strength exercises, throws with kettle bell
	10	C	Development of speed	Runs over 50–80 m
Wednesday	20	A	Warm-up	Game
	30	B	Development of strength	General strength exercises with barbell
	10		Development of take-off strength	One- and two-leg jumps
	10	C	Development of mobility	Loosening exercises
Thursday	15	A	Warm-up	Running, gymnastics
	45	B	Technique	Throws with competitive implement
	15		Development of take-off strength	Triple jump
	10	C	Development of speed	30 m sprints with different starts

Saturday or Sunday-Participation in Competition (not only in special event)

circling, in sitting and standing; turn-jumps (twist the hips about a fixed shoulder axis; imitate the throwing movement).

Implements: Sandbag, barbell

Examples: Practise the turn with sandbag, lift the arms with barbells sideways, standing on a box, the same in horizontal position, backward swinging of arms.

Throwing exercises with various implements:

Throwing the medicine ball or shot; hammer swinging, hammer throwing with one arm, weight throwing, throws with overweight discus, iron bar or beam from standing position and moving.

● Speed

All the exercises used for the development of speed by sprinters or jumpers can be applied here, e.g. runs over 30 m from a crouch, standing or flying start, acceleration runs, running with changes of tempo, bursts from walking or jogging.

● Mobility and agility

For the development of mobility and agility a host of different exercises from almost all events, particularly jumps and preparatory exercises recommended in Technical Training, can be applied. Throws are also valuable with the sling ball or with the discus in all weathers.

5.4.   The Javelin Throw

No definite rules have been laid down for the length of the run-up in the javelin throw. This distinguishes the event from other throwing events included in the Olympics: shot put, discus and hammer throw.

While in the latter events throwing must be from a circle, the javelin must be discharged from behind the arc of a circle drawn with a radius of 8 m. Such arc shall consist of a strip made of wood or metal (Fig. 125). Competitive rules for the javelin throw contain three restrictive regulations:

1. The javelin must be held at the taped grip.
2. From the beginning of the run-up to the delivery the competitor's body must not be turned completely so that his back would face the direction of the throw.
3. The javelin must touch the ground first with the tip of the metal head.

5.4.1.   The Technique

Javelin technique has undergone several changes in the course of its development. Based on the old Swedish technique prevailing before World War I, the Finns constantly improved

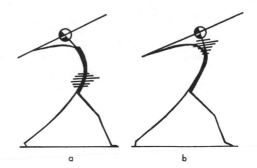

Fig. 126

the technique of the javelin in the years between 1920 and 1938. This progress was continued after 1945 and was mainly determined by Polish and Soviet sportsmen. In recent years the Finns are again among those who have given new impulses to the development of javelin technique.

With few exceptions (e.g. Luusis, USSR) the following view has been accepted for the preparation of the delivery movement: the javelin has to be withdrawn in a straight line as an extension of the axis of the shoulders and the arching of the back required for a good throw must have its centre as close to the implement as possible (Fig. 126b).

The javelin throw comprises the following technical elements:

– The grip and carriage
– The run-up
– The withdrawal
– The impulse stride
– The throwing stride
– The release
– The recovery.

The withdrawal, the impulse stride, the throwing stride and the release form together the five-stride-rhythm.

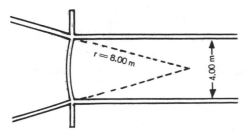

Fig. 125

With the influence of these phases on the throwing result in mind, the following ranking results:
1. The release
2. The withdrawal, the impulse stride and the throwing stride
3. The approach run
4. The grip and carriage
5. The recovery.

5.4.1.1. The Grip

It is practical to grip the javelin at the rear end of the binding. This allows force to be transmitted to the javelin behind its centre of gravity and the fingers find a good resistance on the shaft. In competitive practice two grips have stood the test of time:

The thumb and the two last joints of the index finger are behind the binding of the shaft. The javelin is positioned along the inner edge of the palm (Fig. 127).

The thumb and the two last joints of the middle finger are behind the binding, while the index finger supports the shaft from below (Figs. 128a and b).

Of the two grips the latter offers two minor advantages: one is the somewhat longer and stronger lever offered by the middle finger, which is beneficial to the spin of the implement about a long axis, so important for flight stability. The other advantage is that the index finger on the javelin shaft has a better possibility of controlling the carry.

5.4.1.2. The Carry

The javelin is carried at the height of the forehead above the shoulder parallel to the ground. It does not matter if the point of the javelin is slightly up or down. Many variations could be seen in this respect at the 1972 Olympic Games in Munich. The javelin is not carried at right angles to the shoulder axis, but with its point slightly turned inward (Fig. 129).

With the javelin carried in this position, it can be more easily withdrawn behind the body in a straight line. The purpose of a correct carry is to ensure smooth running, leading the athlete to the release without any delay.

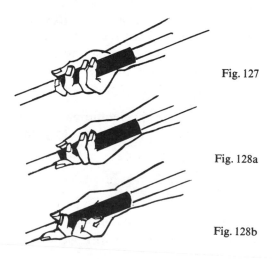

Fig. 127

Fig. 128a

Fig. 128b

Fig. 129

5.4.1.3. The Approach

After the release and the withdrawal the run-up is the most important part in the javelin throw. The results of top-class performers show that with a proper run-up the range of throw can be increased by 25 to 29 m as compared with a standing throw. The run-up has two parts:

1. the cyclic and
2. the acyclic part.

While the first part is a pure acceleration run over about $^2/_3$ of the total distance (20 m), the second part includes the withdrawal and the release (between 9 and 11 m). During the first part speed is built up sufficiently so as to allow for a further increase over the last strides. The initial speed depends therefore on the technical skills of the thrower. If a thrower with a poor technique accelerates too much during the first third of the approach, an inevitable slow-down on the last strides will ensue. The run-up should be easy and relaxed, leading the thrower to a powerful, explosive all-out release.

5.4.1.4. The Five-Stride-Rhythm

Of the three known stride rhythms— the three-stride-, the five-stride- and the seven-stride-rhythm—it is the five-stride-rhythm which is the most widely accepted. This last part of the complete movement serves the immediate preparation of the release, which comprises the following phases:

1. The withdrawal of the javelin
2. The impulse stride
3. The throwing position
4. The release.

We should mention here that some of the world-best throwers prefer the seven-stride-rhythm. They introduce between the third and the fourth of the five strides two further strides with an extended arm, so that in this variation the impulse stride becomes the 6th stride.

● The withdrawal phase

This phase is introduced by a preliminary stride (for the right-hand thrower from right to left). The withdrawal starts at the second stride of the five-stride rhythm and ends at the third stride.

The throwing arm is drawn back in alignment with the shoulder axis. The palm of the hand is turned upwards and extends the forearm. The axis of the hip remains almost at right angles to the direction of the throw. When the withdrawal is completed, the athlete's body has a marked backward lean, so important for a sustained application of force during the release (Fig. 131, Pos. 1–5).

In recent years some of the world's best performers have been seen starting the withdrawal during the first and ending it after the second stride.

● The impulse stride

The technique of the penultimate stride was controversial and subject to many

Fig. 130

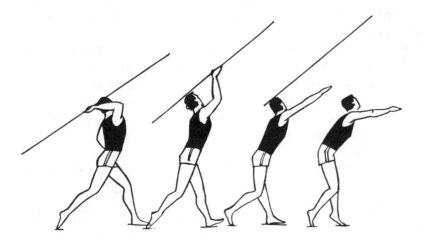

Fig. 131

changes in the historical development of the javelin throw. According to advanced techniques a fast and active but low fourth stride is required. In technically experienced throwers this fourth stride has at least the length of the third one. This technique is conducive to an economic landing rhythm of the legs and to a good backward lean associated with a longer effect of the energy on the throwing action. The toes of the right foot must not deviate more than 30° from the run-up direction. The hip axis is turned about 20° to the right.

The left leg presses the body down low into the fourth stride, preventing the body's centre of gravity from lifting at the landing of the right leg, which must be allowed to bend when it receives the body weight. This is important for a good landing, since any "lift" at this juncture would delay the release (Fig. 131, Pos. 6).

● The throwing position

The throwing position in this event comes at the instant at which both legs have come to the ground after the fifth stride. BAUERSFELD [54] writes: "We define the throwing position as the moment when the athlete's right foot makes contact with the ground after the impulse stride." This is a more precise definition but in our view it would be still more exact to describe as "throwing position" the moment at which the right leg has taken the weight of the body in the fifth stride, because this phase, starting with the landing of the right foot and ending when the centre

54 K.-H. Bauersfeld "Leichtathletik II – Wurf und Stoß" (Track and Field II–Throwing), in the Series "Kleine Bücherei für den Übungsleiter und Sportlehrer", vol. 10, 2nd ed., Sportverlag, Berlin 1963

of gravity is well over the right leg, is la relatively passive one. This phase is very important because its duration influences the beginning of the release. The longer and the more passive it is, the later the right leg can start to extend and in doing so introduce the release (Fig. 131, Pos. 7–8).

The arm and the javelin have not changed position during the impulse stride and the throwing position. In this phase the full extension of the forearm by the hand is important; under no circumstances must the arm be flexed at the wrist.

● The release

The release is initiated by a forward and upward stretching of the right leg at the knee and ankle joints, driving the right hip forward. The left bent leg lands over the heel. It has first a supporting and then a lifting function. The shoulder and the hip axes now run parallel and almost at right angles to the direction of the throw. The throwing arm is not yet stretched. The arching of the back reaches its maximum, having its centre of tension in the shoulder region. While the right leg is extended, the heel is raised, allowing the pressure of the ball of the foot to act longer on the body. The left leg continues its stretching action as soon as the body's CG comes into its sphere of action. The throwing arm now comes into its own, thus releasing the tension. The left leg must complete its extension only when the body's CG is over this leg, since otherwise the bracing effect would be too strong. When the throwing arm begins to strike, the elbow is raised until it is level with the head and pointing in the throwing direction. At this point the lower and the upper arms form a right angle (see Fig. 131, Pos. 9–13). During the release the left side of the body must be in a fixed position. This is achieved by a sudden arrest of the backward movement of the left arm just when the right side of the body overtakes the left side. The angle of release is between 32 and 36°. The thrower should attempt to keep the angle of incidence of the javelin—the javelin forming one arm and the track the other arm of the angle—as near to the angle of release as possible (Fig. 130)

Ideally the angle of release will coincide with the angle of incidence. A higher angle of incidence affords a greater surface of attack to te flow of fair.

● The recovery

The recovery stride has no influence on the length of the throw, but merely checks the forward speed of the body, thus preventing the athlete from fouling. A distance of at least two metres from the arc will be required for this. After the release the right leg is led forward in a springing movement; now the reverse takes place. To avoid stepping over, three conditions must be complied with:

1. The right foot must be planted transversely to the throwing direction; landing is over a flexed leg.
2. The upper body must lean forward (low centre of gravity).
3. The left leg is raised and brought back into the direction of the run-up.

5.4.2.   Technical Training

The javelin throw is an overhand throw. Its technique is difficult to learn because of the length of the implement. The beginner should therefore be allowed to learn the sequence of movements under simplified conditions. Since the release movement is almost identical with a long throw with a cricket ball or a club, the use of these or similar implements in the preliminary exercises will accelerate the learning process. Mastering the overhand throw with these implements should be the first aim of the beginner. By comparison with other throwing events, the javelin throw requires less maximum strength, but a lot of explosive force, agility and mobility. The two latter attributes are frequently underrated in learning the event. The importance of agility is particularly marked in the performance of boys and girls throwing a cricket ball. The best results are here not always achieved by the strongest and toughest, but by throwers possessing excellent agility and flexibility. In the javelin the proportions change in favour of strength, but agility and flexibility remain valuable attributes of the javelin thrower.

5.4.2.1.   Special Preparatory Exercises

The purpose of this group of exercises is to prepare the thrower directly for the overhand throw under technically simple and easy conditions. The implements to be used are: cricket balls, small iron shots (up to 700 gr), clubs and small medicine balls. All the exercises and instructions assume a right-handed thrower.

Training Examples:

1. The release is performed from an easy straddle position—the legs are slightly bent at the knee joint; in this

position forward and upward stretching of legs and release of the implement overhand.

2. Throws from stride position—the left leg is set forward, the shoulder axis is square to the direction of the throw. The right arm is swung backwards over the right shoulder for the throw. Release as in exercise 1.

3. Throws from stride position—the body weight is over the flexed right leg. The throw is initiated by the extension of this leg.

4. Throws after two-stride approach. The initial position is either the stride position—right in front of left—or with feet parallel. The upper body now turns to the right and the throwing arm extends backwards at shoulder height. All the exercises quoted can also be done by aiming at a target.

5. All exercises under 1 to 4 are repeated with a medicine ball of 3 to 4 kg, using both hands. Maintain the same release rhythm.

5.4.2.2. Basic Exercises of Technical Training

The chief aim in the basic training is to arrive at a flawless transmission of the speed built up during the first part of the run to the implement. In the early stages throwing for distance should be replaced by throwing at targets. It makes learning easier and prevents injuries. We recommend the following set of exercises:

– Exercise 1: Learning the grip and carry.

The javelin is held level with the head and stuck vertically into the ground. The hand glides down the shaft until it meets resistance at the lining with the index and the thumb or with the middle-finger and the thumb. Practise the carry by gripping the javelin with the throwing hand.

Points to note: Beginners are advised to hold the javelin with the tip slightly down and the tail slightly up. This allows the wrist to remain loose.

– Exercise 2: Standing throw.

Stand in stride position and turn the trunk to the right until the left shoulder points in the throwing direction. Stretch the right arm backwards at shoulder level so that the javelin is almost parallel to the ground. The right leg is a little more bent than the left. Introduce the release by a stretching and turning movement of the right leg.

Purpose: Proper coordination of the movements at release.

Points to note: The right leg remains on the ground as long as possible. The reverse should take place only after maximum extension. The right arm must not come into action too soon.

Hint: The throw from a static position should be practised only for a short time.

Auxiliary exercise: If the beginner has difficulties in executing this exercise, he should repeat exercises 1 and 2 of the special preparation but with the javelin.

– Exercise 3: Throws from a throwing stance.

In a stride position—the right foot is in front of the left; the throwing arm is stretched to the rear behind the line of the shoulders. From this position perform an active stride with subsequent release (Fig. 131, Pos. 6–13).

The body weight remains over the right leg until the athlete's centre of gravity is in the area affected by the action of this leg.

Purpose: Allow the athlete to find out

for himself the right moment for the release.

Points to note: In the initial position the body must have a slight backward lean of about 10 to 15°. The axis of the hip and the right foot turn 30 to 40° to the right. On landing the left leg should be flexed.

– Exercise 4: Take two walking strides before throwing with an extended arm. The throwing arm is stretched back at shoulder height. Two initial positions may be assumed:
a) feet in parallel position
b) stride position with the right leg in front of the left. The order for either basis is right before left.

Purpose: Learning the rhythm of movements at release.

Points to note: Execute the two strides at increasing speed. The throwing arm remains extended until release. The second stride–left–right–is a low but very active stride. The same exercise can be performed with three strides, starting with feet either parallel or in striding position (right before left). The sequence of strides is left-right-left.

– Exercise 5: Training of the withdrawal.

Withdraw the javelin over two strides, first in walking, then in jogging or running. The withdrawal is started when the right leg moves forward. It ends during the next stride. This exercise can be repeated several times with gradually increasing speed.

Purpose: Preparation for the five-stride-rhythm.

Points to note: Withdrawal of the javelin must be in a straight line. The grip must not be changed or loosened. Pronounced backward lean.

– Exercise 6: Learning the five-stride-rhythm.

One of the main aims in the technical training of the javelin throw is to master the five-stride-rhythm. After a preliminary stride and withdrawal perform further strides until release; blend all the movements together.

The complete five-stride-rhythm can be trained first in walking, then in jogging and finally in running.

Purpose: Flawless sequence of movements from the run-up to the release.

Points to note: Accelerate over the last three strides. After the third stride withdrawal must be ended (the first stride initiates the rhythm). The fourth stride, also called the impulse stride (cf. 5.4.1.4.) is a low but active stride.

Auxiliary Exercise: In the last stride beginners tend to lean to the left side in the attempt to avoid too much arching of the back. Novices should therefore practise the run-up inside a narrow lane marked with chalk lines.

Sketch of the five-stride-rhythm:
1st stride – preliminary stride
2nd stride – beginning of the withdrawal
3rd stride – end of the withdrawal
4th stride – impulse stride
5th stride – release.

– Exercise 7: Practise the complete movement.

The complete movement should always be trained from jogging or running and end with the release. Emphasis must be on the acceleration over the last five strides. At first accelerate only over the last two strides, then over strides 3–4–5–, later 2–3–4–5 etc.

Purpose: Work up to optimum speed over the last two strides.

Points to note: If the right leg has been well extended this becomes apparent by the dragging of the right foot after the fifth stride. A deviation of the left in this dragging should only be slight. The coach should observe the complete movement from different angles: from the side—a well straightened launching arm and a good lean back—then from the rear—run-up and withdrawal along a straight line.

5.4.2.3.   Ancillary Exercises

1. Determine the distance of the run-up. The exact length of the run-up should be determined when preparing for a competition.

a) To determine the distance from the start to the beginning of the five-stride-rhythm, have the thrower to do several acceleration runs, then put check-marks. Let him always start with the same leg.

b) After this measured run-up-there follows the five-stride-rhythm (same course of speed) and finally the release. Now measure the distance from the beginning of the five-stride-rhythm to the last step after recovery.

c) The markings on these two distances must be used in competition.

Complete movement and check-marks (x): Two forms of putting check-marks are outlined in the following scheme:

           x
— — — —1–2–3–4–5
           x

The check-mark will be either on the landing point of the left leg after the first of the five strides on the left side of the thrower or on the landing point of the last run-up stride before the five-stride-rhythm on the right side. It is assumed that the two athletes are of the same standard. The first type of marking offers beginners the advantage that hitting the mark coincides with the commencement of the withdrawal. No special drill is required for learning the recovery in the javelin. If the release has been properly executed, the reverse will be correct.

2. A series of throws from a three-stride approach. Special tasks are set to help improve the individual elements of the complete movement.

3. In stride position—the thrower drives the javelin head at release height into a tree. The right flexed leg then extends forward and upward. The arching of the back resulting from this movement gives the athlete the "feel" for the correct trunk action. The shoulder and hip axes move parallel to each other and in a line vertical to the longitudinal axis of the javelin.

4. Dummy throws against resistance. Exercises 2 and 3 of the technical training are repeated but without release; the javelin is pulled back by a partner. This gives the thrower the "feel" for the right movements in the extension of the leg.

5. Throws from astride position with left arm.

6. Practise the five-stride-rhythm in front of a mirror. This helps to coordinate the movements (space and time). Note that in the mirror you obtain a mirror inverted image.

5.4.2.4.   Fault—Reason—Correction

— Fault: Slow-down at the beginning of the five-stride-rhythm.

Reason: a) Too fast start and no proper acceleration;

b) The withdrawal is not well timed with the running cycle but begins from right to left.

Correction: a) Five-stride-rhythm from jogging; increase speed only when starting withdrawal.

b) Acceleration runs with javelin, ending with five-stride-rhythm.

5.4.3.   Club Throwing

The club throw is another overhand throwing event; it is identical with the javelin throw with respect to the sequence of movements and of the separate phases and in their fundamental course. Thus club throwing differs from the javelin throw only in certain details. The training of this throw is nevertheless justified. It is a competitive event, particularly for boys, girls and young athletes, but is also popular elsewhere. It is taught in sports lessons of upper classes in schools and is appreciated for its contribution to the premilitary training of the young generation. The novice javelin thrower uses it for training the overhand throw.

5.4.3.1.   Technique

Since club throwing has much in common with the javelin throw, we can omit a detailed description of the technique. We only emphasize certain special features of the different phases.
The five-stride-rhythm is also applied in the club throw. It may be used with a run-up, but can also be started with the first of the five strides or after a few preliminary strides.
This depends mainly on the standard of the athlete, e.g. on his ability to continue acceleration in the five-stride-rhythm and to master the movements at a higher speed.
The *grip and carry of the club* is analogous to that of the javelin throw. The implement is held with the thumb, the index and the middle finger in such a manner, that the knob of the shaft lies in the palm of the hand. The club is carried above the shoulder and slightly above the head (Fig. 131a, Position 1). Withdrawal should be on a straight line, as in the javelin throw.
The components of a good withdrawal are:
– a well-timed beginning and ending of the withdrawal on the third of the five strides;
– a complete straightening of the arm (long launching arm) on a short path, i.e. on a straight line continuing the shoulder axis;
– a backward rotation of the shoulder axis until it points in the direction of the throw;
– after withdrawal the club must be in a good position for the throwing movement; it should not be much below or

Fig. 131a

above the extension of the shoulder axis; the club must not be allowed to hang down by cocking the wrist. After withdrawal the shoulder, the extended arm and the club must form a straight line (Fig. 131a, Pos. 3).

The *task of strides 3 and 4* is to further accelerate the thrower and the implement and to set up a sound position for the release. The vigorous impulse stride in which the body assumes the backward arched position plays an important role in producing a long acceleration path. Strides 3 and 4 (impulse strides), if they are to be effective, must bring the legs ahead of the trunk by a powerful leg action. The position of the upper body and the implement must, however, be changed as little as possible.

Throwing position (Fig. 131a, Pos. 4). At this stage the body's CG should be over or still behind the supporting leg. The shoulder is turned backwards and forms a straight line with the well-extended throwing arm. As the backward lean increases, it changes its angle to the horizontal, so that this angle tends to that of the angle of release.

The release. Force must be applied in the proper order (foot, leg, hip, shoulder, arm) and finally be imparted to the implement via the hand. The following factors characterize an effective delivery:

The right leg begins to extend in the throwing direction (the right heel has turned out and the knee points forwards-downwards) before the left leg has grounded in a blocking action.

The shoulder and trunk are introduced into the movement only when the knee and hip extension is almost completed and the hip axis is at right angles to the direction of the throw.

The arm movement begins when the torque between the upper and the lower body is released by bringing the shoulders forward until the chest shows in the throwing direction (Fig. 131a, Pos. 5). The elbow must come to the front completely to produce the "whip-lash"-effect of the trailing forearm.

After landing the left-leg action must not produce a bracing but a levering and stretching effect (Fig. 131a/6).

5.4.3.2. Technical Training

The technical training for club throwing is basically the same as for the javelin event. The rounder throw can also be included in preparatory exercises. In fact the club throw is a good way of preparing the athlete to throw the javelin. By using this simple and handy implement training is facilitated; it is particularly useful in coaching boys and girls. If the club throw is used as a preliminary exercise for javelin throwing or, if other implements are not at hand to replace the javelin, make due allowance for the following aspects of the club throw. The first part of the cycle is included in the run-up. The transition from the run-up to the five-stride-rhythm must be given special attention.

The club must be held in such a manner that one part of the shaft shows below the hand (in the second third of the shaft), thus avoiding the wrist tilting backwards; the grip is rather similar to that for the javelin. When training the delivery, pay attention to a technically correct delivery above the shoulder. An accurate vertical rotation of the longitudinal axis of the club in the air gives a good visual check on the quality of the delivery.

5.4.4. Physical Requirements and Training Methods for Improving Performance

5.4.4.1. The Importance of Physical Condition

If we look at the physical qualities which determine performance in the javelin throw in order of their importance, we arrive at this ranking:
1. Throwing power (Explos. strength)
2. Speed
3. Special agility
4. Special mobility
5. Height and weight
6. Special endurance

● Throwing power

While maximum strength is essential for the shout putter, the javelin thrower must develop mainly explosive strength. It is the fundamental and decisive quality for attaining proficiency in this event. This is due to the fact that the competitive implements are of different weight.

● Speed

The speed of a javelin thrower cannot be measured exclusively by his performance over 100 m. What determines his performance is the capacity to accelerate over the first 30 m and more particularly to achieve the optimum speed at release.

● Special agility

For improving performance in learning and mastering the javelin technique special agility and good coordination ability are important. After a cyclical run-up and five acyclical strides the thrust must be conveyed to the javelin. Here with the given external conditions (for example wind conditions) it is a matter of finding the optimal angle of incidence and angle of release.

● Special mobility

Mobility in the javelin throw is the athlete's ability to fully utilize the range of movement at his hip and shoulder joints. With plenty of suppleness at the shoulder joint the athlete can lengthen the path of propulsion and transfer force on a straight line at release.

● Height and weight

Of all the athletes competing in the throwing events javelin throwers (men and women) had the least weight. The height is not so important since the height of release hardly influences the length of throw. Apart from long distance runners and race walkers the six best javelin throwers (men) averaging 27.5 were the oldest participants in the athletics events at the 1960 Olympic Games. The average age of women finalists competing in the same events was 26.8. They were the oldest participants in competitions for women. These figures reveal that the javelin thrower attains top form at a technically mature age. This is further emphasized by the fact that the gold and silver medal winners at the Olympics were already 30 years old.

From these figures we can deduce the

Table 66 Mean Values of Age, Height and Weight of the 6 best Performers at the Olympic Games 1972

	Men	Women
Age (years)	26.6	23.3
Height (cm)	180	176
Weight (kg)	89.9	69.0

following physical characteristics for javelin throwers: they are of medium weight (75 to 85 kg), medium height (1.75 to 1.85 m) endowed with rapid strength, agility and mobility.

Experience shows that top results are generally achieved by athletes having similar characteristics.

● Special endurance

Endurance is important for the javelin thrower only insofar as he has to execute 3 or 6 throws, often at intervals of 30 minutes and more, with all-out effort.

5.4.4.2. Means for Developing Physical Properties

● Strength

1. General strength exercises
a) Exercises with barbell—e.g. snatching, pushing, pressing, knee-bends.
b) Other strength exercises, e.g. gymnastics with medicine ball or kettle bell, hammer swings, rope-hanging by one hand etc.
2. Special strength exercises
a) Throwing shots (weight up to 2.5 kg) from approach run of 3 or 5 strides.
b) Practising the delivery phase on a rope with additional load (Fig. 132a).
During training many throwers try to achieve the same effect by using an expander. The movement will be fast only in the initial part. With increasing resistance it becomes a sheer strength exercise. Javelin throwers should be discouraged from doing this exercise frequently, as the velocity pattern is markedly different from that required for the javelin throw.
c) Series of throws with iron tubes and heavy javelins up to 2.5 kg.
d) Axe throwing with implements weighing 2 to 3 kg (Fig. 132b).
e) Jumps with and without additional load and jumps over obstacles.

● Speed

a) Runs over 30 and 40 metres from crouch and standing starts, as well as "flying dashes" with all-out effort.
b) Acceleration runs over 80 m. For improving the final effort in throwing exercises lighter implements (stones and rounder ball) should be used at longer intervals.

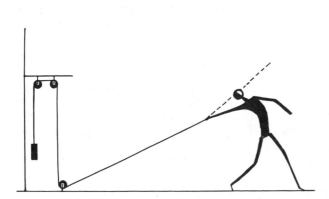

Fig. 132a

Fig. 132b

● Agility

The agility required in javelin throwers can be developed by ball games: basketball, volleyball and hockey are best suited for this purpose. The latter is particularly effective, because handling a hockeystick is a good preparation for the acyclic movement in the five-stride-rhythm. The javelin thrower should also try hurdling and hanging by the hand from bars and ropes.

Further training means:
1. Throws from surfaces of varying consistency
2. Throws with shoes having different size spikes (short and long spikes)
3. Throws with head and following wind. It would be wrong to practise throws only with a following wind. In competitions weather conditions vary greatly. Bearing this in mind during training will save the athlete problems in competition. Throws from different surfaces, with different spikes and under different weather conditions require a somewhat different coordination. Only a flexible thrower who has trained under a variety of conditions will be able to adjust himself in competition.

● Mobility

a) Arm circling forwards and back-

Table 67   Weekly Schedule of Training during the Preparatory Period (Foundation Training)

Day	Duration (min.)	Training Task A = Preparation B = Main Part C = Closing		Training Means
Monday	30	A	Warm-up	Jogging and gymnastics
	25	B	Development of strength	Exercises with barbell of medium weight with ten repetitions per series General strength exercises
	30		Development of mobility	Exercises on wall bars
	20	C	Limbering down	800 m jogging
Wednesday	30	A	Warm-up	Jogging and gymnastics
	10	B	Development of strength and endurance	Hammer swinging 200 m and 300 m runs at medium speed using the extensive interval method
	10	C	Limbering down	Jogging
Friday			In the gymnasium	
	30	A	Warm-up	Basketball
	20	B	Development of strength	General strength exercises: – exercises with barbell – exercises on wall bars
	30		Development of agility and mobility	
	15		Development of strength	Hanging and climbing on towrope
	10	C	Limbering down	Game
Sunday	40		Development of endurance	Runs through woods (5–8 km) at medium pace

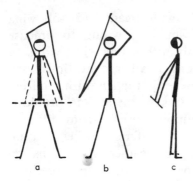

Fig. 133

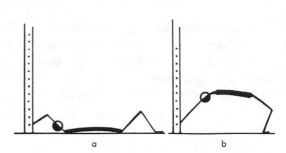

Fig. 134

wards, with arms moving parallel to each other.

b) Trunk bending with feathering. Full extension at knee-joints, fingertips touching the toes.

c) Turn figures of eights with javelin (Fig. 133a and b).

d) Dislocation of shoulders forward and backward with javelin with extended arms, reducing the spacing between handgrips at every trial (Fig. 133c).

e) Exercises on wall bars (Figs. 134 and 135).

f) Exercises with partner (Fig. 136).

● Endurance

General endurance—on which the special endurance is built—should be mainly improved during the first half of the preparatory period by runs through woods. Runs up to 300 m at medium speed on a cinder track can also be included in the programme.

At the beginning of the competitive season the means for improving special endurance receive priority. Make sure that the thrower can execute between 30 to 40 throws in every training session.

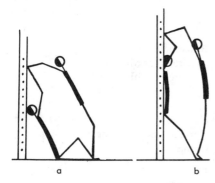

Fig. 135

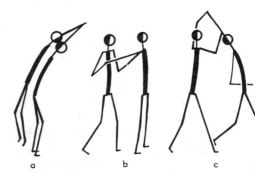

Fig. 136

Table 68 Weekly Schedule of Training during the Competition Period (Foundation Training)

Day	Duration (min.)	Training Task A = Preparation B = Main Part C = Closing		Training Means
Monday	30	A	Warm-up	Jogging and gymnastics with javelin
	15	B	Train quick response	Starts
	20		Development of strength	Throws after three or five strides
	10	C	Limbering down	800 m jogging
Tuesday	30	A	Warm-up	Jogging and gymnastics with javelin
	20	B	Development of speed	Bursts over 30 and 50 m all-out
			Technique	Five-stride-rhythm from jogging with release
	10	C	Limbering down	Jogging
Wednesday	20	A	Warm-up	Game
	30	B	Development of strength	Special strength exercises with barbell
			Development of mobility	Gymnastics with javelin
	30		Technique	Throws with javelin from three strides approach-run
	10	C	Limbering down	Jogging
Thursday	20	A	Warm-up	Jogging and gymnastics with javelin
	15	B	Development of speed and agility	5 × 30 m "flying" with maximum effort
				Hurdle race over 91,4 cm high hurdles
	10	C	Limbering down	Jogging
Sunday			Competition	

5.5. The Hammer Throw

5.5.1. Technique

The technique of hammer throwing is determined by the specific nature of the implement and the measurements of the throwing circle (diameter 2.135 m), which comply with the International Competition Rules. It has improved so much in recent years that today a well trained athlete can throw the hammer almost over 80 m. Crucial for the length of flight of the implement is its initial velocity (v_0). For throwing the hammer 75 m and more, an initial velocity of 27 to 28 m/s must be imparted to it. A complete throw usually consists of two preliminary swings and three turns on the left foot with an active push-off from the right leg at each turn. [55] In the first part of the turn the athlete pivots on the heel and in the second part on the ball of the foot, so that athletes often speak of a "heel-ball-turn", resulting in a forward movement of the thrower across the circle in the throw-

55 All exercises are described as for right-handers.

375

ing direction. The hammer head travels on a plane inclined to the horizontal. The critical points in this plane are the high and low points: their correct location in every turn determines the effectiveness of the technique. The acceleration of the hammer is mainly achieved by the active unwinding of the torque built up in the single-support phase. In contrast to other throwing events, there are several "winds" in the hammer throw (at each turn and just before release).

In the attempt to lengthen the path of propulsion, the best hammer throwers in the world try to keep the effective radius of the hammer sweep as long as possible during the arm swinging phase and the turns. Shorter throwers tend to increase the number of turns from 3 to 4.

Fig. 137

5.5.1.1. The Grip

The inside grip of the hammer handle is laid against the pads of the middle phalanxes of the left-hand fingers. The right hand cuffs the left by putting the four fingers over the back of the middle and basal phalanxes of the left-hand fingers. The hammer must be held firmly but not tensely (Fig. 137).

Fig. 139

5.5.1.2. The Initial Position

The thrower stands at the rear edge of the circle with his back facing in the direction of the throw. His feet are a little more than shoulder-width apart and his knees are bent for stability during the arm swings. The thrower now places the hammer head behind his right leg as far to his rear (inside or outside the circle) as possible. In reaching back his weight shifts to the right foot. His trunk has a slight forward lean. He then turns to the right until the right shoulder points in the direction of throwing. The hammer wire forms a straight line with the extended left arm.

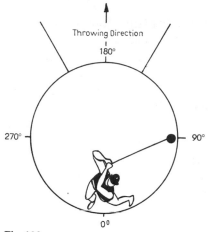

Fig. 138

5.5.1.3. Preliminary Arm Swings

As the upper body of the thrower straightens and begins to turn to the left, the hammer is pulled up and forward (Fig. 139, Pos. 2). With the idea of

377

setting up a rhythm during the preliminary swings, some throwers start differently.

They do not put the hammer head behind to their right, but allow it to swing backwards and forwards through their stradled legs. They then swing the implement back outside their right leg, thus introducing the preliminary arm swings without the hammer having touched the ground.

In order to generate the longest effective radius possible of the plane in which the hammer moves, the thrower will strive to keep his arms straight as long as possible. To comply with this requirement, all good throwers slightly lower the left shoulder. They begin with this movement when the hammer is at its lowest point and end it by turning the trunk to the right. When the right shoulder points in the throwing direction, the shoulder girdle is again in a horizontal position (Fig. 138).

The correct shift of the weight from the hips is highly important during the preliminary arm swings. The thrower must counteract the increasing centrifugal force. He tries to maintain his balance by allowing his hips to turn in opposition to the hammer head. When the hammer is to the thrower's left side, he will drive his hips to the right. When the hammer moves backwards, he presses his hips forward etc. (Fig. 139, Pos. 2–4).

The rotation reaches its highest point when the hammer head is to the left at the rear of the athlete and its lowest point when it falls in front (to the right) of the athlete. After the first arm swing the thrower keeps the lowest point of his hammer well to the right, at around 290 to 300°, and the highest point somewhere around 120°. During the second arm swing both points travel in the direction of rotation. Experience shows that two preliminary swings are sufficient to give the hammer the velocity of 15 to 16 m/s required for beginning the turns. Additional arm-swings have been found to be wasteful.

5.5.1.4. Transition from the Second Arm Swing to the First Turn

A successful turning action depends essentially on the accurate execution of the transition from the second arm swing to the first turn. The transition begins when the thrower has turned to the right in the second arm swing and starts to "unwind" the body torque in a circular unwinding movement and by actively turning the right foot around. The weight is thereby transferred to the left leg and the centre of gravity of the body is slightly lowered.

As the hammer head "hits" the lowest point of its orbit, the left foot begins to turn inwards. When the hammer has passed the lowest point, the right side of the body drives to the left in its entire length (from the foot to the right shoulder) in a powerful circular movement.

Triggered by the pressure of the right leg, the right body side turns firmly about the longitudinal axis of the body.

Throughout the transition phase into the first turn, the upper body is kept as erect as possible and the shoulders are parallel to the ground. At the end of the transition phase the right foot leads the body into the turn by a powerful low movement. The complete body weight is over the left leg when the right foot leaves the ground during a turn of some 50 to 65°.

A too strong or too slight shifting will upset the balance of the thrower and hinder good technical execution of further turns.

5.5.1.5.   The Turns

When the hammer comes close to the lowest point after the second arm swing, the thrower begins to turn the left foot to the left over the heel. In doing so he slightly lifts his toes off the ground. Then the right foot pushes to the left over the ball of the foot. It comes off the ground when the left foot has turned by 95 to 110° away from its initial position in the direction of the turn. The hammer now travels at shoulder height at near 90° (Fig. 139, Pos. 6). This is when the first single-support phase begins. The left foot turns over the outer edge of the ball. The hammer head passes the highest point of its orbit. The left leg is well bent at the knee joint. In order to achieve a new "wind-up" and to create favourable conditions for the further acceleration of the hammer, the right leg is led around the left leg in a tight turn (Fig. 139, Pos. 7).

The double-support phase serves to accelerate the hammer by unwinding the body torque. Figure 144 shows that in the single-support phase the hammer head loses tangential velocity and reaches in the ensuing double-support phase a much higher speed than it had at the beginning of the single-support phase.

The double-support phase begins when the hammer, having passed its highest point, is located to the right of the thrower at head level and the right foot meets the ground again at the same level as the left. At this stage the hammer should have an angle of not more than 270°. The body mass is over the left foot with the heel still off the ground (Fig. 139, Pos. 10).

The best throwers in the world have different ways of setting down the right foot. Those who roll the right foot from the heel to the ball are in the minority. During the turns the throwers tend to feather in the right foot over the ball to the sole of the foot and to ground it over the ball only during the last turn.

5.5.1.6.   Changing Technique in the Different Turns

Due to the velocity of the thrower, which increases after each turn, and the steadily increasing centrifugal force of the hammer, some changes in the technique occur during the second and third turns.

● A stronger twist of the trunk

As the hammer's velocity increases, the centrifugal force of the hammer head increases proportionately after each turn, acquiring in good throwers a value of more than 200 kg after the third turn. The higher centrifugal force is matched by a correspondingly increased centripetal reaction. This is created by the greater twist of the trunk in the opposite direction of the hammer. The angle at the knee- and hip-joints becomes higher. In the third turn, when the hammer has passed its highest point, the centre of gravity of the body is lowered to such an extent that in the single-support phase the lower left leg stands almost horizontally to the ground.

● Changes in the angle of inclination of the path of the hammer

With every turn the angle of inclination of the hammer path gets higher. This is the result of the increased twist of the upper body, while the angle between trunk and arms has remained almost unchanged. But this also reflects the necessity of gradual adjustment of the angle of inclination to the angle of release. The angle of inclination depends to a large extent on the thrower's height. Shorter men are, for instance, at a disadvantage, because they must try to keep the angle of inclination of the hammer path low to prevent it from touching the ground. Due to this they are not able to give the hammer a sufficiently high angle of release (44°).

● Changes in the position of the feet and in the leg work during the turns

The thrower's velocity increases with each turn. Some of the world-best throwers perform the last turn in less

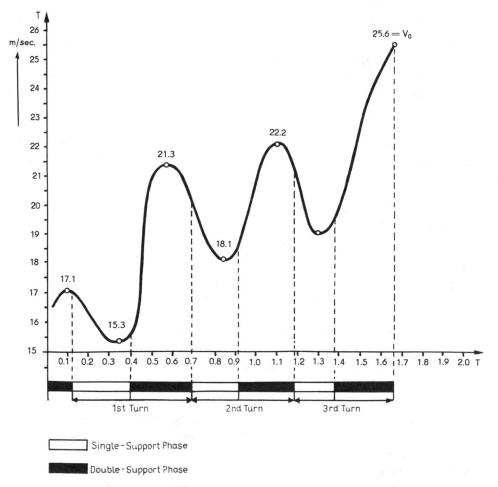

Fig. 140 Graph showing the changes in the hammer's velocity. Throw by Bakarinow (USSR) 66.70 m.

V — Velocity of the hammer head
T — Time in seconds
V_0 — Initial velocity in m/sec.

than 0.5 sec., while they require 0.6 sec. and more for the first turn. Due to the need to get ahead of the hammer in each turn and to give the body a greater twist, the right foot comes closer to the left in each transition to the double-support phase, thus constantly reducing the path of the right leg (Fig. 139, Pos. 1, 16, 22 and Fig. 141). As already mentioned, top-class throwers put the right foot down in different ways. In our opinion the only thing that matters is that after the third turn the right foot comes down with the ball first, thus permitting the right leg to begin sooner with the extension and the thrower to get his hips in a more favourable position for the release.

● Changes in the highest and lowest points

The locations of the highest and the lowest points are not constant. They are shifted more and more in the direction of each turn. Different results were obtained for each thrower by measurements (Fig. 142). A shift of 8 to 12° can be taken as an average. What is important is that in the third turn the lowest point does not go beyond the median line.

5.5.1.7. The Release

The delivery phase begins when the right foot touches the ground after the third turn. When the right leg lands the athlete's weight is over the pivoting left leg which touches the ground only with the ball of the foot. (Fig. 139, Pos. 21). This is done in the attempt to land the right foot as quickly as possible and to start the delivery. The landing of the right foot must be fast and firm in order to match the acceleration of the implement, which is racing down to the lowest point with the beginning of the active straightening of the legs. At the same time the right leg turns left and drives the right hip (pelvis) forward and to the left against the resistance of the fixed left side of the body. When the hammer head has passed the lowest point of the orbit, the rotation movement to the left is accompanied by an active lifting of the chest and the shoulder girdle to the left, while the thrower is still attempting to maintain a long radius. Just before the hammer is released, the left knee straightens. When the implement leaves the hand, the vertical line of projection of the thrower's head should not go beyond the right

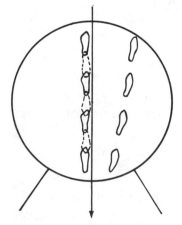

Fig. 141

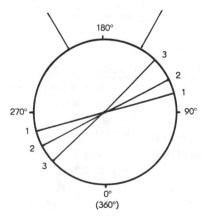

Fig. 142

381

heel. The release ends with a sharp pull of the hand which is transmitted to the hammer. If the feet are in a stationary position, this is a clear proof of a correctly executed delivery. The arms continue their upward swing (Fig. 139, Pos. 26 and 27).

In order to fully utilize the extension forces, the upper body should not be brought into action too soon at the release. The hammer is released at shoulder height at an angle of 90°. The left shoulder points in throwing direction and the back is well arched (Fig. 139, Pos. 26). The most favourable angle of release in the hammer throw is between 42 and 44°.

5.5.1.8. The Recovery

To avoid stepping over the thrower must absorb the impact by reversing the legs and by lowering the body's centre of gravity, thus increasing stability.

5.5.2. Technical Training

The technique of hammer throwing is more difficult to learn than that of other throwing events. The learner should not straight away take up the hammer used by experienced athletes of his age. Until he has acquired the necessary strength he should train with a lighter hammer. Whether to use a hammer with a long or short wire should be decided by the coach. As a matter of principle a short-wire hammer replaces the light hammer and a long-wire hammer the heavy one. Training with a lighter hammer should not, however, be extended over too long a period. The athlete should soon start to turn and

throw with the normal implement, particularly if he has used a lighter hammer at the beginning.

Almost all right-handers turn left and left-handers right in the hammer throw. A left-hander should turn to the left, if in everyday life and in sports he is used to turning left (cycling and skiing).

5.5.2.1. Safety Measures

According to the rules of competition a safety cage must be used in hammer throwing. Experience has shown that such cages do not provide sufficient protection against accidents. Torn-off hammer heads, if released without control, force their way through the wire net of the cage. For training and for competition the following safety precautions should therefore be taken:

1. Make sure the handle and the wire are not damaged. A buckled wire should not be straightened.
2. Make sure the swivel is safely anchored.
3. During throwing athletes and other persons should keep clear of the side of the ascending hammer path.
4. All persons in the vicinity of the hammer thrower should keep their eyes on the hammer.
5. Without the order of the coach to throw, the hammer must not be released, even in the event of failures or falls.

5.5.2.2. Special Preparatory Exercises

● Agility exercises

Agility exercises for hammer throwing should be executed in combination with turns. They must not be exaggerated and should be included into preparation programmes only if the thrower does not get giddy after two or four turns or loses his orientation. Whenever turns are practised, the athlete should turn both to the right and to the left. Turns should be started slowly and with long pauses between the routines. In the course of training the turns should get faster and the double-support phase shorter.

● Training examples

1. Make turns in running along a straight line of 10 to 20 m length.
2. Take final jumps with turns in series of 3 and 6 jumps (between 180 and 360° or more).
3. Do a series of quick turns alternately on the ball and on the heel, ending with a firm stand. The athlete must be able to stop turns in a given direction. The weight must be over the supporting leg (in right-handers the left leg).
4. Make throws with the sling ball after one or more turns.
5. Make discus throws with rotations.
6. Make turns with a light punch ball or a boxer's punch bag, the arms fully extended, footwork at the thrower's convenience.

● Stretching exercises

As a result of strength-work the thrower's back-, shoulder- and hip-muscles tend to get tense. Exercises for making the hip and shoulder girdles mobile should be included from the very beginning.
In every session several stretching exercises should be included in programmes set up for one or two cycles of 3 to 4 weeks each. Such routines should be applied during and after exercises with the barbell.
Examples of exercises:
1. Trunk circling in standing.
2. Hip circling in standing with half knee-bend.
3. Hip circling in the prone and supine leaning rest.
4. Arm circling forwards/backwards.
5. Shoulder circling forwards and backwards.
6. Arms at front horizontal; forward movement of shoulders (hunched back) and backward rotating of shoulders.
7. Leg circling on fixed rings.
8. Hip rotation in the hanging position on wall-bars. The leg introduces the hip rotation by turning the knee around.
9. Feathering in forward line on wall-bars with or without the help of a partner. Grip the wall-bars with one or both hands; the arms are extended.
10. Flexion and tension of the arms from the hang on wall-bars with the help of a partner who stands below the athlete and lifts him on his shoulders. Point of contact: shoulder-girdle.
11. Flexion and tension from backward sitting position with bent knees on the wall-bars. The hands grasp the bar at shoulder-width over the head.

● Exercises with the hammer

When the athlete has been briefed on the dangers and is familiar with safety precautions, he should learn all about the centrifugal forces of the turning hammer. For swings with one arm light hammers should be used initially. For all other exercises hammers of different weights, as well as two hammers together, may be used.
Examples of exercises:
1. Swing the hammer forwards and backwards, then put it down. This exer-

cise can be executed to the right and to the left side of the legs and between straddled legs. The hammer must be held with both hands, the arms should be well extended.

2. Cf. 1, but with alternate hammer swings and swings between straddled legs, without putting the hammer down.

3. Allow the hammer to rotate around the body by reversing hands (danger of accident, leave long distances between athletes).

4. Do turns on the spot with short and fast chassé steps. Hold the hammer with arms extended in front of the body or sideways with one arm. The hammer head must describe wide circles.

5. Preliminary swings with one arm, left and right, with weight shifting.

6. Cf. 5 – change the lowest point deliberately during several preliminary swings with one arm.

Having fixed the throwing direction, the low points are in front and to the right side of the athlete, i.e. at 270 to 360 degrees.

5.5.2.3. Basic Exercises of Technical Training

After a basic training of 5 to 10 sessions the thrower should have command of the hammer and be acquainted with the centrifugal forces it develops. He must then be in a position to release the hammer without being pulled down by it. Great attention must be paid to the turns. Learning the release should be delayed, as it becomes easier when the athlete masters the turns. Sportsmen who intend to specialize in this event should not train the throw with less than three turns. During the basic training all the technical exercises are aimed at the absorption of certain elements of the hammer throw technique.

1. Watch the posture throughout.

2. Shift the body weight on to the left leg.

3. The arms must remain stretched throughout the complete throw ("hanging on the hammer"-effect).

4. Locate the lowest point and define the plane of the hammer sweep.

For a systematic series we recommend the following exercises: start with an explanation and demonstration of the grip of the hammer and the initial position.

– Exercise 1: Arm swings–do 10 to 20 easy arm swings with a hammer, without a break.

Purpose: The arm swings are preliminary elements of the hammer throwing technique. They prepare the athlete for the turns and give him the kinetic "feel" for a smooth transition to the turn with a wide sweep of the hammer head.

Points to note: Hold arms straight out in front of the body. Good timing at lowering the left shoulder accompanied by a turn of the trunk to the right. Position with "sit-in"-effect and knees pushed forward. Rotating movement of the pelvis in opposition to the hammer. The left upper arm brushes the left side oft the thrower's face when the hammer swoops downward. Drive shoulders forward and "hang on the hammer".

Hints: Use a light hammer on the first training day. If the athlete can handle it, he may use a normal hammer in the next session. The first thing to learn is the proper grip. It is tiresome to do many subsequent arm swings. To provide an active break, arm swings should be alternated with dummy turns, which will be the next basic exercise. Corrections and instructions can be given during the arm swings.

Auxiliary exercises:

1. Exercises to be applied if the athlete lacks the proper feeling for a "long arm". Take preliminary swings, alternating the arms.
2. Exercises if the athlete fails to master the twist of the upper body to the right.
The coach stands on the right side of the athlete at a distance of about 5 m. Each time the hammer passes through the highest point in front of the athlete's face, he must focus his eyes on the coach by looking through the small gap framed by the two arms. During these uninterrupted arm swings the coach moves back to the right of the athlete, thus forcing him to turn his upper body back to the right.
3. If the thrower does not have full control at the lowest point, he should repeat several arm swings without a break, consciously changing the lowest point during his swings. Put mark on the ground for guidance.

— Exercise 2: Turns without hammer

The turn will first be practised in two phases, accentuated by the athlete's counting "one-two" or saying "heel-ball".

1. Execute the heel-ball pivot slowly (only footwork).
2. Make slowly two, three or more turns in succession.
3. Cf. 1. In the second phase the right leg gets ahead of the trunk.
4. Cf. 3. Hold arms straight out with hands joined. Allow the right leg to pass the trunk and the arms.

5. Cf. 4, but making two successive turns. A short pause between each turn to help concentration.
6. Cf. 5, but making three turns.
7. Make several turns with various implements (sticks, shots, stones), travelling on an inclined hammer plane, at first with pauses, then without.
8. Cf. 7, but with slight acceleration.

Purpose: Learn first to make turns without the hammer.

Points to note: The first phase "one" or "heel": pivot over the left heel and the right ball by turning about 180° to the left with the CG over the left leg. The second phase: "two" or "ball"—complete the turn over the ball of the left foot. At the same time lead the right foot "tightly" around the left. The right foot lands level with the left. The body's CG remains over the left leg. The legs lead the turns. The body is in an easy "sitting" position. The trunk is erect, the legs are slightly flexed, the knees pushed forward.

Hints: The beginner is introduced in the "heel-ball" turn on the very first day of training.
The throwing direction is marked by a straight line 2 to 3 m long. In the initial position the athlete stands with feet astride this line and arrives at the same position at the end of each turn. The turn must be well demonstrated in its different phases. It is advisable to demonstrate them several times at short intervals, as the technique may appear complicated to the beginner. The turns must be demonstrated at a speed which is adapted to the athlete's standard, so that he may consciously follow the movements. The coach will stand by the athlete's side, so that the latter can easily watch all his movements and copy them.

If the athlete has a good understanding of the mechanics, he should be allowed to do the appropriate trunk, arm and leg actions at the same time. Exercises 5, 6 and 7 are intended for athletes who wish to specialize in hammer throwing.

The "heel-ball"-turn must be repeated many times. An athlete can shorten his training by practising the heel-ball movement at home. Once he has the command of the turns at low speed, he may be allowed to gradually increase speed and reduce the intervals between turns.

– Exercise 3: Turns with hammer

When the athlete has mastered the correct sequence of movements of the heel-ball turn without an implement, he may begin to make turns under the stress of the hammer's centrifugal force and gradually increase the degree of difficulty:

1. Some preliminary arm swings with the turn, putting down the hammer.
2. Two preliminary arm swings, one turn.
3. Two preliminary arm swings, two turns; all turns at an easy constant speed.
4. Two preliminary arm swings, 3 to 6 turns; all turns at an easy constant speed.
5. Two preliminary arm swings, 3 to 6 turns; accelerate on the last turn.

Purpose: Turning with the hammer is the main phase of the hammer throwing technique. The hammer is accelerated to top speed on the longest path possible right through to the release.

Points to note: From the first turn onwards the right foot lands on the ball of the foot. During the turns the eyes are focused on the hammer head. A slight inclination of the head to the left is not wrong. It gives the athlete a better "feel" for the hammer. But if he turns his head too far left he may lose balance and start the next turn too soon. When the right leg has landed, the next turn may be started only when the hammer head has come to the front at about the 0° point.

Hints: Once the athlete has learned to land correctly on the ball of the right foot after the first turn, a lot of future work can be saved. It permits him to shift his centre of gravity on to the left leg. The ability to accelerate at a constant speed requires intensive training and cannot be acquired during the basic training.

Auxiliary exercises:

1. Turns with the help of a partner (coach). The coach holds the athlete by the hands and checks him for the execution of certain phases of the motion right through to the complete turn. The athlete will thus develop the "feel" for the centrifugal force through the partner's resistance. The coach is able to correct faulty movements on the spot, while turning around the athlete in the direction of the hammer path.

The following elements are easily acquired:

a) Firm stand and "hanging on the hammer" (allowing the arms and shoulders to be pulled forward).
b) The understanding for the transfer of the CG on to the left leg.
c) The active and conscious overtaking of the hammer by the right leg.
d) The development of body torque.
e) The unwinding of the torque.

If the athlete has difficulty in the transition from the preliminary swings to the turn, i.e. if he loses control of the sequence of movements, especially of his legs, at the beginning of the turn, he must practise the turn without preliminary swings. This method has the advantage of developing the "feel" for the pull of the hammer and the legs getting ahead of it.

2. Take two preliminary swings, one turn–one arm swing–one turn, etc.

3. Take two preliminary arm swings, one turn–one arm swing, two turns etc.

4. Take two preliminary swings, two turns–one arm swing, two turns etc.

5. Take two preliminary swings followed by turns not alternating with swings.

6. Turns without preliminary arm swings.

Hints: on exercises 2 to 4

The arm swings between the turns in exercises 2 to 4 prevent the uncontrolled acceleration resulting from the turns and permits the thrower to concentrate on the next turn and control his movements.

During the arm swings between turns the beginner can correct the position of his feet.

– Exercise 4: The release

The learner should be allowed to release the hammer now and again in the throwing direction even before he fully masters two or more turns. Finally the active release should be trained:

1. Release after turns at a constant steady speed.

2. Cf. 1, with acceleration in the last turn.

3. With optimum acceleration in all turns.

Purpose: The release is a critical element of the hammer throwing technique. The distance of throw depends largely on the components achieved at the moment of release.

Points to note: Smooth transition from the turns to the release. Powerful straightening of the legs when the right foot has come to the ground. The arms are long. The head is tilted back. The trunk is upright in a vertical position above the feet. The hands let go of the hammer handle at about 90° when they are at shoulder height.

Hints: Only the athlete who allows his upper body and arms to remain relaxed at the release will learn the fast, vigorous and correct release. Successful deliveries are usually those in which the thrower has the feeling that he is in full control of the hammer to the very last moment. Athletes who wish to specialize in hammer throwing will execute at least three turns before the release. Technical elements in the performance of the turns tend to deteriorate after several throws. It is therefore preferable to practise the turns alternately with and without release. Repeated throwing and turning disturb the vestibule and the equilibrium and adversely affect the concentration of the thrower. Frequent pauses should therefore be inserted.

a) Take a short rest after each turn and each throw;

b) Insert longer pauses (5 to 10 min.) taken up with jogging or running, after a series of 15 turns or throws.

Throwing exercises:

1. Delivery of a throwing weight from the low right to the high left with or without forward and backward swinging of the implement between the straddled legs and to the right side of the body. During the initial movement the thrower assumes an easy "sitting" position. During the release he should not turn to the left, but if so only slightly.

2. Throw the weight from a turn of 90°, preceded by a preliminary arm swing. Note: the body must be completely straightened and the thrower must be standing firmly after delivery.

3. Throw the weight as in 2, but from a complete hammer throw turn. Technical execution as in 2.

Hints: The implement used for the auxiliary exercise must be shorter and heavier than the competitive hammer. A heavy hammer with a short wire may be used. Better still are throwing weights as used in weight events on grass (12.5 kg for men, 10.0 kg for youth).

The exercises for training the release must be adapted to the athlete's standard, his qualities and ability. Alternate weight throwing with hammer throwing. There is no limit to the number of repetitions of these exercises.

Exercises with throwing weights are good routines for the footwork, the accuracy of movements of trunk and arms.

5.5.2.4. Ancillary Exercises

Athletes who intend to specialize in hammer throwing should drill the following additional exercises to improve technique:

1. Do three to six turns, accelerating to maximum speed.

2. Cf. 1, with light hammer.

3. Do throws from four or five turns. Alternate easy throws with throws for length.

4. Alternate turns with swings with variations (see exercises of technical training and exercise 3 of ancillary exercises).

5. Cf. 4, with release.

6. Throws using two or three turns. After the arm swing the hammer handle is held with the left hand only. The arm must not go beyond the median plane.

5.5.2.5. Fault– Reason–Correction

Major faults occurring during the technical training are:

1. The thrower pulls the arms in during the arm swings, in the turns and during release.

2. He "falls" on the right leg, i.e. transfers the body weight from the left to the right leg on landing.

3. Wrong location of the lowest point during the preliminary swings and in the turns. All the other mistakes are of secondary importance during the basic training. Athletes and coaches should be mainly concerned with the correction of major faults.

During preliminary swings:

– Fault: The arms are pulled in (bent elbow), the effective radius is too small.

Reason: The movements are tense, the thrower lacks experience.

Correction:

a) Make alternating swings with the right and the left arm.

b) Do swings with both hands holding the hammer; the arms must be fully stretched, the hammer must sweep over a wide plane.

– Fault: The arm swings are angular.

Reason: The work of the upper body is not correct.

Correction: Begin to lower the left shoulder when the hammer is at its lowest point.

– Fault: The lowest point of the hammer head is in front of the thrower. He is swinging his arms like a windmill.

Reason: The thrower does not turn his trunk to the right or turns too late.

Correction: The left shoulder which is being lowered must lead the trunk into the turn.

— Fault: The athlete's body is stiff, he does not counter the pull of the hammer head with his hips (pelvis).

Reason: He lacks understanding of the mechanics. Poor flexibility of the joints (trunk and pelvis).

Correction: a) Do exercises increasing the mobility of the trunk and pelvis. b) Do frequent simulations of the correct hip work. c) Cf. b, including trunk and arm work. d) Cf. c, with half bent knees. e) Cf. d, with hammer.

— Fault: During the preliminary swings the hammer does not come up high enough and does not reach the required plane.

Reason: Not enough initial acceleration.

Correction: Practise a fast, long and vigorous pull of the hammer. Frequent repetitions of one or two arm swings.

In the turns:

— Fault: After the turn the thrower "falls" on the right leg; the body weight does not remain over the left foot.

Reason: The turn is introduced with the head and the left shoulder. The left leg is straightened during the turn.

Correction: a) Arms and shoulders must remain passive. The eyes are on the hammer throughout the turn. Push off vigorously from the ground with the right foot. Drive the left knee and hip forward during the turn.

— Fault: The thrower loses balance.

Reason: He does not sufficiently (or too much) "counter" the pull of hammer and the increasing centrifugal force. The arms are pulled in at the elbow, the legs are stiff.

Correction: Hang effectively on the hammer; keep the arms stretched and do casual turns. Repeat turns, without release.

— Fault: The lowest point has shifted too far in the throwing direction.

Reason: No body torque. The right leg has either not moved ahead of the hammer or too late. The hammer is accelerated together with the trunk.

Correction: Press the right leg into the turn. Get ahead of the hammer and land firmly.

— Fault: No unwinding of the body torque; the thrower drags the hammer.

Reason: He started the next turn too soon.

Correction: After the landing of the right foot delay the next turn until the hammer can be seen in front at the 0° point (draw marks on the ground).

— Fault: The forward movement during one turn is insufficient.

Reason: The "heel-ball"-pivot is sloppy; the thrower pivots either over the heel or the ball of the foot only.

Correction: Frequent turns without the hammer, accentuating the first and the second phase of the "heel-ball" turn.

— Fault: The left leg extends during the turn.

Reason: Lack of strength in the leg muscles, incomplete transfer of body weight to the left leg. The hammer is accelerated on its way from the lowest to the highest point.

Correction: a) A great amount of leg strengthening exercises with weights. b) Repeated "heel-ball" pivots with half-bent knees. c) Make sure acceleration is from the highest to the lowest point.

— Fault: The hammer plane is too

steep, the hammer hits the ground.

Reason: The angle between the arms and the trunk is not kept constant.

Correction: Fix arms and shoulders.

— Fault: The plane of the path of the hammer is too "flat".

Reason: The upper body is not relaxed; the trunk is held too stiff in the single support phase.

Correction: "Hang" against the hammer pull in the single-support phase.

— Fault: During the turn the thrower rotates sideways out of the ring. His turns are not complete.

Reason: The "heel-ball" pivot has been started too soon.

Correction: a) Practise without hammer. Pivot over the heel to 180°, then "rock over" the foot to the ball and complete the turn. b) Turn with the hammer, as in a) but inserting swings. Make several consecutive turns until progressing on a straight line inside the ring. Draw check-lines.

— Fault: During the turns the thrower rotates sideways out of the ring (to the right).

Reason: The thrower finishes the change-over from heel to ball too late. The right leg lands too late.

Correction: a) Make turns first without, then with the hammer. The change-over from heel to ball must set in sooner, at about 150 or 170°. b) During the turns the right foot pushes, then skims in close to the left heel or just behind it, so it will land quickly.

During the release:

— Fault: Too much weight on the right leg.

Reason: The release has been performed with the upper body. After the third turn the thrower "falls" heavily on to the right foot.

Correction: Go over the release with kettle bell and emphasize the leg action. Arms and trunk remain passive and relaxed.

— Fault: Angle of release too low.

Reason: No power is derived from the legs during the release. The hammer plane during turns is too flat.

Correction: Make throws with the hammer and various other implements. Accentuate the leg extension during the release. Correct the hammer's plane (see fault: "Too flat plane of the hammer path").

— Fault: The hammer flies too far left (seen in throwing direction).

Reason: The right foot lands too late. During the landing of the right foot the hammer has travelled on further left beyond the 0° point.

Correction: "Carry" the right foot quickly and close to the left. The last turn should be less than 360°. Get both knees as close together as possible.

— Fault: The thrower is pulled out of the ring.

Reason: The release was initiated by the upper body.

Correction: Standing throws using one turn, with the short-wire hammer. Release by the sheer power of the stretched legs.

— Fault: During the release the hammer hits the ground.

Reason: The throwing arm takes a swing before release; the upper body collapses forward like a jack-knife.

Correction: Power for the release must be generated by the legs, without active participation of the upper body.

Final remarks:

During the technical training, from the very beginning of the systematic work right through to the time when the thrower has full command of the hammer technique, the various phases of the complete movement must be constantly repeated. At the beginning of every training session the thrower must first get used to the hammer again. This continues with learning or repeating the preliminary arm swings, the turns with and without the hammer, etc. In this order the only thing that changes is the time used for the various exercises. It depends on the training background of the individual athlete.

In the sections 5.5.2.2. ("The Special Preparation") and 5.5.2.3. ("Basic Exercises of Technical Training") a host of practical examples has been given for the sake of completeness from which the athlete may choose those which are best suited to his standard and grasp of the event.

5.5.2.6. Specifications for Layout and Implements for the Hammer Throw

The circle from which the hammer is thrown at competitions has a diameter of 2.1357 m (7 feet). The platform is usually of concrete or asphalt. In creating conditions near to those of competition, it is useful to construct a similar ring for training purposes (approx. 2 × 3 m). This allows training in all weathers and the use of 4 to 5 turns, as in competition. In constructing the platform the following materials are required: hard core (broken stones)—10 to 20 cm, coarse graval and concrete (mixture 1:3)—5 to 10 cm. The surface should be slightly stippled when being laid to produce a rough but not ribbed surface. Shoes with leather soles and heels cannot be worn on concrete or asphalt. If the thrower works without

gloves, he will get blisters on his fingers. He should therefore wear an old leather glove with pads of 2 mm thickness sawn to the bottoms of the fingers.

5.5.3. Physical Requirements and Training Methods for Improving Performance

The idea which still prevails that a hammer thrower must necessarily have a powerful upper body and muscular arms is wrong. Of course hammer throwing is the sport in which, more than for any other event, strong leg muscles are required or should be developed. Explosive strength and speed qualities are good criteria for judging the aptitude of an athlete for the hammer.

With regard to height and weight the demands placed on the hammer thrower are not so high as those required for shot putting or discus throwing. An athlete who decides to specialize in hammer throwing should take into consideration the criteria gained by experience. On principle only a sportsman with an actual or potential height of 1.80 m should take up the event. For youths a weight between 75 and 80 kg is sufficient, as it will increase by 20 to 25 kg during the long years of training.

At the Olympic Games of 1972 the finalists in the hammer had an average height of 1.875 m and an average weight of 106.1 kg. This shows that as far as build is concerned, top-class hammer throwers are similar to shot putters and discus throwers. Even older sportsmen can start to throw the hammer and achieve good results when they are in their thirties. This is, however, only possible if they have undergone allround physical training in their youth and come close to the requirements we have given.

5.5.3.1. The Importance of Physical Condition

The most important physical requirements for the hammer thrower are strength and speed.

● Strength

Just how important strength is for the hammer thrower is shown by the mere fact that during the last phase of the release the thrower must control the pull of the centrifugal force produced by the hammer which rises to almost 300 kg. This requires strong leg, back and hand muscles. The best hammer throwers in the world are able to make deep knee-bends with a barbell of 270 kg and more on the neck and to snatch weights ranging from 135 to 150 kg.

● Speed

Strength is, however, not the whole story. One often experiences early stagnation in hammer throwing because of poorly developed speed qualities.
Explosive force (rapid strength) is the decisive factor for long distances in all the throwing events. Good hammer throwers require only 1.7 sec. for accelerating the hammer head from 16 m/s to near 25 m/s. As we have already mentioned, the centrifugal force is thereby increased to more than 300 kg. Such speed and strength performances can only be achieved by sportsmen who are endowed with great explosive force. Thus Bakarinov (USSR), whose characteristics were:

height 1.72 m, weight 105 kg, ran 30 m in 4.0 sec. notwithstanding the limitations to his possible leverage. Connolly (USA) cleared without special training in high jumping his own height and G. Zsivotzky (Hungary) who was Olympic champion in Mecixo-City in 1968 reached almost 15 m in the triple jump without special training.

● Special agility

Since hammer throwing is the most complicated of all the throwing events, it requires more agility than most other track and field events. The three turns require above all a good sense of orientation.

● Mobility

A hammer thrower must be very flexible in the shoulder girdle if he wants to achieve a wide effective radius in the preliminary arm swings. A flexible vertebral column and a wide range of movement at the hip joints are further important assets for a hammer thrower. This permits him to produce a high body torque in the single-support phase.

5.5.3.2. Means for Developing Physical Properties

● Strength

1. General strength exercises
Exercises with the barbell:
Deep knee-bends with barbell on the neck, snatching with and without lunge
Pressing in position on the bench
Pushing from the chest with and without lunge.
Exercises with sandbag:
Jumps from low crouch, trunk-bending and trunk-circling, bringing the trunk

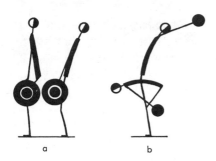

a   b   Fig. 143

to an upright position from prone and supine position.

Exercises for explosive strength:

Triple-jump from short run-up. Stand-ing triple jump, right-right-right and left-left-left, high jump over the bar, one-leg jumps for time (20 to 30 m).

2. Special strength exercises

Exercises with the barbell:

Reverse with and without lunge. Snatching the barbell without reverse (to hips) (Fig. 143a); half knee-bends, trunk circling.

Exercises with kettle bell:

One-arm snatching. Throws over the head backwards with both arms. Throws over the shoulder with one arm (Fig. 143b), arm swings.

Table 69   *Weekly Schedule of Training during the Preparatory Period (Foundation Training)*

Day	Duration (min.)	Training Task A = Preparation B = Main Part C = Closing		Training Means
Tuesday	10	A	Warm-up	Limbering up/Gymnastics
	30	B	Development of speed	General speed exercises
			Development of strength	General strength exercises
			Improve mobility	Stretching and loosening exercises
			Loosening	
	30	C	Development of agility	Game (Basketball)
Thursday	20	A	Warm-up	Circuit training or strength exercises with light weights
	10	B	Development of take-off strength	Exercises with barbell for the development of special strength
			Development of strength	
		C	Loosening	Game or running
Saturday	15	A	Warm-up	Moving with ball
	45	B	Improving technique	Throwing the hammer, every fifth throw for length
	20		Improving take-off strength	Jumping exercises (high jump right and left)
	40	C	Improving general mobility and agility, loosening, gymnastics, jogging	Other track and field events (hurdles and throwing events)
Sunday	25	A	Warm-up	Running and gymnastics
	25	B	Improving technique	12 throws-all-out
	60		Development of physical qualities	Running through woods or cross-country
	10	C	Loosening, limbering down, jogging, gymnastics	

393

Table 70   Weekly Schedule of Training during the Competition Period (Foundation Training)

Day	Duration (min.)	Training Task A = Preparation B = Main Part C = Closing		Training Means
Monday	20	A	Warm-up	Strength exercises with light
	10	B	Development of speed	weights, general speed exercises
	45		Improving technique	Four or five turns with hammer
	25		Development of take-off strength	Jumping exercises (high jump)
	10	C	Limbering down	Jogging
Tuesday	15	A	Warm-up	Game/Gymnastics
	60	B	Development of strength	General and special strength exercises with barbell
	10	C	Loosening	Stretching and loosening exercises
			Development of agility	Game
Thursday	20	A	Warm-up	Running and gymnastics
	10	B	Development of speed	Starts/Special speed exercises
	30		Technique	Hammer throwing (15 throws all-out)
	15		Development of take-off strength	Jumping exercises (triple jump) special strength exercises
	20		Development of strength	
		C	Limbering down	Jogging
Saturday or Sunday			Participation in competitions (hammer throw and other throwing events 100-m hurdles, high jump)	

The above exercises can be executed with a throwing weight, but partly also with shells, stones, beams and other implements.

● Speed

1. General speed exercises
Starts up to 30 m. Tempo-changing runs, acceleration runs, runs with commands (changing direction or exercise during the runs upon a command). Running on the spot at maximum speed.

2. Special speed exercises
Turns while running or jumping, without hammer; turns with light (6 to 7 kg) or short-wire hammer; during winter in the gymnasium: throws with the sling ball or sandbag into the net (hammer throw turn). For developing agility and mobility the same preparatory exercises as recommended for the technical training (see Chapter 5.5.2.3.) can be applied.

6.   The Combined Events

6.1.   General Principles

Various kinds of multi-disciplinary competitions, for which records are recognized, are catered for by the Amateur Athletics Association of the GDR (DVfL). The international combined events in athletics are the Decathlon for men and the Heptathlon for women. While the decathlon has been in the

Table 71   Combined Events

Age Group (Years)		Events
Female and Male		
8	Triathlon	60 m–long jump–throwing the ball
9		
10		
11	Pentathlon	60 m–60 m hurdles–long jump–throwing the ball–800 m
12		
Female		
13	Heptathlon	1st day: 80 m hurdles–shot put–long jump–200 m
		2nd day: high jump–javelin throw–800 m
14		1st day: 100 m hurdles–high jump–shot put–200 m
15	Heptathlon	2nd day: long jump–javelin throw–800 m
16/17		
Women		
Male		
13	Decathlon	1st day: 100 m–long jump–shot put–high jump–400 m
		2nd day: 100 m hurdles–discus throw–pole vault–javelin throw–1,500 m
14		1st day: 100 m–long jump–shot put–high jump–400 m
15		
16/17	Decathlon	2nd day: 110 m hurdles–discus throw–pole vault–javelin throw–1,500 m
Men		

In the hurdle and throwing events the competition rules of the Amateur Athletic Association of the GDR (DVfL) on measurements and weights of equipment are valid (see Tables 35 and 56).

Olympic programme since 1912, the women's pentathlon was held for the first time as an Olympic event in Tokyo in 1964. In 1981 this was replaced by the heptathlon.

Although in recent years the combined events have been recognized as independent competition events, the number of heptathlon and decathlon specialists is rather small compared with other athletic events. This is mainly due to the difficulty of training for several events, which is the most complicated training in athletics.

In spite of the great versatility required in modern training, the specialist in one event can, with time, concentrate his efforts on the preparation of his special event only and the pattern of movement involved. Heptathletes and decathletes, however, must prepare for several events and learn a great number of different skills. If they were to do the same amount of training for each single event as the corresponding specialists do, this would go beyond their physical and mental capacity. The training plans and methods of specialists in one event can therefore not be adopted for the combined events without considerable modifications.

6.2.   Special Features of a Combined Training

The specifications arise from the need to train for seven or ten events so as to produce top performances in all of them and from the order in which these events must be completed on competition days.

6.2.1.   Planning for Several Years

It is essential to set up plans for several years since it takes a very long time to master the mechanics and skills of various events. The idea that talented decathletes and heptathletes can reach the top in only a few years is erroneous. If an athlete in one particular event requires several years to become an outstanding specialist in this event, clearly a decathlete will need several more years to reach perfection in the skills of all ten events and to attain superior results in all of them. As it is impossible to perfect several techniques simultaneously, heptathletes and decathletes have to concentrate their training on specific essential aspects.

6.2.2.   Focused Training

This is the only effective method for reaching in time good results in all the events. The training extending over many years must be split up in such a way that attention is concentrated on certain specific events in each of these training sectors. Only when the mechanics of these priority events have been sufficiently stabilized to ensure good results, attention can be switched to other events which have so far been trained for more casually. If necessary the athlete may devote two or even three years of training to the perfection of one event only. It is better to achieve good results in one or some of the seven or ten events rather than to have average results in most events or not to get on at all.

6.2.3. Combined Training

This form of training is a further aspect of multi-disciplinary training. Excellent single results are significant for the heptathlete or decathlete only if achieved within the framework of a multi-disciplinary contest. Practice has proved that athletes with excellent results in individual events need not necessarily be good decathletes. Many of them have difficulty in switching over from one event to another. This handicap can best be overcome by training the events, especially in the immediate preparation, in the order they are held during competition. Even though only those talented individuals who are the most diligent, persistent and strong-willed athletes can reach international class in several events, all those others who do not belong to this highly talented minority should not refrain from doing heptathlon or decathlon training, because it is the best means for achieving all-round fitness. It is also the best preparation for later training in a special event.

6.3.   Decathlon

Of all the track and field events decathlon requires the greatest versatility. The decathlete must not only acquire skills for ten different events, but learn simultaneously several complicated patterns of movement: hurdles, javelin, discus, shot put, high jump, long jump and pole vault. This requires great fitness, considerable adaptability and coordination, which are partly innate but must also be evenly developed by thorough training and competition.

6.3.1.   Physical Condition

So far decathletes have been characterized according to their special ability either as the sprinter-jumper or the jumper-thrower type. Whereas the first group produced their best results in the running and jumping events, the others were top performers in jumping and throwing.

Experience has proved that today neither one nor the other of these types is equipped to advance to the top, because the results achieved by some of the world-best decathletes require an allround type, fitted for the achievement of outstanding results in all events with the exception of the 1500 m, which occupies a special position. The modern decathlete is a man with all-round athletic qualities. The world-best

Table 72   Mean Values of Age, Height and Weight of the 8 best Performers at the Olympic Games 1972

Age (years)	25.3
Height (cm)	184.0
Weight (kg)	83.0

Table 73 *Average Results achieved by the 6 best Decathletes at the Olympic Games 1960, 1964, 1968 and 1972*

	Rome 1960	Tokyo 1964	Mexico-City 1968	Munich 1972
100 m	11.1	11.0	10.7	10.76
110-m Hurdles	15.0	15.2	15.0	14.87
400 m	50.0	49.1	49.0	48.60
Long Jump	7.10	7.03	7.63	7.26
High Jump	1.82	1.88	1.97	1.96
Pole Vault	4.02	4.21	4.31	4.51
Shot Put	13.92	14.11	14.65	14.11
Discus Throw	47.05	43.71	45.21	44.43
Javelin Throw	65.64	61.50	65.11	58.20
1,500 m	4:48.2	4:31.8	5:05.1	4:24.8

decathletes are superior sprinters, jumpers and throwers all in one.

It follows from Table 71a that tall and fairly heavy athletes are best suited for the decathlon. That there are also remarkable exceptions is proved by Yang Chuan-Kwang (Taiwan), 184 cm tall and weighing 77 kg, who was the smallest and lightest decathlete among the best.

Physical fitness is, however, not the only criterion for a good decathlete. The best specialists in this event were without exception very fast, agile athletes with unusual explosive power (Table 73).

An athlete with superior functional as well as structural qualities and who is also endowed with strong will-power, diligence, persistence and combativeness may be considered to be apt for decathlon.

6.3.2. Special Features of the Decathlon Training

6.3.2.1. The Focused Training

Once a coach has decided to train a young athlete for the decathlon, he must outline a plan for several years, specifying the events on which training will be concentrated in each training year. During the first two years emphasis should be on developing basic speed and on learning the most complicated mechanical skills—the pole vault and hurdling. Speed is essential for all the decathlon events, as it mainly decides the performance not only in the jumping events but also in the throws. A young athlete who has not yet specialized in a particular event should do hurdling or pole vaulting, as these are the most propitious training and competitive events for the decathlete. They help to develop not only speed and endurance, but also strength and agility, in short, the most important qualities for the decathlete. Intensive pole vault training will at the same time improve the performance in the throwing events, even if the latter are not trained for specifically. Furthermore routines with complicated rhythms develop tenacity, a quality which helps in the subsequent learning of other movements.

Naturally the events initially given priority must also be further developed and consolidated over the following years, even if not with the same intensity and frequency. On the other hand events which do not have priority at a given time must not be neglected completely, but trained for occasionally and moreover not unsystematically.

Once the novice decathlete has sufficiently progressed in the sprints, hurdles, pole vault, he may give priority to another event. The time allotted in the plan for the priority of an event is, of course, not sacrosanct. If one finds that the perfection of one or other event requires less (or more) time, the timetable for the concentrated training can be amended accordingly.

The build-up of superior performance of a decathlete takes about eight years, so that long-term training plans should be outlined for eight years during which each one of the ten events should be given priority at some time, until the different techniques are completely mastered. While the beginner who trains for the improvement of basic speed usually concentrates his efforts exclusively on one event, the advanced athlete can train for three or four events at the same time, because he has better physical condition and experience than the beginner. If a decathlete is to be developed systematically it would be wrong to neglect the concentrated training and allow the athlete to train for many events at the same time just for winning or defending a title, i.e. to reach a required standard. Walter

Meyer, who would have greatly improved his results in pole vaulting and long jumping if he had focussed his training on these events proved that even good decathletes commit this error. This would undoubtedly also have influenced his decathlon performance. Concentrated training is one of the main tasks during the preparation phase. Decathletes and their coaches should therefore strive for long-term aims, concentrate their efforts on the perfection of skills and excellent results in all ten events in order to achieve top decathlon performances in their best athletic years.

6.3.2.2. The Combined Training

Preparation for the best results in the different decathlon events is only one of the objectives to be aimed at by this type of sport. Development of the capacity to achieve best results within the framework of decathlon should be another target. Practice has shown and investigations have confirmed, that most decathletes remain far from their best possible results in some of the ten events. These are generally the long jump, hurdling and discus throw.

While poor results in hurdling are generally due to fatigue resulting from the efforts of the first competitive day and insufficient warm-up, the reasons for poor results in the long jump and discus throw are due to the athlete's inability to switch over from one event to another. Obviously the preceding 100-m run affects the sense of rhythm for the long jump and a 110-m hurdle race has a negative effect on the subsequent discus throw. In order to avert this danger, the decathlete must organize his training so as to combine preparations for the events involving the greatest "conversion" difficulties. Sprint/long-jump and hurdles/discus-throw are usually the events which should be linked. It has proved useful in this respect, especially in the immediate preparation for a decathlon contest, to start the sprint training, which follows the long-jump training, with some jumps as if in a competition and then only to turn to the usual routines for the main training session. Similarly after the hurdle-training that in the discus throw should be concluded, here again starting with some competitive throws. It follows from these indications that combined training is the method to choose during the competition phase.

It should be understood that combined training must be carried out systematically; a merely haphazard training of this kind will not yield positive results. It is not a coincidence that N. Avilov (USSR), one of the best decathletes of the world, achieved decathlon results which came up to his best performances in the long jump and the discus without any adaptation difficulties. Avilov trained for years according to the combined method. A decathlete who has difficulty in consecutively performing two other events, should also apply the combined training method for them.

6.3.2.3. The Efficiency Factor

Efficiency in several events is defined as the relationship between the total of best results in single events—in points—and the results in pentathlon or decathlon expressed as a percentage.

It must be considered in this respect that the best results in five or ten single

events should have been achieved in the last two years, as otherwise this would make the relationship unrealistic. The relationship expressed as a percentage in fact indicates the coefficient in the utilization by a sportsman of his potentials. For B. Pollack (GDR) the efficiency of her world record of 4932 points was 99.45 per cent. The Olympic champion Peters (GB) reached 99.7 per cent in Munich 1972.

Among the men Avilov (USSR) reached 98.8 per cent, Kirst (GDR) 96.8 per cent. Hedmark (Sweden) 98.1 per cent and Toomey (USA) 97.2 per cent. The efficiency achieved by women is better at present than that of men. A high degree of efficiency expresses that a further increase of performance could only be achieved by improving individual results, while efficiency of less than 97.0 per cent implies reserves for stabilizing performance in groups of events.

6.3.2.4. Specific Aspects in Improving Condition

It has already been mentioned that decathletes cannot train according to plans and methods of specialists in the individual events. Decathlon is not a straightforward addition of ten events; it is an independent competition in its own right and requires its own specific methods.

Speed training which takes up the main part of the complete training of a sprinter cannot be carried out to the same extent in decathlon training. But since speed is an important prerequisite for a good decathlon result, the decathlete must look for ways and means of ensuring the best development possible of speed without neglecting the build-up of other qualities. For this reason the decathlete will undertake special sprint training only to improve the crouch start, running in the starting phase and speed endurance, mainly connecting sprints with the other elements of training. This includes all the drills for the run-up, the long jump and pole vault as well as running at submaximum and maximum speed for hurdle training. All these routine exercises will not, however, provide him with the speed endurance required for the 400 m and could not, therefore, be a substitute for fast races; these must, of course, be trained separately.

The speed training of the decathlete should follow approximately the following pattern:

February/April (end of the preparatory period)

Work on the crouch start and running in the starting phase: 30 per cent of the total speed training;

acceleration and speed races over distances ranging between 100 and 300 m: 40 per cent of the total speed training;

runs improving sprinting qualities in combination with other events (hurdles, long jump, pole vault): 30 per cent.

May/September (competition period)

Work on the crouch start and running in the starting phase: 40 per cent of the total; Acceleration and races over distances ranging between 100 and 300 m: 20 per cent. Runs improving sprinting qualities in combination with other events: 40 per cent.

The endurance training should take place mainly during the preparatory period.

In that phase the decathlete must lay the foundation for the endurance required in summer, since endurance work in summer would adversely affect his speed. Without doing middle-distance training the decathlete must improve his general endurance to such an extent that he is able to run 1 500 m in between 4:20.0 and 4:40.0. For this he must start the preparatory period with long runs (fartlek) and reduce them gradually from month to month to racing distances of about 300 m.

The following programme may serve as a pattern:

November/December

Runs through woods in the form of fartlek or continuous runs of 6 minutes with 6 to 3 minutes rest. The number of runs as well as the length of rest intervals should be adapted to the age, training background and standard of the athlete. The breaks can be taken up with gymnastics. When half of the runs are absolved, a longer break should be inserted, which can be taken up with gymnastics, jumps on soft ground, pull-ups as well as throws (stones or tree stumps).

Alongside this training over woodland trails the decathlete should put in a further day of speed races, in which he runs over distances ranging between 200 and 500 m. These runs should be at an easy pace with 6 (beginners) or 12 (advanced) repetitions. Rest intervals must be gradually cut down to a minute and taken up with walking; even the experienced decathlete cannot be expected to do jogging during the intervals like a middle-distance runner.

January/February

The continuous runs through woods and over cross-country will be reduced to 4 minutes and the pace will be gradually increased. Rest intervals will be cut down to 2 or 3 minutes. For longer recovery the programme of the preceding phase applies; here again the number of repetitions (pull-ups, jumps etc.) should be stepped up.

The number of speed races between 200 and 500 m remains approximately the same, but with times nearing the average of 1500-m run. A decathlete who does the 2500 m in 4:50.0 min. will do the 300-m runs in some 55.0 to 57.0 seconds. Here also the rest intervals should be gradually cut down to 1 minute.

March/April

In March runs over woodland trails will be cut down to 2 or 3 minutes but at a faster speed, while gradually lengthening the breaks between runs. Thus the speed of runs through the woods is adapted to fast races, so that end of March runs through woods can disappear from the programme and be replaced by speed races. In this segment of training the athlete switches from general to special endurance training. The number of speed races is reduced (in the case of 100-m runs e.g. from 10 to 8 and finally to 6), the pace is stepped up and rest intervals are extended to allow for recovery in spite of the higher tempo. Preference should now be given to 200-m and 300-m distances.

Competition Period

In this period running to improve general endurance is deleted and the decathlete runs exlusively to improve special endurance, i.e. he concentrates on the speed endurance essential for the decathlete. These runs over various distances (mainly 150 to 300 m) should be at sub-maximum intensity. At regular intervals runs at maximum speed should be inserted, as this gives the athlete guidance for the 200-m and 300-m intermediate times in the 400 m.

The decathlete should not hesitate to do some 800- and 1500-m runs in the preparatory period and out of season for checking his standard for the 1500 m without being fatigued by preceding events. He must do a sufficient number of 1500-m runs in order to gain experience in the distribution of strength and to assess his endurance over this distance. Most decathletes have poor times over 1500 m because they underrate their potentials, do not adequately distibute their forces or lack will-power. The strength training of decathletes does not differ greatly from that of specialists in the individual events. Not all current exercises can be integrated into the strength programme. From a host of normal routines the decathlete should choose those exercises which involve several groups of muscles simultaneously. These are e.g. snatching the barbell, knee bends with barbell followed by pushing, hopping or springing, at the same time doing shot puts and so on. This programme can be rounded off by special strength exercises of other events (see sections 5.2.3.2., 5.3.3.2., 5.4.4.2. and 5.5.3.2. in the chapter "The Throwing Events").

Since strength, above all speed strength, is of decisive importance for the decathlete, each week's training in the preparatory phase should include two or three sessions for the improvement of strength. Weight training, twice with heavy weights and once with light weights (strength gymnastics) has been shown to be effective.

In order to avoid slackening of effort during the competition phase, strength exercises should not be limited to the preparatory phase. Strength training once a week is usually sufficient to maintain the strength the athlete has acquired in the winter. As soon as he feels that this strength is declining, he should take up a forced strength training again in the way of an "impetus training". This usually becomes necessary when preparing for a major decathlon competition. The trained athlete can generally recover lost energy in two or three weeks by including two or three strength training sessions in the weekly programme.

In winter the decathlete should, as a matter of principle, begin his strength training with light weights and long series, but gradually increase weights and reduce the number of repetitions. During the competition period he should train with weights near his maximum, yet at the same time still be able to handle them rapidly.

The training of skills takes up a great part of the total decathlon training, because a decathlete must master many techniques at the same time. If he cannot devote the same amount of time to each event as a specialist in one event, this should not, however, lead him to stick to old techniques and to ignore new achievements. It is the trainer's task to see that while the athlete is learning a new technique he does not, or only when it cannot be avoided, start in a decathlon competition. When the basic elements of the new technique have been acquired, he should participate in as many contests as possible to drive it home.

The training for improving skills should be extended over the whole training year. The preparatory period should be mainly used for laying the foundations; this does not mean that technique should be completely neglected during this time. The winter months are the best time for working on a new technique or for learning new skills. At the end of the preparation phase the intensive technical training is begun in the form of concentrated training, which will be continued throughout the competition phase (see the relevant paragraphs on the technique of the various events).

The proper relation between the development of physical qualities and skills has been the subject of many investigations during recent years. In the preparatory period a distribution of 70 to 30 per cent in favour of physical qualities seems adequate. During the competition phase this relation shifts to some 55 : 45 per cent.

Training for the improvement of mobility is often wrongly considered to be part of the warming up. Yet strength, speed and endurance cannot be fully utilized, if the range of joint movement is reduced because of a lack mobility. Mobility, which undoubtedly plays an important role in all athletic events, is an essential prerequisite for some technical events such as hurdling and javelin throwing. Workouts for improving mobility must become part and parcel of the decathlete's training, meaning that he must devote at least 30—40 minutes to it, not counting the gymnastic exercises during warm-up. Intermittent gymnastic exercises after a series of strength programmes or sets of runs have a beneficial effect. They should include loosening and stretching exercises for the legs and for muscles in the region of the hips and shoulders (cf. gymnastics for hurdlers and throwers, in particular for javelin throwers).

6.3.3.   Competition

6.3.3.1.   How often can a Decathlete start?

For a long time the opinion prevailed that a decathlete should only start twice or three times in a season. Meanwhile it has been proved, especially by Soviet decathletes, that the thoroughly trained decathlete is well able to start successfully in 6 to 8 contests. This naturally depends on his standard. After only one year of training for this sport the novice decathlete can naturally not start as often as the experienced athlete who has done 6 or more years of regular training. There is no objection to a well prepared youth (15 or 16 years) taking part in a decathlon contest, provided he has undergone a proper all-round training. Versatile young men and women should try to take part at least once in a decathlon meeting, even if they still have marked shortcomings in some of the events.

As a rough guide one may say that a decathlete can participate the same number of times in meetings as the number of his decathlon training years, i.e. twice in the second training year and six times in the sixth. A three-weeks' rest period is usually sufficient for a well-trained decathlete to recover from the strain of the preceding contest and to get prepared for the next. Two weeks suffice in exceptional circumstances. Prior to important decathlon contests such as championships and international competitions, the preparatory period should be not less than four weeks. In the case of an interval of three weeks the training should be intensified to maximum load (possibly by a speed training) and then gradually reduced to complete rest just before the competition.

6.3.3.2.   Preparation for Competition

Even if a decathlete takes part in six decathlon competitions in a year, this number is small compared with the possible starts of a specialist in a single event. His chances of best performances are correspondingly reduced. Unfavourable weather conditions, poor competition layout or physical condition under par may negatively influence the results and a flop in only one of the ten events may be critical for the overall result. The decathlete should therefore strive to get the best results possible in each decathlon competition. For him there can be no fighting for victory only; he must participate in each meet with the firm intention of improving his best performance! For this he must be well prepared—psychologically and physically. In the first place the decathlete must try to compete in his "weak" events and participate in "small" decathlon meetings with emphasis on the events in which he still has difficulties when beginning a new event.

It is not advisable to take part in general athletics meetings and to start in four or five events which overlap, as this does not give the athlete sufficient time to concentrate on each single event. The upshot will tend to be unsatisfactory results which frequently discourage a man and make him doubt the value of his training. Less would be better in this situation! Another drawback is that by taking part in many events pole vaulting comes off badly. If a decathlete does concentrated training in this event, he should during this time start some fifteen times in pole vault competitions, which forces him to compete also in the middle of the week. If suitable meetings are not scheduled, decathletes should organize "internal" competitions for their own sake. At these meetings pole vaulting and high jumping should occupy a central place, these being the events that take up the longest time in competitions. Thus decathletes can start in the ordinary week-end competitions without having to neglect these highly important jumping events.

It should also be stressed that coaches should not be reluctant to let their decathletes start against stronger opponents. An athlete who wants to be successful in the decathlon must first learn to accept defeat in single events! The preparation for a decathlon contest should not be done "sparingly". It is not his placing in the individual event but his final position that counts (number of points); he may become the winner in a decathlon contest without having won in one of the ten events!

The number of rest days prior to a competition will be decided individually. During this time the athlete must keep away from sports grounds and do some intensive warm-up runs one or two days before the start. Training sessions in the preparatory period should, if at all possible, match the timetable of the competition programme; this means that if decathlon meets start at 9 a. m, training should be scheduled for the same time.

6.3.3.3. Warm-up before and during Competition

Although the importance of a good warm-up for producing top results is generally known, this fact is not always properly allowed for before decathlon competition. One of the most experienced Soviet decathlon trainers, G. V. KOROBKOV [56] meant what he said when he spoke of the "art of warming up" and postulated that decathletes should give as much attention to the improvement of warm-up as to the perfection of skills. The correctness of his assertion is proved by the fact that the decathlete must warm up for ten events every day. He should discover the type of warm-up that will make him fully ready for performance with the least possible effort. Many questions have to receive a clear answer before outlining a warm-up programme. What race distance should he cover before the 100 m and at what speed? How many trials should he perform? How long should the interval between trials and the beginning of competitions be? How many rounds are required for achieving the best results in the long jump? Which exercises should he do before shot putting and how long should the rest interval between the trials be? At what height should he start in the high jump? Many hours of training are required for an answer to all these questions and for finding out the best pattern for the individual out of a host of variations. The decathlete should therefore consider the warm-up not only as a preparation for the training, but as part and parcel of the training itself. In the course of his training the decathlete must find out the warm-up programme best suited for each single event. If he requires e.g. 5 (10) puts for obtaining

56   G. V. Korobkov "Zehnkampftraining" (Decathlon Training), Sportverlag, Berlin 1954.

results near his best, he must without fail perform these puts before shot putting in a decathlon competition. If recovery between the long jump and the shot put is not long enough, he must include some trial puts in his warm-up programme before the 100 m. If he has found that he can achieve his longest throw by using intervals of not more than 2 minutes between the trials, he must try during the decathlon competition to time his throws to the same rhythm. If there are no such proper facilities, simulated puts or playing with the shot help.

The decathlete will proceed in a similar way for the other events. Keeping warm in the time between throws or jumps is just as important as warming up before competitions. Normally rest intervals are so short, that they can be taken up with jogging, playful gymnastics or some trials. If the breaks are longer (e.g. in the case of a large pool of competitors) it is advisable to lie down during one part of the break and then to get ready again by exercises which have been shown to be effective in workouts and in competition. Warm-up becomes more of a problem in major competitions when intervals between the starts last one hour or more. In this case it is preferable to leave the competition area, take a rest in the dressing-rooms and ask for a massage. All that matters is to be on the spot again in due time for an effective preparation. In general some short acceleration runs, starts or jumps will do for getting ready again after a short time. It goes without saying that between starts the athletes must keep warm by dressing warmly.

During lunch breaks which usually last over three hours, the decathlete should refrain from sleeping, as it is often difficult to get ready again after a short sleep. He should eat according to his appetite but preferably stick to light meals. He may quench his thirst but must not forget that every drop he drinks is a further load on his body and reduces his potential performance. Yoghurt sweetened with honey is an adequate food on such occasions as it has the dual effect of stilling the hunger and quenching the thirst.

Warming up after a lunch break takes longer, because first signs of fatigue appear after the morning efforts and these must be overcome by an intensive warm-up. The high jump, which may take several hours, demands great concentration from the decathlete. He must be able to assess his performing capacity accurately and not waste energy by jumps over low heights, since he may run the risk of knocking the bar down three times at the starting height. Good high jumpers have the disadvantage of having had to compete for a long time in this event and of possibly being prevented from being properly ready for the subsequent 400 m. They are well advised to do some easy acceleration runs even between jumps, so that once the jumps are completed, they will require only few starts and sprints round the bends by way of preparation. If it is at all possible they should avoid starting in the 400 m directly after the high jump, because the relatively short and slow approach-run for the high jump is not the right preparation for the 400 m.

Once the decathlete has sufficiently limbered up after the 400 m, he should take a shower, get a massage and eat a full meal. Although he can have drinks, he should never drink more than is necessary to quench his thirst. If he is nervous and cannot go to sleep because he is worrying about the next day's competition, he should take a sedative rather than toss about sleeplessly in his bed. The effect and possible after-effect of the drug must be fully understood to avoid a possibly harmful effect on the next day's performance. The decathlete should get up at least three or four hours before starting in the second day's competition, because his body needs time to be fully timed again. A short morning stroll and some easy gymnastic exercises will improve his readiness. An intensive warm-up before the hurdles race is crucial for the course of the whole day. If the warm-up is incomplete, this will not only spoil his hurdles result, but also have a bearing on his competitive spirit. The warm-up for the subsequent events is much the same as already outlined for the first day of competition.

A decathlete should never forget that it is not the single event that is exacting, but the time between the events. Only by properly taking up the rest intervals can the ten events be brought together into a real decathlon!

6.3.3.4. The Equipment

The decathlete's kit is also a vital factor for success. During competition the decathlete is for a long time completely on his own and cannot expect any outside help. He must therefore carry everything needed for the competition in his sports bag: running shoes, spikes for sprinting, long and high jumping (the second day of the competition he needs spikes for the javelin throw), an extra pair of shoe laces, elastic bands, adhesives, insulating tape, liniment for rubbing in on a cold day, check-marks for the run-up, a cloth for cleaning-up, a cloth for cleaning or drying implements, a measuring tape, some fruit and cakes for taking the edge off his appetite and a refreshing drink (warm tea). He also needs a woollen blanket and, if available, a rubber mattress, especially on cold days and for the long intervals between the individual events. Warm sports wear goes without saying as it is a natural prerequisite for keeping warm and for changing if the sports wear is soaked by sweat.

6.3.4. Training Examples

6.3.4.1. Preparatory Period

1st segment November/December
Frequency: five times a week.
Sunday—runs for improving general endurance: runs (1 min.) or fartlek; long distances, easy pace. During active rest work-outs for the improvement of mobility: pull-ups, roll-ups, climbing, running jumps, hopping on one leg, throws using stones and tree-stumps.
Monday—work on the technique of a "focussed" event. Exercises with barbells, sandbags and so on for improving general strength (primarily snatching, pushing, pressing and knee-bends). During breaks between serial runs loosening and stretching exercises.
Tuesday—rest
Wednesday—exercises for improving explosive action, jump squats, clearing the crossbar, jumps on one leg, triple-jumps, jumps clearing obstacles and hurdles, jumps for technique, starts from various starting positions to improve response to the gun; climbing

and hanging by one hand from ropes or uprights.

Thursday—practise the technique of a "concentrated" event. Exercises for improving general strength (repeat Monday's programme), loosening and stretching exercises.

Friday—pace races over distances ranging from 200 to 500 m, great number of runs, easy pace, short intervals.

Saturday—rest

2nd segment January/February

Frequency: seven times a week.

Sunday—runs for improving general endurance by using runs or fartlek; intensify pace, increase number of runs and length of distance as under 1st segment; take up intervals as under segment 1; do 30 to 50m uphill dashes.

Monday—work on the technique of a "concentrated" event; do exercises for improving general strength. Step up the number of repetitions.

Tuesday—practise other events for completing the athletic training, do gymnastics with apparatus (cross-beam and parallel bars), games (basketball and football).

Wednesday—work on the technique of a "concentrated" event: do exercises for improving general strength (repeat Monday's programme).

Thursday—do exercises for improving explosive action; increase the number of repetitions; do jumps for improving jumping form; start from various starting positions for improving reaction to gun. Climbing and hanging by one hand as well as preparatory exercises on ropes and uprights.

Friday—pace-races, doing distances between 200 and 400 m; increase the number of runs, same pace, same length of intervals.

Saturday—work on the technique of a "concentrated" event; do exercises for improving special strength (for the respective "concentrated" event).

If facilities for training twice a day are available, the Friday programme may be shifted to another day to obtain a day of rest.

3rd segment March/April

Training frequency: seven times a week.

Sunday—change-over from running for improving general endurance to running for improving special endurance. Reduce number of runs and distances and intensify pace. Breaks can be taken up as before.

Monday—work on the technique of a "concentrated" event. Do exercises for improving general strength, cut down number of repetitions, easy weights; do loosening and stretching exercises during breaks.

Tuesday—gymnastics with apparatus and games; practise the technique of another event.

Wednesday—perfect the technique of a "concentrated" event; do exercises for improving general strength (repeat Monday's programme).

Thursday—do exercises for improving explosive action; increase the number of jumps for perfecting skills. Work on crouch start and short sprints (15 to 30 m).

Friday—speed races over distances ranging from 100 to 300 m, intensify pace, reduce time of rest and cut down number of repetitions.

Saturday—work on the technique of a "concentrated" event; do exercises improving strength for the "concentrated" event.

If an open-air track is available, the basic element of the warm-up should be hurdling.

6.3.4.2. Competition Period

May/September
Training frequency: four to five times a week.
Sunday—competition; do sprint-race distances and "combined" training.
Monday—rest.
Tuesday—work on the technique of a "concentrated" event; do exercises for improving explosive action and throwing power. Reduce number of repetitions, raise loads to near maximum.
Wednesday—work on the crouch start, do runs for improving speed and sprints from standing and flying starts. Practise the long jump.
Thursday—work on the technique of a "non-priority" event. Clear three to five hurdles (10 times). Do one or more runs at maximum speed over 150 to 300 m.

Friday—work on the crouch start and do runs for improving speed in connection with run-ups for long jumps and pole vaults; train a technical event. Do runs (submaximum) for improving the running technique.
Saturday—rest.
In preparation for a decathlon contest it is advisable to train the events in the sequence specified by competition rules and to pair the events: sprint/long jump, hurdles/discus throw.

6.3.4.3. Transition Period

October—during the transition period the decathlete should recover from the strenuous competition phase but not stop training altogether. Games and runs through woods should have priority in this phase. It is sufficient to train three or four times a week.

6.4. Heptathlon for Women

As of 1981 the heptathlon has replaced the pentathlon in national and international championship programmes (see Table 71 and Section 6.1.). This takes into account the performance development and capabilities of women in track and field events and in combined events. This leads to even closer comparisons to training methods in the men's decathlon. The following can be limited to the basics and peculiarities for training for the heptathlon. For a more comprehensive survey the passages on the men's combined events and the special events in the chapters on running, jumping and throwing events are indispensable.

6.4.1. Physical Condition

The make-up of the heptathlon places technical demands and demands on the condition of the athlete. For example, sprinting ability has a substantial influence on performances in the 100-m hurdles, the 200-m race and in the long jump. In the high jump, long jump, shot and javelin acceleration and jumping power—two physiologically similar qualities—are the decisive basis for condition. On the other hand the 800-m race places demands on the endurance (short duration) and as far as training methods are concerned forms a certain contrast to the other events.

Table 74   Performances in Heptathlon

Name	Country	100 m Hurdl. (sec.)	Shot Put (m.)	Long Jump (m.)	200 m (sec.)	High Jump (m.)	Javelin Throw (m.)	800 m (sec.)	Points
Neubert (1982)	GDR	13.59	15.10	6.84	23.14	1.83	42.54	2:06.16	6772*
Neubert (1981)	GDR	13.70	15.41	6.82	23.58	1.86	40.62	2:06.72	6760
Gratchova (1982)	USSR	13.80	16.18	6.65	23.86	1.80	39.42	2:06.59	6611
Frederick (1982)	USA	13.70	15.25	6.07	25.09	1.85	51.62	2:13.84	6457

* World Record

Learning and applying techniques in the individual events requires an ability to learn motor qualities. On this account the heptathlon is particularly suited to those athletes who are versatile in sport and who enjoy and are interested in combined events.

With regard to physical conditions there are no essential differences to those of pentathletes. In the high jump, the long jump, the shot and the javelin taller women—around 1.75 m — have certain advantages. The emphasis on such events requires that the women be strong. To date average weight has been around 65 kg.

6.4.2.   Special Features of Training

The programme for heptathlon training is drawn up for several years (see chapter 2.13), specifying the main tasks for each year. The main tasks in developing abilities in condition and coordination are:
—Broad training of these abilities according to the principle of versatility (specific training and competition vers-

atility: see section 2.2.1.) during basic and preparatory training.
— Concentration on developing specific abilities in condition, in particular speed and explosive power during preparatory and further training.
—Concentration on technical training in selected heptathlon events during the preparatory and further training.
The heptathlon requires good basic sports training in which performance in speed, power (in particular explosive power), stamina, agility and mobility are improved. This applies mainly to the basic and in part to preparatory training. When a good level of condition and coordination skills have been reached emphasis is then placed on developing skills and abilities in techniques and condition needed for the heptathlon. Reference will be made to certain peculiarities of this training process.

6.4.2.1.   On Running Training

To develop specific running abilities training should correspond to the principles of training methods for sprinting (see section 3.3.4.2.). The first two segments of the preparatory period aim to improve general endurance. Improving this quality creates more favourable condition for increasing load in sprint and dash training. At the same time increased endurance increases performance in the 800-m race. Partly in the second and in the third segment of the preparatory phase a periodical increase in the intensity of tempo runs develops specific sprint endurance. The distance varies from 100 m to 300 m. To prepare for the 800-m race tempo runs of between 500 and 1000 m should be included from time to time using the intensive intervals or the duration method. To maintain and improve sprinting ability more sprints (technique runs, starts, etc.) at a submaximum speed should be included in the second segment of the programme.

6.4.2.2. On Strength Training

In modern training exercises for developing strength take up the largest part in the preparatory period. Work-outs with and without additional load to the body weight, with barbells, kettle bells, sandbags, medicine balls, routine on wall-bars and jumping exercises should form the main part of two training sessions in the weekly schedule.

The main target of strength exercises should be improving explosive power. They should therefore be performed at great speed using medium additional load to the body weight (every exercise should be repeated six to ten times).

Exercises for developing general and specific strength must be included in the strength training programme: they can be taken from one of the seven events having particular priority in that particular year. Since the training tasks of a heptathlete are much more complex than those of a specialist competing in one of the individual events, the precise effect of each strength exercise should be well known before integrating the most important exercises into a special strength programme.

General strength exercises must, on principle, be emphasized in the first, special strength exercises in the third segment of the preparatory period. In the second segment they should be applied in roughly equal parts. Strength exercises should be chosen according to the degree of physical fitness of the athlete. General strength exercises take precedence in the training schedule for beginners, while advanced athletes will mainly do special strength exercises.

During the preparatory period strength is at first trained according to the extensive interval method but gradually substituted by intensive interval work and partly by repetition work. The methods should be adapted to the standard of each individual athlete. This extensive internal work is recommended for the beginner while advanced athletes should use the intensive interval method (see 2.7.2.).

During the competition phase the strength acquired through training should be maintained by appropriate exercises. Several general and specific strength exercises should be included once or twice a week in the training programme.

6.4.2.3. On Technical Training

The following principle is valid for technical training: do not do everything at once but plan concentration on certain events taking into consideration the individual technical training level.

With regard to training methods emphasis should be placed on technical training in the sprint, hurdles and long jump for training here is linked for the most part to sprint training. Further inclusion of one or several events in technical training depends on the level of technical training of the athlete and her ability to learn. Training should be geared to those events where technical training is difficult for here the training process is more complicated and takes longer time. For many women the javelin is one such event.

6.4.2.4. On Competition

In preparing for a heptathlon contest the athlete will, especially in the early part of the competitive season, train for two or three of the events. Sprints should be given preference.

In the competitive season heptathletes can take part in several competitions even those in which they still have technical short-comings. A recovery period of some three to four weeks, depending on the standard of the athlete, should be planned between competitions.

We will refrain from offering training examples for heptathletes since suggestions for the specification of a multi-disciplinary training can be derived from the decathlon schedule. Due allowance should be made for particular problems in training women (cf. Section 2.4.3.).

Reading List

Bauersfeld, K.-H.:Leichtathletik II – Wurf und Stoß. Vol. 10 in the series "Kleine Bücherei für den Übungsleiter und Sportlehrer".–2nd ed., Berlin: Sportverlag, 1963

Birkemeyer, H.: Hürdenlauf für Frauen.–Berlin: Sportverlag, 1958

Carl, G.: Kraftübungen mit Geräten.–4th ed., Berlin: Sportverlag, 1983

Donath, R.: Mittelstrecken- und Hindernislauf.–Berlin: Sportverlag, 1960

Donath, R.; Schüler, K.-P.: Ernährung der Sportler.–2nd ed., Berlin: Sportverlag, 1979

Donskoi, D. D. (Donskoy, D. D.): Grundlagen der Biomechanik.–Berlin: Sportverlag, 1975

Gain, W.; Hartmann, J.: Muskelkraft durch Partnerübungen.–5th ed., Berlin: Sportverlag, 1982

Harre, D., and others: Principles of Sports Training. Introduction to the Theory and Methods of Training.–Berlin: Sportverlag, 1982

Hoke, R.: Handbuch des Leichtathleten.–Wien: Globus-Verlag, 1951

Jäger, K.; Oelschlägel, G.: Schülersport – Kleine Trainingslehre.–4th ed., Berlin: Sportverlag, 1980

Köhler, H., and others: Lauf dich gesund! (Und andere Programme für das Ausdauertraining).–3rd ed., Berlin: Sportverlag, 1981

Kossakowski, A.: Psychologische Grundlagen der Persönlichkeitsentwicklung.–3rd ed., Berlin: Volk und Wissen, 1982

Krestownikow, A. A. (Krestovnikov, A. A.): Physiologie der Körperübungen.–Berlin: Volk und Gesundheit, 1953

Kunath, P.: Sportpsychologie. Lehrmaterial der Deutschen Hochschule für Körperkultur Leipzig.–Leipzig, 1975

Kusnezow, W. W. (Kusnetzov, V. V.): Kraftvorbereitung. Theoretische Grundlagen der Muskelkraftentwicklung.–2nd ed., Berlin: Sportverlag, 1975

Lohmann, W.: Schülersport – Lauf, Sprung, Wurf.–4th ed., Berlin: Sportverlag, 1981

Lompscher, J.: Theoretische und experimentelle Untersuchungen zur Entwicklung geistiger Fähigkeiten.–2nd ed., Berlin: Volk und Wissen, 1975

Löscher, A.: Kleine Spiele für viele. Übungssammlung.–3rd ed., Berlin: Sportverlag, 1979

Matwejew; Kolokolowa (Matveyev; Kolokolova): Allgemeine Grundlagen der Körpererziehung.–In the series "Sporterfahrungen des Auslands", Berlin: Sportverlag, 1962

Matuszak, F. S.: Weight Training in a Junior High School.–Scholastic Coach, USA, 1960

Morgan; Adamson: Circuit-Training. London: Bell & Sons, 1959

Nabatnikowa, M. J. (Nabatnikova, M. Y.), and others: Ausdauerentwicklung. Theoretische Grundlagen.–Berlin: Sportverlag, 1974

Nett, T.: Das Übungs- und Trainingsbuch der Leichtathletik.–2nd ed., Berlin-Charlottenburg: Verlag für Sport und Leibesübungen Harry Bartels, 1952

Nett, T.; Jonath, U.: Kraftübungen zur Konditionsarbeit. Leichtathletisches Muskelkrafttraining.–Berlin-Charlottenburg: Bartels und Wernitz, 1960

Neuner, G., and others: Pädagogik.–Berlin: Volk und Wissen, 1978

Osolin, N. G. (Ozolin, N. G.): Das Training des Leichtathleten.–2nd ed., Berlin: Sportverlag, 1954

Puni, A. Z.: Abriß der Sportpsychologie.–Berlin: Sportverlag, 1961

Rubinstein, S.: Grundlagen der allgemeinen Psychologie.–9th ed., Berlin: Volk und Wissen, 1979

Rudik, P. A.: Psychologische Aspekte der sportlichen Tätigkeit.–Berlin

Schafrik, J., and others: Leichtathletik in Vergangenheit und Gegenwart.–2nd ed., 2 vols., Berlin: Sportverlag, 1976

Scholich, M.: Kreistraining.–2nd ed., Berlin: Sportverlag, 1982

Simkin, N. W. (Zimkin, N. V.): Physiologische Charakteristik von Kraft, Schnelligkeit und Ausdauer.–In the series "Sport im Sozialismus", Berlin: Sportverlag, 1959

Team of Authors: Beiträge zu Trainingsfragen.– In the series "Sport im Sozialismus", Berlin: Sportverlag, 1960

Team of Authors: Kleine Enzyklopädie – Körperkultur und Sport.–5th ed., Leipzig: Bibliographisches Institut, 1979

Team of Authors: Leichtathletik in der Schule.–Berlin: Volk und Wissen, 1977

Team of Authors: Pädagogische Studientexte. Berlin: Volk und Wissen, 1961

ARTICLES FROM *"DER LEICHTATHLET"*

Journal of the DVfL of the GDR
Annex "Der Leichtathletik-Trainer", Sportverlag, Berlin

Volume 1960

Kunath, Willenserziehung und Leistungsbereitschaft (No.10)

Schmolinsky, Der Laufrhythmus des 400-m-Hürdenlaufes (No. 15)

Bauersfeld, Die Technik des Speerwurfes (No. 16)

Israel, Das Übertraining. Seine Entstehung, Erkennung, Behandlung und Verhütung (No. 18)

Golm, Meine Erfahrungen mit jugendlichen 400-m-Läufern (No. 21)

Büttner, Zur frühzeitigen Spezialisierung der männlichen und weiblichen Jugend im Mittelstreckenlauf (No. 24)

Geißler, Meine Erfahrungen im Training mit jugendlichen Mittelstrecklern (No. 25)

Djatschkow, Zur Anlaufgestaltung im Hochsprung (No. 29)

Dähne, Die Technik des Hammerwurfes (No. 30)

Kretzschmann, Zur speziellen Wettkampfvorbereitung des Langstreckers (No. 32)

Donath, Ist das Intervalltraining wirklich überholt? (No. 32)

Drechsel/Siebmann, Wie steht es um unseren Nachwuchs? (No. 34)

Grundlach, Die Stabübergabe in der Sprintstaffel (No. 35/36)

Bauersfeld, Die Technik des Kugelstoßens (No. 37/38)

Kowalenko, Der Zehnkampf braucht Nachwuchs (No. 39)

Höfke, Für eine rechtzeitige Spezialisierung im Zehnkampf (No. 42)

Rabbel, Übergangsstufen sind nötig (No. 46)

Drechsel, Sinnvolle Vorbereitung ist wichtig. Zur Diskussion über die Nachwuchsentwicklung im Zehnkampf (No. 46)

Büsser, Schnelligkeitstraining auch im Winter (No. 50)

Volume 1961

Wolf, Das Sprinttraining mit Jugendlichen in der Vorbereitungsperiode (No. 2)

Pöhlitz, Das Training der Deutschen Jugendmeisterin Waltraud Kaufmann (No. 2)

Djatschkow, Spezielle Sprungübungen des Hochspringers (No. 6)

Bauersfeld, Kraftentwicklung – eine wichtige Aufgabe der Leichtathleten (No. 7)

Gundlach, Alter, Größe und Gewicht der Teilnehmer an den Olympischen Spielen 1960 (No. 9)

Sgonina, Die Entwicklung eines jugendlichen Stabhochspringers unter den Bedingungen einer KJS (No. 11)

Mallek, Zum Training mit jugendlichen Stabhochspringern (No. 11)

Israel, Über die Verkürzung der Erholungsvorgänge (No. 14)

Thieß, Kindertraining und Pubertät (No. 15)

Israel, Die Belastbarkeit der Jugendlichen in der Pubertät (No. 15)

Gehmlich, Freudbetont trainieren (No. 15)

Pöhlitz, Zum Mittelstreckenlauf der weiblichen Jugend (No.17)

Siebmann, Sowjetische Erfahrungen über Nachwuchsarbeit (No.18)

Wolf, Sprinttraining mit Jugendlichen im Frühjahr und im Sommer (No. 18)

Donath, Wo liegt die Grenze zwischen allgemeiner und spezieller Ausdauerarbeit? (No. 19)

Themel, Zum 600-m-Lauf der weiblichen Jugend A (No. 19)

Bäskau, Jugendrekord und gute Zensuren (No. 21)

Kuhn, Waldlauftraining der "Spezialisten" (No. 22)

Götze, Die Schuljugend den Wälzer lehren (No. 31)

Gundlach, Zur Technik der weltbesten Dreispringer (No. 33)

Mertens, Das Training im Mittelstreckenlauf (No. 37)

Kautz, Trainingsanleitung für Nachwuchsspringer (No. 47)

Volume 1962

Hoffmann, Intervalltraining, Intervallarbeit, Intervallmethode? (No. 8)

Rieger, Die Grundmethode im Dreisprung (No. 14)

Gundlach, Das Neue im Training der Neuseeländer (No. 17)

Lydiard, Meine Trainingsmethode im Mittel- und Langstreckenlauf (No. 18)

Bartušek, Ein Beitrag zu den Problemen des Tiefstarts (No. 25)

Lohmann, Der Dreisprung der Schüler (No. 28)

Hoffmann, Kondition oder Technik (No. 33)

Grundmann, Systematisierung des Gesamttrainingsprozesses (No. 37)

TRINIDAD HIGH SCHOOL
LIBRARY

Hillebrandt, Technische Probleme des Diskuswerfers (No. 13)

Ostapenko, Spezialübungen des Hürdenläufers (No. 15)

Kühn, Hinweise für junge Sprinter (No. 16)

Reiß, Mittelstreckentraining für 16- bis 18jährige Frauen (No. 22)

Reiß, Bemerkungen zum Ausdauertraining im Kinder- und Jugendsportalter (No. 23)

Fruktow, Spezialübungen des Gehers (No. 23)

Samozwetow, Spezialübungen der Hammerwerfer (No. 32)

Grigalka, Spezialübungen der Kugelstoßer (No. 40)

Tschistjakow, Die Ausbildung der Absprungtechnik (No. 41)

Djatschkow, Spezialübungen für Hochspringer (No. 42)

Tschistjakow, Der Anlauf der Hochspringer (No. 43)

Volume 1967

Zbobysam, Die Proportionen der Springer beim Dreisprung (No. 3)

Mittag, Ausdauertraining für Sprinter (No. 4)

Goltschenko, Ungenutzte Reserve im Zehnkampf (No. 17)

Sabow, Schnelligkeit und Kraft bei Anfängern im Wurf (No. 22)

Jagodin, Varianten moderner Technik im Stabhochsprung (No. 23)

Ter-Owanesjan, Die Kunst des Weitsprunges (No. 24/25)

Jonow/Tschernjajew, Dynamik der Schnelligkeit im Sprint (No. 26)

Stschennikow, Armarbeit der Hürdenläuferinnen (No. 28)

Horlemann, Schrittlänge und -frequenz beim Gehen (No. 29)

Derg, Kontrolle der Kraftentwicklung bei Werfern (No. 33)

Grigalka, Grundlagen der modernen Kugelstoßtechnik (No. 33)

Petrow, Krafttraining der USA-Werfer (No. 34)

Konstantinow, Das Training zukünftiger Werfer (No. 35/36)

Mallek, Weitsprungtraining der Jugend (No. 41)

Kautz, Technisch-methodische Hinweise zur Schulung des Tiefstarts (No. 42)

Popow, Vervollkommnung der Weitsprungtechnik (No. 44)

Kosinin, Vervollkommnung der Hürdentechnik (No. 47)

Schmolinsky, Hürdenausbildung gehört in jedes Trainingsprogramm (No. 49)

Volume 1968

Planck, Die räumliche Gestaltung der letzten Anlaufschritte im Weitsprung (No. 9)

Karikosk, Junge Weltklasseläufer und ihre Lehren (No. 10)

Werchoschanski, Zur Beurteilung der Absprungqualität des Dreisprunges (No. 12)

Hirth, Was gibt es Neues im 400-m-Hürdenlauf? (No. 14)

Kreer, Dreisprünge von Solotarjew und Sanejew (No. 17)

Solotarjew, Vom Sprint zum Dreisprung (No. 20)

Kovar, Anlauf – Absprung – Schwungbeineinsatz (No. 23)

Jeremi, Training des Weitspringers (No. 25)

Rasumowski, Ausdauer eines 400-m-Läufers (No. 29)

Kusnezow, Besonderheiten der modernen Sprinttechnik (No. 37)

Schorez, Umfang und Intensität beim Langstreckenlauftraining (No. 45)

Sulijew, Besonderheiten der Speerwurftechnik (No. 47)

Hornauf, Frühzeitige Hürdenausbildung (No. 51/52)

Volume 1969

Gundlach, Fosbury-Technik hat Perspektive (No. 9)

Werchoschanski, Neue Wege im Dreisprung (No. 11)

Vostatek, Die 4 × 100-m-Staffel (No. 13)

Jonow/Tschernjajew, Die Abhängigkeit der Schnelligkeit von Länge und Frequenz der Schritte (No. 16)

Lonski, Entwicklung jugendlicher Hochspringer (No. 17)

Rawson, Der 800-m-Rekordläufer der Zukunft (No. 18)

Ostapenko, Der Hürdenlauf (No. 19/20/21)

Mullak, Die Ausdauer eines 400-m-Läufers (No. 25/26)

Bulantschik, Beobachtungen bei weltbesten Hürdenläufern (No. 42)

Ilijew/Nikonow, Stab und Kraft (No. 43)

Papyschewa, Schnellkraft-Training der Hochspringerin (No. 45)

Kriwonossow, Der Hammerwurf (No. 46/47)

Moc, Der vollkommene Gehstil (No. 48)